Japan and Germany as Regional Actors

The end of the Cold War and the bipolar era constituted a significant change in Germany's and Japan's foreign policy settings, granting both countries greater leeway to pursue policies divergent from Washington's strategy. This important book fills a gap in the existing literature by employing an explicitly comparative framework for analyzing and evaluating Germany's and Japan's post-Cold War regional foreign policy trajectories. Recent non-comparative studies diverge in their assessments of the extent to which the two countries' foreign policies are characterized by continuity or change, as while the majority of analyses on Germany find overall continuity in policies and guiding principles, prominent works on Japan see the country undergoing drastic change. Through a qualitative content analysis of key foreign policy speeches, this book traces and compares German and Japanese national role conceptions by identifying policy-makers' perceived duties and responsibilities of their country in international politics. Further, through two case studies on missile defence policies and textbook disputes this study investigates actual foreign policy behaviour in order to question the assertion that post-Cold War Germany and Japan are following very different paths.

Providing a much needed new analysis of German and Japanese foreign policies, this book will be of great use to students and scholars interested in Japanese politics, German politics, comparative politics and international relations more generally.

Alexandra Sakaki is a Robert Bosch Foundation research fellow at the German Institute for International and Security Affairs (Stiftung Wissenschaft und Politik) in Berlin, Germany.

Routledge Politics in Asia series

Formerly edited by Michael Leifer
London School of Economics

Japan and Germany as Regional Actors

Evaluating change and continuity after the Cold War

Alexandra Sakaki

Routledge
Taylor & Francis Group

LONDON AND NEW YORK

First published 2013
by Routledge
2 Park Square, Milton Park, Abingdon, Oxfordshire OX14 4RN

Simultaneously published in the USA and Canada
by Routledge
711 Third Avenue, New York, NY 10017

First issued in paperback 2014

Routledge is an imprint of the Taylor & Francis Group, an informa business

British Library Cataloguing in Publication Data
A catalogue record for this book is available from the British Library

Library of Congress Cataloging in Publication Data
Sakaki, Alexandra.
Japan and Germany as regional actors : evaluating change and continuity
after the Cold War / Alexandra Sakaki.
    p. cm. – (Politics in Asia series)
  Includes bibliographical references and index.
  1. Japan – Foreign relations – 1989– 2. Germany–Foreign relations –
  1990– 3. Comparative government. I. Title.
  JZ1592.S34 2012
  327.43-dc23   2012004440

ISBN 978-0-415-69749-1 (hbk)
ISBN 978-1-138-85745-2 (pbk)
ISBN 978-0-203-10478-1 (ebk)

Typeset in Times New Roman
by HWA Text and Data Management, London

Contents

Acknowledgements

There are many people I wish to thank for their assistance in the genesis of this book, a significantly revised and updated version of my dissertation at Trier University, Germany. First and foremost, I am grateful to my advisor, Professor Dr Hanns W. Maull of Trier University for his thoughtful, probing comments on draft chapters and his support and encouragement during the research and writing process. I owe him my sincere appreciation for his knowledgeable suggestions and help in arranging interviews. Without his guidance, this book would not have been possible.

I am indebted to numerous experts, scholars and government officials, who provided me with helpful insights and comments during interviews. Please note that I omit all academic titles in the following list for better readability. For sharing their perspectives and views on German policy, I would like to thank Hans-Peter Bartels (Member of Bundestag), Kinga Hartmann (Educational Agency of Saxony), Christos Katsioulis (Friedrich-Ebert-Foundation), Patrick Keller (Konrad-Adenauer-Foundation), Hans-Ulrich Klose (Member of Bundestag), Sascha Lange (Stiftung Wissenschaft und Politik/German Institute for International and Security Affairs), Robert Maier (Georg-Eckert-Institute), Rolf Mützenich (Member of Bundestag), Falk Pingel (Georg-Eckert-Institute), Jürgen Schnappertz (German Foreign Ministry), Benjamin Schreer (Aspen Institute), Svenja Sinjen (German Council on Foreign Relations), Thomas Strobel (Georg-Eckert-Institute), Karsten D. Voigt (SPD), as well as a staff member of the CDU/CSU parliamentary grouping and a defence expert, who wish to remain unnamed. For generously taking time out of their busy schedules to discuss Japanese policy, I would like to thank Katayama Yoshihiro (Keio University), Kondo Takahiro (Nagoya University), Okonogi Masao (Keio University), Tanaka Hitoshi (Japan Center for International Exchange), Togo Kazuhiko (Temple University Japan), Ueki Chikako Kawakatsu (Waseda University), Yoshizaki Tomonori (National Institute for Defence Studies), Yuzawa Takeshi (Japan Institute of International Affairs), and three experts from the National Institute for Defence Studies as well as a member of the Japan–Korea Joint Research Commission on History, who wish to remain unnamed.

For assistance and advice I would furthermore like to thank Alexander Bukh (Tsukuba University), John Campbell (formerly University of Michigan),

Robert Dujarric (Temple University Japan), Thomas Heberer (University of Duisburg-Essen), Andrew Horvat (Tokyo Keizai University), Christopher W. Hughes (University of Warwick), Nakai Yoshifumi (Gakushuin University), Karen Shire (University of Duisburg-Essen), Tanaka Akihiko (University of Tokyo), Gabrielle Vogt (University of Hamburg) and Klaus Vollmer (Ludwig-Maximilians-University Munich). Special thanks to Gilbert Rozman of Princeton University, who nurtured my interest in Japanese foreign policy during my undergraduate studies.

I am deeply grateful for two and a half years of generous support and funding by the German National Academic Foundation (Studienstiftung des deutschen Volkes) as well as for a seven-month research stay at and sponsored by the German Institute for Japanese Studies (Deutsches Institut für Japanstudien) in Tokyo. Without this assistance, I would not have been able to conduct my research.

Finally, I would like to thank my family in Germany and Japan for continuous support and help. I am grateful to my mother, Martina Wittig, who patiently read through all my draft chapters and made valuable editing suggestions. Thanks to my husband Akio Sakaki for his moral support throughout the project and for our discussions about Japanese politics.

Alexandra Sakaki
Duisburg and Berlin, December 2011

Abbreviations and special terms

Abbreviations

ABM	Anti-Ballistic Missile (Treaty)
APEC	Asia-Pacific Economic Cooperation
ARF	ASEAN Regional Forum
ASEAN	Association of Southeast Asian Nations
AWACS	Airborne Warning and Control System
BdV	German Association of Expellees (Bund der Vertriebenen)
CDU	Christian Democratic Party (Germany)
CIA	Central Intelligence Agency
Corps-SAM	Corps Surface-to-Air Missile
CSCE	Conference for Security and Cooperation in Europe
CSU	Christian Social Union (Germany)
DPJ	Democratic Party of Japan
EU	European Union
FDP	Free Democratic Party (Germany)
FSAF	Future Surface-to-Air Family of missiles
GDR	German Democratic Republic (East Germany)
GEI	Georg-Eckert-Institute (Braunschweig, Germany)
GPALS	Global Protection against Limited Strikes
HAWK	Homing All-the-Way to Kill (Missile)
IAEA	International Atomic Energy Agency
ICBM	inter-continental ballistic missile
IR	International Relations
IRIS-T	Infra Red Imaging System Tail (Missile)
ISEI	International Society for Educational Information (Japan)
JDA	Japan Defense Agency
JSDF	Japan Self-Defense Forces
JSP	Japan Socialist Party
LDP	Liberal Democratic Party
MD	missile defense
MEADS	Medium Extended Air Defense System
MoD	Ministry of Defense (Germany/Japan)

MoE	Ministry of Education (Germany/Japan)
MoU	Memorandum of Understanding
NATO	North Atlantic Treaty Organization
NIDS	National Institute for Defense Studies (Japan)
NGO	non-governmental organization
NMD	national missile defense
NPT	(Nuclear) Non-Proliferation Treaty
NRC	national role conception
NTWD	Navy's Theater Wide Defense
ODA	official development aid
OSCE	Organization for Security and Cooperation in Europe
PAC-3	Patriot Advanced Capability-3 (surface-to-air interceptors)
PKO	peace keeping operation
PRC	People's Republic of China
ROK	Republic of Korea (South Korea)
SDI	Strategic Defense Initiative
SDP	Social Democratic Party (Japan)
SM-3	Standard Missile-3
SORT	Strategic Offensive Reductions Treaty
SPD	Social Democratic Party (Germany)
START	Strategic Arms Reduction Treaty
TFT	technology-for-technology (framework)
THAAD	Theater High Altitude Area Defense
TMD	theatre missile defence
UN	United Nations
UNESCO	United Nations Educational, Scientific and Cultural Organization
WESTPAC	Western Pacific Missile Defense Architecture Study
WEU	Western European Union
WMD	weapons of mass destruction

Frequently used terms

Article 9	Article 9 of the Japanese Constitution is an article that renounces war
Bundeswehr	German for 'Federal Defence Force'
Bundestag	German for 'Federal Diet' (lower unicameral house of the parliament)
Land/Länder	States within German federal system (also *Bundesland*)
Neighbourhood Clause	1982 Criterion for textbook screenings, according to which Japan pledges to take into consideration the feelings of neighbouring countries in reviewing the depiction of recent history in textbooks
Ostpolitik	Policy of expanding West Germany's social, economic, and political ties with communist countries of the Eastern bloc

	during the Cold War, often associated with Chancellor Willy Brandt
Prime minister	Term used for the position of 'Ministerpräsident', the political leaders of the *Länder* in Germany
Tsukurukai	Japanese Society for History Textbook Reform (Atarashii rekishi kyōkasho o tsukurukai)
Senshu bōei	Japan's concept of an exclusively defence-oriented security policy

Introduction

Germany and Japan in the post-Cold War era offer superb opportunities to examine the factors and forces that shape and guide a country's foreign policy. The end of the Cold War lifted the structural constraints and limitations placed upon both countries' external strategies by the rigid bipolar system. The new environment gave them more freedom in formulating and pursuing their own policies. West Germany and Japan had previously been tied firmly to the strategies of the US-led 'capitalist camp', allowing them only minor deviations in their own policies. Following the Second World War, Washington had exercised direct control as an occupying force, later it retained indirect power over Bonn and Tokyo as the most important ally guaranteeing national security against the Soviet threat. The end of the bipolar era thus constituted a significant change in the external setting, granting Germany and Japan more leeway to pursue foreign policies divergent from the strategies of Washington and its partners. In policy speeches, decision-makers from both Germany and Japan clearly recognized the expanded latitude in their foreign policy in the early 1990s.[1]

Germany and Japan were widely examined and analysed – often through comparative studies – in the academic literature on international relations and politics in the early to mid-1990s.[2] The pressing question was how the two countries would behave in the new international environment. What would determine the foreign policy trajectories of Bonn and Tokyo once the forces that held Germany and Japan in place during the Cold War had fully faded? Would the two countries stake out new foreign policy courses with more unpredictability and the potential for disruption or would they continue to stick to their traditional policy lines of self-restraint and consideration for other countries' concerns? Many scholars were particularly interested in how Bonn and Tokyo would act vis-à-vis their regional neighbours in Europe and East Asia. Would their regional security postures be characterized by old habits of power balancing and the quest for dominance?

Comparative studies addressing these questions were inspired by the striking commonalities between Germany and Japan. Both are populous, democratic and formidable economic powers and they retain strong alliance relationships with Washington, sustained by a substantial American military presence. Germany and Japan share an overwhelming interest in regional and global stability, due to their dependence on international trade and in particular on imported natural resources. Their histories moreover exhibit obvious parallels: Germany as well as Japan went through delayed, rapid processes of industrialization in the late 19th century, setting the stage for the development of militant nationalism and expansionary and aggressive foreign policies in the first half of the 20th century. After their defeats in 1945, Germany and Japan progressed from their former *Machtbesessenheit* (self-aggrandizement before 1945) to *Machtvergessenheit* (low profile in international diplomacy and abstention from traditional power politics after 1945) (Schwarz 1985; Inoguchi 2005: 185). The legacies of the past and residual mistrust among neighbours continued to weigh heavily on the two countries' foreign policies. Especially in the early 1990s, politicians in Bonn and Tokyo faced contradictory expectations from neighbouring countries and partners. On the one hand, they were criticized for enjoying the 'free ride' through reliance on the US security shield; on the other hand, moves to expand their international contributions were met with watchful eyes and calls to exercise restraint.[3]

Most studies in the early 1990s predicted that Germany and Japan would pursue similar foreign and security policies, although scholars disagreed on the direction the two would take. Realist theorists expected Bonn and Tokyo to seek dominating political leadership positions in their respective region commensurate with their economic strength. They argued that the two countries would inevitably act more aggressively in their own national interest, demand autonomy in foreign policy decisions, and strive to acquire greater military capabilities including nuclear weapons. As a result, they foresaw the emergence of regional instability and power rivalries (Waltz 1993; Mearsheimer 1990a, 1990b; Layne 1993). Kenneth Waltz, for example, wrote: 'Ironically, Japan in Asia and Germany in eastern Europe are likely in the next century to replay roles in some ways similar to those they played earlier' (1993: 63). In contrast, constructivist scholars were more optimistic about the prospects of the two countries as regional and global actors, emphasizing the importance of collectively shared ideas and values. They pointed out that Germany's and Japan's normative foundations were overhauled after 1945, based on their experience as aggressors in World War II, their defeat, and their subsequent economic and political rehabilitation. Hanns W. Maull argued that Germany and Japan at the end of the Cold War were emerging as 'civilian powers' (1990/1991: 92). Their foreign policies, he asserted, would be characterized by an acceptance of the need to cooperate internationally, a strong preference for non-military means in dealing with other countries, and a willingness to develop supranational structures (ibid. 92–3). Thomas Berger similarly argued that both Germany and Japan would continue to be reluctant to use military means in international affairs. He based his prediction on a comparative analysis of what he called the 'politico-military cultures' (1998).

Now, roughly two decades after the end of the Cold War, a fresh look at German and Japanese regional security behaviour since 1990 promises new insights into the fundamental question: what factors have guided and shaped the foreign policies? An initial examination of actual behaviour reveals an intriguing picture of distinct and consistent patterns in each country's policies and strategies over the past two decades. One can observe similarities as well as differences. It is evident that the two countries have explicitly rejected unilaterally dominating regional roles that realist scholars predicted. Both have demonstrated a pronounced aversion to the use of military force, thus reassuring neighbouring countries of their peaceful intentions. They gradually expanded their support for UN missions by contributing military personnel, though only after intense domestic debates and considerable soul-searching. The differences between Germany's and Japan's foreign and security policies are, however, as notable as the similarities. Japan has restricted the use of force in UN activities much more than Germany has. Although both countries have contributed to regional cooperation, Germany has done so more enthusiastically, often acting as a key initiator and advocate. It supported formal multilateral institutions and regional cooperation vigorously and was willing to transfer sovereignty to the supranational level. Even among European partner countries, this was unparalleled (Pond 1992; Aggestam 2004). Japan, by contrast, has taken a more hesitant stance in regional security cooperation, preferring bilateral and less formal, issue-specific multilateral cooperation. Furthermore, Tokyo has consistently given priority to relations with the US in its foreign policy (Hughes and Fukushima 2004). The comparative study at hand examines the factors that have driven these distinct foreign policy approaches in the post-Cold War era.

A second motivation for the present comparative analysis on Germany and Japan is linked to the recent scholarly literature on the two countries' foreign policy trajectories. A central question that pervades in the discussions is the degree to which the post-Cold War foreign policies have been marked by continuity versus change. The majority of recent books and articles avoid comparative perspectives in seeking to answer this question.[4] In the predictions of the early 1990s, scholars foresaw similar foreign policy lines for Germany and Japan, but current assessments tend to diverge considerably. Whereas the majority of recent accounts on Germany find *overall continuity* in the Federal Republic's foreign policy course after the Cold War, prominent works on Japan contend that the country has been undergoing a *fundamental and extensive transformation*. The different assessments provoke a number of questions, which will be addressed in this comparative study. But first, a closer look at the academic debates on Germany and Japan is warranted.

Studies on Germany find substantial continuity, especially in the foreign policy *goals* pursued by subsequent administrations.[5] Most scholars assert that policy continuity is anchored in a stable set of normative guidelines and principles that has developed among policy-makers and the public since 1945. As a leading study in 2001 asserted, German foreign policy after unification 'is best explained as norm-consistent foreign policy behavior' (Rittberger 2001: 7). However, the analyses also point to important behavioural adjustments – particularly in the choice of policy *instruments and means* – implemented to meet the new requirements of the post-Cold War world order. The most significant adaptation was made with regard to the use of military force, with Germany now playing a more proactive role in international peacekeeping missions than during the Cold War and in the early 1990s. Most scholars conclude that the adjustments represent attempts to harmonize Germany's foreign policy traditions with the conditions of the post-Cold War world. As August Pradetto attests, the adaptations retain their roots in the normative and politico-cultural traditions of the Federal Republic and can thus be seen as 'modifications below the threshold of fundamental change' (2006: 22).

The question of change was particularly debated with the inception of the coalition government between the Social Democratic Party (SPD) and the Green Party in 1998. Gerhard Schröder was not only the first SPD chancellor since 1982 but also the first leader of the 'post-war' generation.[6] Observers realized that he referred to German foreign policy differently from his predecessor Helmut Kohl, not hesitating to voice 'national' interests and exhibiting more pragmatism. Schröder's policy in the lead-up to the Iraq War in particular gave rise to academic debates. In the midst of an election campaign in January 2003, Schröder declared that Germany would not send troops to Iraq, no matter what the UN Security Council decided. His stance seemed to go against the traditional German emphasis on multilateral decision-making and the attachment to international institutions. Nevertheless, most studies concluded that – with the possible exception of the Iraq case – the substance of Schröder's foreign policy revealed 'little evidence of fundamental change' in Germany's basic orientation, although the policies were 'dressed up rhetorically with a new sense of self-importance and self-confidence' (Maull 2006a: 273). Some observers argued that Schröder's different style reflected German 'emancipation', but not a new direction in Berlin's foreign policy (Forsberg 2005).

Continuity has also been detected in the policies under the leadership of Chancellor Angela Merkel of the Christian Democrats, first in governmental coalition with the Social Democrats and then with the Free Democrats. For example, Gisela Müller-Brandeck-Bocquet argued that Merkel's European policy reflects clear continuity with past administrations (2010: 257) Christian Hacke similarly observed that the policy of keeping a low profile, seeking compromise and mediation, and maintaining good transatlantic relations was consistent with past practices (2008: 2). Some studies remark that German traditional commitment to multilateralism has been in decline, as policy-makers increasingly focus on domestic issues.[7] Despite these reservations, the overwhelming majority of studies conclude that the Federal Republic's foreign policy in the post-Cold War era can be described as 'modified continuity' (Harnisch 2001: 48).

In contrast, prominent studies on Japanese foreign policy find significant change and even transformation since the end of the Cold War. Two books, each by a foremost authority on Japan, see fundamental change in Tokyo's policy. Historian Kenneth Pyle contends that Japan today is 'on the threshold of a new era' (2007a: 374), preparing to 'become a major player in the strategic struggles of the twenty-first century' (ibid. 17). He holds that Tokyo's current shift will be major, similar to previous 'abrupt changes and wide swings of international behavior' during such times as the Meiji Period in the 19th century or the post-1945 era (Pyle 2007a: 19). Similarly, political scientist Richard Samuels sees a 'transformation' in Japan's foreign policy strategy, as a new national security consensus is emerging (2007b: 64). Both Pyle and Samuels point out that

Japan's stance on the use of military force has changed considerably, as reflected in the recent proactive dispatches of Japanese troops to the Indian Ocean and Iraq. Samuels observes that Japanese leaders today are 'slicing in earnest' at the 'pacifist loaf' (2007b: 91), baked before by such politicians as Yoshida Shigeru, an influential post-war prime minister. Moreover, Pyle and Samuels argue that nationalistic Japanese leaders such as Prime Ministers Koizumi Junichiro or Abe Shinzo have displayed more assertiveness and self-confidence in their foreign policy. In both Pyle's and Samuel's accounts, the changes in Japan's policy were in large part precipitated by the end of the Cold War.[8]

Several specialists agree with the view that Japan is undergoing a fundamental transformation. Kevin Cooney, for example, argues that changes in Tokyo's foreign policy are 'not merely incremental course corrections but also major shifts in national policy' (2007: 8). In his opinion, Japan is in the 'midst of a maturation process in which it is seeking to present itself as a great power' (ibid. 3). Others, however, are more cautious – seeing important changes in Japan though not necessarily an outright transformation. Former Japanese Foreign Ministry official Tanaka Hitoshi maintains that Tokyo's policy reflects a 'process of adapting to the changing domestic and international strategic environment' and cautions against exaggerating and misinterpreting current trends (Tanaka 2008a: 1). At the same time, he concedes that Japan's foreign policy style and form have undergone significant mutation. Similarly, political scientist Soeya Yoshihide argues that Japan has not made a turnaround in its policy from traditional principles and norms, but is rather in a phase of adjustment and reformulation (Soeya 2005: 207–8).[9]

These assessments, which place Germany and Japan far apart on the spectrum between continuity and change in foreign policy, raise several essential and interrelated questions. First, if we adopt a comparative perspective, which allows us to critically reflect on our evaluation of continuity versus change in one country through the parallel analysis of the other country, will we come to the same conclusion? In other words, would we still find a significant discrepancy between the two countries, with prevailing continuity in German policy and fundamental transformation in Japanese policy? Secondly, can we specify more precisely the extent and type of change (or adjustment) taking place in either country? For example, the 'new era' that Pyle professes in Japan's international orientation implies a significant shift in the country's policies. Does this mean a complete break with former policy goals and established policy instruments? Or have the changes in Japan been more comparable to the 'adjustments' that are seen in Germany's case – with core policy objectives remaining unaffected? Conversely, we can ask whether German adjustments have perhaps been underestimated and the country has in fact experienced a more fundamental 'transformation' with significant policy elements being altered. A third question arises if we assume that recent assessments seeing continuity in Germany and a far-reaching 'transformation' in Japan are correct: what has determined and driven the divergent paths in foreign policy? Where is Japan going and what kind of policies should we expect from Tokyo in the coming years?

Surprisingly, the studies asserting extensive change in Japan's foreign policies hardly provide an answer to the last question of how Tokyo is likely to behave in the future. Kenneth Pyle maintains that it is too early to tell what the new strategy will be, although he implies that policy-makers tend to respond in line with elements of Japan's traditional 'style' (2007a: 1) 'Given the uncertainty in the region,' he argues, 'it is impossible to predict what the new strategy may be or when it will coalesce' (Pyle 2007b: 210). Richard Samuels goes further in his characterization of Japan's new policy course. He sees a domestic consensus emerging, which he calls 'Goldilocks' preference', based on a hedging strategy in which 'Japan's relationship with the US and China will be neither too hot nor too cold, and its posture in the region will be neither too big nor too small' (Samuels 2007b: 132). He also insists that Tokyo's policy will be defined by more assertiveness and 'greater strength and independence' (Samuels 2007a: 205). At the same time however, Samuels contends that the domestic debate is still in flux, and that the 'final shape of Japan's new security consensus is still up for grabs' (2007b: 203). In his view, the future of the US–Japan relationship in particular is still open for discussion. He points out that Tokyo's and Washington's divergent strategic preferences have become more visible and that these 'combine with Tokyo's preferences for autonomy and prestige in ways that may threaten the currently close relationship' (ibid. 191).

On a basic level, observers who see a fundamental change or transformation in Japan seem to agree that the normative constraints on Tokyo's security policy are loosening and that future behaviour will be bolder and more focused on military force. Yet there seems to be little agreement on what objectives Tokyo will pursue through military means. In this respect, neither Pyle nor Samuels give clear answers.[10] Other observers, such as Eugene Matthews, are concerned about nationalist tendencies affecting Japan's military policy, which in their view could destabilize the whole East Asian region (Matthews 2003).

Using an explicitly comparative framework for analysis, this study reassesses the issue of change and continuity in German and Japanese foreign policies. The chosen analytical framework helps to illuminate the causes and reasons for each country's distinct policy strategy and style. Furthermore, the comparative approach facilitates the characterization of the extent and type of change under way in each country. Based on the analysis, the study wants to shed new light on the question of where Germany and Japan may be going in their policies in the coming years.

Theoretical approach and key questions

This book employs and further develops a role theoretical approach to compare and analyse how Germany and Japan have formulated their foreign policy goals and strategies in the post-Cold War era. Role theory – as a strand of constructivist thinking in the discipline of international relations – assumes that state behaviour is guided by *role conceptions* encompassing a body of attitudes, beliefs, assumptions and ideas shared within society. Role conceptions define and circumscribe the aims, the perceived responsibilities and the instruments or tactics judged appropriate and legitimate in a country's foreign policy. They serve as reference frames for policy-makers when considering behavioural options and formulating goals and strategies (Boekle *et al.* 2000: 11; Hyde-Price and Aggestam 2000: 253). Each country is assumed to have a distinct set of role conceptions, which distinguish it from other countries and lead to different foreign policy orientations, strategies and preferences.

Based on this theoretical approach, the study at hand argues that the international structure does not determine state behaviour, but that material factors are only given meaning through social processes, ideas and shared knowledge. We depend on our social interpretation and construction of reality and on our ideas and subjective knowledge about the world to determine appropriate foreign policy behaviour. Structural configurations such as the distribution of power are thus filtered through a 'cognitive lens' with which actors are endowed (Berger 2003: 262).

Role theory can provide valuable insight into the question of continuity and change in foreign policy. By observing the predominant role conceptions over a length of time, it allows the tracing of shifts and modifications in stated policy goals and strategies, and examination of changes in declared motivations and rationales. It permits investigation of how policy-makers reflect on the current international environment, and whether ongoing experiences confirm or challenge existing role conceptions. Based on a role theoretical approach, this study thus presents a dynamic account of change and continuity in German and Japanese foreign and security policies, drawing on policy-makers' own perspectives.

This book seeks to answer a number of empirical and theoretical questions, focusing on Germany's and Japan's regional security policies in the time period since the end of the Cold War from around 1990 to the present. First, regarding the empirical aspects, it identifies and characterizes the content of each country's role conceptions and reveals similarities and differences. By taking an actor-focused perspective, it addresses the question of continuity and change in German and Japanese foreign policies in the post-Cold War era. Secondly, regarding the theoretical aspects, this book sets out to examine the factors and forces that shape and guide a country's foreign policy, treating Germany and Japan as two pertinent examples. It considers and probes whether a role theoretical approach can provide convincing explanations for German and Japanese post-Cold War foreign policy behaviour observed in particular policy fields.

Methodological overview

Identification of role conceptions

Dominant role conceptions can be analysed by referring to foreign policy speeches of political elites in which they indicate their commitment to particular behaviour, functions and responsibilities of their country (Aggestam 2000: 97). Thus, in the context of this study, a qualitative content analysis of major foreign policy speeches from Germany and Japan was conducted. A minimum of three foreign policy speeches per year and country were chosen for the time period from 1990 to 2011.[11] The speeches were delivered by principal decision-makers such as prime ministers, chancellors or foreign ministers, who serve as the most authoritative sources for defining national conceptions of identity and role. In the content analysis, all assertions referring to the conceptions held by decision-makers of the duties and responsibilities of their state with relevance to the region were inductively coded and classified in a categorization system. After coding German and Japanese speeches separately, aggregate labels were devised by identifying areas of correspondence and thematic similarities in the speeches of both countries. This procedure ensures that both similarities and differences in the role conceptions of Germany and Japan can be identified and compared.

In the coding process, two important criteria were applied in identifying statements to be included in the analysis. First, statements had to focus on political, diplomatic and security issues falling into the traditional narrow definition of security studies (Katzenstein 1996: 10). This limitation was made both to keep the scope of this study within manageable proportions and to analyse social determinants of national security policy – a policy field traditionally dominated by studies relying on utilitarian and structural approaches. Secondly, only statements focusing on duties and responsibilities within each country's region, i.e. Europe for Germany and Asia for Japan, were included in the coding process. This second criterion was chosen both for practical reasons, i.e. to further limit the scope of the study, and for analytical reasons, as the two countries are key regional players. The application of the two criteria to the content analysis will be explained in more detail in the first chapter.

Approach to case studies

Based on two case studies, this book examines actual German and Japanese foreign policy behaviour and tests the explanatory power of role theory. Case studies were chosen with three selection criteria in mind. First, the cases had to have relevance for regional security issues, corresponding to the focus applied in the coding process of the content analysis. Secondly, German and Japanese policymakers had to be confronted with similar strategic questions and difficulties in the chosen policy fields. If the two countries deviate significantly in their behaviour despite being faced with similar circumstances and challenges, the influence of role conceptions can be analysed effectively. Thirdly, to test the role theoretical approach, the chosen case studies had to cover different aspects in German and Japanese regional security policy.

Two case studies were selected for analysis.[12] The first covers German and Japanese policies on missile defence systems – an issue of enormous significance in the current defence strategies of both countries. It arguably represents a 'hard' test case for the explanatory power of ideational variables and role conceptions. As noted above, policies closely related to traditional defence and security questions have been explained mostly through reference to utilitarian and structural variables. Because missile defense (MD) policy covers a broad range of issues, this case study is divided into three sub-studies: the first looks at MD strategies for *national territorial defence*, the second examines MD policies for the *protection of soldiers* deployed abroad and the last deals with the two countries' stance on using their MD capabilities to *support partner countries*. Each of these sub-studies is intricately linked to the broader regional security strategies of either country, as the discussion will show. The second case study investigates Berlin's and Tokyo's policies on joint textbook commissions with neighbouring countries. In Europe and even more so in Asia, the treatment of history in school books has the potential to destabilize security relations. Because of analytical reasons specified in the case study's introduction, the German–Polish and Japanese–South Korean textbook disputes were selected for comparison.

Each case study involves several analytical steps. First, German and Japanese behaviour is examined separately, highlighting the developments in foreign policy strategies and dominant themes in the political debates. Characteristics and distinct patterns of behaviour of each country are analysed and compared. Then follows a discussion of whether role conceptions provide convincing explanations for German or Japanese foreign policy conduct. Finally, the analysis considers other factors which may have influenced German and Japanese strategies and behaviour.

Relevance and existing literature

Germany and Japan are two key powers in regional and international security dynamics. Both countries wield formidable economic strength and consequently play important roles in shaping their respective environments. For Washington in particular, Berlin and Tokyo remain essential partners and allies in international affairs. A deeper understanding of how Germany and Japan define their interests and roles is thus indispensable. Furthermore, as pointed out above, they are pertinent examples to examine the explanatory potential of role conceptions. Although a systematic comparison of Germany and Japan as post-Cold War regional security actors promises fundamental insights into the forces shaping and guiding foreign policy strategies, theoretically grounded studies are scarce. IR scholarship has primarily focused on one region rather than engaging in cross-regional research. Without doubt, language requirements have been a major obstacle to tackling such cross-regional studies and specifically comparisons between Germany and Japan.

The work of Peter Katzenstein perhaps comes closest to this book's endeavour of comparing German and Japanese regional security policy strategies. His valuable research examines European and East Asian regionalism, in which Germany and Japan are seen as 'intermediaries' (Katzenstein 2005: 3) linking each region to the 'American imperium' (ibid. 4). However, Katzenstein's work differs from this book in the analytical focus and in the theoretical approach. He studies the characteristics of European and East Asian regionalism and investigates the interaction between the forces of globalization and internationalization. While he pays particular attention to Germany and Japan as core regional powers, he does not present an actor-specific outlook by examining the political debate or speeches of decision-makers. Rather, he explores the complex forces shaping regional characteristics and German and Japanese foreign policy behaviour. His research is based on an eclectic approach drawing on all three main theories in IR scholarship: realism, liberalism and constructivism (Katzenstein 2005: 39). This allows him to analyse a range of factors possibly affecting policy strategies. In the end, however, the reader is left somewhat bewildered by the complexities and interdependencies presented in the study, and it remains unclear which forces Katzenstein considers most important in shaping policies. Therefore, this book wants to contribute to the research on German and Japanese regional security behaviour through a systematic comparative approach focusing on the actors' perspectives.

Comparative role theoretical work on Germany and Japan has also been rare, and – apart from some older work from the mid-1990s – a direct comparison between the two countries is lacking.[13] Recently, Lisbeth Aggestam (2004) has examined German, British and French conceptions of regional security roles based on a qualitative content analysis of policy speeches from each country. One of the key questions underlying her work is whether the three countries' conceptions are converging around a European identity through socialization processes. Building on Aggestam's research, this book sets out to gain further insight into Germany's regional role conception. The cross-regional comparison carried out in the analysis below seeks to expose characteristics about German and Japanese thinking patterns that may not be as conspicuous in intra-regional comparisons or single-country studies. Moreover, this book examines the explanatory power of role conceptions through several case studies – a field Aggestam did not investigate. In another lately published study, Hanns W. Maull (2007) evaluates recent German foreign policy behaviour in light of the civilian power role concept that he developed earlier in his comparative research. Although he provides rich and multifaceted insights into current policies, his study does not include a detailed examination of foreign policy speeches.

The only role theoretical study about Japan is that by Bert Edström (2004). In his short, non-comparative study, Edström examines continuities and changes in speeches before and after the 1993 political upheaval, in which the governing Liberal Democratic Party (LDP) lost power. Although Edström provides some initial insights into Japanese role conceptions, a more detailed analysis focusing on the developments in the post-Cold War era is required to identify the forces shaping and guiding foreign policy strategies. Aside from Edström's study, two other works deserve mention. Susanne Klien (2002) explored Japan's international role including some recent domestic debates among policy-makers, but her research is not based explicitly on a role theoretical approach and does not examine foreign policy speeches. A Japanese study by Tanaka Akihiko of Tokyo University quantitatively analyses 133 Diet speeches held by Japanese prime ministers between 1945 and 1999. Although the study presents interesting results, its scope is limited, as it only surveys the different concepts of 'region' used in speeches, such as 'Asia', 'Asia-Pacific' or 'Southeast Asia' (Tanaka 2000).

Argument and structure

Both qualitative content analysis and case studies presented in this book demonstrate the influence of normative and ideational variables in German and Japanese foreign policy-making. National role conceptions provide a robust and compelling explanation for observed patterns of foreign policy behaviours. Overall, the analysis finds overwhelming continuity in the role conceptions and policies of Germany and Japan. Incremental adaptations in foreign policy preferences and attitudes can be found in both countries, but they are anchored in established normative guidelines and represent attempts to harmonize existing preferences with the conditions of the post-Cold War era. The most visible change has been the two countries' expansion of their military capabilities and global involvements through the dispatch of troops. However, rather than signifying the return to power politics, this change reflects the desire by decision-makers to make international contributions in a changed environment. Politicians in both Berlin and Tokyo continue to abjure unilateralism in foreign policy and display caution about the use of military force. Due to the persistence of German and Japanese role conceptions, this book argues that scholars have overstated and misconstrued the changes under way by asserting that Japan is undergoing a sweeping transformation in its foreign policy.

This book is organized as follows. Chapter 1 presents the theoretical and methodological frameworks and is followed by a discussion in Chapter 2 of the German and Japanese role conceptions found in the content analysis. Chapters 3 and 4 present the findings from the case studies about actual foreign policy behaviour of Germany and Japan in the post-Cold War era. The Conclusion summarizes key findings, draws inferences about both countries' foreign policy trajectories and assesses the analytical value of role theory.

Terminology

In line with convention, Japanese names are written with the family name followed by the first name. Western names appear with the given name appearing before the family name. Japanese text passages and terms are transcribed according to the *Hepburn romanization system,* with slight modifications. For instance, I write shinbun instead of shimbun. The text refrains from using macrons or inflection marks such as ō or ū in names of Japanese individuals and in names and terms that are commonly used in English, such as the city name Tokyo (instead of Tōkyō). Furthermore, when using the term 'Germany' in descriptions of the Cold War era, this book refers to the Federal Republic of Germany, or West Germany.

1 Theoretical and methodological frameworks

Introduction

This chapter describes the theoretical and methodological foundations of this book. The first part introduces role theory, revealing strengths and weaknesses and exploring key issues such as change and continuity in role conceptions. It concludes by considering role conflicts and coping strategies, an area that has received insufficient attention in role theoretical accounts thus far. The second part focuses on the method used to identify and compare national role conceptions in this study. It explains the choice of empirical material and describes the labelling and categorizing process employed in the content analysis.

Theoretical approach

National role conceptions and their function

Role theory assumes that a country's foreign policy behaviour is decisively shaped by national role conceptions (NRCs). NRCs are defined as intersubjectively shared, value-based expectations about the appropriate role a state should play in international affairs – or for the purpose of this study, in regional security affairs. Kalevi Holsti, who introduced role theory to the study of international politics in a 1970 article, relied on a similar definition: 'A national role conception includes the policymakers' own definitions of the general kinds of decisions, commitments, rules and actions suitable to their state, and of the functions, if any, their state should perform on a continuing basis in the international system or in subordinate regional systems' (1970: 245–6).

Role conceptions are products of countless domestic and international influences and they have both ideational and material roots (Holsti 1970; Wish 1980; Maull 2007; Aggestam 2004). They stem from environmental factors such as geographic location and natural resources, from domestic and international socialization processes, and from material factors such as economic power and capabilities, which may open up or rule out certain policy choices. Role conceptions are fundamentally shaped by collective experiences and societal learning based on formative events, past failures and successful policies. Just like individuals, nations act based upon past experiences and the resulting shared convictions and perceptions. Role conceptions reflect a negotiated understanding of the world and represent the collective memory and normative ideals and beliefs of a society.

By specifying objectives, delimiting the range of policy options and tactics, and establishing standards of proper behaviour, NRCs provide foreign policy-makers with orientation and conceptual 'road maps' (Aggestam 2000: 87). They facilitate decision-makers' understanding of the highly complex world of international relations and provide guidelines for appropriate behaviour. Faced with both time constraints and cognitive limits, political elites have little room to rethink basic strategies on a day-to-day basis. The following quote by an official from the Japanese Ministry of Foreign Affairs illustrates the significance of role conceptions (here referred to as 'principles'):

> Having principles saves contemplation and time. If we have an established principle, ... we won't have to doubt it each time we debate something. In my case, I never doubt ... that the development of the Japan–US alliance is in Japan's interest. My rationalization is to concentrate efforts on managing that alliance.
>
> (Tanter and Honda 2006)

NRCs thus ensure that decision-makers can swiftly react and focus their energies on policy implementation and the realization of established objectives.

According to Ulrich Krotz, NRCs affect state behaviour in three dimensions: first, they *prescribe* by motivating wills and goals, secondly, they *proscribe* by ruling out certain courses of action as inappropriate, and thirdly, they *induce processual preferences* by defining the tactics and instruments seen as legitimate and morally acceptable in foreign policy (Krotz 2002: 8–9). NRCs thus identify and delineate a country's goals, interests, the perceived responsibilities and duties as well as the instruments judged appropriate in foreign policy. Furthermore, they shape and condition how policy-makers evaluate their present external environment, their policy alternatives and the likely consequences of their conduct. However, it is important to note that NRCs do not directly cause state behaviour. Rather, they provide reasons or motives for particular conduct. Role theoretical research thus cannot explain foreign policy behaviour in a conventional positivist sense (Aggestam 2004: 19). As an interpretive approach, it can expose and highlight the perspectives and views of decision-makers and register apparent linkages to foreign policy behaviour.

Role theory in the discipline of international relations

In international relations, role theory belongs to the constructivist research agenda. Constructivists criticize the dominant theoretical approaches and especially neo-realism for assuming that the behaviour of states is dictated exclusively by the material-structural context and the distribution of power in the international system. For constructivists, the material world is given meaning only through an actor's 'cognitive lens' comprising his subjective understandings and ideas (Berger 2003: 390).

Role theory's focus on the subjective perspective of the role holder allows the researcher to assess the interplay between internal and external variables and pinpoint the cognitive outcome. NRCs thus provide an analytical bridge between the ideational, material and institutional realms. Role theory does not stand in outright contradiction to other theoretical approaches in IR. Rather, it acknowledges the influence of factors that realist or liberal accounts emphasize. According to role theory, the effect of such variables on foreign policy behaviour may vary both in extent and in type, depending on the cognitive predispositions and beliefs in each state. Even though role theory emphasizes normative-ideational factors, states are not seen as irrational actors. Rather, policy-makers act in accordance with their *subjective, value-based rationality* and their *perceptions of reality*. Societal norms and beliefs influence and condition the definition of national interests, and hence there is no value-free rationality.

Role theory opens the door for a methodical examination of normative factors in foreign policy-making. This is perhaps its greatest contribution to the discipline of IR. Numerous constructivists have highlighted the influence of values and ideas, using terms such as 'identity' or 'political culture' to conceptualize their effect in shaping policies.[1] These studies have provided valuable insights, but they face the inherent difficulty of systematically exploring and capturing a country's 'identity' or 'political culture'. Role theory can identify more precisely the impact of norms and ideas on a country's behavioural preferences and strategic outlook. Through a content analysis of key speeches or other pertinent material, the analyst can investigate a society's conceptions of role, which indicate how identity and culture are translated into action templates. Role theory thus serves as an invaluable analytical tool and effective extension of mainstream constructivist approaches.[2]

Role theoretical terminology

Role theory distinguishes between ego-part and alter-part conceptions. Ego-part conceptions consist of the rights and obligations that a country's politicians perceive on behalf of their *own* state. Alter-part conceptions, on the other hand, denote the behavioural expectations held by *other* states or by international organizations. While both ego- and alter-part conceptions have some effect on the behaviour of states, this study considers the ego-part as the one with more immediate and substantial impact, and hence the more relevant realm for examination. As Michael Barnett points out, when a state does not comply with alter-part expectations, its survival is rarely at stake, 'but the government's domestic standing frequently is' (Barnett 1993: 278). This study furthermore assumes that a country's ego- and alter-part conceptions may consist of multiple distinct behavioural expectations. This assumption is in line with Kalevi Holsti's study, which found an average of 4.5 ego-part role conceptions in one country per source he investigated (Holsti 1970).

When referring to the sum total of a country's role conceptions, Lisbeth Aggestam's term *role set* will be employed. According to Aggestam, a role set represents the school of thought predominating in foreign policy (Aggestam 2004: 67). A country's overall approach to foreign policy can be characterized and described by analysing this role set. Finally, *role behaviour* or *role performance* is defined as the actual behaviour of the role holder. This book empirically tests role theory's assumption of a general correspondence between NRCs and foreign policy conduct.

Continuity and change in role conceptions

NRCs are relatively stable understandings regarding the proper behaviour of a state, but they are not unchangeable. Their temporal stability makes NRCs a useful tool for explaining typical patterns of international actors' policy behaviour while remaining attentive to changes in these patterns (Holsti 1970: 306–7). The temporal stability of role conceptions within the ego-part has several roots. First, by definition, NRCs are collectively shared beliefs and ideas that are considered legitimate and appropriate within society. Such widespread conceptions become 'sticky' and cannot easily be replaced by alternative sets of ideas. Secondly, for politicians, NRCs are useful reference frames providing consistency and authority in foreign policy decisions. Political leaders cannot treat NRCs as infinitely malleable and elastic because that would 'make the world seem random and beyond control' (Chafetz *et al.* 1996: 736). Thirdly, the endurance of NRCs is reinforced by the psychological phenomenon of consistency seeking. To minimize uncertainty and anxiety and to speed up decision-making processes, actors tend to incorporate information that reinforces their existing views, while ignoring or distorting data that are inconsistent with dominant beliefs (Duffield 1999: 770). Consequently, NRCs – resting on normative-ideational beliefs about proper conduct – are not easily disconfirmed by new information.

Role change is nevertheless conceivable, and it is most likely to occur gradually. As Chafetz *et al.* argue, 'states do not usually abandon role conceptions outright. Instead they slowly downgrade their centrality. Rapid shifts in role may, however, occur in states undergoing internal upheaval ... or in new states' (1996: 736). Shifts in background factors and issues arising from interaction between states may induce changes in dominant role conceptions within a state. If new information continually challenges and contradicts societal views, significant cognitive dissonance may arise. In the medium term, policy-makers will not be able to ignore or deny these contradictions. A role conflict, in which a country is faced with competing or conflicting behavioural expectations, may also trigger role change. Different types of role conflict will be discussed in further detail below. While role theory generally assumes stability, it also acknowledges various instances of role change. This makes NRCs an ideal tool for studying continuity and change in foreign policy.

Role conflict and coping strategies

A role conflict arises when a state faces two or more incompatible or contradictory behavioural expectations. Ego- and alter-part conceptions represent socially negotiated understandings emerging from multiple sources, and thus behavioural expectations will not always coincide or align. Conflicting pressures may occur either within the ego-part role set or between ego- and alter-part NRCs.

States cope differently with situations of role conflict. If the two role conceptions are in tension but not in outright contradiction, the simplest strategy for policy-makers is to draw on conceptual ambiguities to ameliorate friction and conceal problematic points. Because role conceptions are broad categories relevant to a variety of circumstances, they can be interpreted with some flexibility. If this fails however, policy-makers need to adopt more elaborate forms of coping behaviour. There are four conceivable coping strategies. The first three are particularly useful in the short term as they do not require adjustments in the two conflicting role conceptions; the last strategy calls for extensive efforts in modifying NRCs and is appropriate for the mid- to long term.

First, to avoid changes in the conceptions, a country may escape the situation that gave rise to the role conflict. It may do so by either withdrawing completely or by proactively seeking to change the problematic situation itself. This strategy will be illustrated and discussed in more detail in the case study on Germany's missile defence policy and the protection of allies and partners.

Second, a country may decide to enact one role at the expense of another (Walker and Simon 1987: 142). In so doing, policy-makers leave the content of both role conceptions rhetorically unchanged, but in actual behaviour they violate one in favour of the other. Role theoretical research suggests that policy-makers are guided by a hierarchy of preferences within their role set in deciding which role to adhere to and which to defy (Edström 1988). The specificity of the two NRCs in question may also be a factor. If one NRC distinguishes appropriate from inappropriate behaviour more precisely, politicians may find it more difficult to violate this particular NRC. If they need to react rapidly or the role conflict is expected to be a one-time occurrence, policy-makers may find this second strategy convenient. In the long term however, this strategy leads to significant cognitive dissonance and legitimacy problems, and it is thus unlikely to be used for extended periods of time.

A third strategy that leaves the NRCs essentially unchanged is for politicians to search for a compromise between the two conflicting conceptions (Backman 1970: 318; Biddle 1986: 83). Policy-makers may meet both behavioural expectations in part or adhere alternately to one and the other. However, in the long term, this strategy is also problematic, because government behaviour is likely to be criticized as lacking direction and consistency.

The final coping strategy involves policy-makers' efforts to negotiate a new understanding of the competing conceptions. To eliminate frictions, it may be enough for government leaders to suggest small adjustments in one or all affected conceptions. In other cases, it may be necessary to initiate more fundamental changes or to introduce new role understandings – processes that will likely be accompanied by extensive domestic debates.

Cases of role conflict present both challenges and opportunities for theorists. As seen above, it is difficult to predict state behaviour in any of these situations for there are various coping strategies, and states may also rely on a combination thereof. On the other hand, role conflicts present opportunities to examine in detail the impact and influence of NRCs and the circumstances which lead a state to choose one coping strategy over another. For these reasons, close attention will be paid to such conflicts when examining German and Japanese foreign policies.

Methodological approach

Content analysis

The empirical material for the content analysis consists of speeches delivered by the highest level German and Japanese decision-makers on questions of regional foreign and security policy.[3] The selection of speeches generally follows criteria commonly used in other role theoretical studies. To ensure continuous analytical coverage, a minimum of three foreign policy speeches per year and country are chosen for the time period from 1990 to 2011. In total, the empirical material comprises 129 German and 130 Japanese speeches made by principal decision-makers such as prime ministers or chancellors, foreign and defence ministers who articulate conceptions of role with the greatest political authority and salience. Furthermore, the selected speeches target both domestic and international audiences. They range from policy speeches addressing parliament (the *Bundestag* in Germany and the *kokkai* in Japan) to speeches held at international organizations such as the United Nations. Availability and easy access through such sources as diplomatic Bluebooks were other criteria in choosing material for analysis. Finally, foreign policy speeches were selected according to their relevance for the research question. The chosen speeches address the general or region-wide strategic outlook, while material with a narrow focus on a particular policy field was exempted to minimize potential bias.

Indications about a country's role conceptions can be gathered from a variety of sources, such as public opinion data, key legal documents (such as constitutions), representations in the media or interviews. However, the reliance on fundamental foreign policy speeches has several essential advantages. These speeches provide rich data and insights into the beliefs and ideas of principal political players, who are responsible for formulating concrete policies. Speeches by important decision-makers are likely to reflect only those role conceptions supported by a critical mass within society. Another advantage of using policy speeches is that this data occurs naturally, i.e. without the analyst's or someone else's prompting. Rather than gathering data through interaction with officials in interviews, for example, speeches allow the analyst to rely exclusively on *unobtrusive* research methods to investigate how the speaker views his social world.

While divergent views within a society are not ruled out, role theory suggests that there will be broad areas of correspondence within and across parties and groups on the core set of foreign policy role conceptions. Indeed, a number of studies have confirmed that politicians from the same country hold similar conceptions about foreign policy conduct, based on shared ideas such as collectively held historical understandings and common evaluations of successful and unsuccessful past policies (Wish 1980; Weske 2006; Duffield 1999).

Qualitative content analysis

The selected speeches were subjected to a qualitative content analysis in order to identify dominant role conceptions. According to Ole R. Holsti, content analysis can be broadly defined as 'any technique for making inferences by systematically and objectively identifying special characteristics of messages' (quoted in Berg 2004: 267). Content analysis seeks to reduce the amount of text material by highlighting recurrent arguments or themes that are relevant to the research question. In analysing the material, the researcher seeks to establish representative categories to capture text characteristics and features. Qualitative content analysis in particular focuses on the *meaning* of texts. It allows the researcher to examine how issues are presented, contextualized and evaluated by the subject. While some role theoretical studies have relied on quantitative methods, it is far from clear whether frequency of articulation is directly correlated with the relative importance of role conceptions. Thus, this book only employs the qualitative approach.

The coding scheme was developed inductively, involving the formulation of categories through identification of recurrent themes and referencing of passages relevant to the research question. An inductive approach has several advantages. First, this book does not aim to test a specific theory-related hypothesis and thus the deductive approach with pre-defined categories used in some other role theoretical studies is not suitable. Secondly, an open, flexible approach to the definition of categories can avoid biases from forcing data into existing schemes. The analyst can thus maintain maximum sensitivity to policy-makers' specific conceptions as well as conceptual shifts over time.

Defining categories and assigning labels to particular passages in the text material remains an act of interpretation.[4] Therefore, the process of coding text passages should be 'rule-governed and explicit to the greatest extent possible' (Mayring 2005: 11). Philipp Mayring distinguishes between three basic forms of interpretation in content analysis: summary, explication and structuring (Mayring 1990: 54). This study relies primarily on the first and to some extent on the second type. The purpose of the first, summary, is to reduce the text material to basic contents and themes. In other words, this approach seeks to create a 'manageable corpus' of concepts that reflects the meaning of the original material (ibid.). It does so by relying on an iterative process that includes paraphrasing, grouping, integrating and abstracting. Explication was employed as a supplementary tool only after the analysis of speeches was concluded. This form of interpretation involves

① Development of subcategories (behavioural expectations)

Germany

- Selection of speeches
- Definition of criteria for coding
- Formulation of subcategories
  - Preliminary analysis of two speeches per country and year
  - Formulation of categories reflecting as closely as possible specific behavioural expectations
  - Analysis of all speeches; testing and adjustment of categories
- Result: 11 subcategories

Japan

- Separate analysis of Japanese speeches
- Same procedure as in case of Germany
- Result: 13 subcategories

② Development of aggregate categories (role conceptions)

- Group subcategories thematically and seek areas of correspondence
- Define and label aggregate categories which reflect areas of correspondence
- Test and adjust aggregate categories by checking if other role theoretical studies provide more appropriate categories or labels
- Result: 6 aggregate categories for Germany and 7 for Japan

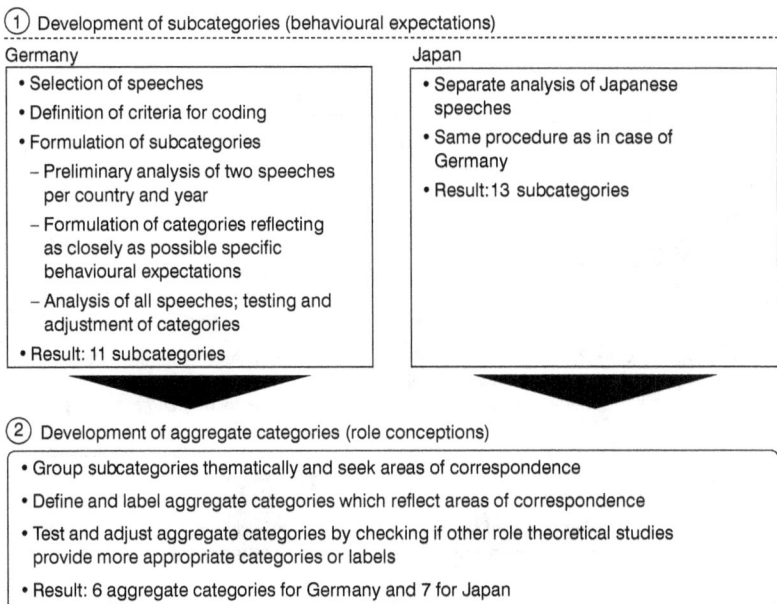

Figure 1.1 Process for development of comparative categories

the consideration of additional material (such as publications by and interviews with foreign policy elites) that may help to illuminate and explain particular aspects or text passages. The third form of interpretation distinguished by Mayring, that of structuring, draws on the deductive approach with pre-defined categories and is therefore not applicable to this study.

Comparative coding process

Previous comparative role theoretical research relied on deductively defined categories as thematic domains to contrast and compare countries (Aggestam 2004; Frenkler *et al.* 1997; Kirste 1998). This book introduces an alternative method for defining comparative categories inductively. Coding schemes were developed through an iterative process of defining preliminary labels, testing them and then making necessary adjustments or reformulating categories. After coding German and Japanese speeches separately, aggregate labels were devised by identifying areas of correspondence and thematic similarities in the speeches of both countries (see Figure 1.1). This procedure reduces unintended bias and ensures that both similarities and differences in the role conceptions of Germany and Japan can be identified and compared.

As explained in the Introduction, only statements with a focus on political, diplomatic and security issues falling into the traditional narrow definition of security studies were considered in the analysis (Katzenstein 1996: 10). Secondly, assertions also had to focus on the conceived duties and responsibilities within

Subcategories

	Germany	Japan
① Exporter of Security	• Contributor to international security with focus on regional issues • Supporter and propagator of international security regimes • Promoter of regional cooperation and integration (building, deepening, widening)*	• Global contributor to international security in partnership with the US • Supporter and propagator of international security regimes • Supporter of regional cooperation (including ad-hoc/issues specific cooperation)*
② Promoter of Universal Values	• Promoter and defender of universal values including democracy and human rights	• Promoter and defender of universal values including democracy and human rights
③ Non-Militarist Country	• Advocate of diplomatic and economic means to settle disputes and conflicts • Supporter of military means only as last resort and in multilateral context	• Advocate of diplomatic and economic means to settle disputes and conflicts • Exclusively defense-oriented country*
④ Reliable Partner	• Opponent of unilateral action • Collective actor/partner to the US and France as well as European countries ('Sowohl-als-auch')	• Opponent of unilateral action • Reliable US ally as well as supporter of cooperation with other countries (US-Bilateralism plus)
⑤ Regional Stabilizer	• Promoter of bargaining, compromise and mediation • Propagator of interdependent interests • Promoter of regional cooperation and integration (building, deepening, widening)*	• Stabilizer through alliance relationship with the US • Exclusively defense-oriented country* • Supporter of regional cooperation (including ad-hoc/issue specific cooperation)* • Economic stabilizer through ODA
⑥ Contributor to Regional Cooperation	• Promoter of regional cooperation and integration (building, deepening, widening)* • Supranationalist	• Supporter of regional cooperation (including ad-hoc/issue specific cooperation)*
⑦ Respected, Trusted Country	• Not found in German speeches	• Recipient of respect and trust due to *own* international contributions • Country, whose foreign policy engenders trust and respect • Partner at 'eye level' with the US through 'global partnership'

Figure 1.2 Aggregate categories and subcategories found

* Starred subcategories are assigned to several aggregate categories

each country's region. Keywords signalling regional importance facilitated the process of determining whether assertions would be included. The keywords used were: *region, regional, neighbourhood, neighbours* for both German and Japanese texts, and *Asia* (including Asia-Pacific, East Asia and Northeast Asia) for Japanese texts, and *Europe* (including European Community and European Union) for German texts. By relying on these keywords, the study remains flexible and sensitive to differing conceptions of the precise geographical scope of 'regions'.

Six role conceptions were found in the case of Germany and seven in the case of Japan. Figure 1.2 shows the categories with the corresponding behavioural expectations for both Germany and Japan. As explained above, the frequency of articulation of particular role conceptions was not taken into consideration; therefore the order in which they appear in Figure 1.2 does not reflect a hierarchy within the role set.

2 Role conceptions in German and Japanese speeches

Introduction

The aim of this chapter is to provide a detailed description of the role conceptions found in the content analysis of German and Japanese foreign policy speeches. The discussion begins with the six NRCs found to apply to both Germany and Japan, followed by an examination of the seventh NRC, identified only in Japanese speeches. In the chapter's final section, Germany's and Japan's overall role sets are compared and evaluated. The section argues that at first sight the two countries seem to share many similarities, but a closer examination finds significant differences in policy-makers' perspectives. The section also reconsiders the question of change and continuity in German and Japanese foreign policy-making, arguing that rapid shifts in policy goals and strategies have not occurred in either country in the post-Cold War era and appear unlikely for the foreseeable future.

Translated quotes from speeches in this chapter often include phrases or keywords in the original language in parentheses to allow interested readers to understand particular connotations in the original text material. Unless noted otherwise, italics in quotations were added by the analyst to highlight certain aspects.

German and Japanese role conceptions in comparison

1. Exporter of security

The role conception of 'exporter of security' refers to Germany's and Japan's willingness to contribute to international security, encompassing both regional and global security. It provides insight into how much importance each country attaches to playing a role in regional security affairs. The analysis of speeches demonstrates that the willingness to bear greater regional and international responsibility grew among both German and Japanese policy-makers after the Cold War. Government leaders reasoned that their countries had long benefited from the Cold War international order without making substantial contributions. In 1995, Defence Minister Volker Rühe called on Germany to abandon its role as 'importer of security' (*Importeur für Sicherheit*) and become a 'responsible contributor country' (*verantwortliches Beitragsland*) (Rühe 1995a). In the same way, Japanese Foreign Minister Watanabe Michio argued in 1993 that Japan 'must not just benefit (*jueki suru*) from the international order, but also contribute and strengthen it' (Watanabe 1993).

Carving out a more active role was seen as a delicate task in Germany and Japan, given negative historical legacies and lingering suspicions among neighbouring countries. In early 1993, German Foreign Minister Klaus Kinkel explained: 'it is necessary to accomplish [the task that] we have twice failed to do: to find a role in harmony with our neighbours (*im Einklang mit unseren Nachbarn*) that corresponds with our desires and our potential' (Kinkel 1993d). In a similar vein, Japanese Prime Minister Kaifu Toshiki urged fellow politicians in October 1990 to make a determined effort 'to identify what we can do in the cause of building a new world order of peace and prosperity' (Kaifu 1990a). Decision-makers from both countries sought to expand regional and international contributions in a gradual and cautious manner, while emphasizing their support for multilateral cooperative efforts, such as the United Nations. While policy-makers particularly called for non-military, diplomatic contributions to regional and global security in the early 1990s, they have increasingly stressed the need to dispatch military personnel (Kohl 1991a; Schröder 2001b; Steinmeier 2007b; Kaifu 1991a; Koizumi 2002c; Noda 2011).

Despite apparent similarities, German and Japanese conceptions of being 'exporters of security' differ significantly in the relative importance that politicians attach to regional versus global contributions. Especially in the early 1990s, the role conception had a distinctly *European focus* for German decision-makers, while Japanese leaders conceived of their role primarily in *global terms*. This gap between the two countries is still evident today, but it has narrowed.

German political elites have seen their chief responsibility in the dedication to regional stability and to the creation of a 'European peace order' (*europäische Friedensordnung*), while an independent global leadership role is rejected (Kohl 1990d; Genscher 1992). Chancellor Gerhard Schröder explicitly declared in 1998: 'we do not claim the role of a leading power in the international context' (Schröder 1998b). If anything, a global role is envisioned only indirectly: Germany may contribute to worldwide security by means of a strong and united Europe. When explaining their focus on Europe, policy-makers refer to the stipulation in the preamble of the Constitution, stating that Germany 'as an equal member' shall 'serve the peace in the world *in a united Europe*' (Kohl 1990d; Genscher 1990b). Especially in the past decade, policy-makers have also acknowledged the pragmatic reason that the combined force of the EU states represents the best chance for Germany to make its voice heard in global affairs (Fischer 2001; Merkel 2006c; Westerwelle 2011). Despite overwhelming continuity in this European-focused conception of Germany's role, politicians have increasingly highlighted the necessity for Europe to become a major force in worldwide security matters (Merkel 2010a; Steinmeier 2009a; Westerwelle 2010c). While Foreign Minister Joschka Fischer voiced his hope in 1999 that a united Europe would become the 'global partner' of the United States, Guido

Westerwelle, in the same position in 2011 called for the EU to become a 'power shaping the world' (*globale Gestaltungsmacht*) (Fischer 1999b; Westerwelle 2011).

In marked contrast to Germany, Japanese leaders focus on the global scope of their role as 'exporter of security', seeking to 'demonstrate international leadership' (Nakasone 2009; also see Okada 2010). In the early 1990s, they envisioned their country working jointly with the US towards the establishment of a stable international order. This was clearly reflected in a 1992 speech by Prime Minister Miyazawa Kiichi, in which he made three references to global ambitions in just one sentence: 'I think the true *global* partnership between [the US and Japan] lies in the joint fulfillment of our responsibility on a *global* scale towards the building of a *worldwide* peace order by joining the strengths of both countries' (Miyazawa 1992a). Like their German counterparts, Japanese officials referred to constitutional passages in justifying their policy focus. The Constitution instructs Tokyo to play an active role in international affairs and strive 'for the preservation of peace, and the banishment of tyranny and slavery, oppression and intolerance for all time *from the earth*' (Watanabe 1992a; Koizumi 2006a). In the minds of many decision-makers in Tokyo, the terrorist attacks on the US in 2001 vindicated their stance to think and act globally (Koizumi 2002d). While speeches throughout the time period investigated refer to Japan's global responsibilities, a trend towards growing attention to East Asian affairs is discernible. As the potential for regional instability became apparent with events such as the North Korean nuclear crisis in 1993–4 and the Taiwan Straits crisis in 1995–6, politicians in Tokyo began to place more emphasis on the need for Japan to engage regionally (Koizumi 2001c; Noda 2011; Maehara 2011). As Senior Vice-Minister for Foreign Affairs Shiozaki Yasuhisa explained at the 42nd Munich Conference on Security Policy in 2006, Japan now intends to 'act as a constructive component in Asia *and* the international community' (Shiozaki 2006).

The analysis of German and Japanese speeches furthermore reveals remarkable similarity in the *justifications* policy-makers from both countries provide for their commitment to the role of 'exporter of security'. Three key arguments can be identified. First, elites in both countries express their *own desire* for more active roles, citing perceived moral motivations and referring to constitutional passages (Schröder 2001a; Steinmeier 2007c; Westerwelle 2010b; Koizumi 2003b; Hatoyama 2009b; Kan 2010a). Secondly, political elites speak of the need to respond to the *expectations of partner countries* for more proactive foreign policies, especially in speeches discussing the potential dispatch of military forces to international missions (Kinkel 1994e; Miyazawa 1992c). Thirdly, elites point to the influence of a *combination of ego- and alter-part beliefs* by arguing that the contributions in foreign and security policy should match each country's enormous international weight and potential. Japanese policy-makers in particular argue that Tokyo's contributions must be 'commensurate' (*fusawashii*) with Japan's economic power. (Obuchi 1998g; Komura 1999c; Fukuda 2007; Abe 2007a). By demonstrating proactive leadership and presenting initiatives, they seek to replace the perceived reactive and passive policy-making (Kan 2010b; Noda 2011).

2. Promoter and defender of universal values

The role conception 'promoter and defender of universal values' refers to the importance that Germany and Japan attach to 'universal values' such as human rights, individual freedom and democracy in their foreign policy. Both countries strongly identify with these values, which form the basis of their domestic order, and seek to promote them globally. However, this role conception has different implications for each state's regional policy: The attachment to universal values *reinforces* Berlin's orientation towards integration policies in Europe, while it *dampens* Tokyo's enthusiasm for regional cooperation in East Asia. At the same time, the importance of these values serves to bolster both countries' relationships with the US.

German policy-makers acknowledge in speeches that their support for regional cooperation is strongly motivated by the shared attachment of EU nations to universal values. In their perspective, the EU's success rests on common normative ground, uniting the region's countries in a 'community of values' (*Wertegemeinschaft*) (Schröder 2004b). Chancellor Angela Merkel proclaimed the importance of values in her regional outlook in a speech in 2006:

> If one asks what Europe, what the European Union keeps together, it is clear to me: above all, Europe rests on the common values, which the member states of the European Union share: On freedom, justice, democracy, the rule of law and the respect for human rights. These fundamental values have grown in Europe over centuries.
>
> (Merkel 2006c)

Particularly in the 1990s, German policy-makers emphasized the need to encourage regional countries – especially former Communist countries – in their efforts to establish and solidify democratic governance. They sought to create incentives by offering the prospects of EU membership or by providing support through 'neighbourhood policy' (*Nachbarschaftspolitik*) for those states not considered viable candidates for the EU. As Rudolf Scharping, chairman of the SPD (and later Defence Minister), argued in a 1995 speech:

> It is the fundamental values of Western democracy and human rights that shape our policy and [our] relations [with other countries] and therefore constitute the basis for our peaceful character. We have to and want to help those countries, which are shaking off their legacy of communism, to progress on the same path.
>
> (Scharping 1995b)

Since the successful EU accession of many former Communist countries in 2004 and 2007, German policy-makers have reduced their references to spreading universal values in Europe. Nevertheless, speeches reflect the continuing importance of common norms in relations with both European countries and the US (Westerwelle 2010a; Merkel 2011b). Chancellor Gerhard Schröder for example maintained that the 'set of shared fundamental values' (*gemeinsamer Wertekanon*) was an essential element in the strong transatlantic ties between European states and North America's democracies (Schröder 2004c). Similarly, Chancellor Angela Merkel described the common norms as 'indispensable' (*unverzichtbar*) as a basis for effective cooperation between Europe and North America (Merkel 2008b).

In contrast, the attachment to universal values discourages and restrains policy-makers' espousal of regional cooperation in Japan's case, although this is rarely acknowledged explicitly in official statements. Government representatives have difficulty identifying with a region that does not share Japan's fundamental norms. In speeches, they draw attention to East Asia's diversity and point out that there is no uniform commitment to the values cherished by Japan (Koizumi 2002f; Hatoyama 2009b). In 2005, Foreign Minister Machimura Nobutaka insisted that multilateral cooperation in East Asia required a willingness to 'maintain shared values' (*kyōtsū no kachikan o iji suru*), including democracy and human rights (Machimura 2005b). In books and interviews, Japanese policy-makers are more frank about the implications of their role conception. In an interview, former Prime Minister Miyazawa Kiichi compared bilateral consultations with the US and with China, observing: 'dialogue is difficult when the values are different. In this respect, it is easier [to hold dialogue] with the US – it is uncomplicated. Europe is alright as well. Indeed, it is Asia that is difficult' (Iokibe *et al.* 2006: 50). Apparently, Japanese politicians perceive the greatest difficulty in holding dialogue with Beijing. Former Deputy Foreign Minister Tanaka Hitoshi asserted:

> Regarding [cooperation in East Asian] security policy, it is a prerequisite that the values that are defended are the same [among all countries]. Thus, the answer to the question of whether [Japan] can establish a security policy framework (*shikumi*) with China is clearly 'it cannot'. The values which both countries seek to defend are different.
>
> (Tanaka and Tahara 2005: 221)

The majority of Japanese policy-makers thus contend that their country must strive to 'advance democratization' (*minshuka no zōshin*) in the region, in order to create a basis for better bilateral and multilateral cooperation (Miyazawa 1993a).[1] In the view of Prime Minister Mori Yoshiro, securing peace and prosperity in the region based on 'universal' values continues to be a 'priority issue' (*yūsen kadai*) for Japanese diplomacy (Mori 2001). In seeking to foster such values, Japanese policy-makers intend to build on Japan's own insights as an 'experienced democracy' (Shiozaki 2006). According to Foreign Minister Aso Taro, Japan is a 'veteran player' (*shinise*) in the area of democracy and human rights and thus should play the role of an 'escort runner' (*bansō ranā*) supporting democratization in the region (Aso 2006c). Similarly, Prime Minister Hatoyama Yukio argued neighbouring states could 'benefit from Japan's store of knowledge and experience', such as in democratic development (Hatoyama 2009a). Due to the shared attachment to universal values, Japanese politicians furthermore place importance on the US as Tokyo's global partner and on regional countries like Australia and New Zealand (Miyazawa 1993b; Obuchi 1999a; Kawaguchi 2002b). Foreign Minister Aso reflected on the strong relationship between Japan and the US, stating 'At the core of this alliance is our shared embrace of the universal values of freedom, democracy, and free markets' (Aso 2006e).

Japanese policy-makers – like their German counterparts – thus strongly rely on universal values as guiding principles in their foreign policies. This finding contradicts Kenneth Pyle's argument that officials in Tokyo tend to eschew political ideals such as democracy as 'anathema' (2007a: 351). In Pyle's view, Japan's 'readiness to tighten cooperation with the United States is not the result of shared values, so much as it is the realist appraisal of the value of the alliance' (2006: 22). However, the content analysis of speeches demonstrates that decision-makers' perceptions of other countries – including the US – are decisively shaped by the role conception of 'promoter of universal values'.

3. Non-militarist country

The role conception 'non-militarist country' implies the rejection on the part of Germany and Japan of a strong military capability that may be used aggressively to defend or promote the national interest. It reflects the two countries' preferences for using diplomatic and economic means to settle disputes. The analysis of speeches reveals the centrality of this role conception in regional foreign policy behaviour of the two countries. Restraint in the use of military force is seen both as a moral imperative and a measure to confront suspicions of neighbouring countries about a possible resurgence of Germany's and Japan's pre-1945 militarism (Kinkel 1994e; Schröder 2003a; Westerwelle 2010a; Miyazawa 1992c; Kono 2001a; Aso 2006c). Chancellor Kohl indicated such considerations, promising in 1990 that there would be no 'nationalistic going-it-alone' (*nationalistische Alleingänge*) for his country, since Germans sought to be 'good neighbours' (Kohl 1990d). In a similar vein, Japanese Foreign Minister Watanabe Michio in 1992 declared Japan's resolve 'never to become a military power that might pose a threat to its neighbours', given the 'deep-rooted apprehension stemming from the past and from Japan's sizeable [economic] presence' in the region (Watanabe 1992a). Despite the parallels in this role conception, policy-makers in Berlin and Tokyo exhibit radically different views regarding the use of military means for purposes other than pure self-defence. Whereas German political elites *perceive a need* to use military force under certain circumstances, their Japanese counterparts tend to *reject* this possibility.

Provided that military force is used as an ultima ratio, German elites accept their own state's participation in multilateral operations with the aim of preserving international security. They emphasize that such operations should always take place under the leadership of an international organization to ensure legitimacy. Foreign Minister Klaus Kinkel remarked in 1992: 'When all other means have failed, if necessary, justice has to be defended by military means against the one violating justice (*Rechtsverletzer*). That is one of the lessons of a – particularly for us Germans – disastrous past' (Kinkel 1992b). In the early 1990s, many politicians were sceptical whether the *Bundeswehr* should be deployed outside the geographic area of NATO or the Western European Union (WEU). However, global dispatches became broadly accepted following the ruling by the Federal Constitutional Court in Karlsruhe on 12 July 1994, which declared such missions constitutional. German officials continue to stress that military force should only be employed as a last resort and in a multilateral context. While Foreign Minister Klaus Kinkel following the court ruling pledged there would be 'no militarization of German foreign policy', Chancellor Schröder asserted in 1998 that the use of military force would 'remain the ultima ratio of peace policy' (Kinkel 1994b; Schröder 1998b). More recently, Foreign Minister Guido Westerwelle declared in 2010 'German peace policy stands for the peaceful resolution of regional crises' (Westerwelle 2010b). Despite adjustments in the geographic scope, Germany's role conception thus reflects overall continuity in core elements.

Japanese political elites, in contrast, hold a significantly more constraining and limited conception of being a 'non-militarist country', in line with constitutional stipulations. Japanese leaders emphasize their country's determination never to become a threatening military power again. Asserting their commitment to an 'exclusively defence-oriented policy' (*senshu bōei*), they highlight Japan's stance of using military means solely for the purpose of self-defence, i.e. in response to an attack on Japan (Miyazawa 1992c; Kono 2001a; Aso 2006c; Kan 2011). They furthermore pledge to retain only a minimum of defence capabilities. Prime Minister Kaifu clearly expressed this stance in a 1990 speech:

> In the 45 years since the end of the war, Japan has repeatedly declared its determination *not to become a military power* that *might once again threaten other countries*, it has renounced war as a sovereign right of the nation, and it has rejected the threat or use of force as means of settling international disputes. There is a broad consensus in support of these ideals, and I am certain that this Japanese stance has contributed significantly to the peace and stability in the Asia-Pacific region.
>
> (Kaifu 1990a)

The Japanese conception thus *rules out* the threat or use of military force in cases other than self-defence, such as peace enforcement missions under the UN.

With the emergence of new conflicts including the Gulf War of 1990–1 and the growing US pressure for Japanese military contributions to international security, political leaders in Tokyo felt the need to reconcile their restrictive role concept with the new requirements of the post-Cold War era. They realized that Japan's desire to be an active 'exporter of security' and a 'reliable partner' to the US was in tension with the strict ban on overseas deployments of the Japan Self-Defence Forces (JSDF). As a result, a consensus gradually emerged in favour of a more proactive understanding of Japan's role conception of 'non-militarist country'. For example, Prime Minister Fukuda Yasuo in 2008 described Japan's desire to become a 'peace fostering nation' (*heiwa kyōryoku kokka*) that 'spares no efforts' (*rōku o oshimazu*) in the pursuit of regional and global stability (Fukuda 2008). Despite revising its legislation to facilitate UN peacekeeping dispatches, Tokyo continues to adhere to the principle of using weapons only for self-defence and thus is unable to deploy forces to peace enforcement missions. In speeches decision-makers declare that Japan should never again become an aggressive military power that wages war and should contribute internationally through peaceful means (Koizumi 2001c; Aso 2006c). Prime Minister Kan Naoto for example pledged his country would 'uphold the fundamental principles of its defense policy, including its exclusively defensive defense policy' although he warned against pacifism that is oblivious to international security issues (Kan 2011). Compared to the 1990s, however, speeches of the past few years, including those by recent DPJ leaders, have made fewer references to this role conception, focusing instead on the need to be an 'exporter of security'.

4. Reliable partner

The role conception of 'reliable partner' refers to Germany's and Japan's determination to work and act together with other countries. Officials from both countries stress the importance of avoiding unilateral foreign policy conduct. The analysis of speeches reveals two similar motivations for acting as 'reliable partners'. First, political elites from both countries express their hope that, by acting together with other countries, they will avoid stirring fears among neighbouring countries about unilateral and national interest-driven foreign policy courses (Kohl 1990a; Fischer 2000a; Westerwelle 2009; Watanabe 1993; Koizumi 2001a). Secondly, policy-makers in both Germany and Japan consider it unrealistic to achieve various policy objectives alone in today's globalized world. Surveying today's complex international security problems, Chancellor Merkel in 2006 concluded, 'No country in the world can handle the dangers alone. For that reason, German security policy is always ... a policy of partnership (*partnerschaftliche Politik*). German security policy cannot be thought of as a national policy' (Merkel 2006b). In a similar vein, Prime Minister Obuchi Keizo contended in 1999, 'In the world of today, no nation can stand alone', urging Japan to act jointly with other countries in confronting transnational challenges (Obuchi 1999b).

Despite the parallels in the motivations, the role conceptions of Germany and Japan differ with respect to the *choice of countries* with which principal partnerships are pursued. While German politicians attach *equal weight* to two countries, the US and France, Japanese elites attach the *highest single priority* to the US. Decision-makers in the Federal Republic identify the US and France as the two most important partners, although they also name other relevant states such as Great Britain and Poland (Fischer 2000a; Westerwelle 2009). For German elites, it is essential to refrain from choosing or prioritizing relations with either Paris or Washington. They assert that partnership with the two countries is compatible ('*sowohl-als-auch*'), despite the often contrary perspectives. In 1993,

Foreign Minister Klaus Kinkel contradicted accusations that Germany after the Cold War would begin to prioritize France and Europe in its foreign policy over its relations with the US. He declared:

> The bridge of friendship across the Atlantic was the key for the conclusion of the Cold War and [Germany's] reunification. We will never forget what we owe to our American friends. The maintenance of a close and a trustful German–American partnership is more than a debt of gratitude, however. The demonstration of unity and solidarity (*Schulterschluss*) across the Atlantic remains the cornerstone of our foreign policy and *cannot be pitted against* (*ausspielen*) our relationship with our closest neighbour France.
>
> (Kinkel 1993d)

Political scientist Holger Mey called this policy of equidistance in relations with Washington and Paris 'Germany's preference not to make a preference', adding 'even if this includes a danger of doing the splits and sitting between all chairs' (Mey 1995: 205). The difficult balancing act has also held an advantage, however, as Germany has wielded significant power in shaping compromises involving the two partner countries. As Foreign Minister Joschka Fischer acknowledged in 1998, Germany's concurrent attachment to transatlantic relations and to Europe helps to create 'new room to manoeuvre' (*neue Spielräume*) for Berlin (Fischer 1998).

For German leaders, relations with France have particular significance in the European context, because the two former 'arch enemies' have become the bedrock of the integration process in Europe (Schröder 2002b; Westerwelle 2010c). German elites conceive of the bilateral relationship as an indispensable 'motor' of integration that provides ideas and proposals to further regional cooperation (Kohl 1993a). In 2003, Foreign Minister Joschka Fischer described the partnership with France as follows:

> German–French cooperation is the *core* and the *flywheel* (*Schwungrad*) of European development and – I contend – will remain so under the conditions of an EU of 25 [member states]. ... When Germany and France agree, it was *never exclusive or targeted at others*, but it has always functioned as a flywheel. ... It is the task of the German–French motor to advance such compromises.
>
> (Fischer 2003a)

Decision-makers see Paris and Berlin as particularly qualified to propose initiatives in the EU, because the two countries can reach balanced compromises based on their diverging standpoints (Westerwelle 2010c). As Foreign Minister Fischer argued in another speech, 'The dynamism that Germany and France have unfolded in the European integration is based not on similarity, but rather on a complementarity between our peoples' (Fischer 1999d).

Decision-makers in Tokyo also emphasize the compatibility of relations with the US and with regional partners. However, in contrast to Germany, they conceive of the US as their most important partner and hence number one priority. The alliance relationship is seen as the backbone of Japan's relations with neighbouring countries. As Prime Minister Koizumi Junichiro stated in a press conference in November 2005, 'There is no such thing as a US–Japan relationship [that is] too close. ... the closer, more intimate it is, it is easier for us to ... improve relations with China, with South Korea and other nations in Asia' (Koizumi 2005d). Elaborating on his statement in the government's publication *Cabi-Netto*, Koizumi rejected allegations that his policy neglected neighbouring countries, while acknowledging that for Tokyo 'there is *no single relationship that is as important* as the one between the US and Japan' (*nichibei kankei hodo jūyōna kankei wa nai*) (Koizumi and Jijigahosha 'Cabi Netto' Henshubu 2006: 135).

Other foreign policy elites similarly describe Washington as Japan's central partner. In 2008, Prime Minister Aso Taro contended that 'the strengthening of the US–Japan Alliance ... should *always come first*' (*nichibei dōmei no kyōka ... wa tsune ni dai ichi de arimasu*), before considering relations with neighbouring countries (Aso 2008). In speeches, the importance of the US is reflected in the expressions used to describe the alliance relationship: 'cornerstone' (*kijiku*), 'linchpin' (*yō*), 'basis' (*kihon*), 'foundation' (*kiban*), and 'foundation stone' (*ishizue*) (Nakayama 1991b; Hata 1994b; Koizumi 2004a; Aso 2007; Fukuda 2007; Nakasone 2009; Okada 2010; Noda 2011). The order in which politicians refer to other countries in their speeches further underlines the primacy of the US alliance in foreign policy thinking. In practically all general policy speeches analysed in this study the US was mentioned *before* neighbouring countries or multilateral regional security institutions.

As the statements above illustrate, Japanese policy-makers see a functioning security relationship with the US as the *prerequisite* and *platform* for good relations with neighbouring countries. Japan's conception of being a 'reliable partner' may be described as a policy of 'US-bilateralism plus',[2] as decision-makers attach the highest priority to the US, while other relationships play a secondary – though nevertheless important – role. The reasons for Japan's strong attachment to the US are similar to those of Germany. Policy-makers emphasize the common attachment to universal values and interest in international stability (Miyazawa 1991; Kawaguchi 2002b; Kan 2011). The alliance furthermore provides Tokyo's leaders with the psychological reassurance that Japan will remain integrated in the international community (Koizumi 2001a). Above all, however, Japanese elites stress that the alliance fosters stability in East Asia by deterring potential aggressors, a point further considered in the next section (Kawaguchi 2002a).

5. Regional stabilizer

Both German and Japanese policy-makers expect their respective country to play the role of a 'regional stabilizer'. Their objective is to foster steady and predictable relations among neighbouring states. Despite sharing this overarching objective, German and Japanese politicians conceive of their roles in markedly different ways, based on distinct foreign policy perspectives and reasoning. As a result, differences clearly outweigh similarities in Germany's and Japan's role conceptions of 'regional stabilizer'.

German politicians focus on the need for multilateralism and regional institutions, stressing two interrelated aspects (Scharping 1995a; Fischer 2003c; Steinmeier 2009a). First, they perceive an obligation to promote stability through the deepening and widening of multilateral regional institutions, especially the European Union as well as NATO. To them, integration provides the best means to overcome dangerous nationalist tendencies in Europe and 'pacify nations that have been rivals for hundreds of years' (Rühe 1995b). In the 1990s, German policy-makers emerged as a staunch 'advocate' (*Anwalt*) of countries in Eastern Europe seeking membership in the EU (Schröder 2003a; Kinkel 1994c). As noted above, however, German enthusiasm for further geographic widening has weakened since the enlargement rounds in 2004 and 2007, as the challenge of cooperating in a union of 27 members has become evident.

Secondly, German decision-makers believe their country must make efforts to mediate multilaterally among regional states to prevent instability arising from unresolved clashes of interest. In speeches, decision-makers promise to demonstrate a 'willingness to compromise' (Herzog 1995), to 'build bridges between opposing positions' during multilateral negotiations (Kohl 1997a) and to refrain from 'pushing through national maximum demands by hook or by crook' (*nationale Maximalpositionen auf Biegen und Brechen durchsetzen*) (Fischer 1999a). However, Germany's policy of mediation and compromise is not without pitfalls – as decision-makers have realized. Following the failed referenda on the proposed EU Constitutional Treaty in France and the Netherlands, Chancellor Angela Merkel commented in early 2007 that Germany would 'endeavour a compromise' on the issue, but warned against 'a minimalist approach' based on lowest common denominator decisions (Merkel 2007a).

In their policy of mediation and compromise, German leaders place particular emphasis on the engagement of Russia (Jung 2008; Westerwelle 2010c). Speeches reveal concern about the possible re-emergence of tensions with Russia, based on traditional balance of power thinking and perceptions of exclusion. As Foreign Minister Klaus Kinkel argued,

> In the future, security must be defined more broadly and must be organized *not against one another but jointly.* ... Security with and not against one another – above all that means acknowledging *Russia's rightful and legitimate place* [in the European security architecture].
>
> (Kinkel 1995b)

German elites believe Moscow might feel isolated and perceive the EU as an ever-growing American sphere of influence, as it is itself not a candidate for membership in either the EU or NATO (Schröder 2001a).

While the German conception of being a 'regional stabilizer' emphasizes multilateralism, Japanese policy-makers in contrast focus primarily on the military balance of power as an essential determinant of peace and stability. In their view, Japan's contribution to a favourable balance of power is twofold. First, Japan's position as a US ally is considered a key aspect of Japan's stabilizer role (Kakizawa 1992; Tanaka 2001b; Shiozaki 2006; Kan 2010a). In the words of Foreign Minister Aso Taro, Japan's position as a 'built-in stabilizer' in regional security 'clearly stems from the "weight" that the Japan–US military alliance holds' (*nichibei dōmei ga motsu 'omoshi' toshite no yakuwari ni yotte, jimei de aru*) (Aso 2005). Washington's commitment to Asia is seen as a decisive factor in securing peace and stability in Asia in political and military terms. The 'forward deployment' (*zenpō tenkai*) of US troops in Asia is indispensable, according to Japanese politicians, as it demonstrates the alliance's credibility and 'deterrence power' (*yokuseiryoku*) (Komura 1999a; also see Okada 2010; Koizumi 2005b; Kakizawa 1992; Kaifu 1990c: 32).

In most speeches, politicians avoid naming specific regional threats, but instead describe the alliance as 'a public good' (*kōkyōzai*) for the nations in the Asia-Pacific region (Aso 2006a; Okada 2010; Kan 2011; Matsumoto 2011). As Prime Minister Fukuda Yasuo explains, the 'Japan–US alliance is now not only a means for ensuring the security of Japan, but it serves as an instrument for the stability of Asia-Pacific' (Fukuda 2008). While attaching fundamental importance to the alliance, politicians attribute security dialogue among regional countries a supplementary (though increasingly important) function in ensuring stability in East Asia (Nakasone 2009; Kan 2011). This was reflected in a statement by Vice Foreign Minister Abe Masatoshi in 2004, who observed that, 'although there have been efforts' towards establishing multilateral security mechanisms including the ASEAN Regional Forum (ARF), regional stability continued to be primarily 'maintained through bilateral security agreements centred on the United States' (Abe 2004).

The second contribution to a favourable regional balance of power is Japan's pledge never to become a military great power. This aspect was particularly prevalent in speeches of the early 1990s, when decision-makers maintained that Tokyo's non-threatening posture helps to prevent arms races otherwise triggered by the fear of Japanese power (Watanabe 1992a; Kono 1995a; Shiozaki 2006). The bilateral alliance to the US with its guarantee for Japanese security heightens the credibility of Tokyo's pledge to never become a military power, they argue. Nevertheless, with the military modernization efforts by neighbouring countries, statements focusing on this aspect of Japan's stabilizer role have decreased since around the mid-1990s. Documents and statements issued by the Ministry of Defence (MoD) have instead warned against the danger of Japan becoming a 'power vacuum' (*chikara no kūhaku*) that triggers instability, due to the failure to respond adequately to regional military build-up (Ministry of Defence Japan 2007). In speeches, policy-makers also point out the need to respond actively to shifts in the regional power balance and particularly China's rise (Kan 2010b; Maehara 2011). This view points to an attentiveness to shifts in the regional balance of power and threat perceptions regarding North Korea and China.

Aside from the military dimension, Japan's conception of being a 'regional stabilizer' also has economic and normative dimensions. In the Japanese view, economic disparities are a major cause of international disputes and conflicts, and thus decision-makers perceive a responsibility for Japan as the region's economically most advanced country to foster development (Kakizawa 1992; Komura 1999b; Koizumi 2003a; Kan 2011). By helping to lower the economic disparities in the region through official development aid programmes, Japanese politicians hope to contribute to regional stability in the traditional security area. Moreover, decision-makers also maintain that Japan's promotion of democratic values and of the rule of law in East Asia will reinforce stability and peace (Aso 2005; Hatoyama 2009a).

6. Contributor to regional cooperation

The role conception 'contributor to regional cooperation' refers to Germany's and Japan's willingness to actively shape regional multilateral cooperation. Policy-makers in both countries emphasize the importance of fostering security dialogue and cooperation among regional countries. However, speeches reveal considerable differences between German and Japanese conceptions with regard to *three aspects*: the *priority* attached to the promotion of cooperation, the *type* of multilateral framework envisioned, and the specific *role* Berlin, respectively Tokyo, should play therein.

German politicians reveal a remarkable consensus on the high priority in foreign policy to actively expand and intensify regional cooperation and European integration. They envision a network of overlapping and interlocking multilateral institutions with three main pillars constituted by the EU, NATO, and the Conference (later Organization) for Security and Cooperation in Europe (CSCE/OSCE) as a basis for a European peace order encompassing Europe and North America (Kinkel 1994f; Steinmeier 2009b). In the words of Foreign Minister Hans-Dietrich Genscher, Germany aspires to the 'replacement of confrontational politics by cooperative politics in Europe' (Genscher 1992). Repeatedly, decision-makers have expressed their desire to create a 'pan-European peace order (*gesamteuropäische Friedensordnung*) that bans war as an instrument of politics permanently (*dauerhaft*) from our continent and ensures equal cooperative security for all' (Fischer 1999b; also see Scharping 1999b; Steinmeier 2008b; Westerwelle 2010c).

Regarding the second aspect – the type of multilateral framework envisioned by policy-makers – German thinking is characterized by a notable preference for enduring, formal and legally binding supranational structures. Supranationalism is seen as an essential means to make the European integration process irreversible, thereby ensuring long-term stability and peace. The desire for institutional permanency was reflected in the repeatedly used metaphor of seeking to 'build the house of Europe' (Süssmuth 1990). As Chancellor Kohl stated, 'The building of the "house of Europe" (*Haus Europa*) is the decisive prerequisite for peace and freedom in the 21st century in Europe. ... The federal government that I lead does its utmost ... to further advance the European unification (*Einigung*) – I deliberately say: to make it irreversible (*unumkehrbar*)' (Kohl 1996b). The 'house' metaphor was also used by politicians from the subsequent Red-Green government, with Foreign Minister Joschka Fischer promising to '[build] new floors for the house of Europe' through the deepening and widening of the EU (Fischer 1998). In their conception of building this house, German policy-makers accept and indeed advocate institutional integration that involves sacrificing important aspects of state sovereignty. Supranationalism is seen as an effective insurance against the re-emergence of nationalistic tendencies in Europe (Fischer 2000b). In Chancellor Merkel's view, international cooperation requires 'giving up a piece of our own sovereignty' (Merkel 2010a). This mode of cooperation also has enabled the Federal Republic to overcome the mistrust of neighbours while at the same time expanding the country's international influence and room to manoeuvre (Fischer 2000a; Haftendorn 2001: 436; Duffield 2003: 268).

Regarding the third point, German politicians perceive a special responsibility for their country to play a leading role in advancing and promoting European integration together with France, although they reject a unilateral or exclusive leadership role (Fischer 2003a; Westerwelle 2010c). Foreign Minister Klaus Kinkel evoked the notion of Germany as a 'good team player' (*guter Mannschaftsspieler*), a 'player with special responsibility' but without the 'captain's armband' (Kinkel 1994b). In light of this activism reflected in German thinking, the country's role conception may perhaps be more accurately termed '*promoter of regional cooperation*' rather than just '*contributor*'.

Overall, German speeches reflect remarkable continuity in the stated *goal* of fostering European integration and cooperation, but the cited *motives* for this policy have unmistakably *shifted* from predominantly emotional and history-focused reasoning in the early 1990s to more practical and 'rational' arguments beginning with the Schröder government and continuing with the Merkel government. While Chancellor Kohl repeatedly described European unification as a 'question of war and peace' (*eine Frage von Krieg und Frieden*) in the early 1990s, politicians since the late 1990s have focused on the need to tackle global and transnational challenges by seeking a common stance with other European nations. History-focused arguments that dominated under Kohl have become less common, although they have not vanished (Fischer 2000b; Merkel 2008b; Westerwelle 2010a). European integration policies are increasingly portrayed as a conscious and rational choice rather than an inescapable destiny or obligation.

Japanese policy-makers also conceive of the role conception of 'contributor to regional cooperation' as an important foreign policy element. However, as was seen in previous sections, regional security dialogue is only accorded a supplementary function in ensuring peace and stability. By stressing that the alliance is an indispensable platform for regional efforts, Japanese political elites display little confidence in security cooperation as a viable *alternative* for ensuring stability (Obuchi 1998c; Koizumi 2005d; Aso 2008). Compared to their German counterparts, Japanese policy-makers refrain from articulating an ambitious goal like building a pan-Asian multilateral peace order based on cooperative security. While regional cooperation is believed to 'enhance the sense of mutual assurance' (*otagai no anshinkan o takameru*) between neighbouring countries (Miyazawa 1992d), Japanese elites reveal a cautious outlook on the effectiveness of ongoing endeavours. In referring to the ASEAN Regional Forum (ARF) – the most prominent regional institution for security dialogue – Prime Minister Hashimoto Ryutaro remarked in 1997 that 'we shall have to see how effective the ARF process is' (Hashimoto 1997b).

On the second aspect, the type of regional framework envisioned, Japanese policy-makers exhibit preferences that are markedly different from those of their German counterparts: They seek informal, flexible and consensus-oriented forms of cooperation or ad-hoc regional initiatives that deal with specific security problems. Prime Minister Hatoyama Yukio for example called for 'a multilayered network of functional communities' (Hatoyama 2009a). Speeches reveal three motivations for the preference for soft and flexible approaches to regional cooperation. First, policy-makers frequently cite Asia's diversity in terms of values, culture, ideology, political systems and economic development as an impediment to more formal integration (Miyazawa 1993a; Kono 1994b; Koizumi 2002f; Hatoyama 2009b). As Vice Foreign Minister Sugiura Seiken explained in 2001, in light of 'Asia's rich diversity', Japan is making efforts to achieve 'cooperation through stratified and *soft* multilateral frameworks, with bilateral relationships as the foundation' (*nikoku kankei o kihon toshite, jūsōteki de yuruyakana takokukan wakugumi o tsūjita renkei*) (Sugiura 2001). Secondly, Japanese policy-makers believe that an approach based on sub-regional and ad-hoc frameworks may be well suited to deal with many of the security issues that need to be addressed in Asia, including North Korea, Taiwan and territorial disputes (Kono 1995a; Shiozaki 2006). Thirdly, Japanese leaders prefer soft and informal frameworks of regional dialogue, because they do not draw such stark lines between members and non-members. Fearing a possible exclusion of the US, Japanese policy-makers stress the need to remain 'open' (*hirakareta*) to cooperation with countries around the globe (Watanabe 1992b; Hashimoto 1997a; Koizumi 2002e; Hatoyama 2009b).

Regarding the third point, Tokyo's specific role in regional cooperation, Japanese leaders – like their German counterparts – reject a unilateral leadership position in regional cooperation. In comparison, however, Tokyo's elites envision a more low-profile role, deferring key initiatives to others. Politicians reject regional cooperation in which more powerful countries 'such as the US, China, or Japan' dominate smaller and weaker countries (Kono 1995a). In describing Japan's role, elites emphasize that Tokyo seeks to act in tandem with others and engage with neighbours based on 'the consciousness as equal peers' (*taitō no nakama ishiki*), while refraining to view others 'as above it or below it' (*jōge gainen o mochikomanai*) (Aso 2005). On numerous occasions, Japanese politicians have highlighted their support for the initiatives taken by the Association for Southeast Asian Nations (ASEAN) in fostering sub-regional and region-wide dialogue. Japan seeks to play the role of a constructive sparring partner, 'thinking and acting together' with the Southeast Asian countries, but leaving ASEAN in the 'driver's seat' (Shiozaki 2006; Kakizawa 1992; Koizumi 2002e; Fukuda 2008). In contrast to the German expectations of acting as a 'promoter of cooperation', Japanese leaders continue to see their country play a largely supportive role in regional cooperation and Japan's role conception may thus be more accurately termed 'supporter of regional cooperation'.

7. Respected and trusted country (Japan only)

The final role conception 'respected and trusted country' was found only in Japanese speeches. Policy-makers express their desire for Japan to be a country treated with admiration and recognition by other states. The conception reflects a long-held aspiration to rehabilitate and rebuild the country's post-war reputation, coupled with a widespread perception that Tokyo's international efforts and contributions have so far received insufficient credit from the international community. Prime Minister Hata Tsutomu for example articulated the desire for respect in 1994, when he stated that he sought to make Japan a country that is 'trusted and loved by international society' (*nihon o kokusai shakai no naka de shinrui sare, ai sareru kuni to suru*) (Hata 1994b). In referring to this role conception, many Japanese elites cite the Preamble of the Constitution, which stipulates that Japan shall strive to 'occupy an honoured place in international society' (*kokusai shakai no naka de, meiyo aru chii o uranaitai*) (Watanabe 1992a; Mori 2000c; Koizumi 2003c, 2004a; Kan 2010a). Most decision-makers focus on the perceived lack of respect from other countries, but a few politicians including Prime Minister Abe Shinzo also voice dissatisfaction about what they see as insufficient self-esteem and self-confidence (Abe 2006b; Noda 2011; Hatoyama 2009b).

Below, three aspects regarding Japan's role conception will be discussed. First, the analysis will consider how politicians seek to earn trust and respect for their country by examining the textual context in speeches. Secondly, four reasons are identified as having contributed to the perception of a lack of international recognition for Japan. Lastly, the analysis compares Japan's case with Germany, highlighting reasons why politicians in Berlin generally do not express a comparable role conception, even though the immediate post-war time period was characterized by a similar desire to rebuild Germany's international reputation.

The content analysis revealed that two related ideas dominate in Japanese thinking about how to gain international respect. Decision-makers first of all call on Japan to expand its involvement in initiatives for international stability and peace, as reflected in the role conception of 'exporter of security' (Obuchi 1999b; Kan 2010a). In a 2004 speech, Prime Minister Koizumi referred explicitly to the need for an active contribution to international stability in order to be treated with respect:

> It is natural that a country should *act for world peace* by helping those people and countries that are struggling to overcome difficulties. Surely that is the kind of attitude that will allow us to *occupy 'an honoured place* in international society' as described in the Preamble to the Constitution of Japan.
>
> (Koizumi 2004a)

Similarly, Prime Minister Noda maintained in 2011 that the Japanese people can only 'regain hope and pride' by 'not becoming "inward-looking" [but] aspiring to engage actively overseas' (*'uchimuki' ni ochiirazu, sekai ni yūhi suru kokorozashi o idaku*) (Noda 2011). The second, related idea for gaining international respect is to establish Japan as a *role model* for other states, especially for Asian neighbours. In this view, Japan is in a unique position to advise and help others due to its experience as the region's oldest democracy and most advanced economy that has had to grapple with various problems such as pollution or nationalism at an earlier time than its neighbours (Aso 2005, 2006e; Fukuda 2008; Hatoyama 2009a).

Despite efforts to establish Japan as a 'respected and trusted country', decision-makers in Tokyo appear dissatisfied about the current level of international recognition for their country. Four interrelated causes of this frustration are identified. Because Japanese policy-makers tend to avoid addressing these issues explicitly in formal speeches, the analysis draws on public statements and interviews by policy-makers as well as Japanese academic literature.

First, in the post-Cold War era it became clear that Tokyo had failed to instil trust and respect for Japan in the international community by adhering to a pacifist policy based on the concept of 'defensive defense' (*senshu bōei*). As political scientist Iokibe Makoto observes, after 1945 'the Japanese thought that their stance of not fighting against another country and not becoming involved in a conflict between other countries would receive praise (*shōsan sareru*) from international society as good pacifist behaviour' (Iokibe 2006: 237). However, rather than earning respect from other countries, Japan faced severe criticism during the Gulf War of 1990–1 for its passivity and refusal to send troops to the conflict (Koizumi 2004a; Fukuda 2008). Moreover, when Japan began to expand its military contributions to UN missions in the early 1990s, its policy elicited suspicion and concern among regional countries (Watanabe 1992a). These reactions confirmed that Tokyo's purely defensive security policy had failed to engender trust and confidence among former victims of Japanese aggression.

Secondly, the enduring recession following the burst of the bubble economy in the early 1990s has seriously damaged self-confidence in Japan, a country that has above all prided itself on its economic achievements since 1945. International attention has shifted to the rising economic power China – pushing Japan to the sidelines. Due to economic stagnation, Tokyo has also been forced to cut back on its foreign development aid – an important source of national pride for many policy-makers. As Foreign Ministry official Oe Hiroshi noted with concern, Tokyo has relinquished its position as the world's number one provider of aid, with the US surpassing Japan in 2001 and England taking second place in 2007 (Oe 2007: 237–8). In 2011, Prime Minister Noda Yoshihiko explicitly mentioned the need to rebuild the economy in order for Japan to become a country in which every person can have pride (Noda 2011).

Thirdly, Japanese politicians are frustrated that Tokyo's handling of its militarist past continues to attract widespread criticism regionally and globally. Many Japanese decision-makers, especially of the post-war generation, seek to move beyond the humiliating memory of war, and some question the need for new apologies and redemption. Recurrent controversies over the treatment of history undermine Tokyo's international reputation. In a 2001 speech, Foreign Minister Kono Yohei therefore warned that 'relationships of trust' could only develop with an attitude 'that does not turn its eyes away from [historical] facts' and is based on a 'feeling of humility' (Kono 2001a). Nevertheless, a clear consensus on the treatment of history has not emerged among Tokyo's lawmakers.

Fourthly, decision-makers appear frustrated about Japan's subservient role in the alliance with the US, which they see as contributing to the general lack of trust and respect from other countries (Tanaka 2008b, interview with A. Sakaki). As Mori Takeo, Chief of the Policy Coordination Division of the Foreign Policy Bureau at the Foreign Ministry, observed in early 2009: 'There exists an unmistakable criticism or frustration within Japan that [this country] is not really independent and acting too subserviently towards the US (*taibei tsuijū*)' (Akita *et al.* 2009: 48). Fearing potential disagreements in the alliance relationship, political elites rarely express their discontent openly in speeches. Nevertheless, some politicians allude to the desire for a more balanced relationship by calling for Tokyo's own 'subjective' (*shutaiteki*) foreign policy initiatives (Miyazawa 1992a; Ikeda 1997; Koizumi 2001a) and the establishment of a 'global partnership' with the US (Kaifu 1990a; Miyazawa 1992b; Machimura 2005a). In an October 2009 speech, Prime Minister Hatoyama Yukio clearly described his goal of an equal relationship 'in which the Japanese side too can actively make proposals' (Hatoyama 2009b).

In publications or interviews, policy-makers more explicitly voice frustration about the unbalanced relationship. In his 2006 book, Prime Minister Abe Shinzo declared the goal to make Japan an 'independent country' (*jiritsu suru kokka/ dokuritsu kokka*), which in his view required the loosening of the strict limitations on using military force (Abe 2006: 43, 123). Fellow LDP party member Ishiba Shigeru similarly argued in 2005 that Tokyo was in a 'follower' position vis-à-vis its alliance partner, because of the unrequited US defence pledge for Japan, symbolizing the one-sidedness of the relationship (Ishiba 2005: 17). The uneasiness about the lopsided relationship was expressed most clearly by Ozawa Ichiro, at the time the leader of the opposition party Democratic Party of Japan (DPJ). During a meeting with US Secretary of State Hillary Clinton in January 2009, Ozawa warned against a 'subservient relationship in which one side always obeys the other' (*ippō ga ippō ni shitagau jūzokutekina kankei*), while at the same time stating his support for close alliance cooperation (*Tokyo Shinbun* 2009). The remark reflects the widespread concern that Japan – as a US junior partner – lacks the ability to influence international affairs independently and on its own initiative.

While Japanese policy-makers strive to lessen the reliance on the US, it is crucial to note that the vast majority do not seek genuine independence, including an abrogation of the alliance. Political elites seek to 'equalize' the US–Japan alliance by creating a more independent policy-line, but they simultaneously advocate continued cooperation with the US (Hughes 2004a: 51). The majority of decision-makers – including moderate nationalists – do not perceive a contradiction between loyalty to the US and the desire to gain an independent voice in international affairs. By taking a more proactive stance in international issues, decision-makers hope to shift the US–Japan alliance from a focus on 'burden sharing' to a mutual commitment in 'power sharing' (Yamaoka and Shiozaki 2000: 29).

Overall, the analysis of German speeches did not yield a comparable role conception widely shared among elites. Arguments corresponding to some aspects of Japanese thinking can be found in speeches and statements by Chancellor Gerhard Schröder. During his chancellorship, Schröder repeatedly declared that Germany was a 'self-confident country' (*selbstbewusstes Land*) and a 'great power' (*große Macht*) that would not unquestioningly follow others but that would assert its own ideas (Hellmann 2004: 32; Le Gloannec 2004: 34; Rittberger 2001: 12; Schröder 1998b). In September 2002, Schröder also voiced resentment about US pressure to dispatch troops in the lead-up to the war on Iraq. He contended that the 'existential questions of the German nation' would be decided in Berlin 'and nowhere else' (Schöllgen 2005: 5). The statement made it clear that Germany would not bend to US pressure – similar to Japanese declarations that Tokyo would take its decisions 'independently'.

The analysis of speeches shows that the majority of German policy-makers do not share Schröder's perspective. In fact Foreign Minister Joschka Fischer explicitly rejected Schröder's notion of asserting 'national' interests more forcefully, explaining in a November 1998 interview:

> A stronger attention to our own ego, to our own prestige, would only harm our interests and generate mistrust. … Germany has benefited much from the integration of our interests into the European network of interests (*Einbindung unserer Interessen in das europäische Interessengeflecht*). We should continue to adhere to this [policy].
>
> (Fischer 1998)

Furthermore, it seems that German policy-makers on the whole feel content with the respect and trust Germany receives from other countries and the leeway and influence that Berlin has in international circles. Chancellor Schröder himself acknowledged in 2002, 'Our Germany *enjoys respect and esteem* in the world. Because we are partner and role model. Because we are building the Europe of the people and help to secure and protect peace and human rights globally' (Baumann 2006: 185).

Why then have German policy-makers – compared to their Japanese counterparts – generally felt more satisfied with the level of trust and respect their country receives? Three important reasons can be deduced from the discussion in this chapter. First, post-war Germany has been successful in gradually establishing itself as an equal partner with its European neighbours (Risse 2001: 209). In the process of integration, the Federal Republic was able to build up relationships of trust and become a privileged link and mediator between the US and France. Japan, on the other hand, did not develop a comparable strategy for gaining influence and equality. Secondly, German post-war foreign policy initiatives have generally met with international approval and even praise – a fact that has not gone unnoticed among lawmakers. The Federal Republic is recognized as an indispensable contributor to the European integration process. Furthermore, Germany has won acclaim for its post-war policy of *Vergangenheitsbewältigung* (coming to terms with the history of Nazism and aggression). Thirdly, Japanese policies of self-restraint especially in the military field continue to be justified by the need to reassure neighbours and learn from the negative historical legacy of militarism. German policy-makers, by comparison, have been able to establish more forward-looking justifications for traditional policies of self-restraint, thereby projecting a positive and self-confident image of their country. For example, to explain policies of institutional binding they have increasingly cited practical reasons, such as the need to cooperate in a globalized world.

Overall comparison of the German and Japanese role sets

The German and Japanese role conceptions found in this study are characterized by a number of broad similarities in the goals formulated by policy-makers. Neither country seems to aspire to a unilaterally dominating leadership position in their region focused on maximizing national power, as realist scholars had suggested in the early 1990s. Both countries perceive a historical and moral responsibility as former aggressors in the Second World War and a duty as two of the largest economies worldwide to contribute to international and particularly regional security. They both seek to do so by fostering cooperation and stability in their respective region. Policy-makers in both countries emphasize the general importance of universal values, the preference for non-military instruments in conflict resolution and the need to act together with partners.

Despite these similarities in the stated policy goals, the analysis of German and Japanese speeches reveals significant differences in the specific behavioural expectations held by decision-makers. The greatest discrepancy was found in the way politicians from both countries seek to ensure stability in their respective region. Japanese policy-makers focus on the deterrence function of the US presence in the region while their German counterparts stress formal multilateral institutions as well as mediation and compromise as a way to transcend narrow-minded nationalism and balance of power thinking. On the whole, the German role set indicates a conviction among policy-makers that the traditional security dilemma between sovereign states can be overcome through multilateral institution-building. Germany's decision to provide global support to military missions under UN or NATO command reflects this German faith in multilateral institutions. The results of the content analysis suggest that the German role set is based largely on a 'transformationalist' understanding of international relations (Aggestam 2004: 241), in which political elites seek to transform the security dilemma rather than accept it as a given. In comparison, the Japanese role set reflects more of a 'traditionalist' mindset regarding international relations (Aggestam 2004: 241), as decision-makers pay more attention to realist concepts such as the balance of power and deterrence. However, some aspects in the Japanese conception do not fit traditional realist behavioural prescriptions focused on power maximization. In particular, policy-makers attach importance to universal values, suggesting a certain degree of idealism and hope for a more peaceful world order. Furthermore, Japanese leaders seek to minimize the risks posed by the security dilemma by exercising self-restraint in the maintenance of military capability. Overall, the Japanese role set thus seems to be based on a mixture of traditionalist and transformationalist thinking.

These results allow some reflection on the degree to which Germany and Japan may be characterized as 'civilian powers'. In the early 1990s, Hanns W. Maull formulated the hypothesis that the two countries bore many similarities to the ideal type of a 'civilian power'. He characterized the behaviour of a civilian power in various dimensions, including a general willingness to shape international relations, a focus on absolute rather than relative gains in economic affairs, a tendency to promote regime and institution building including a partial transfer of sovereignty, the avoidance of unilateral action, the promotion of universal values, and a reticence to use military force (Frenkler *et al.* 1997: 22ff.). The civilian power ideal type was formulated as a general role concept against which the national role conceptions of specific countries can be compared. The results of this study do not allow an ultimate judgement to be made on the civilian power orientation of Germany and Japan, as the content analysis only considered statements that refer to a regional context and fall into the traditional narrow definition of security studies, two limitations that do not apply to the civilian power concept. Nevertheless, some inferences can be drawn, based on the analysis. The German transformative role set exhibits a remarkably close resemblance to the civilian power ideal. Politicians state that they are willing to transfer sovereignty to multilateral institutions and seek to mediate among partner countries to achieve compromises. Furthermore, they express a willingness to provide military support to multilateral missions to solve conflicts, if other measures have failed. At least on the declaratory level, Germany's role set is by and large consistent with the civilian power ideal type. The Japanese role set on the other hand bears some, but not all the characteristics of a civilian power. The transformationalist elements, such as the emphasis on universal values and the need to act with partners, suggest some similarity to the civilian power ideal type. However, the traditionalist components in Japan's role set, especially the attachment to the US alliance and the focus on deterrence and the balance of power, do not fit the civilian power ideal as formulated by Maull. Furthermore, Japanese policy-makers do not display a willingness to delegate sovereignty to the supranational level, one of the characteristics of a civilian power. Japan's role set also diverges from Maull's concept regarding the use of military force as a last resort in settling disputes, as a civilian power would be expected to lend support to multilateral missions.

The analysis of speeches furthermore finds that German and Japanese role sets since the end of the Cold War are characterized by strong continuity, coupled with gradual modifications and adjustments in some role conceptions. The most perceptible change in both countries took place with regard to the role conception of 'non-militarist country', as policy-makers sought to make a more active contribution to UN missions in crisis areas. Nevertheless, decision-makers remained wedded to existing norms and values in considering possible changes in the role conception. German politicians thus focused on the importance of international institutions as a framework for their country's military support, while Japanese elites retained the notion of Japan as an 'exclusively defense-oriented country' that could not participate in peace-enforcing missions, in which soldiers would have to use military force for purposes other than pure self-defence.

Continuity in declared goals and national role conceptions was found across different administrations in both countries. In post-Cold War Germany, different parties led the federal government, starting with the CDU/CSU-FDP coalition, and followed by the SPD-Greens, the grand coalition between the CDU/CSU-SPD and finally again a CDU/CSU-FDP coalition. Particularly with the assumption of office by the SPD-Greens coalition in 1998, there were speculations about potential changes in the Federal Republic's foreign policy, following the 16-year chancellorship of Helmut Kohl. In Japan, the election victory of the DPJ in 2009 after 54 years of almost continuous rule by the LDP was seen as an even greater turning point, raising uncertainty over the country's foreign policy course. While slight shifts in emphasis between different administrations can be discerned, the speeches overall reflect an endurance of existing NRCs in each country. Prime Minister Hatoyama Yukio, the DPJ's first prime minister, for example stressed the promotion of regional cooperation and the development of an 'East Asian community' more so than other leaders (Hatoyama 2009a, 2009b). Nevertheless, he underlined the primacy of the US alliance in speeches, signifying continuity with previous governments. This finding seems to confirm Naomi Bailin Wish's observation that there exist 'greater similarities among role conceptions expressed by leaders from the same nations than from different nations' (Wish 1980: 549–50).

Despite overwhelming continuity in the role conceptions of Germany and Japan, further changes and adjustments are conceivable in both countries. In the face of economic difficulties and fiscal constraints, the German public is increasingly wary about the government's fixation on multilateral solutions and compromises, and many demand that Berlin pursue the national interest more assertively instead. Public and budgetary pressure could thus presage a German foreign policy that is 'weaker, leaner, [and] meaner' in the context of regional institutions (Harnisch and Schieder 2006: 95). On the Japanese side, domestic pressure is building to re-evaluate Japan's stance as an exclusively defence-oriented country, a notion that is seen as placing severe limits on Tokyo's contribution to both the UN and to the bilateral alliance with the US. Speeches in the past few years have also reflected a growing frustration about Japan's subservient status in the alliance relationship with the US. Though rapid shifts in policy goals and shared norms remain unlikely in either Germany or Japan, gradual and incremental change will thus continue.

3 German and Japanese missile defence policies

Introduction and background

This chapter presents the first case study on German and Japanese policies regarding missile defence, thereby enabling an evaluation of the explanatory power of role conceptions. As US allies, both countries have had to formulate approaches to this policy field, particularly since US President Ronald Reagan's 1983 inception of an ambitious US missile defence programme called Strategic Defense Initiative (SDI) and popularly known as 'Star Wars'. Subsequently, US policy has shifted in terms of focus and commitment, but the quest for a more effective and comprehensive missile defence system has persisted until today. Germany and Japan have thus been pressed to assess their own need for such a system, determining its technological feasibility, the costs and the desirability given their particular foreign policy goals. Focusing on the post-Cold War era, this chapter examines the two countries' missile defence (MD) policies in three areas of potential use: (1) territorial protection of Germany's/Japan's *homeland*, (2) protection of German/Japanese *soldiers abroad*, and (3) *assistance to other countries* in defending territory or troops through loan or lease of MD equipment.

The analysis reveals consistent differences in how decision-makers in Berlin and Tokyo perceive these three policy areas. Despite a growing Iranian missile threat, German politicians have been strikingly reluctant to consider the strategic requirements for territorial defence. They emphasize instead the need to consider Russian security interests and concerns. Their Japanese counterparts reflect confidence in the benefits of a territorial MD shield. The immediacy of the North Korean threat has of course affected Japanese thinking, but normative factors play an equally important role in the evaluation of policy choices, as the chapter will demonstrate. Compared to the first policy area, attitudes to the protection of soldiers abroad are reversed: while Berlin has been highly supportive of building a missile defence system for its troops deployed abroad, political elites in Tokyo have not publicly discussed the need for such protection. Normative factors again play a key role in these different outlooks. In the third policy area, decision-makers in the two countries are faced by similar quandaries. Political elites feel obligated to assist allies and partner countries with their MD equipment, but given their desire to be 'non-militarist countries' they are selective about providing such support, especially in Japan's case. In sum, the chapter argues that each country's distinct approaches to the three policy areas can be best understood by considering the relevant role conceptions.

The remainder of this introduction provides a background on US missile defence policy during and after the Cold War. The following six sections of the chapter analyse Berlin's and Tokyo's post-Cold War policies with respect to the three potential uses of MD, as specified above. The chapter begins with a discussion of Germany (sections 2–4), and then examines and compares Japan (sections 5–7). The analysis pinpoints important characteristics in lawmakers' attitudes, identifies key phases in the domestic debates and examines how far role conceptions help understand observed behaviour. The chapter concludes (section 8) by assessing the overall explanatory power of role conceptions in German and Japanese MD policies. This part also discusses the two countries' coping strategies when faced with role conflicts.

US missile defence during the Cold War and German and Japanese reactions

In a March 1983 speech, US President Ronald Reagan proposed the Strategic Defense Initiative (SDI), comprising a system that could 'intercept and destroy strategic ballistic missiles before they [reach] our own soil or that of our allies' (Reagan 1983). The plan to use both ground- and space-based devices for interception was revolutionary, as previous programmes by the US and other countries had been designed only for limited geographic coverage with ground-based systems. The US planned to devise a layered missile defence system with global reach and interception devices for each of the three flight phases of a ballistic missile: (1) the boost phase, which begins immediately after launch while the rocket motor is burning and before the missile has reached space, (2) the midcourse phase, when the missile flies in space, and (3) the terminal or re-entry phase, when the missile re-enters the atmosphere before impact on the target.

Initially, Reagan's plan was met with suspicion and caution, as allies feared the US might upset the strategic balance with the Soviet Union and breach the ABM Treaty. To make the proposal more acceptable to others, the US recast it as a big research programme in which both industry and civilian scientific research could benefit. Allies were officially invited to participate in March 1985 (Miller 1985; Kawakami and Jimbo 2002: 263). Germany and Japan indicated interest, while emphasizing the importance of maintaining the strategic balance between the US and the Soviet Union. They both had to negotiate a possible participation in the project cautiously due to strong anti-militarist sentiments and doubts about the technological feasibility among their publics.

Germany first sought consultations and agreement with other Western European countries, in accordance with its traditional multilateral inclination. However, due to divergent views, ranging from full support for MD by Great Britain to scepticism by France, efforts to stake out a common European position on SDI failed (Xinhua News Agency 1985; Filipiak 2006: 91–2). In March 1986, Bonn and Washington thus reached a bilateral agreement, stating that German private companies and research institutions would be allowed to participate in US research activities, while the German government would remain uninvolved. With this arrangement, Bonn hoped to secure profitable SDI contracts for private companies, gain insight into this innovative research area and ensure good alliance relations with the US (Miller 1985).

Based on similar reasoning and seeing the German compromise as a useful solution, Tokyo concluded a comparable agreement with Washington in July 1987, enabling private companies to participate in SDI. Specifically, the two governments approved a joint research project between Japanese and US companies, called Western Pacific Missile Defense Architecture Study (WESTPAC), which began in December 1988 (Kaneda *et al.* 2006: 87–8).

US missile defence policy after the Cold War

After the Cold War, the US continued to push for the development of an MD shield. Differences between administrations existed regarding the approach to MD development and the stated rationale, resulting in shifts of focus regarding particular components of the layered system. While some administrations put more emphasis on the protection of partner countries and US facilities and troops abroad, others have stressed territorial defence for the US mainland as the primary concern. The distinction was reflected in President Bill Clinton's definition of national missile defence (NMD) and theatre missile defence (TMD). NMD was to intercept long-range missiles targeted at the United States, while TMD was for shorter, 'theatre'-range missiles aimed at deployed troops or US overseas facilities. For Clinton, this distinction was particularly important, because the TMD programme he promoted was compatible with the Anti-Ballistic Missile (ABM) Treaty signed between the US and the Soviet Union in 1972, whereas NMD was more problematic. Because of technological overlap between NMD and TMD, the George W. Bush administration abandoned this division. Nevertheless, shifts of emphasis in the declared rationale continued, with important effects on German and Japanese perceptions of MD, as will be seen in this chapter.

The early 1990s: the George Bush and Bill Clinton administrations

With the winding up of Cold War tensions, the George Bush (senior) government initially attached lower priority to the SDI project, as reflected in the substantial reduction of the missile defence budget (Kaneda *et al.* 2006: 28–9). However, the Gulf War in 1991–2 stimulated new discussions on missile defence, when Iraq fired Scud missiles at Israel in the hope of drawing the Jewish state into the war. In response, Bush shifted the priority of SDI from the defence of North America against large-scale missile strikes to theatre missile defence, calling his project 'Global Protection against Limited Strikes' (GPALS).

In 1993, the Clinton administration reviewed US anti-missile policy, announcing continued focus on theatre missile defence to protect US overseas facilities as well as allied countries. Compared to his predecessor, Clinton called for more involvement of US allies like Germany and Japan in the research and development of missile defence systems. Furthermore, Clinton pursued bilateral talks on missile defence with Russia, resulting in several declarations including a mutual pledge in May 1995 not to develop a TMD system that could upset the nuclear balance (Matsui 2000: 51). However, Clinton's policy came under pressure from the Republican Party, which in the November 1994 elections won the majority of seats in both Houses of Congress. The Republicans called for a shift in priority towards NMD, threatening to defeat budgetary proposals for TMD programmes. Advances in missile technology by countries like North Korea and Iran in the late 1990s seemed to confirm Republican warnings about a growing threat to US territory. In spite of these developments, President Clinton remained cautious about the NMD programme. In September 2000, he deferred a decision on whether the US should deploy an initial MD capability to protect its territory, citing technological problems and other reasons.

The George W. Bush administration

His successor, Republican George W. Bush (junior) accelerated the development of a missile defence system, especially for the protection of US homeland (Kubbig 2005b: 416). Although his policy focused on building a territorial missile defence shield, he announced in May 2001 that he would no longer distinguish between NMD and TMD programmes. One of the reasons for eliminating this distinction was that Bush hoped to assuage European fears of a 'de-coupling' of US and European security (Morimoto and Takahashi 2002: 318–19).

Although no missiles were used, the 11 September 2001 terrorist attacks provided an opportunity for Bush to accelerate the development of MD technology. With Congress united behind him, the president decided to withdraw from the ABM Treaty on 13 December 2001, thus eliminating one of the hurdles to a territorial missile defence shield. Signing the National Security Presidential Directive No. 23 on 16 December 2002, Bush promoted preparations for a US missile defence system. The directive stated the US would begin with the initial deployment of the system in 2004–5. After completing the installation of more than ten interceptors in Alaska and California as well as radar systems in the UK and in Greenland, the Bush administration in early 2007 officially embarked on bilateral negotiations with Poland and the Czech Republic on stationing missile defence components on their territories. The US concluded two agreements, one in July 2008 with the Czech Republic to place a radar system in the Brdy district and the other with Poland to install ten missile interceptors near Koszalin (Shanker and Kulish 2008). With these devices, Washington sought to counter a potential threat from longer range Iranian missiles aimed at the US East Coast and parts of Western Europe.

The Barack Obama administration

Following a review of missile defence plans, President Obama decided to shift the programme's primary focus back towards protecting targets abroad. In September

2009, Obama announced he would prioritize the development of components designed to shoot down short- and medium-range missiles, which presented the most immediate concern for partner countries and US facilities abroad. His policy recalibration, he explained, was based on new intelligence assessments, which do not see an immediate threat to the US from intercontinental ballistic missiles of states such as Iran or North Korea (Harvey 2009; Collina 2010). Consequently, Obama proclaimed his new 'phased adaptive approach', according to which only MD components with a proven track record in interception tests would be deployed. Bush's planned installation of ground-based interceptors in Poland was judged to be premature, as this technology had failed in numerous tests (Lange 2010). Instead, the administration announced its plan to deploy the more successfully tested Standard Missile-3 (SM-3) land-based interceptors in Romania in 2015 and in Poland in 2018, thereby extending the area of missile defence coverage into southern Europe (Kaufman 2010). At the same time, the Obama administration was forced to cut funds for some MD projects due to severe budgetary constraints and concerns about the rising national debt. As will be seen in section 3, this included a joint project with Germany and Italy, which was terminated in February 2011.

Compared to his predecessor, Obama stressed the need for multilateral cooperation on missile defence, calling for more extensive NATO consultations. He furthermore sought to mend relations with Russia, which had deteriorated amid Bush's unilateral MD policy and the planned installations in Poland and the Czech Republic (Collina 2010). Bilateral relations with Moscow subsequently improved, culminating in the signing of a new Strategic Arms Reduction Treaty (START) on 8 April 2010. However, in late 2010 and 2011, frictions re-emerged due to the lingering Russian fears about losing deterrence power amid US and European plans for an MD shield (Dempsey 2011).

German policy on territorial missile defence

Introduction

Amid an increasingly fluid security environment and a growing number of countries with missile technology, Germany's protection from a potential attack has been an important strategic issue after the Cold War. A key question has been whether the country should seek to develop and acquire MD technology offering full territorial protection, rather than relying only on systems for point-defence. During the Cold War, the Federal Republic had already acquired a limited capability to defend important strategic points within its territory from missile attacks with the Hawk and Patriot systems.

This part of the case study will examine the evolution of German post-Cold War territorial MD policy. First I identify three phases in the political debate: (1) the period from 1990 to 2000, characterized by a remarkable reluctance to consider the need for territorial MD, (2) the period from 2000 to 2006, during which politicians initially voiced strong opposition to US territorial MD plans, but then shifted to subdued reconsideration concerning Germany's strategic needs, and (3) the period from 2007 until 2010, when politicians in Berlin again shifted from opposition to US plans to further strategic reconsideration. Overall, the analysis finds that role conceptions provide a good explanation for the dominantly sceptical attitude regarding territorial MD in Germany.

1990–2000: reluctance to discuss homeland security

In the early 1990s, numerous German government publications cautioned of a growing threat from weapons of mass destruction and missiles. Surprisingly however, politicians rarely considered the need for a territorial missile defence system. In part, this hesitant stance can be explained by the widespread scepticism about the system's technological feasibility among decision-makers. More importantly however, politicians feared upsetting the regional balance of power, an anxiety stemming from the Cold War debate about Reagan's 'Star Wars' project.

Spurred by the Bush senior and Clinton administrations, NATO allies debated the need for missile defence after the Cold War. Members of the alliance agreed that the proliferation and use of shorter range ballistic missiles and the potential development of missiles with longer ranges were a growing menace in the new strategic environment. This view was reflected in the new Strategic Concept of November 1991, which observed a growing risk posed by 'weapons of mass destruction and ballistic missiles capable of reaching the territory of some member states of the Alliance' (Martin 1996). A NATO Senior Defence Group on Proliferation in November 1995 stated the need for a territorial defence system to protect alliance territory against longer range tactical ballistic missiles (Martin 1996). This assessment was essentially confirmed by a October 1999 report by the German Federal Intelligence Service (*Bundesnachrichtendienst*), warning that 'several states in the Near East are working on missiles with a range of more than 1,000 km', which can be classified as medium- and long-range (Scheffran and Hagen 2001).

Nevertheless, both the Kohl and Schröder governments displayed reluctance to engage in discussions about the potential need for a missile defence shield for Germany and for NATO territory (Krause 2000: 38; Cambone *et al.* 2000: 28–9). The only indication that the German government considered territorial missile defence was its participation in the development of a Medium Extended Air Defense System, MEADS, to which it committed in a May 1996 memorandum of understanding (MoU) with the United States and Italy. However, the system is primarily intended for point protection of troops deployed abroad (as will be discussed in more detail below) and it is of limited strategic value in territorial protection, since it intercepts only missiles with a range of up to 1,000 kilometres (Kubbig and Nitsche 2005: 529).[1]

Even after Iran tested its Shahab-3 medium-range ballistic missile with an estimated range of about 1,300 kilometres in July 1998, German political elites, like the politicians in most other European countries, remained reluctant to discuss territorial defence. Rather, they displayed confidence that engagement policies would be successful in moderating the regime's behaviour. A senior British official characterized the general aversion of Europeans in the late 1990s to discussing territorial missile defence as a 'severe case of ostrichitis', suggesting their stance resembled the behaviour of an ostrich that hides its head in the sand when in danger, believing itself to be unseen (Cambone *et al.* 2000: 15–16). In examining European attitudes on MD, a group of experts under the auspices of the Atlantic Council concluded in July 2000 that the German political elite in the late 1990s was the 'least inclined' of the major European countries to engage in discussions on the strategic issues related to territorial missile defence (Cambone *et al.* 2000: 29). One reason for the German reluctance was that politicians were not wholly convinced of the technological feasibility of MD (Schnappertz 2010). Furthermore, decision-makers after the Cold War continued to fear that a missile shield would disrupt the strategic balance between the US and Russia. This aspect will become clear in the sections below.

2000–2006: from vocal opposition to subdued reconsideration

The time period from 2000 to 2006 witnessed a shift in attitudes among German policy-makers. Following a parliamentary inquiry by the Free Democratic Party (FDP) in 2000, a majority of politicians initially voiced strong opposition to US missile defence plans. Berlin's leaders rarely seemed to consider whether MD was necessary to respond to the strategic changes after the Cold War and Iran's development of weapons of mass destruction (WMD). Towards the end of the period, Iran's steadfast pursuit of its nuclear and missile programmes cooled German confidence in diplomatic efforts, triggering some reconsideration regarding the need for a territorial MD system.

In 2000, the Free Democratic Party (FDP) initiated a parliamentary inquiry, calling on the German government to clarify its stance on territorial defence, thereby challenging the vagueness and aversion to engaging in discussions on the topic (Krause 2001: 478). The Red-Green coalition government reacted with scepticism about US National Missile Defense (NMD) plans, warning in an internal paper that 'The cohesion of NATO could be affected; moreover such a system – even if technologically feasible – would not cover the entire spectrum of threats presented by risk states' (*Spiegel* 2007a). Members of the government, most prominently Foreign Minister Joschka Fischer, raised three objections about US plans, namely (1) the need to ensure NATO cohesion, (2) the importance of continuing diplomatic efforts for non-proliferation, and (3) concern about an imminent arms race.

German government leaders worried that the NATO alliance might weaken over the NMD issue, due to two interrelated concerns. First, there was apprehension that the NMD debate in the US might indicate unilateral tendencies in the strategic thinking, a concern that spread with the inauguration of the George W. Bush administration (Cambone *et al.* 2000: 16). Politicians in Germany saw the US pursuit of NMD as a *fait accompli*, which left little room for consultations and compromises with US allies. Secondly, decision-makers suspected that isolationist tendencies in the US were rising and the deployment of a missile defence system would further intensify this trend. Foreign Minister Fischer reflected such suspicions, when he warned at the Munich Security Conference in February 2001 that the US must remain a 'European power' (Filipiak 2006: 272). As a result of such concerns, German politicians urged multilateral consultations on missile defence. Although some politicians initially sought discussions among EU members, in the end, a majority favoured NATO as the primary channel for deliberations to ensure US inclusion from the beginning. To that end, Defence Minister Rudolf Scharping argued that 'it is much more important to talk about [missile defence] in NATO' than to find a common European position. He continued: 'It makes little sense if the Europeans sit down together and afterwards talk to the Americans. Right from the start, we have to do so in the Alliance' (Filipiak 2006: 277).

The second major objection in German discussions on US NMD plans focused on a possible US withdrawal from the ABM Treaty, which had ensured strategic stability between the two superpowers during the Cold War. To politicians in the Federal Republic, the treaty retained a symbolic value in the post-Cold War era, symbolizing détente, cooperation and international support for diplomatic and agreement-based variants of arms control. Confronted with the US intention to abrogate the treaty, German politicians reacted with shock, perceiving it as evidence of Washington's weakening commitment to diplomatic non-proliferation policies (Cambone *et al.* 2000: 26).

The third major objection, raised most prominently by Foreign Minister Fischer and Chancellor Schröder, was that the US NMD project would endanger global strategic stability and initiate a new arms race with Russia. In May 2000, Schröder dismissed the US programme as politically dangerous, claiming that it was a 'counterproductive containment policy against Russia' that is 'anything but in the European interest' (*Spiegel* 2007a). In June 2000 in the newspaper *Berliner Zeitung*, Schröder furthermore warned, 'Neither economically nor politically can we afford a new round of arms race' (Neuneck 2001: 165).

In line with this view, German politicians remained exceptionally attentive to Russian concerns and proposals. This tendency was reinforced by Berlin's desire to patch up relations with Moscow after bilateral ties had soured over contentious issues such as Russian actions in Chechnya and NATO's involvement in Kosovo in the late 1990s (BBC 2000). A June 2000 proposal by Russian President Vladimir Putin to establish pan-European multinational intervention troops that would be rapidly deployable to provide point-defence against incoming missiles was received positively by Schröder (Lisagor 2000). Subsequently, a number of analysts queried whether Russia was sincere in its proposal for a mobile missile defence squad, suggesting that Moscow mainly sought to cause a rift among NATO allies and increase its leverage (Adomeit 2001; Arnhold 2001). The US only expressed polite scepticism about the Russian idea, which was strategically rather different from Washington's plan for a permanent strategic missile shield intended to ward off unexpected attacks from 'rogue' states or terrorist groups. Moreover, many observers in the US viewed the German fear of a new arms race as outdated and inadequate for the new post-Cold War strategic environment. American observers generally assumed that Russia was neither willing nor capable of engaging in a new arms race with the United States. Moreover, the planned US missile defence system would for the foreseeable future not provide a credible shield against the thousands of nuclear missiles in the Russian arsenal, some pointed out (Krause 2001).

In contrast to their American counterparts, German policy-makers rarely debated whether the changing strategic environment required new policy approaches. Most leaders in the Federal Republic were furthermore optimistic about the possibility of discouraging rogue states or terrorist groups from using their missile and WMD capabilities by diplomatic means. In this context, politicians warned against isolating the Iranian regime, with Foreign Minister Fischer advising in February 2000 that 'Iran should be included in the international community' (Neuneck 2001: 165). This comment was made well before the inauguration of the George W. Bush administration, which named Iran together with Iraq and North Korea an 'axis of evil', triggering considerable concern about a potential military conflict between the US and Iran.

German leaders hesitantly became more accepting of the US plans in the course of 2001. On 26 February 2001, Schröder warned that, considering its 'imminent economic interest', Germany should 'not be left out' of the missile defence plans (Scheffran and Hagen 2001: 437). During his first meeting with President Bush in Washington in late March 2001, Schröder even conceded that missile defence in combination with other policies might help reduce nuclear arsenals. Thereby, he revoked his previous position that US plans would inevitably trigger an arms race (Filipiak 2006: 280). Nevertheless, Schröder refrained from any commitment to participate in missile defence.

Several factors help explain this gradual change. First of all, the Bush administration, inaugurated in early 2001, left little doubt that it would pursue missile defence, despite protests from allies. The British government reacted by casting aside previously held doubts and demonstrated support for US plans. This move brought about some rethinking in Germany (Scheffran and Hagen 2001: 436). Secondly, Bush's policy of merging the NMD and TMD programmes lessened German suspicion and fear of a Fortress America, whose security would be 'de-coupled' from European security. Thirdly, in the aftermath of the 11 September 2001 terrorist attacks in the US, Russia seemed to adopt a more constructive posture and barely objected when Washington in December announced its intention to withdraw from the ABM Treaty. Lastly, the US decision to conclude a formal arms control 'equivalent' by signing the US-Russian Strategic Offensive Reductions Treaty (SORT) in May 2002 also encouraged adjustment in the German position on the US plans (Kubbig 2005c: 338).

In 2002, the German government helped initiate discussions on missile defence at NATO level during the Prague summit. Member states decided to conduct a feasibility study on missile defence for NATO territory and charged a consortium of industry representatives and experts with this task. The study, concluding that missile defence for NATO territory was viable, was presented at the November 2006 summit in Riga. Despite growing concern among NATO states about the proliferation of weapons of mass destruction, an ultimate decision on the need for the system was postponed. Germany remained ambivalent on territorial missile defence and refrained from concrete policy steps (Schreer 2010).

In the meantime, German and international anxiety about Iran grew markedly as a June 2003 report by the International Atomic Energy Agency (IAEA) stated the regime had failed to comply with the Nuclear Non-Proliferation Treaty (NPT). The Federal Republic decided to launch a diplomatic initiative together with Britain and France, forming the so-called EU-3. Negotiations twice seemed to yield results when agreements were reached in October 2003 and November 2004, but on both occasions it quickly became clear that Iran was unwilling to follow words with deeds. At the same time, the regime's advances in missile technology generated concern. In February 2006, German intelligence circles reported that Iran had received 18 Soviet-built BM-25 (SS-N-6) rockets from North Korea with a range of approximately 2,500 kilometres, equipped to carry nuclear warheads (*Focus* 2006). A number of politicians in Berlin reflected unease, noting that the distance between Iran and the southern city of Munich was only 2,760 kilometres (von Klaeden 2007). While not mentioning Iran explicitly, the 2006 White Book warned that 'The proliferation of weapons of mass destruction and their means of delivery … are increasingly developing into a potential threat for Germany … State and non-state actors are trying to obtain high-tech for criminal purposes' (Bundesministerium für Verteidigung 2006: 16).

2007–2011: from vocal opposition to a gradual reconsideration – a rerun?

After the 2000–1 hype, public attention regarding homeland missile defence faded. A speech by Russian President Vladimir Putin during the Munich Conference on Security Policy in February 2007 reinvigorated the German debate. As during the previous phase, the time period between 2007 and 2010 was characterized by a shift in German attitudes. Following Putin's speech, Berlin's decision-makers showed themselves remarkably attentive once again to Russian concerns about the US MD shield, although compared to before more politicians – particularly from the CDU-CSU – questioned Moscow's motives. With the heightening Iranian security crisis and the Obama administration's new multilateral efforts, German politicians began to take a more positive attitude to the US programme.

Following the US announcement on the planned stationing of MD elements in Poland and the Czech Republic, Moscow responded by denouncing this policy as a provocation aimed at 'encircling' Russia (Schnappertz 2010; Bartels and Kröger 2007: 39). In February 2007, President Putin asserted that 'Plans to expand certain elements of the anti-missile defence system to Europe cannot help but disturb us. Who needs the next step of what would be, in this case, an inevitable arms race?' (Putin 2007). If Moscow intended to cause a rift between NATO members, the strategy worked well. In Germany, policy-makers debated almost exclusively the prospect of an arms race, as Putin had suggested. Leading the debate, politicians from the Social Democratic Party vigorously backed the Russian assessment.

Kurt Beck, chairman of the SPD, opposed the missile defence system with the words 'We do not need more rockets, rather we need efforts to build trust and reduce distrust.' He furthermore called for Germany to 'do everything to prevent another arms race (*Rüstungsspirale*)' (*Süddeutsche Zeitung* 2007).[2] Fellow SPD member and foreign minister, Frank-Walter Steinmeier, similarly expressed concern, arguing that 'disarmament, not armament' should have priority in foreign policy (*Spiegel* 2007e). In general, SPD members concurred that a missile shield would not contribute to an improved security environment in Europe as long as Russia felt threatened by this system (Katsioulis 2010). Most members of the Green Party, including the party's vice chairman Jürgen Trittin, shared the critical attitude of the SPD (*Stern* 2007). The FDP took a more ambiguous stance, although comments by party chairman Guido Westerwelle suggested that he too had misgivings about US missile defence policy (Busse 2007).

Members of the CDU-CSU were generally more cautious about the Russian criticism of US missile defence.[3] Foreign policy spokesman of the CDU-CSU fraction Eckart von Klaeden went so far as to denounce Putin's allegations of the MD system being targeted at Russian missiles as 'propaganda' (*Süddeutsche Zeitung* 2007). While not all members of the CDU-CSU were as outspoken in their criticism as von Klaeden, most doubted the likelihood of a new arms race (Staff member of the CDU/CSU parliamentary grouping 2010; Keller 2010).

Noteworthy is German Chancellor Angela Merkel's conduct in the debate on US missile defence plans. Rather than stating her opinion clearly, she maintained a low profile, seeking to act as a mediator and reconciling the various views within Germany and in the international community. Using somewhat ambiguous rhetoric that occasionally left open whether she was addressing fellow domestic politicians or the international community, Merkel stated that 'everything must be done to avoid unilateral actions (*Alleingänge*) and to discuss issues concertedly' (*Spiegel* 2007d). She also said she favoured resolving the dispute within NATO and hoped for open talks with Russia.

Overall, the majority of policy-makers and commentators failed to address key strategic questions such as how Berlin should react to the global proliferation of missile technology. As commentator Nikolas Busse noted in the newspaper *Frankfurter Allgemeine Zeitung*, German politicians presented the issue to the public 'as if it was primarily a problem of strategic balance between the US and Russia'. Busse's criticism was that virtually nothing was said about the developments that had prompted US policy, and that the central question of whether Germany needed a missile defence system was not raised (Busse 2007). According to former NATO General Klaus Naumann, the debate reflected 'almost incredible ignorance' about the strategic environment (*Spiegel* 2007b). Naumann argued that an arms race was inconceivable since the few planned interception missiles were ineffective against the large quantities of sophisticated Russian missiles. Moreover, he pointed out that Russian rockets fired towards the US mainland traversed the North Pole, not Europe. Therefore, interceptor missiles deployed in Eastern Europe were futile for defending US territory against such attacks. Later, a high-ranking Russian official admitted that Putin's opposition to

US MD plans derived more from shrewd power politics and the desire to increase leverage than from strategic concerns. Observing the debate in Germany and other NATO countries following Putin's speech in Munich, the Russian official appeared pleased with the effect, noting: 'Now, they listen to us' (*Jetzt hört man uns zu*) (Bittner 2008).

Beginning in the spring of 2007, German decision-makers gradually shifted towards a more positive evaluation of the US MD programme. Four key reasons for this change can be identified: (1) an escalation of tensions regarding Iran's nuclear and missile programmes, (2) intensified consultation and growing support within NATO regarding MD, (3) the Obama administration's new policy approach, and (4) the positive reputation of Obama in Germany.

First, international concern about Iran intensified with the announcement by President Mahmud Ahmadinezhad on 9 April 2007 that his country was now enriching uranium on an industrial scale (*Stern* 2007). Further cause for alarm was the regime's apparent progress in developing multiple-stage missile technology, needed to increase rocket ranges. Recurrently, Iran test-fired its Sejil-2 and improved Shahab-3 missiles, with estimated ranges of about 2,000 kilometres (BBC 2009). A growing number of politicians in Berlin, especially from the CDU-CSU, began speaking in favour of a missile defence shield for Germany and Europe (*Stern* 2007). For example, Defence Minister Franz Josef Jung commented, 'I think that the current developments confirm that it is prudent to decide for such a [missile] defence [system]' (*Spiegel* 2007c). SPD members also began to evaluate territorial MD more positively. In an interview in June 2010, Rolf Mützenich admitted that he had shifted towards a cautiously supportive stance on missile defence, because Iran had made rapid progress in missile technology, as demonstrated by the development in late 2008 of a solid-fuel rocket with improved accuracy (Mützenich 2010).[4] SPD member Hans-Ulrich Klose confirmed a general tendency among policy-makers to reconsider the need for MD amid the growing Iranian threat (Klose 2010).

Secondly, the gradual shift in German views on MD was influenced by a series of NATO consultations, leading to more support for the US project. At a special meeting of high-level representatives in April 2007, member states agreed to back US plans, since the missile defence system did not present any danger to Russia in their view (Deutsche Welle Online 2007). Moscow's protests against the US missile shield lessened somewhat after the announcement. Furthermore, President Putin surprised the US in early June 2007 with the offer to build a joint anti-ballistic missile system in the former Soviet Republic of Azerbaijan. The proposed system would guard against a missile attack from Iran. Thus, Putin acknowledged a potential threat from the regime. Despite US scepticism, the Azerbaijan proposal helped temporarily to lessen bilateral tensions between Washington and Moscow. At the November 2010 Lisbon summit, NATO leaders finally committed themselves to the development of a missile defence capability, agreeing that the defence of 'our populations and territories against ballistic missile attack' was 'a core element of our collective defence' (NATO 2011). They furthermore concurred to seek MD cooperation with Russia.

Thirdly, the new approach in US MD policy, announced by President Obama in September 2009, appealed to politicians from parties across the political spectrum in Germany. In particular, the emphasis on multilateral consultations and engagement with Russia met with support from both CDU-CSU and SPD politicians.[5] Chancellor Merkel greeted Obama's policy shift as a 'hopeful signal for overcoming the difficulties with Russia' (Nassauer 2009). As Moscow toned down its criticism of MD, German decision-makers felt reassured that the cooperative approach would prevent the emergence of an arms race based on new antagonisms. They were also pleased that the new US strategy would extend the area of MD coverage to countries in southern Europe. As Foreign Ministry official Jürgen Schnappertz explained, this helps to avoid zones of varying security in the region, and therefore strengthens cohesion and facilitates cooperation within NATO and the EU (Schnappertz 2010). Finally, German politicians supported Obama's policy of installing only those MD elements that had been tested successfully. They viewed this approach as more pragmatic than Bush's seemingly rushed deployment plan (Schnappertz 2010).

Fourthly, Obama's positive international reputation played an important role in German decision-makers' reconsideration of MD. In stark contrast to his predecessor, President Obama – as a Nobel Peace Prize winner – was perceived as a leader who would make more efforts at cooperation. Prior to his presidency, many German politicians expected him to abandon the MD project upon taking office. When Obama thus announced his intention to continue developing MD capabilities, German elites were more inclined to seriously deliberate the US project (Sinjen 2010).

Despite the trend towards a more positive evaluation of MD among German policy-makers, the country's role in NATO's missile defence project is yet to be clearly defined. Alliance members have not yet worked out concrete details on implementing the November 2010 decision to develop an MD shield. Furthermore, Berlin's leaders will carefully monitor Russia's stance on the MD project, which throughout 2011 has been characterized by scepticism and concern about the possible loss of deterrence capability (Dempsey 2011). Negotiations on a Russian involvement in the development of MD will likely face significant challenges (Sinjen 2010). Given the severe budgetary constraints, Berlin's politicians will also consider the costs of acquiring MD (Bartels 2010). At the NATO summit in April 2008, a German representative expressed concern that his country would 'probably [have to] contribute 20 Cents for every Euro spent' on the project (Bittner 2008).

Explaining German policy

German policy-makers have been strikingly reluctant to deliberate the need for a comprehensive missile defence system, although in recent years a trend towards growing support is discernible. Thus far, the public discourse has focused on the assumed negative aspects of an MD system. What accounts for the German aversion to engage in discussions? In seeking to answer this question, this section will consider three key policy aspects: (1) decision-makers' assessment of a threat to their country, (2) their appraisal of the technological feasibility and costs of the proposed system, and (3) the relation between German role conceptions and the country's policy regarding territorial MD.[6]

Threat assessment

An ambivalent picture emerges from public statements and documents assessing the ballistic missile threat to Germany. On the one hand, official documents such as the White Book and various NATO declarations have noted a growing threat from the proliferation of missile technology since the mid- to late 1990s. In particular, Iran's missile and nuclear programmes, pursued with ambition and provocative rhetoric, have elicited apprehension in Germany. On the other hand, in deliberations on missile defence, Berlin's leaders have avoided debates on the strategic changes that induced US policy, such as the tensions with Iran. The German public shows low concern about an external threat from missiles and other weapons of mass destruction. In a spring 2006 public opinion survey, only 1 per cent of respondents answered that they thought terrorism was an urgent topic for Germany (European Commission 2006: 34).

Those politicians who oppose MD generally take an optimistic stance regarding Iran. First, some politicians argued it was better for Germany to refrain from joining the US project and accept a certain amount of vulnerability. SPD foreign policy expert Niels Annen argued that participation in the MD programme 'would signal to Iran that we already now assume that the diplomatic efforts will fail' (*Spiegel* 2007c). Secondly, several decision-makers argued that Iran did not possess missiles capable of reaching Germany at this stage. For example, Foreign Minister Steinmeier argued in February 2007 that Europe was not threatened 'under the current state of Iranian weapons technology' (Frühling and Sinjen 2007: 3). Such assessments leave two questions unanswered, however. First, they do not indicate what Germany should do if Iran possesses missiles of greater range in the future. Secondly, the strategic consequences of an Iran possessing missiles capable of reaching the southern parts of the EU or NATO territory remain unclear. Berlin could be confronted with serious quandaries if Teheran attempted manipulation by holding one of Germany's regional partners hostage with nuclear-armed missiles.

Technological feasibility and cost-effectiveness

German decision-makers do not give much consideration to the technological feasibility and the cost-effectiveness of a missile defence shield, two aspects that are interrelated. Politicians rather tend to reject such a system altogether, presuming Germany's foreign policy goals would be ill served by participating. Nevertheless, some ambivalence in views regarding feasibility and cost can be discerned, similar to the diverging threat assessments discussed above. The official government position in communiqués or agreements suggests the entire range of MD technology could work and help increase Germany's security (Kubbig and Nitsche 2005: 522). On the other hand, individual German politicians appear sceptical about technological aspects of MD systems. Repeatedly, officials pointed out that 100 per cent security was unattainable and a missile defence shield could never cover the entire spectrum of threats presented by risk states. German leaders also seemed to have qualms about the potential costs of an MD system, as seen in the above-mentioned comment of a government representative, expressing fear of a hefty bill if Germany participated.

Policy goals and role conceptions

The contradictory threat perceptions and ambivalent assessments of technological feasibility and cost-effectiveness of an MD system may explain to some extent Germany's overall hesitant posture towards missile defence. Nevertheless, Berlin's inconsistent handling of the issue remains puzzling. Why did German policy-makers criticize the US MD programme so harshly when they perceived some benefits for German security? How come German policy-makers were so susceptible to apparently unfound Russian criticism about US missile defence policy? Why did they ignore strategic changes prompting the US to expedite its MD programme? This section will determine whether and how far German role conceptions can explain Germany's evaluation and approach to the missile defence issue.

The two role conceptions 'regional stabilizer' and 'anti-militarist country' help to explain Germany's reluctant posture on MD and the sensitivity to Russian objections. First, in accordance with the role conception of 'regional stabilizer', decision-makers seek to mediate multilaterally between the interests of various partner countries, paying particular attention to Russian concerns and requests. As a result, Berlin strongly urged the US to consider carefully Putin's proposals for a pan-European mobile missile defence squad in 2000–1 and for a joint missile interception base in Azerbaijan in 2007. However, focused on Russian criticism of US policy, Germany's leaders have failed to adjust their strategic thinking to the new security challenges after the Cold War. By assuming that a new arms race could ensue, they underestimated the size of Russia's arsenal of nuclear missiles while overestimating the capability of the planned US defence system. At the same time, German lawmakers misconstrued Moscow's tactics. As seen above, Russian objections derived mainly from a widespread frustration over the country's declining international power and over US unilateralism. Putin thus hoped to stir a divisive debate within NATO in order to increase his international leverage. The role conception of 'regional stabilizer' triggered a reflex among German policy-makers to pay heed to Russian criticism, especially after Reagan's SDI plans had already caused considerable controversy during the Cold War (Schreer 2010; Katsioulis 2010).

Secondly, in line with the role conception of 'anti-militarist country', lawmakers have displayed a profound faith in the effectiveness of diplomacy, seeking to achieve security through cooperation rather than through military means. The anti-militarist norms were clearly reflected in public discussions on MD, as political leaders emphasized diplomacy as ethically superior to military steps. Thomas Bauer observed that the term 'arms race' was 'being referred to from a ... moral point of view, describing the dominance of military actions over political or diplomatic solutions' (Bauer 2007: 6). According to SPD politician Karsten Voigt, deterrence is seen by many as a political problem, signifying distrust between countries. Mutual suspicion and insecurity between countries therefore requires diplomatic efforts rather than technical developments and a defensive capability build-up (Voigt 2010). The faith in diplomacy also explains the German shock about the Bush administration's withdrawal from the ABM Treaty and the fear of upsetting the cooperative ethos with Russia. Even with regard to Iran, Berlin's policy-makers did not lose confidence in multilateral talks, despite the regime's continuously provocative rhetoric.

The role conceptions of 'contributor to regional cooperation' and 'regional stabilizer' furthermore explain Berlin's emphasis on multilateral consultations on MD within the EU and especially NATO. Both supporters and opponents of MD agreed on the need for regional negotiations to reduce tensions and to ensure the cohesion of NATO. For example, when US plans to install radar equipment and interceptor missiles in Eastern Europe prompted protests in Russia and Europe in 2007, Chancellor Merkel pursued a multilateral mediation strategy.

However, aside from Merkel, politicians did not act entirely in compliance with the role conceptions 'contributor to regional cooperation' and 'regional stabilizer'. Despite professing NATO solidarity, German policy-makers ploughed ahead with their criticism of missile defence, rather than exercising restraint and considering carefully each country's opinions and interests first. By opposing the US so firmly from the start, Germany hampered a consensus within NATO and contributed to a rift among allies – apparently to Russia's delight. There are several reasons why political elites did not behave in a fully role-adequate manner. First, one may argue that the behaviour did not completely break with the dominant norms of Germany's role conceptions, since MD criticism was rooted in the anti-militarist foreign policy tradition, as explained above. Having witnessed the Cold War in the front line, Germans tend to be highly sceptical about large military projects that could upset the regional balance of power. Secondly, criticism of US MD plans arose from a widespread disappointment over Berlin's marginal influence on Washington's policy. The US consulted Germany neither on abrogating the ABM Treaty nor on installing missile defence elements in Poland and the Czech Republic. Public criticism thus reflected frustration about dealing with a superpower that did not share Berlin's inclination towards multilateralism. In fact, some policy-makers admitted that they did not oppose missile defence per se, but objected to the US approach to the issue (Howland and Stoyanov 2007). Lastly, some German politicians might have worried that there could have been consequences for the Russian leadership if its proposals on missile defence were completely ignored by West European countries and the US. It would not have been in the German interest for Russian hardliners to gain the upper hand in the Kremlin as a result (Katsioulis 2010).

All in all, role theory offers a useful explanation to Germany's hesitant stance in territorial MD and its handling of the issue. Berlin tended clearly towards multilateralism and non-military means, consistent with traditional foreign policy norms. With regard to Russia, the effect of the German role conception of 'regional stabilizer' is particularly obvious, as policy-makers responded reflexively to Moscow's criticism. The Federal Republic also seemed to face a role conflict, as politicians failed to advance NATO cohesion and solidarity by raising criticism of US policy. Consequently, German behaviour deviated somewhat from the ideal of being an unprejudiced multilateral mediator and a dependable partner both within NATO and to the US. The balance appeared to tip in favour of the swift critical response due to other considerations, such as mounting frustration about US unilateralism.

German policy on missile defence for soldiers abroad

Introduction

In the post-Cold War era, German policy-makers have also debated procuring a mobile missile defence system for point-defence, especially for soldiers stationed abroad. This part of the case study explores the Federal Republic's policy in this area, identifying three phases in the debate: (1) the period from 1990 to 1999, when Germany quietly began to participate in a project called MEADS (Medium Extended Air Defense System) under US leadership, (2) the period from 2000 to 2004, when first doubts about the project emerged, but the government opted to continue its support, (3) the period from 2004 to 2011, when public criticism against MEADS peaked, but then fell again following two important parliamentary decisions in favour of developing MEADS. At the end of this third period, a US decision in February 2011 to terminate the country's participation in the project triggered a rethink in Germany about whether MEADS should continue.

The analysis finds that German policy since the mid-1990s has been characterized by a remarkably high degree of support for the MEADS project, despite significant difficulties in the cooperation with the US and lingering doubts about the strategic need for this MD capability. As will be seen, Berlin's strong commitment can be well explained by the influence of several role conceptions, most importantly the roles of 'exporter of security' and 'reliable partner'.

1990–1999: a quiet start to participation in the MEADS project

During this time period, German defence specialists first recommended participation in a US-led project developing a new MD system called MEADS in the mid-1990s. The decision in favour of joining the project was driven by two considerations: first, decision-makers were encouraged by the wish to play a greater role in multilateral missions abroad, necessitating better defence systems for troops, and second, they hoped to strengthen transatlantic ties. Despite significant problems in the cooperation with the US in the late 1990s, German lawmakers continued to back the project.

In the late 1980s and early 1990s, calls emerged among German policy-makers for a defence system that would not only provide point-defence for German territory, but also help protect troops stationed abroad against incoming missiles, unmanned aerial vehicles or aircrafts. Iraq's use of Scud missiles during the Gulf War in 1990–1 substantiated fears about the vulnerability of troops deployed to conflict areas. Subsequent deliberations resulted in the proclamation of the 'Military-Technical Objectives' in 1992, which called for a mobile tactical anti-missile defence system that could protect German troops on missions abroad (Schäfer 1996).

At around the same time, important partner countries of Germany were considering the introduction of similar new air defence systems. France and Italy had begun joint work on a system with mid-range surface-to-air interception missiles called 'Famille de missiles Sol-Air Futurs' (Future Surface-to-Air Family of missiles or FSAF) in 1989 (Grams 2003: 52). A year later, the United States initiated the Corps Surface-to-Air Missile (Corps-SAM) programme, investigating the possible development of an interception system that was to be rapidly deployable, highly mobile and effective against a range of targets.

Given the conceptual overlap and worried about high development costs, the US approached policy-makers in Bonn in February 1994 about the possibility of a collaborative effort. The German government signalled interest, but insisted on multilateralizing the project so that interested European partner countries could participate. Bonn was concerned that the good relations with France would be jeopardized if they agreed to an exclusive bilateral project with the US, especially since French leaders had previously sought the inclusion of Germany in their own project (Covault and Morocco 1994). US officials accepted the Federal Republic's demand and invited France, Italy, as well as other interested countries to participate in the collaborative effort. As a result, the US, Germany, France and Italy signed a statement of intent on 20 February 1995 in Paris to cooperate on the development of a mobile air defence system, which they called Medium Extended Air Defense System, or MEADS. The four parties agreed that MEADS would be designed as a mobile system that could ward off aircraft, unmanned aerial vehicles, cruise missiles, and ballistic missiles with a range of about 100 to 1,000 kilometres.

Domestically, the rationale for joining the MEADS project was left somewhat ambiguous. According to the Ministry of Defence, MEADS was needed 'for point-defence of vital assets and the protection of maneuver forces against the ever increasing threat in the field of tactical ballistic missiles and other targets including cruise missiles' (Boehmer 1995). However, this statement contradicted common wisdom about the security problems Germany faced. First, the threat to German territory of missiles with a range of 100 to 1,000 kilometres was decreasing rapidly, as Eastern European countries – which had presented a security risk during the Cold War – were strengthening their relations with Bonn. Secondly, the number of German soldiers deployed abroad in the mid-1990s was small, calling into question the rationality of embarking on an expensive air defence project for the protection of troops, even if the threat from missiles was increasing.

Interviews conducted for this study reveal two reasons for German interest in MEADS. First, from around the mid-1990s, there seems to have emerged a tacit awareness among decision-makers that their country would need to increase its contribution to multilateral missions abroad and thus a growing number of soldiers would be exposed to missile threats (Voigt 2010; Staff member of the CDU/CSU parliamentary grouping 2010). Officials concurred that public opinion could present a significant obstacle in expanding the role of the *Bundeswehr*, especially if troops deployed abroad faced overt security risks, such as from missiles. In public statements, decision-makers generally avoided drawing an explicit connection between MEADS and an expanded military role, fearing public discussions about the *Bundeswehr* becoming an international 'intervention force'. A 1995 report of an experts' seminar organized by the Defence Ministry warned: 'An emphasis on [the] capability [of MEADS in the context of international military missions] could obstruct efforts to establish a more mobile German armed forces culture (*Streitkräftekultur*)' (Kahler 2001: 51).

Secondly, German politicians also saw MEADS as a key project to strengthen transatlantic cooperation on security (Schreer 2010; Katsioulis 2010; Schnappertz 2010). In April 1996, Defence Minister Volker Rühe praised MEADS as 'an important programme between Europe and the United States', underlining that it was one of the few transatlantic military projects in the post-Cold War era (Muradian 2000a). German decision-makers furthermore emphasized that, due to NATO oversight of MEADS, the project would be managed on 'full equality' based on the 'one country, one vote system', regardless of the financial contributions made by each member (Kahler 2001: 54, Filipiak 2006: 262). This aspect, they knew, was particularly important to French politicians, who had voiced scepticism about the prospects for a true partnership with the US.

Despite German efforts to convince French policy-makers to participate, Paris opted to drop out of the MEADS project in May 1996. Officials cited various reasons, including the high expected development costs, diverging air defence requirements and uncertainty about US willingness to share technological insights (Grams 2003: 56). The US, Italy and Germany were thus the only signatories of the 1996 Memorandum of Understanding, in which the three agreed to jointly begin a project definition and validation phase for MEADS. Furthermore, they decided that the US would bear 60 per cent of the project's costs, while Germany would contribute 25 per cent and Italy 15 per cent of the total budget. At the time, experts estimated that the total development costs of MEADS would be around US$2 billion (Boehmer 1995).

After a quiet start to the trilateral project, first problems in the cooperation for MEADS emerged in 1998. Holding a majority in US Congress, the Republican Party challenged President Clinton's focus on TMD over NMD. In mid-1998, Congress suspended funding for MEADS and called for a re-examination of the project's scope and financial budget. German politicians displayed serious irritation with US policy and warned Washington against dropping out of the project. One senior German official cautioned,

For Germany, and certainly … France, [US withdrawal from the project] would confirm the suspicions of those who have always had a distrust regarding the US sincerity to enter into truly collaborative arms cooperation alliances. … We view MEADS as a test case for defense cooperation between NATO allies.

(*Armed Forces Newswire Service* 1998)

In autumn 1998, US policy-makers signalled their willingness to continue with MEADS, but only on the condition that Germany and Italy accepted a key change. Rather than developing a new type of interception missile as originally planned, the US now demanded the adoption of a modified version of the US Patriot PAC-3 (Patriot Advanced Capability-3) missile, which was already under development as a fixed anti-aircraft and missile system for the US Army (*Aviation Week and Space Technology* 1995). Decision-makers in Washington hoped this would reduce the country's financial burden in MEADS. Political leaders in Berlin were dismayed, however. A German defence official angrily described US pressure as a case of extortion, saying it was like 'having a pistol put to one's head' (Kubbig 2000: 5). Other defence experts questioned whether MEADS would still be a multinational project based on equality if Germany accepted US demands. As one official observed, MEADS 'is a NATO system for the time being. The question is, will it be a NATO system with PAC-3 or is it a US programme with minor shares for the allies?' (Kahler 2001: 61). Officials were particularly concerned that the US would not share technological know-how on PAC-3, pointing to strict Pentagon security guidelines on information disclosure (Muradian 2000b).

In the end, Germany and Italy grudgingly gave in to US demands in order to ensure the continuation of the MEADS project. However, they made it clear that they would only participate if the US laid out a plan for technology transfer regarding the PAC-3 interception missile – a request that Washington met in April 2000 with a proposal for a phased technology transfer plan (Kahler 2001: 63). Germany and Italy also acquiesced in 1999 to a request for a new cost-sharing agreement that would decrease the US financial burden. According to the new arrangement, the US contribution to the budget was decreased from 60 to 55 per cent, while the German share was increased from 25 to 28 per cent and the Italian from 15 to 17 per cent (Krause 2000: 18). The first crisis in the MEADS project was surmounted without attracting much public attention or parliamentary debate.

2000–2004: critical voices emerge

German doubts about MEADS unexpectedly emerged around 2000–1, at one time bringing the Federal Republic close to withdrawal from the project. However, following US pressure, the *Bundestag* approved the country's continued participation, with the majority of parliamentarians showing only limited interest in the topic.

Interest in MEADS was sparked by the May 2000 report of an independent commission charged with making recommendations to the government on reforming the German *Bundeswehr*. The commission 'Shared Security and the Future of the Armed Forces' – also called Weizsäcker-Commission after its chairman, former President Richard von Weizsäcker – acknowledged a growing danger to soldiers from missiles and airplanes, but voiced reservations about MEADS. In its report, the commission warned that the complexity of such a mobile system 'involves unusually high technical and financial risks' and therefore careful deliberation was needed (Nachtwei 2005: 3). Subsequently, critics challenged the cost estimates for MEADS. They raised doubts about the decision to accept US demands on a modified PAC-3 missile, arguing the unit price of this missile might reach US\$5 million – five times the amount the German government was prepared to pay for its missiles (Muradian 2000a). Only two years after Washington had been on the verge of withdrawal from MEADS, Germany's participation now suddenly seemed uncertain. In addition to fears about costs, leading defence officials voiced frustration about US policy on sharing technological know-how regarding the PAC-3 missile (Muradian 2000b). In their view, this would force European contractors into a subordinate role, preventing them from taking part in the sophisticated engineering work.

German discontent culminated in a November 2000 letter written by Undersecretary of State of the Defence Ministry Walter Stützle, announcing Germany's intention to withdraw from MEADS. Stützle justified the decision by arguing that the ballistic missile threat facing Germany remained limited. Moreover, he maintained that the MEADS concept did 'not ... satisfy the requirements for coping with the future spectrum of emerging threats in national defence and international military operations' (Hagen and Scheffran 2001). Pentagon officials reacted with fury, reminding the German side that they had fought a series of internal battles with the US Army and the Ballistic Missile Defense Organization to ensure the survival of the programme and secure adequate funding. US officials put intense pressure on Stützle's superior, German Minister of Defence Rudolf Scharping, to revoke the decision. US Defense Secretary William Cohen threatened that if Germany backed out of the programme, there would be no way back in (Muradian 2000b). In a major reversal of policy, Scharping overruled the decision announced by Stützle in early December 2000, pledging to contribute 50 million German marks to the planned risk reduction phase of MEADS (Filipiak 2006: 266).

In order to ensure that Germany could provide further funds to MEADS during the risk reduction phase, the German *Bundestag* voted on the project in June 2001. In the debates preceding the vote, two SPD members, Volker Kröning and Verena Wohlleben, particularly criticized MEADS, citing doubts about the strategic-military rationale for the project and the difficulty of cooperating with the US (Kubbig 2005a: 3). Apart from these two individuals, few parliamentarians showed a deeper interest in MEADS (Landmann 2005: 5). Chancellor Schröder sought to dispel lingering doubts, insisting Germany should not miss out on the 'material' gains and on the 'technological know-how' in the NATO project (Rundfunk Berlin-Brandenburg Online 2003). In the end, the *Bundestag* approved Germany's continued participation in MEADS, allotting a budget of 145.5 million German marks to the risk reduction phase (Krause 2000: 19). However, several conditions were attached to the approval, including a requirement for the government to make further efforts in cost reduction by searching for cost-effective alternatives to the PAC-3 missile during the next project phase. Following this decision, the three-year risk reduction phase proceeded relatively quietly with few public discussions on MEADS.

2004–2011: vivid debates about MEADS

The MEADS project finally received extensive public attention in 2004–2005, following a critical report by the Peace Research Institute. Parliamentarians vigorously debated the rationale for participation. Despite widespread doubts among politicians, the *Bundestag* approved the continuation of MEADS in April 2005 as well as a related development project in January 2007. The analysis of the debates shows that the importance of MEADS for the transatlantic relationship was a key reason for supporting participation.

Following the conclusion of the risk reduction phase in July 2004, policy-makers in Washington and Rome quickly signalled their readiness to begin with the next phase of the joint project. Due to established project rules and regulations for MEADS, 26 March 2005 was set as the deadline for Germany to decide on its further participation in the design and development phase.

In order to prepare the impending decision on the next MEADS phase, the Defence Committee of the German Parliament established a rapporteurs group called 'Ground-based Air Defence' in November 2003. The group, charged with discussing German ground-based air defence systems and evaluating MEADS, consisted of seven parliamentarians, one civil officer and five air force officers from the German Ministry of Defence (Berichterstattergruppe Bodengebundene Luftverteidigung 2004). After nine meetings, the seven parliamentarians in the group issued their final report on 19 October 2004, based on a 'virtually identical' draft that had previously been prepared by the group's members from the Ministry of Defence (Kubbig and Nitsche 2005: 528).[7] Parliament's Defence Committee in turn accepted the final report unanimously on 10 November 2004. This report, which later leaked to the public, observed the threat from ballistic missiles and aerial vehicles was growing globally and recommended going ahead with the MEADS project, since the project involved an 'acceptable residual risk' (Berichterstattergruppe Bodengebundene Luftverteidigung 2004: 10).

A major public debate was sparked not by this report, but rather by a critique of the MEADS project, published by Bernd Kubbig of the Peace Research Institute in Frankfurt on 21 December 2004. Kubbig raised severe doubts about MEADS, arguing that the project was too expensive and strategically irrational. He observed that cost estimates by the Defence Committee were not transparent, as the Committee had failed to release publicly information on the number of systems it sought. He also argued that, depending on the scope, the costs of procuring MEADS could easily reach a double digit billion euro sum, rather than the €2.85 billion estimated by the committee (Kubbig 2005a: 5). Kubbig questioned the strategic rationale of MEADS, maintaining that the greatest security threat to soldiers deployed abroad emanated from small weapons and artillery and not from missiles (2005a: 10).

In the ensuing public debate, politicians particularly from the Green Party and FDP as well as individuals from the SPD voiced scepticism about MEADS. Green Party spokesman on defence issues Winfried Nachtwei stated that MEADS was 'not an appropriate reaction to the alleged threat' and was 'exceptionally expensive' (Agüera 2007: 127). SPD disarmament expert Rolf Mützenich similarly contended in January 2005: 'Abroad, we are confronted with non-state actors, with gangs that threaten our soldiers with small weaponry. MEADS neither provides protection against this [threat] nor against the proliferation of missiles' (*Welt* 2005).[8] Critics of MEADS received high-level backing when the German Federal Accounting Office (*Bundesrechnungshof*) issued a report on the cost-related aspects of MEADS on 1 March 2005. According to the paper, cost estimates were not transparent and likely too low. In particular, the Accounting Office criticized the lack of inclusion of spending caps in the project plan (Kubbig 2005d: 11).

Proponents of the MEADS project could be found among members of the SPD and CDU-CSU, and they generally stressed three aspects. First, the most commonly employed argument for MEADS was the potential harm a German withdrawal would have on the transatlantic relationship. For example, Defence Minister Peter Struck called MEADS 'indispensable' for Germany's reputation in NATO and the relationship with the US (BBC 2005). Many political leaders were clearly concerned about the state of US–German relations in the aftermath of the bilateral dispute about the US invasion of Iraq (Mützenich 2004). Secondly, proponents contradicted claims that MEADS was strategically inadequate. Jürgen Hermann of the CDU argued that MEADS was necessary because German soldiers had the 'right to be equipped adequately' (*NGO Online* 2006). Similarly, an SPD expert for defence issues stated in March 2005 that Germany would acquire the capability to 'defend peace' and assume international responsibility through MEADS (Agüera 2007: 139). Although some supporters pointed out that MEADS could protect at-risk objects in Germany in addition to increasing the security for soldiers, this was not a major point in the debate. Thirdly, some politicians highlighted opportunities for research work on sophisticated technology. Social Democrat Elke Leonhard maintained the project was providing Germany with 'high-tech jobs' (Arbeitsgruppe Friedensforschung an der Universität Kassel 2005).

Because of the intensity of public discussions, the German government was forced to request an extension of the deadline for its decision on participating in the development phase.[9] A new deadline was set for the end of April 2005. With growing urgency, MEADS proponents in the SPD called on the coalition partner, the Green Party, to support the project. Defence Minister Peter Struck asked whether the coalition needed another politically damaged minister – alluding to the already weakened Foreign Minister Fischer (Kubbig and Nitsche 2005: 539). In the end, leader of the Green Party's parliamentary group Katrin Göring-Eckard announced on 19 April 2005 that the party's parliamentarians would vote for MEADS, as the 'balance of forces in the coalition was such that the project could not be averted' (*Spiegel* 2005). As a result, the Budget Committee of the Parliament unanimously accepted the MEADS plan on 20 April 2005, and two days later the majority of the *Bundestag* voted in favour of the project. However, parliamentarians also demanded more transparency and annual updates on the state of development and project costs (Kubbig and Nitsche 2005: 535).

After the 2004–5 clash between MEADS supporters and opponents, parliamentary interest regarding the project evaporated. A funding request to the parliament for the development of a secondary missile for MEADS, the IRIS-T (Infra Red Imaging System Tail) missile, as a less sophisticated and allegedly cheaper missile, in January 2007 elicited little parliamentary debate – in stark contrast to the April 2005 MEADS decision. The planned IRIS-T missile had been severely criticized by the Federal Court of Auditors in 2004 for its high costs, and the Court had demanded that the development of the IRIS-T be deliberated together with the full MEADS plan in parliament in April 2005, since the missile was an integral part of the German project plan. However, supporters of MEADS apparently feared complications if IRIS-T was included in the initial funding request, and thus succeeded in delaying the decision until 2007. The *Bundestag*'s Budgetary Committee approved the development of the secondary missile worth €123 million in January 2007, without attracting significant public attention.[10]

Soon after the decision, suspicion emerged about whether important information had been withheld from parliamentarians by the Ministry of Defence (MoD). On 8 February 2007, only eight days after the German decision on IRIS-T, US acquisition chief for military equipment Kenneth Krieg officially informed Germany and Italy that budgetary pressures forced the US to scale back its funding for MEADS. The resulting changes and adjustments in the MEADS project would likely mean delays and cost increases in the overall project, including the planned German secondary missile IRIS-T. Some observers questioned whether the MoD had in fact known of the US problems prior to the parliamentary decision (*Inside Missile Defense* 2007).

Since the inception of the MEADS project, Berlin's leaders have thus fought a series of internal battles about their country's participation, each time opting for continued support. However, given the need to cut government spending, Washington decided in February 2011 to terminate its involvement in the programme, with significant implications for the German stance. The Obama administration announced its intention to withdraw from MEADS on 14 February, citing schedule delays and expected cost increases to the tune of US$1 billion (Donahue 2011). In line with trilateral agreement, it pledged to provide continued funding until the end of the development phase in 2013, however. Germany, where doubts about MEADS had re-emerged in debates about budgetary cuts in 2010, quickly reacted by stating it would join the United States in abandoning the project. The MoD elaborated that current circumstances suggested 'a realization or acquisition of MEADS' after the development phase would 'not occur' (*Tagesschau* 2011). Politicians from the Green Party and FDP reiterated their criticism about MEADS, calling for a quick termination of the project (*Frankfurter Allgemeine Zeitung* 2011). CDU politician Philipp Mißfelder on the other hand reflected disappointment about the US decision, stating MEADS was 'very important, because it was the only transatlantic armaments project' (*Frankfurter Allgemeine Zeitung* 2011).

The US and German withdrawal announcements cast doubts on the future of MEADS. Nevertheless, at the time of writing it is still too early to tell whether the project has been brought to a definitive end. First, Germany is in the process of revising a plan for its air defence capabilities, considering different options such as the modernization of the country's Patriot MD systems (*Frankfurter Allgemeine Zeitung* 2011). Secondly, led by Lockheed-Martin, the industry consortium involved in the development of MEADS is seeking to fill the US void by convincing NATO and non-NATO states to join in the programme (Hegmann and Steinmann 2011). Reportedly, Qatar has shown interest in participation as the Gulf state looks to security requirements ahead of its hosting of the 2022 soccer World Cup (Kington and Hoffman 2011). Finally, it is conceivable that MEADS may receive more attention and support in NATO discussions, especially since alliance members agreed on the development of an MD shield in November 2010. As a German MoD official emphasized in February 2011, MEADS would be the most important German contribution in the development of such a missile defence system (*Frankfurter Allgemeine Zeitung* 2011).

Explaining German policy

A striking feature of German MEADS policy since the mid-1990s has been the high level of support for the trilateral project among decision-makers, despite frustration about the difficulty of cooperating with the US. On numerous occasions Germany's commitment to MEADS was put to the test, as US policy-makers downgraded the importance of the project and cut funding or changed important project parameters. Each time, German policy-makers decided to make significant and costly concessions to the US in order to continue with the project. Politicians first consented to an increase in Berlin's share in the project funding from 25 to 28 per cent, then they gave in to US demands on using the PAC-3 as the primary missile for MEADS, and finally they quietly accepted that Germany would have to develop the secondary, less sophisticated missile on its own, without US participation and financial support. Only in 2011 did Berlin's stance change, following the US announcement of its MEADS withdrawal. Given the US determination to drop out and amid widespread domestic criticism of the project, the German MoD quickly followed suit by abandoning the project. The following sections seek to explain why German lawmakers were so committed to MEADS until 2011. The analysis considers three aspects: (1) politicians' threat assessments, (2) their evaluation of the technological feasibility and cost-effectiveness, and (3) the relation between German role conceptions and the country's MEADS policy.

Threat assessment

In contrast to the ambivalent assessment regarding a territorial missile threat, there seems to be a widely shared consensus among German policy-makers that soldiers deployed abroad face a danger from ballistic missiles and other aerial vehicles. Until the 2004–5 debate, even those experts and politicians critical of the MEADS project hardly ever challenged this assumption. Based on the experience from the Gulf War of 1990–1, German politicians assumed that multilateral forces in crisis areas would be exposed to a growing threat from short- and medium-range missile technology in the post-Cold War era.

The 2004 Kubbig report for the first time fundamentally challenged the notion that missiles and aerial vehicles presented a considerable threat to soldiers. Kubbig claimed that small conventional weapons and primitive devices used by suicide bombers were a considerably greater danger for troops than missiles. While some decision-makers agreed with this view, many others continued to insist on the strategic need for MEADS. If *Bundeswehr* forces are deployed in the Middle East, according to SPD member Elke Leonhard, it should be taken into account that there is 'no country in that region, which does not possess missile technology' (Arbeitsgruppe Friedensforschung an der Universität Kassel 2005). Furthermore, Foreign Ministry official Jürgen Schnappertz maintained that MEADS was also important for the protection of German territory, as missile attacks launched from ships in the North Sea were a conceivable threat (Schnappertz 2010).

Technological feasibility and cost-effectiveness

As discussed above in the section on territorial defence, German politicians generally seem to believe that the entire range of MD systems is technologically feasible in principle. However, in specific deliberations on MEADS, supporters and opponents alike hardly ever consider the question of whether the MEADS architecture is viable. Undoubtedly, the complexity of the system makes it extremely difficult for officials to judge and comment on the technological capability and setup. Furthermore, politicians may have felt encouraged to support MEADS without knowledge of technical details by the 2004 rapporteur group's report, originally drafted by experts from the Defence Ministry. The report uses reassuring language to describe the capability of the system and potential technological challenges. For example, the report argues that the system's 'hit-to-kill' capability is 'necessary to ensure' that multiple warheads can be 'effectively combated'. The resulting system 'will have the capability [to defend] against the whole range of expected aerial threats in the lower tier' (Berichterstattergruppe Bodengebundene Luftverteidigung 2004: 7).

The question of the cost-effectiveness of the MEADS project has presented a similar challenge for German policy-makers. Without in-depth technological knowledge, officials apparently find it difficult to judge whether cost estimates submitted by the Defence Ministry are adequate. As seen in the analysis above, policy-makers increasingly focused on the budgetary question when the US was insisting on the use of the Patriot missile from the late 1990s. According to the report by the rapporteur group in 2004, this risk reduction phase of the project helped to establish firmer cost estimates that would eliminate major financial risks for the participants. Again, the report in reassuring language stated that Germany's financial contribution to the development of MEADS would be 'limited to a total of 847 million euros' (Berichterstattergruppe Bodengebundene Luftverteidigung 2004: 11; Kubbig 2005d: 10).

Nevertheless, due to growing concern about the potential procurement costs, the Ministry of Defence was forced to release a more detailed spending plan in March 2005. According to this plan, the MoD seeks to procure 12 MEADS batteries, 216 PAC-3 missiles and 504 IRIS-T missiles, at a total estimated cost of €2.85 billion (Agüera 2005). These figures have been widely criticized even by supporters of MEADS as both not transparent and too low (Kubbig and Nitsche 2005: 530; Bauer and Agüera 2005). The Federal Court of Auditors estimates expenditure could amount to €6 billion, while Kubbig warned of even higher costs between €10 and €12 billion (Agüera 2007: 137; Dehéz 2005: 4). Germany's February 2011 decision to terminate MEADS participation can be understood in light of these ongoing doubts about the project's costs.

Policy goals and role conceptions

German policy demonstrates that the assessment of the strategic need for MEADS has been linked to foreign policy goals and hence the role conceptions held by decision-makers. At the time when Bonn began to negotiate cooperation on the project in the 1990s, Germany did not have a sizeable contingent of troops deployed abroad that would have justified participation in this costly project, aimed primarily at increasing security for soldiers. In line with the role conception of 'exporter of security', German MEADS participation was driven by politicians' aspiration to contribute more actively to international security. First, officials sought to enhance the aerial defence capabilities for NATO troops, especially given that Germany had been one of the main benefactors of NATO's integrated air defence system during the Cold War (Krause 2005: 7). Secondly, officials apparently hoped to facilitate future deployment decisions by raising the level of security for soldiers abroad.

However, the role conception of 'exporter of security' does not provide a full explanation for German policy. There is a striking inconsistency in how policy-makers evaluate the utility of comprehensive territorial missile defence and of MEADS. Officials opposed territorial MD, pointing out that complete security was unattainable, as the full range of threats could not be covered. Germany would have to live with a certain level of vulnerability, they maintained. This reasoning is not found in discussions on the security of soldiers, however, suggesting that other factors may have influenced the assessment.

Reflecting the importance of the role conception of 'reliable partner', policy-makers contended that MEADS would serve to strengthen transatlantic relations between the US and European countries within NATO. This argument often dominated debates, with the protection of soldiers playing a secondary role

(Kubbig and Nitsche 2005: 537). Germany's willingness to make a number of concessions in order to ensure continuation of the MEADS project attests to the importance attached to transatlantic cooperation and the perceived need to keep the US involved in European security through NATO.

Particularly in the mid-1990s, German leaders actively sought to involve France and other European countries in the joint project. In doing so, German officials followed the traditional approach of mediating between the contrasting interests of the US and France. Officials consciously pursued MEADS under NATO auspices, which helped to deflect criticism of exclusivity from non-participants. Furthermore, this setup allowed them to keep the door open for France – at least symbolically – to rejoin the project after dropping out in 1996. Germany's emphasis on a multilateral, inclusive approach to MEADS was thus in line with traditional foreign policy norms reflected in the role conceptions 'reliable partner', 'regional stabilizer', and 'contributor to regional cooperation'. At the same time, the multilateral approach matched budgetary needs for financing such an expensive military project jointly with as many partner countries as possible.

Even though German politicians praised MEADS as a multilateral project within NATO, in reality it seems questionable whether it may be called a truly collaborative venture. In fact, even among some of Germany's strongest supporters of MEADS, doubts have emerged about the extent to which the project could be called a NATO project, as US policy-makers took advantage of their dominant position in financial and technological terms. Officially, decisions among the three participating nations were taken under the NATO principle of 'one country, one vote', but the analysis of German policy demonstrates the significant US pressure on its two partners to acquiesce to various demands. In 2003, US leaders went so far as to float the idea of eliminating the NATO MEADS Management Agency in Huntsville, Alabama – a proposal that was vigorously opposed and thwarted by German officials (Agüera 2003).

Given that MEADS is an armaments project, it seems surprising that German policy-makers rarely made references to the possible tensions with the role conception 'non-militarist country'. Strikingly, the government was able to begin participation in MEADS without stirring a major controversy in the mid-1990s – at a time when there was considerable concern within Germany about expanding the military's role overseas. Several factors help to explain the fact that officials did not exhibit more reluctance to join the project. First, MEADS possesses two important qualities that correspond to the German conception of 'non-militarist country': the project is a multilateral project under a formal institution, and the system is a defensive rather than offensive military system. MEADS has been less contested compared to armaments projects such as the Eurofighter, which may be classified as an offensive system. Secondly, especially during the early phases of the MEADS project, the ruling coalition was careful not to overemphasize the utility of the missile defence system for German troops on overseas deployment. They argued that MEADS could be used both for point protection of German territory and for the defence of NATO troops, two points that were uncontroversial. By the time the fierce public debate on MEADS broke out in 2004–5, policy-makers had gained considerable confidence about Germany's role in international military missions.

Overall, the influence of Germany's role conceptions is clearly reflected in German foreign policy on MEADS. The roles of 'exporter of security' and 'reliable partner' strongly affected the evaluation of the joint project by decision-makers. However, other factors also impacted German behaviour. As the analysis shows, the stance by Green Party members in the April 2005 vote on MEADS was significantly influenced by domestic consideration about the coalition with the SPD and the need to avoid a rift between the two parties. Furthermore, German MEADS policy was driven by material interests, as politicians sought to gain access to technological know-how and to secure contracts for Germany's defence industry. Major defence companies involved in the development of MEADS have also made massive financial donations to all major parties in Germany, possibly in the hope of receiving favourable treatment by politicians in return. For example, one study estimates that, in 2002, the defence company EADS and its major shareholder Daimler Chrysler donated about half a million euros to political parties (Arbeitsgruppe Friedensforschung an der Universität Kassel 2005). Such financial backing may have provided policy-makers with further incentive to participate in MEADS.

German policy on assisting other countries with MD

Introduction

Aside from cases of individual self-defence, missile defence systems can be used to assist other countries in protecting their troops or territory. Should Germany procure MEADS, it is likely to face lending requests, because these interception batteries are highly mobile and can be deployed rapidly to crisis areas. Moreover, Germany had already had to respond to demands for its Patriot MD systems, which are not as light and mobile but nevertheless can be transported, to protect strategically important points.

This part examines how Berlin's policy-makers reacted in four request cases: the Israeli call for Patriot systems during the 1990–1 Gulf War, and similar demands for MD protection of Israel, Turkey and the US in the run-up to the Iraq War of 2003. The analysis finds that the Federal Republic has selectively provided MD capabilities, due to a role conflict between the conceptions of 'exporter of security' and 'anti-militarist country'. While German leaders sought to aid allies and partners in their defence needs, they were concerned about becoming involved in potential offensive moves by partner countries. Furthermore, in the case of Israel, the perceived German historical responsibility also played an important role in deliberations.

The 1990–1 Gulf War: Patriot request for the protection of Israel

After the invasion of Kuwait by Iraqi troops in August 1990, the international community led by the United States sought to pressure Iraq's withdrawal through a series of UN resolutions and economic sanctions. In November 1990, a resolution was passed, authorizing the use of military means if Iraqi troops did not leave Kuwaiti territory by 15 January 1991. One day after the deadline, a coalition of international forces launched a massive air campaign on Iraq under the codename 'Operation Desert Storm'. In retaliation, Iraq began firing Scud missiles at Israel in the hope of drawing it into the war and thereby prompting the US's Arab allies to withdraw from the coalition forces out of reluctance to fight alongside the Jewish state. This strategy was unsuccessful, however.

Because of low accuracy, the Scud missiles targeting Israel were not very effective. Still, a total of 39 missiles landed in Israel, causing extensive property damage, two direct deaths, and injuring a number of people (Freedman and Karsh 1993: 331ff.). By late January 1991, leaders in Germany increasingly felt the need to help Israel in protecting its territory from missile attacks. The perceived duty to provide support was based on several interrelated considerations. First, German policy-makers recognized both the need to prevent the escalation of the conflict and a special historic responsibility to defend Israel from missiles.

Secondly, leaders in Berlin felt particularly uncomfortable abstaining from the conflict after newspapers reported that German companies had been involved in helping Iraq build up its chemical weapons industry. The news cast a shadow over German–Israeli relations. Some Israelis condemned German behaviour, comparing the chemical gas threat they faced to the deadly gas used in concentration camps by the Nazi government (Brinkley 1991a). On a visit to Israel in January, Foreign Minister Hans-Dietrich Genscher asked how his country could help and in response Israel drew up a list of military equipment, including additional anti-Scud Patriot batteries to supplement those provided by the US (Brinkley 1991b).

A third consideration behind Genscher's offer to aid Israel was the need to respond to growing criticism by members of the coalition forces about Germany's limited support in the conflict. Bonn had rejected US calls to send troops to the conflict area, which was outside the NATO domain. Instead, it had opted to provide financial assistance to the coalition effort – a policy that was denounced as 'checkbook diplomacy' by some US decision-makers. In seeking to counter this criticism, the Kohl government pledged US$670 million in military aid to Israel in late January, and German military-transport aircrafts began delivering the equipment including Patriot batteries on 1 February (Brinkley 1991b). Adhering to its policy of not sending soldiers to the area, Bonn sent the Patriot batteries without a German squadron for operation, however.

The majority of Bonn's policy-makers supported the decision to assist Israel – particularly those in the ruling conservative coalition. The high level of consensus among politicians helps explain the quick delivery of the military aid. Even the majority of Green Party politicians backed the provision of support to Israel, despite the strong pacifist sentiments among members. The spokesman for the Green Party's executive committee, Hans-Christian Ströbele, caused a major controversy within his party when he voiced disagreement in an interview first published in the *Jerusalem Post*. Ströbele spoke out against German assistance, describing Israeli policies as provocative vis-à-vis its Arab neighbours. He furthermore asserted that no weapon was purely defensive in nature (Luppes 2005: 9). Fellow party members, including rising star Joschka Fischer, were infuriated by these comments and eventually forced Ströbele to step down following the Gulf War.

The Iraq War of 2003: Patriot requests for protection of Israel, Turkey and US

In late 2002 and early 2003, Washington accused Iraq of possessing weapons of mass destruction that posed a serious and imminent threat to the national security of the US, its allies and partner countries. Repeatedly, President Bush demanded full compliance with UN resolutions requiring international weapons inspectors' unrestricted access to suspected weapons production facilities. Despite widespread doubts within US intelligence circles and the international community about the immediate danger posed by Iraq, the US government announced in March 2003 that diplomacy had failed and therefore it would proceed with a coalition of allied countries to rid Iraq of its alleged weapons of mass destruction. The military campaign against Iraq began on 20 March 2003 with a coalition of forces from the United States, the United Kingdom, Australia, Denmark, Poland and other nations.

In keeping with his promise made during the federal election campaign in the spring and summer of 2002, German Chancellor Schröder remained adamantly opposed to the war, refusing to send *Bundeswehr* troops to Iraq and voicing doubts about US intelligence estimates. However, Berlin's leadership was also faced with the question of whether to supply Patriot missile defence systems to countries located in the immediate neighbourhood of Iraq or involved in the conflict. With the looming US-led war on Iraq in late 2002 to early 2003, the governments of Israel, Turkey and the US sought the deployment of German Patriot missile defence batteries against potential strikes by Iraq. The following paragraphs will detail German policy responses to each of these requests.

Patriot request for protection of Israel

Israel, concerned about possible Iraqi missile attacks based on the experience in the Gulf War of 1990–1, officially requested the provision of a Patriot system on 26 November 2002. Among the German political elite, an overwhelming majority favoured the assistance to Israel. Two arguments dominated the discourse among proponents: first, the historic responsibility to Israel and, second, the purely defensive nature of providing the system to a state that was not directly involved in the war. In a late November 2002 interview with the newspaper *Die Zeit*, German Chancellor Schröder stated he would be happy to help Israel, declaring 'If the Israeli Government feels it needs this added security, we will help – and [do so] promptly.' Alluding to Germany's Nazi past, Schröder furthermore maintained that 'The security of the Israeli state and its citizens is of utmost importance to us' (BBC 2002). Green Party members echoed such sentiments about the moral duty to help Israel, while sustaining their firm opposition to the US-led war. The executive of the Green Party fraction (Geschäftsführer der Grünen Fraktion) Volker Beck acknowledged that Germany could 'not principally turn down security requests by Israel', especially since the Patriot was a defensive weapons system (*Spiegel* 2002a).

Although the support to Israel generally drew widespread backing, some German politicians including left-wing SPD members pointed out potential inconsistencies that such a policy line entailed (Landler 2002). The problem was that the assistance to Israel could be seen as an indirect contribution to the US-led war, thus contradicting Schröder's election promise not to join the conflict. The chairman of the SPD parliamentary group in the *Bundestag* Michael Müller argued the situation could be particularly problematic if the US withdrew some of its missile defence systems stationed in Israel to use for the protection of its own troops during the war (*Spiegel* 2002a). Prime Minister Edmund Stoiber criticized Schröder's stance as the 'greatest election lie' (Zettel 2003: 7). On the other hand, foreign policy expert Gernot Erler defended the assistance to Israel, reasoning that Israel itself was not a participant in the war (*Spiegel* 2002a).

On the whole, an overwhelming majority of German policy-makers favoured the assistance to Israel. Hence, the Federal Security Council (*Bundessicherheitsrat*) approved the lease of a pair of Patriot missile defence batteries to Israel on 16 January 2003.[11] The key factor that apparently tipped the balance in favour of assisting Israel was that the Patriots could be viewed as purely defensive systems. In concurrent discussions about whether Germany should also deliver so-called 'Fuchs' tanks to Israel, opposition quickly formed among politicians, because these tanks were seen as an offensive military capability (Zettel 2003: 9).

Patriot request for the protection of Turkey

US defence specialists anticipated that in the looming US-led war on Iraq in 2003, Turkey would be critical in military terms because they hoped to open a second front in Northern Iraq, using Turkey as a base for the attack. Consequently, the country was assumed to be a likely target of retaliatory attacks by Iraq (Bernstein 2003; Bender 2003). Because of the potential risk to Turkey, US Deputy Secretary of Defence Paul Wolfowitz in December 2002 called on NATO members to provide support to ensure the country's security (Zettel 2003: 10). In mid-January 2003, the US made an official request to NATO for alliance preparations for war (Bender 2003). One of the key demands was that Germany should provide Patriot missile defence systems along with AWACS airplanes for the security of Turkey.

Compared to the Israeli case, the question of whether to send Patriot missiles to Turkey was more problematic for German decision-makers, especially since it had been Washington – not Ankara – that had requested assistance (Overhaus 2005: 29). Political leaders worried that war planning by NATO allies would signify an abandonment of diplomatic efforts and endorsement of US attack plans. Chancellor Schröder also feared he would be criticized for breaking his election promise not to contribute to a war in Iraq. On the other hand, Berlin's leadership felt that Germany had to meet its alliance obligations to ensure the security of fellow NATO member Turkey.

In formulating their policy response, politicians sought to skirt this underlying contradiction in policy goals. Initially, Berlin did not respond to the request in NATO directly, adopting a wait-and-see posture while continuing to oppose the US confrontational course with Iraq. But when in late January and early February a number of European countries publicly declared their solidarity with Washington, German leaders came under pressure to clarify their position. In a surprise move, Defence Minister Peter Struck announced on 8 February that Berlin would deliver Patriot missiles to Turkey via the Netherlands. Struck emphasized his country was responding to a Dutch demand for the missiles and not the US request (*Stern* 2003; *Frankfurter Allgemeine Zeitung* 2003a). Furthermore, he pointed out that Dutch troops would operate the Patriots and thus no German soldiers would be involved.

At the same time, Germany continued to oppose US war planning. Berlin's resistance culminated in a declaration on 10 February that, along with the governments of France and Belgium, it would veto a decision in NATO on beginning alliance war preparations. The three states argued that they wanted to avoid providing the US with an indirect legitimization for attacking Iraq and insisted on diplomatic efforts in the UN Security Council. Washington criticized this veto decision, insisting the three countries were evading their obligation to defend fellow NATO members (*Frankfurter Allgemeine Zeitung* 2003a). Germany's seemingly contradictory policy caused confusion internationally, as it was initially not clear whether the country was backing away from Struck's promise to supply Turkey with Patriots via the Netherlands. However, Chancellor Schröder rejected such allegations, stating on 13 February: 'For us, solidarity with Turkey and our solidarity within the alliance are beyond question' (Bernstein 2003).

Few decision-makers in Berlin challenged the policy line taken by Schröder and Struck. Most focused on the parallel discussions about whether Germany should provide AWACS planes and accompanying crews to Turkey. This question was much more controversial, as AWACS planes could potentially be used for information gathering as part of offensive strikes (Zettel 2003: 9). Nevertheless, Bavarian Prime Minister Edmund Stoiber criticized the federal government's veto decision in NATO, arguing it weakened the alliance and the transatlantic relationship. He also warned that Schröder was pushing Germany towards 'isolation' in foreign policy (*Spiegel* 2003).

Due to US insistence, NATO members renewed efforts to reach a joint stance as the war loomed. On 16 February, they agreed upon a declaration, focusing on the defence of Turkey rather than general war preparations. It reflected the stance of Germany, France and Belgium, as it stated 'We continue to support efforts in the United Nations to find a peaceful solution to the crisis. This decision relates only to the defence of Turkey, and is without prejudice to any other military operation by NATO, and future decisions by NATO or the UN Security Council' (NATO 2003). The compromise was a face-saving tactic that allowed the US and European countries to signal a basic agreement and alliance cohesion amid diverging views on the looming US-led war. Following the NATO agreement,

Germany supplied 46 Patriot interceptor missiles to Turkey via the Netherlands on 1 March. In accordance with earlier plans, the missile defence systems were operated by Dutch troops, and political leaders in Berlin continued to stress that the Patriots were intended for defensive purposes only (Kubbig and Nitsche 2005).

Patriot request for protection of US troops

A third request for German Patriot missile defence systems was made in mid-November 2002 by the US in support of a possible war with Iraq. In addition, Washington asked for logistical support, humanitarian help and access to German airspace (Kubbig and Nitsche 2005: 525). In contrast to the Israeli and Turkish cases, German politicians concurred from the start that providing any direct aid to the US was impossible, since this would amount to participation in an offensive military strategy. However, policy-makers worried about the precarious state of bilateral ties in the aftermath of Schröder's election campaign that had focused on his opposition to US war plans. The first reaction of the German government was thus cautious, with a spokesman stating, 'We will examine [the request] carefully on the ... basis of German non-participation in a possible military campaign in Iraq, our alliance duties, and [our] legal options and obligations' (*Spiegel* 2002b).

On 28 November, Chancellor Schröder made public the government's stance. He granted the US access to German airspace, while denying other support, including the delivery of German Patriot missile defence systems. Schröder explained that he was 'clear as a glass' in his stance against a war and insisted the Federal Republic would not take part in a US pre-emptive strike (Landler 2002). The ambivalent response triggered criticism from opposition parties, who saw Schröder backtracking on his anti-war stance (Kubbig and Nitsche 2005: 525–6). Others defended Schröder's policy, arguing that the Chancellor had little choice on the question of airspace, as bilateral agreements gave the US broad latitude in such matters. Nevertheless, a senior German official conceded that Schröder might have had legal grounds to restrict American access, but that he was driven by the desire to heal the rift in the relationship (Landler 2002).

Explaining German policy: policy goals and role conceptions

Summary of cases and consideration of role conflicts

The analysis of the four cases in which partner countries requested missile defence capabilities shows Germany as a 'selective exporter' of security (Kubbig and Nitsche 2005: 526). Officials strove to fulfil their perceived responsibilities to aid allies and partners in their defence needs. At the same time, they sought to distinguish German support from any potential offensive military strategies by partners. The question of whether to deliver Patriot systems to Israel during the Gulf War of 1990–1 was the least controversial in the eyes of German politicians. Iraq was clearly the aggressor in the conflict as it had breached Kuwaiti sovereignty by annexing the country in 1990, and the immediate danger to Israel from Iraqi Scud missiles was undisputed. Embarrassment about the involvement of German companies in Iraq's weapon programmes, coupled with a perceived historical responsibility, prompted Berlin's leadership to quickly decide in favour of sending the Patriot systems to Israel.

At the other end of the spectrum, the request for support by the US in 2002 was the most problematic for German politicians. In this case, the policy goal of being a 'reliable partner' collided with deeply entrenched norms reflected in the role conception of 'anti-militarist country'. In contrast to the Gulf War of 1990–1, the planned US-led war on Iraq could not be justified as a direct multinational response to the conquest of a sovereign state and it was also not legitimized by a UN resolution. Schröder's government thus clearly sought to distance itself from making any obvious contribution to the looming military strike, emphasizing the need for diplomatic efforts. As a result, Berlin rejected direct aid including the provision of Patriots. However, in accordance with the role conception of 'reliable partner', the government decided to permit US use of German airspace in its planned attack on Iraq in order to prevent bilateral relations from plummeting further.

The requests for support to protect Israel and Turkey amid the looming Iraq conflict in 2002–3 were answered affirmatively, with policy-makers arguing that missile defence equipment would be used in a 'purely defensive' manner. In essence, politicians insisted that the Patriot provision was consistent not only with the role conceptions of 'exporter of security' and 'reliable partner' but also with that of a 'non-militarist country'. Chancellor Schröder asserted that, although he had approved the delivery to both Israel and Turkey in order to increase their security in the looming Iraq conflict, this did not constitute German support of Washington's offensive strategy. He maintained, 'there will be no direct or indirect [German] participation in a war' (*Spiegel* 2003).

However, it is questionable whether the distinction between non-participation and participation in the conflict was as clear as Berlin's leadership argued. Germany arguably made an indirect contribution to US war plans, because Washington had to consider the security of Israel and Turkey before launching an attack on Iraq. Nevertheless, the decision in favour of providing support was likely influenced by the desire to be a reliable partner and ally for Israel and Turkey, as well as the need to patch up relations with the US. As the deputy director of the German Council on Foreign Relations, Bernhard May, observed regarding the support for Israel: 'This helps to get the German government out of a corner. They [the Germans] can help without changing their language on Iraq. Schröder will have to stand by his refusal to participate, but the definition of participation [changes]' (Landler 2002).

Furthermore, in the case of Turkey, it became increasingly clear that Germany's argument of 'purely defensive' support could be easily challenged. In the first days after the US launched strikes against Iraq, reports appeared that Turkish troops had entered Iraqi territory along the border (Burkeman and Howard 2003). According to media reports, Turkish Foreign Minister Abdullah Gul announced the incursion on 21 March. However, Germany was saved from being tested on its verbal threats to withdraw the Patriots if Turkey became embroiled in the conflict. After NATO allies voiced strong criticism of Turkey's incursion, Ankara modified its stance, denying that its soldiers had entered Iraqi territory (Castle 2003).

Throughout the crisis with Iraq in 2002–3, Berlin engaged in a delicate balancing act between maintaining the anti-war stance while satisfying at least some US requests. Alliance considerations played a key role in the above-mentioned decision to allow US use of German airspace for its attack on Iraq. Berlin did not want to give the impression it was obstructing military preparations (Schnappertz 2010). Although the Schröder government politically clearly condemned the war, it remained deliberately vague in legal terms about whether the US attack was a 'war of aggression' (*Angriffskrieg*). If not for this ambiguity, a German permission for US use of its airspace would have been highly problematic (Voigt 2010).

Given the veto policy regarding the US request for support in NATO, one could take the view that Germany violated its role conception of 'reliable partner'. For example, Philip H. Gordon and Jeremy Shapiro of the Brookings Institution accuse the Federal Republic of departing from alliance norms and 'damaging the notion of NATO as a defence alliance on which its members could rely' (Rudolf 2005: 144). However, as the discussion above shows, the broader context does not justify such an assessment. Germany's decision to veto the request together with France and Belgium derived clearly from the fear that the US might interpret a NATO agreement on preparatory measures for war as an endorsement of its Iraq policy. In other words, the trilateral veto was an attempt to entice Washington to make further diplomatic efforts. It would be misleading to infer that Germany was evading its alliance obligations or even beginning to distance itself from NATO (Overhaus 2005: 30). Rather, Berlin's leaders indicated clearly from the start that they would assist Turkey.

German officials were infuriated by the fact that the US – not Turkey – had made the request for help and interpreted this as a trap. They would either have to accept that war was imminent and Germany would have to play a role in it – a position that would undermine the Chancellor's own position against the war – or they would face accusations of lacking solidarity in the alliance (Rudolf 2005: 144). Policy-makers sought a way out of the dilemma by vetoing the original US request and only consenting to a NATO compromise that narrowed the focus of war preparations to the assistance of Turkey.

One may criticize German policy however as being inconsistent with regard to the United Nations during the Iraq crisis of 2002–3 – and thus not being fully in line with the role conception of 'exporter of security', which places importance on this international institution. Ostensibly, Germany vetoed the NATO decision on war preparations in order to allow more time for diplomatic efforts in the UN. On the other hand, Schröder declared in January 2003 that, no matter what the UN Security Council decided, his government would not send troops to Iraq (*Frankfurter Allgemeine Zeitung* 2003b). As the statement was made during an election rally, it seems likely that Schröder was trying to secure votes for his party by taking advantage of anti-war sentiments among the population. However, in refusing to make German policy contingent upon a UN decision, Schröder contradicted his own arguments that this international institution should be the main authority in the conflict.

In sum, role conceptions offer a convincing explanation for German policy in the four cases when partner countries requested Patriot MD equipment. The comparison clearly exposes the role conflict between the conceptions of 'exporter of security' and 'reliable partner' on the one hand and that of 'anti-militarist country' on the other hand. Berlin sought to comply with all three roles at least to some extent, although this aspiration led to some policy ambiguity. The role conceptual violation, identified in Schröder's stance on the UN in the war on Iraq in 2003, can be explained in the context of the domestic election campaign at the time.

Japanese policy on territorial missile defence

Introduction

Like their German counterparts, Japanese politicians considered the need for a territorial missile defence shield in the post-Cold War era. Three phases in the Japanese debate can be identified: (1) the time period from 1990 to 1998, when interest in MD grew steadily due to regional security concerns and burden-sharing debates in the alliance with the US, (2) the period from 1998 to 2002, when Tokyo's politicians decided to go forward with MD research, conceiving of the shield as the only means for their country to respond to the growing missile threat while upholding the traditional self-defensive security policy, and (3) the period from 2002 to 2011, when decision-makers took swift steps to deploy MD, finding that such a move would not only strengthen relations with Washington, but – paradoxically – also serve as a hedge against Japanese overdependence on the US for security.

The analysis finds Japan's MD policy can be characterized as highly pragmatic. The emergence of overt threats to Japanese security has driven the country's commitment to missile defence. However, it would be mistaken to discount the influence of norms and values on the formulation of policy. The analysis demonstrates that role conceptions can deepen our understanding of how policy-makers in Tokyo have chosen to respond to missile threats.

Law-related issues in Japan's missile defence policy

Three laws or resolutions have stood in potential opposition to Japan's participation in missile defence projects: (1) the Resolution on the Fundamentals of Exploitation and Use of Outer Space (in Japanese *Wa ga kuni ni okeru uchū no kaihatsu oyobi riyō no kihon ni kan suru ketsugi*; hereafter referred to as 'Resolution on the Peaceful Use of Space'), (2) Article 9 of the Japanese Constitution (the so-called peace clause), and (3) the Three Principles of Weapons Export. As these three issues repeatedly come up in debates, the following section will discuss each briefly, highlighting the relevance to missile defence.

Resolution on the Peaceful Use of Space

The 1969 Resolution on the Peaceful Use of Space states that Japan's exploitation and use of outer space must be 'restricted to peaceful purposes' (*heiwa no mokuteki ni kagiri*), to benefit scientific advancement and improvement in human welfare, while contributing to the development of industrial technologies and encouraging beneficial international cooperation (Morimoto and Takahashi 2002: 320). The term 'peaceful purposes' was initially understood as a ban on Japanese use of space for any kind of military reason, whether defensive or offensive. However, the interpretation later changed, as subsequent sections show. According to MD specialists Morimoto Satoshi and Takahashi Sugio, 'If one interprets the resolution on its most basic level, then missile defence is not permitted' for Japan (2002: 308). Specifically, two issues are seen as problematic with regard to the resolution. One is the interception of enemy missiles in outer space, which constitutes a military – though defensive – act. The other issue is the use of satellites, which are necessary for locating and tracking missiles in space.

According to the original understanding of the resolution, Japan's Self-Defence Forces (JSDF) are prohibited from using satellites in their information gathering. However, this interpretation was amended in 1985, when the head of the Defence Agency Kato Koichi maintained that the JSDF could rely on the type of satellites that were commonly used in the commercial field. This interpretation came to be known as the 'Principle of Common Use' (*ippanka gensoku*) (Kaneda *et al.* 2006: 130). When discussion on a territorial MD shield intensified in the mid-1990s, the common resolution of commercial satellites was about 1–3 metres – insufficient for accurately tracking and intercepting an enemy missile.

Article 9 of the Constitution

Article 9 of the Japanese Constitution stipulates that 'the Japanese people forever renounce war as a sovereign right of the nation and the threat or use of force as a means of settling international disputes' and that 'land, sea, and air forces, as well as other war potential will never be maintained' (Kaneda *et al.* 2007: 72). The government's interpretation of Article 9 has long been that Japan may retain a minimum level of armed strength and may exercise military force for self-defence against armed attacks. This understanding is encapsulated in the notion of 'exclusive defence' (*senshu bōei*; generally translated by the Japanese government as 'exclusively defence-oriented policy'). Accordingly, Japan may use force for individual self-defence, while collective self-defence (i.e. helping other countries to protect themselves by military force) exceeds the limits of the Constitution.

As will be seen in the discussion below, the majority of policy-makers see MD as a particularly fitting instrument for Japanese defence, since intercepting missiles is by definition a defensive mission and thus reflects the spirit of Article 9. However, the ban on collective self-defence creates many policy quandaries with regard to missile defence, as will be discussed in section 7.

Three Principles of Weapons Export

The Three Principles of Weapons Export, approved by the Diet in 1967, state that Japan as a peaceful country would not export arms to communist countries, to countries sanctioned for weapons exports under UN resolutions, or to countries involved or likely to be involved in international conflicts (Kaneda *et al.* 2006: 128). In 1976, the government further tightened the regulations, by announcing that hardware technology for arms manufacturing would also be included under the ban and that the restrictions would be applied to all countries. Due to pressure from the Japanese defence industry and advocates of close US–Japan security cooperation, the constraints on arms exports were loosened in 1983, however. An exemption was introduced for Japan's transfer of military technology and know-how to the US, although the supply of hardware elements continued to be banned (Murayama 2002: 286).

In the post-Cold War era, the Three Principles were seen as problematic in the context of joint production of MD equipment with the US, since Japan might be required to transfer related hardware. Furthermore, a potential US desire to sell the jointly developed MD technology and hardware to third-party countries has also been seen as a challenge to Japan's Principles of Weapons Export.

1990–1998: towards a consensus on MD

During this time, Japanese interest in a territorial missile shield grew steadily, as decision-makers realized the potential for instability in the region. Another key reason for the increasing support was US pressure on Japan to contribute more actively to the alliance relationship and to lower bilateral trade imbalances. While sceptics questioned the feasibility and costs of MD, by 1997–8, a latent consensus emerged among security experts in favour of joining US research efforts.

With the end of the Cold War and the disintegration of the Soviet Union, the majority of Japanese politicians did not perceive a major missile threat to Japanese territory in the early 1990s. In 1992, members of the Japanese Defence Agency began calling for a comprehensive territorial missile defence shield, pointing to the North Korean and Chinese missile development programmes (*Aerospace Daily* 1992). Japanese interest in a potential territorial missile defence shield began to grow markedly from around 1993–4. Supporters focused on three aspects in arguing for the necessity of MD: (1) the need to defend against regional security threats, especially North Korea, (2) the desire to strengthen ties with the US and to share more of the burden within the alliance, and (3) the potential benefits for Japanese companies participating in the development of this new technology.

First, the intensifying nuclear crisis surrounding North Korea in 1993–4 spurred a realization within Japan that the post-Cold War world was not as benign as many had assumed. North Korea's test-firing of a Nodong-1 scud-type missile into the Sea of Japan on 29 May 1993 demonstrated the regime's potential to build medium-range ballistic missiles with the capability of reaching large parts of Japan (Ducke 2002: 138).[12] The North's suspected nuclear activities further increased concerns in Japan. Prime Minister Hosokawa Morihiro in October 1993 urged a debate on MD, saying the country needed 'measures to counter a potential threat from the long-range North Korean missiles' (*Aerospace Daily* 1993).

Secondly, Tokyo faced pressure from the Clinton administration to participate in one of the US MD programmes, contributing to research and development. In September 1993, US Secretary of Defense Les Aspin called for Japan to cooperate on MD as a way for the two countries to correct their trade imbalance and decrease bilateral tensions regarding the 'burden-sharing' within the alliance (Kawakami and Jimbo 2002: 280). In Japan, a growing number of officials also stressed MD as a convenient opportunity to improve bilateral relations with the US. As Kawakami Takahashi and Jimbo Ken observe, the characteristic of the Japanese debate in the mid-1990s was that missile defence 'increasingly became framed in the context of the Japan-US alliance' (2002: 270). Although some policy-makers suspected that the US primarily sought access to Japanese technological know-how, Tokyo decided to set up a bilateral working group, TMD-Working Group, in December 1993. The group, which included Defence Agency and Foreign Ministry officials, mostly examined alliance related aspects of cooperating on MD and deliberated technological feasibility (Kawakami and Jimbo 2002: 268). At the same time, Japanese policy-makers emphasized that Japanese participation in the working group did not necessarily mean proceeding with joint development and deployment of a missile defence system.

Thirdly, there were some decision-makers in Tokyo who believed that MD cooperation with the US could be beneficial also to the Japanese side. They stressed that MD cooperation would not result in a one-way transfer of technological know-how, but that Japanese companies could equally gain from joint work on this cutting-edge technology. They furthermore argued that, due to the sophistication of the required system, Japan did not have the option of developing MD technology by itself.[13]

In May 1994, the results of the WESTPAC study, initiated in the late 1980s by US and Japanese companies, stimulated debates about missile defence. The industry consortium concluded that the North Korean Nodong-1 missile presented a threat to Japan and urged the government to join the US Army's Theater High Altitude Area Defense (THAAD) programme, designed to shoot down short- and medium-range ballistic missiles through ground-based interceptors (Kaneda *et al.* 2006: 89–90). The study's results found supporters as well as opponents among policy-makers. In addition to some LDP members, high-level officials in the Japan Defence Agency (JDA), who had already been outspoken proponents of MD following the US requests for a joint project in 1993, backed its recommendations (Goozner 1994). JDA officials hoped to expand the agency's budget through such a project (Sanger 1993).

On the other hand, the Social Democratic Party (SDP), the strongest counterweight to the LDP at the time, opposed participation in MD projects. In August 1993, the SDP was the largest among seven coalition parties that took over power from the LDP, and in June 1994 it entered into a coalition with the LDP. At their annual convention in October 1994, the Social Democrats officially adopted a platform that rejected research on missile defence with the US. Especially after the peaceful resolution of the North Korean nuclear crisis, the party saw itself as vindicated in opposing MD plans (Goozner 1994). Members from other parties, in particular the Komei and Communist Parties, concurred in the SDP's rejection of MD. Parliamentarians raised doubts about the system's costs, the technological feasibility, as well as the potentially destabilizing effect on the regional balance of power.[14] Moreover, they questioned whether Japan's development of a missile shield would be permissible in view of the Resolution on the Peaceful Use of Space.

From around 1995–6, perceptions about the necessity of a missile defence shield began to change, primarily because of the Taiwan Straits crisis. Starting in the summer of 1995 and continuing through the spring of 1996, China conducted several underground nuclear tests and made a show of force by launching a series of ballistic missiles into Taiwanese territorial waters, not far from important commercial ports. Among the Japanese, the crisis highlighted the possible threat posed by China and raised suspicions about the country's military build-up. Under Prime Minister Hashimoto Ryutaro's LDP-led coalition government taking office in January 1996, considerations about participating in missile defence were intensified. The US–Japan Joint Declaration on Security, announced in April 1996, noted both countries' common interest in dealing with missile threats, stating:

> The two governments recognize that the proliferation of weapons of mass destruction and their means of delivery has important implications for their common security. They will work together to prevent proliferation and will continue to cooperate in the ongoing study on ballistic missile defence.
>
> (Aßmann 2007: 77)

By 1997, a latent consensus within the LDP began to emerge that Japan should join the US in technological research on MD. An April 1997 report issued by the Policy Affairs Research Council of the LDP recommended that Japan more actively pursue missile defence studies with the US (Swaine *et al.* 2001: 30). However, policy-makers hesitated to make a commitment to the US due to Chinese criticism, particularly following the announcement of the revised 1997 US–Japan Guidelines for Security Cooperation. Beijing's leaders worried that the US and Japan might opt to provide MD capabilities to Taiwan (Ueki 2008).

Debates within the government accelerated in 1998, as the JDA pushed to commence technological research with the US (Researcher at the National Institute for Defence Studies 2008c). In the summer, news reports suggested that there were concrete plans by the JDA to launch MD research in fiscal year 1999. Later, it was revealed that the JDA had earmarked some 500 million yen for the project in the August 1998 draft budget for the following year (*Independent* 1998). Out of diplomatic considerations in the run-up to the November 1998 Sino-Japanese summit meeting, the allocation was not labelled 'missile defence' but included under the rubric of 'other items' (Ueki 2008). Despite strong support for MD research from the JDA and parts of the LDP, it was not certain that the project would be supported by the Diet, however. Many parliamentarians continued to harbour scepticism about the feasibility and cost-related aspects of the project.[15]

1998–2002: responding to threats defensively

The time period from 1998 to 2002 is characterized by firm commitment among political elites to MD research. After a North Korean missile launch in August 1998, Tokyo's politicians realized that MD was the only means by which their country could actively counter missile threats while remaining committed to the exclusively defence-oriented policy. Korean rapprochement in 2000 was viewed with scepticism in Japan, and thus few politicians called for a reconsideration of the MD project.

The JDA was saved from strenuous efforts to convince Diet members to vote for the missile defence budget by a North Korean missile test-firing on 31 August 1998. The Taepodong-1 ballistic missile crossed over Japanese airspace and landed in the Pacific Ocean, alerting policy-makers to the vulnerability of the country's densely populated urban areas. Doubts emerged among Tokyo's leadership about the effectiveness of the US nuclear umbrella and extended deterrence (Ueki 2008). Diet debates reflected overwhelming frustration about Japan's defencelessness in the face of the North Korean missile threat. LDP member Asano Katsuhito observed 'the missile could have fallen on Japanese archipelago', if something had gone wrong as it crossed over the country (*Kokuritsu Kokkai Toshokan*, 3 Sept. 1998). Asano urged Japan to proceed with technological research on missile defence as soon as possible. Representative of the Liberal Party Nakamura Eiichi similarly called for a quick decision on MD. Japan, he argued, should not be a

> country that cannot deal with an emergency situation at all and that has a legal framework that [obliges it] to sit and wait for its death (*zashite shi o matsu shika nai hōsei*), a country that has to ask for intelligence information from the US and South Korea, and a country that cannot list ballistic missile defence research expenditures in its draft budget in consideration of the [forthcoming] visit of the Chinese Head of State to Japan …
>
> (*Kokuritsu Kokkai Toshokan*, 3 Sept. 1998)

Following the North Korean missile shot, a majority of Diet members favoured the commencement of joint research. Only muted criticism was voiced, mostly by Communist Party members, about the costs, the feasibility, and the legal and strategic issues related to the project.[16] However, prior doubts about cost and feasibility had not suddenly vanished among those politicians who now favoured MD research. Rather, the debates suggest that policy-makers believed Japan was without significant alternatives to deal with the missile threat.

In the two-plus-two US–Japan security cooperation meetings held on 20–1 September 1998, leaders from the US and Japan reached a de facto agreement that they would begin joint technological research on MD (Kawakami and Jimbo 2002: 270). The formal decision by Japan to proceed to the research stage of MD was announced three months later. In August of the following year, the Japanese government signed a memorandum of understanding with the US covering a five-year programme of mutual work. The two countries agreed to undertake joint research on the US Navy's Theater Wide Defense (NTWD) project (now commonly referred to as Aegis Ballistic Missile Defence) with the aim of constructing a ship-based missile defence system with surface-to-air interception missiles that would be able to destroy enemy missiles in the upper tier (Kaneda *et al.* 2006: 90).[17]

Threat perceptions alone do not provide a complete explanation for the Japanese government's swift decision-making after the North Korean missile test-firing. At least three related considerations influenced lawmakers in giving their support for MD. First, policy-makers felt that missile defence was suitable for Japan, allowing the preservation of defence policy norms in line with the Constitution. As Matsui Kazuhiko, a researcher at the Diet's Upper House, explained, MD is 'not an offensive, but a purely defensive system' that does not threaten other countries (Matsui 2000: 54–5). Thus, the system would correspond to Japan's exclusively defence-oriented policy (*senshu bōei*).

Secondly, considerations about the need to strengthen relations to the US through joint research in MD played an important role (Researcher at the National Institute for Defence Studies 2008c). Some observers even contended that the alliance relationship was the main – if not sole – reason for Japanese participation in research. Okazaki Hisahiko, a long-time diplomat, asserted Japan did not need a missile defence system, but since 'America wants the cooperation ... we should always show we are reliable allies. If it costs money, we pay money. For Japan, the supreme target should be the maintenance of the US–Japan alliance' (Struck 2001). Policy-makers furthermore pointed out that Japan did not have the option of buying the MD system off-the-shelf if the US succeeded in development. They maintained such a policy would draw criticism from Washington about Japan being a technological 'free-rider' (*tada-nori*) (Matsui 2000: 54).

Thirdly, Japanese policy-makers viewed missile defence cooperation with the US as an opportunity for their country's defence industry to participate in state-of-the-art research and to win lucrative contracts. In the first half of the 1990s, Japan had shown some interest in the US Army's Theater High Altitude Area Defence (THAAD) programme. However, Tokyo's leadership finally decided on joining NTWD, in part because this programme was still in an early stage of research and development, leaving room for Japanese companies to participate from the start (Kaneda *et al.* 2006: 90).

On 6 November 1998, the Japanese government took another important decision in the context of MD, with the Cabinet adopting a plan to produce and deploy indigenous observation and reconnaissance satellites, setting aside €1.6 billion (US$2 billion) for the development of two optical and two radar satellites (CNN 2005). The four satellites were subsequently launched in 2003 and 2006. In order to process and examine the data, Japan also established an intelligence centre with 320 staff members, including 100 image analysts (Hughes 2004b: 175). The decision in favour of an indigenous intelligence capability was driven by a widespread frustration among officials about Japan's dependence on US services (Researcher at the National Institute for Defence Studies 2008c). An official from the Defence Ministry criticized the strategic dependence, pointing out that, without the US, Japan would have had practically no information about the August 1998 North Korean test-launch (Shibuya 1999: 194).

Given the participation in MD research and the launching of an indigenous satellite programme, how did Japanese officials deal with the afore-mentioned legal issues? Regarding the Peaceful Use of Space Resolution, Tokyo's policy was characterized by contradiction. On the one hand, decision-makers opted to comply with the declaration – at least according to the 1985 interpretation and the 'Principle of Common Use' (*ippanka gensoku*) – by limiting the development of indigenous satellites to those with a resolution comparable to commercial satellites. The resolution of the four satellites launched in 2003 and 2006 was thus about 2–3 metres, which is insufficient for MD interceptions (Kaneda *et al.* 2006: 103). On the other hand, Japanese officials amended their interpretation of the Peaceful Use of Space Resolution in order to allow missile interceptions in space. In their statements, Cabinet members suggested that the term 'peaceful use' meant 'non-invasive' rather than 'non-military'. According to this understanding, Japan as a 'peaceful country' (*heiwa kokka*) could use space as long as the intention was not to invade the territory of other countries (Kaneda *et al.* 2006: 129).

On the Three Principles of Weapons Export and the Constitution, officials took the position that Japan's research efforts did not raise any legislative problems. They argued that the government would make a strict separation into three project phases – research, development and deployment stage – and that before moving on to the next phase, it would re-evaluate the MD project and any associated legislative issues (Kawakami and Jimbo 2002: 271; Researcher at the National Institute for Defence Studies 2008c). During the research phase, technological know-how could be transferred to the US under the existing exemptions from the Principles of Weapons Export, politicians maintained. Furthermore, they argued that concerns about the constitutional ban on collective self-defence in case of deployment should not preclude Japan from at least joining research efforts (Jimbo 2002: 58).

After Japan signed the memorandum of understanding for MD research with the US in August 1999, major public discussions on missile defence faded. While the rapid rapprochement between North and South Korea in 2000 was greeted with high expectations around the world, most Japanese observers felt unease and apprehension about Pyongyang and its intentions. Calls by Social Democratic Party members to re-evaluate Japan's participation in MD research thus received little attention among Diet members (*Kokuritsu Kokkai Toshokan*, 2 Aug. 2000). The announcement in May 2001 that the Bush administration would drop the distinction between NMD and TMD raised some concern in Japan, although it did not prompt a fundamental rethinking on missile defence. The distinction had been important, as it provided credence to the Japanese claim that the missile defence shield under joint study would not be used to protect the US homeland and was thus in line with the constitutional ban on collective self-defence. In

June 2001, Defence Agency Chief Nakatani Gen reflected concern about the legal implications, stating Japan would not participate in MD if that meant violating the Constitution (Jimbo 2002: 58).

2002–2011: acquiring MD capabilities

After 2002, Japan moved swiftly towards the deployment of MD capabilities for territorial defence. The domestic atmosphere was characterized by overwhelming resentment vis-à-vis North Korea, not only because of the regime's nuclear activities, but also because of the dominance of the so-called 'kidnapping issue' in the media. The characteristic of this time period was that decision-makers began to frame MD as an opportunity to hedge against over-reliance on the alliance partner, while also deepening ties with Washington.

In autumn 2002, anti-North Korea feelings peaked among the Japanese public, marginalizing missile defence critics and inducing a swift decision in favour of acquiring MD capabilities from the US. During a bilateral summit meeting with Prime Minister Koizumi Junichiro on 17 September 2002, North Korean leader Kim Jong-Il took a bold step by admitting and apologizing for the abduction of 13 Japanese citizens in the 1970s and 1980s. In Japan, the confession was seen as a confirmation of the regime's malevolent and cruel nature. Resentment against the North increased as tensions surrounding the regime's nuclear programme rose in October 2002. Pyongyang's admission on 16 October that it operated a secret uranium enrichment programme stirred fear in Japan about North Korean nuclear-armed missiles (Researcher at the National Institute for Defence Studies 2008c).

Considering Japan's irrational and erratic neighbour, a missile defence shield seemed a sensible choice to most Japanese, and few politicians dared to challenge this view. Many MD critics who had previously advocated 'soft' policies towards Pyongyang lost credibility amid the second nuclear crisis and the kidnapping issue. Following Washington's announcement of its intention to deploy a preliminary missile defence shield, Japanese Defence Agency Chief Ishiba Shigeru indicated in December 2002 that his country wished to 'study the [joint missile defence] programme with an eye towards a future move to development and deployment' (Fouse 2003: 2). By late February 2003, a US Pentagon official observed that Japan seemed to move 'rather dramatically' towards a decision to acquire a missile defence capability (Sherman 2003). When Prime Minister Koizumi during a US–Japan summit meeting in May 2003 observed that 'missile defence is a very important issue in the defence of Japan', many observers interpreted his statement as a de facto promise on MD deployment (*Asahi Shinbun* 2005b: 256).

Officially, the Japanese government announced its decision on 19 December 2003 to introduce a layered missile defence system that would include Aegis ship-based and PAC-3 ground-based interceptors. The initial plan called for Japan to acquire three Aegis ships outfitted with four Patriot batteries to intercept missiles.[18] The costs for this capability, according to former Undersecretary for Defence Moriya Takesama, were estimated at about one trillion yen (*Asahi Shinbun* 2005b: 275).

The Japanese government also revealed the intention to import the necessary equipment from the US, while working towards an agreement to begin licensed production in Japan at a later date (Kaneda *et al.* 2006: 96–7). With the mounting tensions on the Korean Peninsula, few policy-makers criticized the deployment decision, although some questioned the maturity of interception technology (Toyoshita 2005: 40).

Explanations for the decision on MD deployment reflected the main arguments of the earlier debate: (1) the need to defend Japan and strengthen the alliance with the US, (2) the attractiveness of MD in view of the exclusively defence-oriented policy, and (3) interest in the technological know-how. However, in this period, an additional fourth argument in favour of MD emerged in the debates: while policy-makers in Tokyo hoped MD deployment would serve to strengthen the US alliance, paradoxically, they were also driven by a latent concern about Japanese over-reliance on the US for security.

First, Japanese policy-makers emphasized the missile shield would help protect Japan from North Korean missiles and strengthen the relationship with the US. Missile defence would discourage neighbouring countries from using missiles in a coercive manner. As Prime Minister Koizumi explained, the shield 'is part of our efforts to prevent someone from getting the wrong idea that Japan would give in to threats' (*Japan Economic Newswire* 2003b). Furthermore, MD would offer protection in the event of an accidental or unauthorized missile launch (Ogawa 2002: 48–9).

Secondly, officials underscored that MD matched Japan's exclusively defensive security policy. In a press conference, Chief Cabinet Secretary Fukuda Yasuo stated that the envisaged system would be 'purely defensive in order to protect our citizens' lives and property' and that there was 'no alternative' to dealing with the threat (Kaneda *et al.* 2006: 96–7). Fukuda furthermore highlighted the defensive character of MD by pointing out that the Japanese interception missiles 'would not even carry gunpowder or explosive objects' as kinetic energy would be sufficient to destroy enemy missiles (hit-to-kill technology) (*Japan Economic Newswire* 2003b).

Thirdly, officials in Tokyo felt under pressure to keep pace with the US in the project after Washington decided to deploy MD elements in December 2002. They argued the US would further deepen its technological knowledge, leaving Japan behind. Defence Agency official Moriya Takesama, for example, maintained deployment was necessary to 'close the information gap' with the alliance partner regarding MD know-how (*Asahi Shinbun* 2005b: 273).

Finally, Japan's decision to build up its missile shield was driven by a concern about Japanese overdependence on the US for security. According to Waseda University Professor Ueki Chikako, Japanese policy-makers feared the US – preoccupied with the Middle East after the 11 September 2011 terrorist attacks – might be less willing or unable to help defend Japan in case of an attack (Ueki 2008). An MD shield, many reasoned, would help increase Japan's own capability to defend itself, thereby serving as a hedge against over-reliance on the US (Ishiba 2006). In this context, decision-makers observed that the strategic goals pursued by the US and Japan concerning North Korea differed somewhat. While Washington's primary concern was the proliferation of WMD by the North, Tokyo's fears focused on the existing capabilities of the regime (Ueki 2008). Such different priorities further increased the need to avoid over-reliance on the US.

The Japanese government asserted that there were no major legislative hurdles to the acquisition of a missile defence shield. Cabinet Secretary Fukuda Yasuo denied a conflict with the constitutional ban on collective self-defence, arguing the system had 'the sole objective of protecting our country and will be operated based on [Japan's] independent judgment and will not be used to defend third countries' (Fukuda 2003). Alluding to the Resolution on the Peaceful Use of Outer Space, the Cabinet Secretary reiterated the government's stance that intercepting missiles in space would be for self-defence in response to an armed attack (ibid.). Fukuda did not discuss the Three Principles on Weapons Exports, as these were not affected by the purchase of MD technology from the US.

However, the Japanese desire to go forward with licensed production of MD equipment stimulated debates on the need to revise the Three Principles on Weapons Exports. Representatives from the defence sector, including former Defence Agency member Moriya Takesama, pointed out the potential benefits of licensing for Japanese companies in terms of revenue and know-how gains (*Asahi Shinbun* 2005b: 264). Political leaders in Tokyo feared Washington might demand from Japan the supply of MD hardware in case of production problems in the US, which would be problematic under the Three Principles. After intensive internal debates, the government announced in December 2004 a partial revision to the Three Principles, according to which the export of ballistic missile defence technology to the US was exempted from existing regulations (Hosoda 2004). At the same time, a more controversial change to the Three Principles was revealed, according to which military-related items and technologies could also be transferred to third countries with the prior consent from the Japanese government (Wuebbels 2004: 10). Japan would handle these cases bearing in mind its 'basic philosophy as a peace-loving nation that seeks to avoid the escalation of international conflicts' (Hosoda 2004). Only three months after these changes, the US and Japan reached an agreement for licensed production of MD equipment in Japan beginning in 2008 (Kaneda *et al*. 2006: 96–7).

Amid persistent tensions surrounding North Korea's nuclear and missile programmes, the Japanese government undertook efforts to prepare and speed up the use of its missile defence system. Due to the short flight time of about ten minutes for a North Korean missile targeting Japanese territory, decision-making structures were amended to enable a quick response. In July 2005, the Defence Agency Chief was given the power to order the interception of incoming ballistic missiles based on the Prime Minister's consent, or based on emergency response guidelines approved in advance by the Prime Minister (Masaki 2007).[19] Furthermore, in October 2005 the US and Japan agreed to set up the Bilateral Joint Operation Coordination Centre in order to ensure interoperability and communication on missile defence related issues (National Institute for Defence Studies 2007: 237).

Following North Korea's test-firing of several missiles in July 2006 and the regime's first nuclear test three months later, Washington and Tokyo accelerated their deployment of MD capabilities in and around Japan. The government in Tokyo decided to deploy the first PAC-3 system at Iruma Air Self-Defence Force Base in Saitama prefecture, near Tokyo, in March 2007, and in three other prefectures by the end of 2007, instead of the originally intended March 2008 (Toki 2008). In addition, Tokyo began installing the Standard Missile-3 interceptors on its Aegis destroyers. The first of four Aegis destroyers to be equipped with MD capability by the end of fiscal year 2010 was commissioned in December 2007, three months earlier than originally planned. Starting in late 2007, Japan conducted a series of missile interception tests and drills by the Self-Defence Forces.

On 20 May 2008, soon after the deployment of the initial missile defence capability, the Diet passed the Basic Law on Outer Space (*Uchū Kihon Hō*) – replacing the 1969 Diet Resolution on the Peaceful Use of Outer Space. The law, jointly submitted by the ruling LDP, the coalition partner Komei Party and the opposition party DPJ (Democratic Party of Japan), was passed by an overwhelming majority of 221 supporting against 14 opposing votes in the upper house (Yamaguchi 2008). It states that the development of outer space should contribute to ensuring 'peace and safety of international society, as well as the national security of our country' (Japanese Government 2008). The law formally establishes the legal basis for embarking on space development for self-defensive and non-aggressive purposes, codifying the widespread interpretation among policy-makers since the late 1990s. As a result, Japan could enhance its missile detection capabilities by deploying reconnaissance satellites with better resolution, no longer bound by the aforementioned 'principle of common use' (*ippanka gensoku*). The development of an indigenous satellite capability was attributed importance due to both industry interests and strategic concerns. In particular, policy-makers like DPJ party member Maehara Seiji emphasized the need to hedge against overdependence on US intelligence information (Maehara 2006: 32–3). Japan's own surveillance capabilities would contribute to a more 'mature relationship' (*seijuku shita kankei*) with the US, many politicians maintained.[20] In November 2009 as well as September and December 2011, Japan launched new satellites with increased resolution to replace previously launched satellites (*Japan Times* 2009a; *Defense News* 2011).

On 5 April 2009, Japan came close to utilizing for the first time its MD systems to intercept a North Korean missile. Pyongyang had announced its intention in March to launch what it described as a communications satellite. The Japanese government reacted by dispatching its MD-equipped destroyers *Kongo* and *Chokai* to the Sea of Japan and ordering them to shoot down any parts of the rocket that could cause damage to Japanese territory (Harden 2009; *Japan Times* 2009b). However, Japan decided against interception, because the missile's debris posed no threat to Japanese territory, according to security experts.

The Japanese government moved towards a further relaxation of the Three Principles on Weapons Exports in 2011. Washington had continuously put pressure on Tokyo over previous years, arguing that Japan's requirement of prior consent for transfers of MD equipment to third countries created unnecessary complications (Tanida 2011). The US was concerned that the Japanese position might slow down planned deployments of MD systems in Europe. In January 2011, Washington threatened to call off a joint research programme to develop improved software for the Aegis-based MD system, citing Japan's insistence on prior consent for technology transfer to third parties (Tanida 2011). Faced with this pressure and eager to demonstrate Japan's resolve to deepen alliance ties after the deterioration of relations following the 2009 inauguration of the DPJ-led government, Tokyo promised in June 2011 that it would work out a framework enabling technology transfers to third parties (*Mainichi Shinbun* 2011). In November 2011, the DPJ's Policy Research Committee proposed a compilation of specific exceptions to the ban. For example, it suggested allowing weapons transfer for peacebuilding and humanitarian purposes as well as to NATO member states (*Yomiuri Shinbun* 2011). At the time of writing, a final decision on this proposal has not yet been taken.

Explaining Japanese policy

Japanese missile defence policy in the post-Cold War era seems highly pragmatic, based on obvious considerations about the changing strategic environment. All major decisions to move forward in the MD project followed an intensification of regional tensions, especially with North Korea. Furthermore, politicians adjusted legislative interpretations in order to facilitate Japan's participation in the US missile defence shield. As the discussion below shows, one would be misguided to reject the influence of norms on Japanese policy, however. To the contrary, one would overlook important reasons why Japanese politicians have found missile defence such an attractive policy option. Role conceptions must be considered to understand the way decision-makers in Tokyo have chosen to respond to security threats.

Moreover, while Japanese policy on the whole seems pragmatic and rational, some decisions cannot be understood by solely looking at security threats. The most striking example is Japanese adherence to the ban on collective self-defence. In order to comply with the ban, Japan pledges to refrain from intercepting an enemy missile as long as its destination is uncertain. Given the short flight time of North Korean missiles to Japan, the policy of waiting for target information seems risky. Japan has also refrained from joining US research efforts on boost phase interception, as the flight path of an enemy missile cannot be determined at that stage.

Threat assessment

In the minds of Tokyo's decision-makers, the regional security environment has significantly deteriorated since the end of the Cold War. Doubts have emerged about the effectiveness of the US nuclear umbrella in deterring potential aggressors (Ministry of Defence Japan 2008). North Korea has been the primary source of concern in Japan, especially with the prospect of nuclear-loaded missiles. China's military build-up and its provocative stance during the Taiwan Straits

Crisis of 1995–6 also stirred fears (Morimoto 2002: 13). Based on these threat perceptions, Tokyo's decision to deploy an MD system appears rational.

In this context, it is important to note that – unlike many German officials – the majority of Japanese politicians do not see disarmament, non-proliferation and other diplomatic initiatives as alternative means to deal with the missile threat. Despite support for such initiatives, decision-makers express scepticism about the potential to reduce the existing threat to Japan. In January 2008, for example, the Executive Director of the National Institute for Defence Studies (NIDS) Takesada Hideshi voiced bewilderment at the fact that the US was so keen on carrying out 'complete inspections' of North Korea's nuclear facilities, stating such a goal is elusive (Takesada 2008).

Technological feasibility and cost-effectiveness

While the technological feasibility of MD was an important point of contention in the early to mid-1990s, few politicians raised this issue after the 1998 Taepodong shot. The growing confidence in the system's capability was related to apparent progress in technology, seen for example in successful interception tests. The feeling of defencelessness regarding the North Korean threat also prompted policy-makers to put more hopes into MD technology as Japan's only means to respond. Nevertheless, a minority of defence specialists continued to warn about remaining technological hurdles (*Asahi Shinbun* 2005b: 251; Ogawa 2002: 53).

With regard to the cost-effectiveness of the planned MD system, the trend in the Japanese debate was similar to the one observed above on technological feasibility: while a number of politicians voiced criticism on the costs of the system before 1998, the topic was rarely raised afterwards, despite large expenditure. The price tag of Japan's MD system includes procurement costs of over 1 trillion yen,[21] development costs for the advanced SM-3 missile of about 115 billion yen,[22] development and deployment costs of 195 billion yen for the four 'multi-purpose' surveillance satellites launched after 1998,[23] and additional operation costs for running the MD system and the analytical centre that monitors intelligence data from reconnaissance satellites.[24] Politicians must not only answer the difficult question of how likely a ballistic missile attack is, but also consider what level of security should realistically be sought and at what cost (Researcher at the National Institute for Defence Studies 2008c). Due to these complexities, Defence Minister Ishiba Shigeru entirely rejected debating cost aspects, insisting: 'We can't talk about how much money should be spent when human lives are at stake' (BBC 2007).

Nevertheless, cost-related aspects of MD may again become a focus in the future, due to severe constraints on governmental spending. DPJ member Maehara Seiji noted in an October 2006 article that the cost of MD was substantial, especially given that only 25–30 per cent of Japan's total yearly defence budget of about 4.8 trillion yen was invested in new equipment (Maehara 2006: 32). Japan was not just facing a ballistic missile threat, he observed. Due to the enormous reconstruction costs following the Tohoku earthquake of 11 March 2011, the Ministry of Defence is likely to face budgetary cuts in the coming years.

Policy goals and role conceptions

In formulating their response to the growing regional missile threats, Japanese policy-makers have been guided by four role conceptions reflected in the analysis above: (1) reliable partner, (2) anti-militarist country, (3) respected and trusted country, and (4) regional stabilizer.

First, politicians have felt that Japanese participation in the MD project is desirable in light of the role conception of 'reliable partner'. In the 1990s, when Tokyo faced serious trade frictions with its alliance partner, a number of decision-makers argued that the goal of soothing bilateral relations was in fact the primary reason for joining MD research. Today, MD policy continues to be influenced by alliance considerations. According to an official at the National Institute for Defence Studies, the MD project is both a means of sharing the security burden in the alliance and 'entrapping' the US in Asia by ensuring strong military links (Yoshizaki 2008). Policy-makers also saw cooperation with the US as the only feasible approach for the development of such a complex technology (Nōsei 2007: 179–80).

Secondly, MD appeals to decision-makers, because it fits the role conception 'anti-militarist country' with its focus on an exclusively defence-oriented policy (*senshu bōei*). Tokyo's political leaders have repeatedly highlighted that MD is the only means for Japan to respond to the North Korean missile threat with a non-offensive military system, in line with the constitutional emphasis on a minimal capability needed for self-defence. The amendments in the peaceful use of space and weapons export policies also do not imply dangerous militarization tendencies. Both changes were made in order to facilitate cooperation with the US, but in doing so, policy-makers stressed the continuing importance of the peaceful principles of the Constitution. Furthermore, a key reason for introducing the new Basic Law on Outer Space was to ensure that Japan had its own intelligence information to operate the MD system based on its independent judgement, thereby conforming to the ban on collective self-defence.

Thirdly, Japanese MD policy highlights the importance of the role conception 'respected and trusted country' and the associated desire for a more equal relationship with Washington. Concern among politicians about the alliance's one-sidedness and Japan's high degree of dependence grew due to American focus on the Middle East following the terrorist attacks of 11 September 2001. Tokyo's politicians saw MD as a means to strengthen relations with Washington, while simultaneously expanding Japan's own capabilities to deal with threats in order to hedge against over-reliance. Thereby, they hoped to put bilateral relations on a more equal footing. The role conception of 'respected and trusted country' also explains Japan's desire to lessen dependence on the US by developing and deploying its own surveillance satellites.

Finally, Japanese MD policy is guided by the role conception 'regional stabilizer'. Unlike their German counterparts, Japanese policy-makers generally do not consider a regional arms race a likely outcome of MD development. This different evaluation rests on the diverging understandings of how to achieve regional stability: German politicians seek stability mainly through multilateral cooperation and believe that even a defensive MD system would signal distrust towards countries like Russia or Iran. Japanese decision-makers, on the other hand, hope to achieve stability by relying on a minimal self-defensive capability. Few opinion leaders thus believe Japan could cause instability and incite an arms race by acquiring a non-offensive MD shield (Fukuda 2003). In fact, many Japanese defence specialists insist on missile defence fostering stability and peace by ensuring a regional balance of power. They insist that Japan should avoid becoming a destabilizing 'power vacuum' due to a lack of adequate capabilities (Morimoto and Takahashi 2002: 306). Thus missile defence is seen as a means of dealing with the shifting power balance caused by the build-up in capabilities by North Korea and China.

In sum, role conceptions offer important insights into why decision-makers perceive MD as an appealing option for their country. The anti-militarist role conception explains Tokyo's preference for a defensive rather than offensive approach to the North Korean threat. In addition to the relevant role conceptions, two factors help to explain Tokyo's policy choices. First, the analysis has highlighted the persistent influence of industry interests. Japanese defence companies have strongly pushed for participation in MD and for the development of indigenous satellites. Secondly, the domestic mood following the 2002 revelations about North Korea's kidnapping of Japanese citizens had important effects on Tokyo's MD policy. The ensuing atmosphere was characterized by intense resentment against not only North Korea, but also against those Japanese opinion leaders who had supposedly 'underestimated' the North (Morris-Suzuki 2003: 234). Calls by politicians for a missile shield thus resonated with the public.

Japanese policy on missile defence for soldiers abroad

Introduction

Japanese policy-makers have not given in-depth consideration to the protection of Japanese soldiers from missile threats. This section briefly examines both why policy-makers rarely discuss the threats to Japanese soldiers abroad and whether their evaluations of the security situation are in step with reality. It argues that the apparent contradictions within Tokyo's policy can be well understood by considering the relevant role conceptions.

JSDF deployments and 'non-combat' zones

According to Tokyo's official policy line, JSDF contingents are not supposed to operate in areas where enemy attacks are likely. The strict rules on missions abroad are a consequence of the government's interpretation of the Constitution. Since the enactment of the International Peace Cooperation Law in 1992, Japan has allowed the dispatch of the JSDF to UN peace-keeping missions. However, the law required the existence of a ceasefire agreement among the adversaries, so that the region could be declared a 'non-combat' zone (*sentō kōi ga okonawarete orazu*) (Ishizuka 2004: 140). In such areas, Japanese forces would not be required to use military force for offensive purposes, according to officials.

A number of observers have criticized the Japanese government's interpretation of Article 9 as untenable. They point out that the definition of 'non-combat' zone is too vague, because the use of military force cannot be rejected as a possibility. According to Nasu Hitoshi, if there was 'a complete and permanent cease-fire with no possible violations, peacekeepers would be unnecessary' (Nasu 2005: 50–61). The reconstruction efforts by JSDF troops in Iraq from early 2004 to mid-2006 highlighted the ambiguity of the term 'non-combat' area. Even though Tokyo sought to select Iraq's safest zone for the mission, opposition parties questioned whether Samawah – the chosen city – could be classified as a 'non-combat' area. They argued Iraq overall was too volatile to have 'safe zones' where the JSDF could be deployed under the requirements of Article 9. While admitting that 'Nobody can guarantee that it's a "no danger" zone', Prime Minister Koizumi insisted on the government's stance of it being a non-combat zone (Watanabe 2004). As Iraqi insurgencies rose, JSDF troops had no other option than to shut themselves up in a fortified camp under the protection of Australian forces (Hughes 2004c: 436; Szechenyi 2006: 145). Japan's posture provoked international criticism. Observers stressed that JSDF troops would be of little help if they had to be 'babysat' by Australian forces.

The apparent ambiguity of the term 'non-combat' zone subsequently prompted a group of Japanese activists to launch a civil lawsuit against the government in order to determine whether the Air Self-Defence Force's mission to airlift multinational troops between Kuwait and Baghdad was unconstitutional. The Nagoya High Court's ruling in April 2008 was equivocal and contradictory. While it regarded Baghdad as a 'combat area' and the JSDF mission as unconstitutional, it rejected the plaintiffs' demands for suspension of the JSDF deployment and the payment of compensation. Chief Cabinet Secretary Machimura Nobutaka commented that he saw no need to clarify the government's definition of 'non-combat' zones (*Japan Times* 2008a).

Explaining Japanese policy

Even though Japan apparently has sent troops to precarious regions, especially in Iraq, government officials rarely address potential hazards to soldiers abroad, including the threat from missiles. The evasion of such security considerations can be explained by examining the conflicting expectations of Japan's role conceptions of 'non-militarist country' on the one hand and the conceptions of 'exporter of security' and 'reliable partner' on the other hand. In line with the latter two conceptions, Tokyo has sought to respond to demands by the international community and especially the US alliance partner to play a bigger role in resolving international conflicts. As a result, Tokyo passed the 1992 Peace Cooperation Law and subsequently made two amendments to the law, facilitating Japan's cooperation with international UN troops (Ishizuka 2004).

At the same time, the Japanese government sought to act in accordance with its role conception of 'non-militarist country', insisting deployments were only made to 'non-combat' areas and thus consistent with constitutional constraints. By drawing on the ambiguity in the definition of 'non-combat' zone, Japan was able to dispatch the JSDF to Iraq. For policy-makers, this was perhaps the best compromise solution short of having to reject one of the three role conceptions. However, as seen above, the compromise remained on the declaratory level, as Tokyo essentially admitted Samawah was a 'danger zone'. This de facto violation of the traditional interpretation of Article 9 demonstrates Japan's willingness to broaden its international security role, indicating the importance Tokyo attaches to the two role conceptions of 'exporter of security' and 'reliable partner'.

Japanese policy on assisting other countries with MD

Introduction

Due to the ban on collective self-defence, Japan is technically not allowed to assist other countries with its MD equipment. While Japanese politicians have been careful to avoid an overt breach of the ban, they have arguably moved towards a de facto exercise of the right of collective self-defence in actual policy, driven by US pressure. The analysis here argues that the contradictory stance reflects the role conflict faced by political elites.

This part is divided into three main sections. The first section briefly examines the legal stipulations on Japan's assistance to other countries and considers some of the resulting policy dilemmas. As a pertinent example, the second section assesses Tokyo's policy regarding a US request to deploy Aegis destroyers with significant capabilities for intelligence collection in the Indian Ocean in 2002. The final section summarizes the characteristics of Japanese policy and evaluates the explanatory power of role conceptions.

Legal restrictions and policy dilemmas

In accordance with the constitutional ban on collective self-defence, Tokyo has maintained that it may not employ missile defence capabilities for the protection of other countries, if Japan is not endangered. Politicians have thus repeatedly asserted that the system's purpose is to protect only Japan (Fukuda 2003). Negotiations with the US on a bilateral agreement in 2003 for setting up an MD system were reportedly complicated by Tokyo's insistence on describing the Japanese programme as 'independent' rather than as a 'part' of the US concept (Lim 2004).

As highlighted above, Japan's decisions to develop its own information-gathering satellites were clearly influenced by the perceived need to observe the ban on collective self-defence. Defence Agency Chief Nakatani Gen argued that, although Japan was permitted to receive intelligence information from foreign countries, it needed autonomous data to detect and track missiles. Only by having its own data sources, could Tokyo ensure it was able to operate the system 'independently' (*shutaitekina unyō*) and at its own discretion, thereby abiding by the constitutional ban (*Asahi Shinbun* 2001).

While the Japanese government claims MD does not raise any problems with the ban on collective self-defence, debates among policy-makers demonstrate that the situation in fact is more complicated. Most importantly, Tokyo's politicians fear they may jeopardize the alliance relationship with the US if they refuse to share intelligence information or intercept a missile targeted at American facilities. Military affairs specialist Shibayama Futoshi aptly summarizes the Japanese dilemma: 'Suppose a missile was launched from North Korea aimed at the United States. If we didn't shoot it down, that would break up the alliance with the United States. But to shoot it down would be unconstitutional' (Struck 2001). Moreover, Japanese policy-makers also fear difficult policy choices if Tokyo were asked to provide MD equipment to Taiwan, for example, if tensions with mainland China rose like they did during the 1995–6 Taiwan Straits Crisis.

Discussions on the scope of individual self-defence touch upon two main issues: (1) whether the JSDF may under certain circumstances intercept missiles that are possibly not targeted at Japan, and (2) whether Japan may share its intelligence information with the US. The sections below provide an analysis of the discussions on each of them.

Interception of missiles (possibly) not targeted at Japan

Regarding the first issue, the debate deals with the conceivable scenario that Japan has to decide on intercepting a missile without reliable information on the estimated target area. The majority of government officials reject the possibility of utilizing the MD system for such a missile, given the uncertainty about whether the country was in fact being attacked (*Asahi Shinbun* 2005b: 276). Based on this reasoning, the government has also rejected participating in the development of boost phase missile defence systems, since the trajectory of a missile cannot be estimated at this early stage (*Asahi Shinbun* 2006). Nevertheless, some specialists have urged development of boost phase interception systems, because enemy missiles can be easily tracked at this flight stage due to their burning rocket motor (Jimbo 2002: 58).

A related, even more contentious debate deals with the question of whether Japan may under certain circumstances intercept missiles targeted at US territory or at its facilities and forces abroad. Discussions reflect the above-mentioned concern among politicians about jeopardizing alliance relations. Decision-makers distinguish several cases and scenarios. Government officials generally agree that a missile targeted at US forces within or in the vicinity of Japan can be intercepted based on the argument that Japan or the JSDF patrolling in nearby waters may be plausible targets (Oros 2008: 168). The hypothetical case of a missile flying towards the US mainland or a US facility like Guam in the Pacific has been more contentious. Some politicians have strictly opposed intercepting such a missile (*Asahi Shinbun* 2006). Others have argued that an interception may be permissible if the missile flies across Japanese territory (*Japan Economic Newswire* 2003a). In May 2007 Defence Minister Kyuma Fumio furthermore maintained Japan could intercept, if the country that launched the missile had previously attacked Japan. In such a situation, Japan would be reacting to an assault on its territory and thus exercising the right of individual self-defence (Toki and Diehl 2007).

Washington increased pressure on Tokyo to clarify its interception policy in October 2006, after North Korea conducted its first nuclear test. Thomas Schieffer, Ambassador to Japan, made clear that the answer to this question would be 'absolutely critical to the function of our future alliance' (Toki and Diehl 2007). Japanese Prime Minister Abe Shinzo, a well-known hawk in favour of constitutional revision, showed himself receptive to this warning and charged an expert panel to draft recommendations. Subsequent Prime Ministers took a more cautious stance however, ruling out the option of exercising the right of collective self-defence (*Japan Policy and Politics* 2008; *People's Daily* 2008). As a result, clear guidelines on intercepting missiles targeted at areas outside of Japan are still lacking.

Sharing intelligence information with the US

Policy-makers in Japan have also debated the possibility of sharing Japanese intelligence information with the US. The government has taken the stance that it may do so if the information will be used with the sole purpose of ensuring Japan's security or if the information is provided as part of a routine exchange of information (*ippantekina jōhō kōkan no ikkan toshite*) (Morimoto and Takahashi 2002: 307–8). On the other hand, Japan is not allowed to pass on intelligence information if another country requests it to gather data with the intention of utilizing them in a military encounter. This would signify a case of collective self-defence (Kaneda *et al.* 2006: 118).

At first sight, this distinction appears fairly clear-cut. However, Japan's actual policy is characterized by contradictions and ambiguity, as the following analysis of Tokyo's position on the dispatch of an Aegis ship to the Indian Ocean in 2001–2 shows. Although Japan's Aegis destroyers were not equipped with MD capability based on the SM-3 missile at that point, they did feature advanced radar equipment, which later was used for the MD systems installed on these ships. The intelligence systems on the Aegis, including data linkages with the US, were at the heart of the Japanese dispute about a possible deployment. This debate provides a pertinent example of Tokyo's stance on intelligence sharing with a partner country and reveals actual practices in dealing with the ban on collective self-defence.

Japan's policy regarding the dispatch of Aegis ships to the Indian Ocean

Following the 9/11 terrorist attacks in the United States and Washington's call for international support in its 'war on terror', Japan quickly passed the Antiterrorism Special Measures Law on 29 October 2001. This law enabled Japan to send the Maritime Self-Defence Forces to help provide logistical and oil-refuelling services to multinational forces operating in the Indian Ocean against Afghanistan's Taliban regime. Tokyo's policy-makers concurred that Japan's support of multilateral troops would not be 'unified with combat' and therefore not violate the ban on collective self-defence (Ishizuka 2004: 144).

In autumn 2001 and spring 2002, Japanese Diet decision-makers debated whether Tokyo should send Aegis destroyers to the Indian Ocean. Compared to other available ships, the Aegis were equipped with a more sophisticated air-defence radar covering a range of approximately 500 kilometres – about five times that of older destroyers – and would allow the transfer of intelligence information to the US Navy via data linkages (Foreign Press Center Japan 2002). Apparently, not only Washington was interested in such a substantial Japanese presence in the volatile region, but the leadership of the Japanese Maritime Self-Defence Forces also pushed for a deployment in the hope of expanding their scope of activities (Midford 2003: 336; Berkofsky 2002b). However, a number of lawmakers in Tokyo, especially from the LDP and Komei Party, cautioned that the US might use Aegis intelligence data for planning military attacks. In that case, Japanese support would be 'unified with combat' and therefore violate the ban on collective self-defence.[25] Tokyo consequently rejected an Aegis deployment.

Following renewed US pressure on Japan for an Aegis dispatch in the fall of 2002, Tokyo unexpectedly shifted from a reluctant to an affirmative stance on the dispatch, causing bewilderment about this policy 'U-turn' among observers (Berkofsky 2002a). On 4 December 2002, Prime Minister Koizumi announced the government's decision, after considerable controversy in the ruling coalition and extensive Diet debates.[26] At this time, there was ample evidence about the US intention to launch an attack on Iraq, and thus many lawmakers feared the Aegis presence might contribute to a possible war on Iraq, especially through intelligence gathering (Mataichi 2002). Proponents of the dispatch rejected suggestions that US prodding had caused the 'U-turn', emphasizing three arguments in favour of deployment. First, they pointed out that the rotation schedule required an Aegis ship to replace one of the smaller Japanese destroyers returning home. Secondly, they argued the Aegis radar system could better ensure the safety and air defence needs of Japan's troops.[27] Finally, advocates maintained the highly efficient air conditioning system on the Aegis would provide the Japanese crew with more comfortable working conditions in the hot climate of the Indian Ocean (*Japan Times* 2002).

Insisting that the dispatch decision had nothing to do 'with the operation regarding the situation in Iraq' by Washington, the Koizumi government announced that the Aegis destroyers would be allowed to share intelligence information with the US Navy (Ministry of Foreign Affairs Japan 2002). Press Secretary Takashima Hatsuhisa sought to counter criticism of violating the ban on collective self-defence, stating

> The Aegis escort ship is expected to exchange information with American and other naval vessels, which are friendly forces fighting against terrorism. If any other operation is undertaken by American or other naval vessels, the Japanese Aegis escort ship would not participate in it at all.
>
> (Ministry of Foreign Affairs Japan 2002)

Diet debates demonstrated the delicacy of Japan's stance. For example, Defence Minister Ishiba Shigeru maintained Japan's provision of Aegis intelligence data to the US and other multilateral forces was 'not [an act] ... unified with combat', although he conceded that it 'depended on the situation' (*kyokumen ni yotte chigaimasu*). He explained 'it is obviously problematic if [Japan] provides information on the timing and direction of an enemy airplane which is then attacked, however, ... sharing knowledge about objects far away and communicating their nationality is [something other ships do as well]' (*Kokuritsu Kokkai Toshokan*, 29 Oct. 2002). In another debate on the issue, Ishiba openly admitted that it was 'hard to clearly distinguish' intelligence data that Japan could share with the US (*Japan Policy and Politics* 2003a). Despite enduring uncertainty about these issues, the dispatch of a second Aegis destroyer in April 2003 and a third one in January 2004 did not arouse major public discussions. Aegis operations stopped after November 2005, because Japan sought to mount newly developed SM-3 interception rockets on them (Tanter 2006).

Explaining Japanese policy in light of its policy goals

Japan's stance on supporting partner countries and allies through missile defence systems and related capabilities exhibits three characteristics that reflect some inconsistencies. First, the political leadership has shied away from anything that would constitute an overt breach of the ban on collective self-defence. Decision-makers emphasize that the MD system is operated on Tokyo's 'independent judgement' and they refrain from promising interception of any missile targeted at the US homeland. Second, some political elites have sought to stretch the interpretive limits of the meaning of 'individual self-defence' by suggesting for example that intercepting a missile flying towards the US was possible above Japanese territory. Third, while no consensus is apparent in debates, Tokyo has in actual policy moved towards what may be called a de facto exercise of collective self-defence, as seen in the case of Japan's Aegis dispatch to the Indian Ocean. According to Sato Yoichiro, the Aegis controversy illustrates a 'consistent drive' by the Maritime Self-Defence Forces to 'set precedents through overseas deployments', signifying the incremental establishment of a system of collective self-defence (Sato 2003).

The apparent inconsistency in Japan's policy can be explained in view of the role conflict faced by decision-makers. Politicians seek to adhere to the role conception of 'non-militarist country' by observing the limitations set by their Constitution and the concept of 'exclusive self-defence'. At the same time, they feel compelled to transcend these strict constraints, so as to act in accordance with Japan's roles as an 'exporter of security' and, more importantly, as a 'reliable ally' to Washington. By demonstrating support, Japan hopes to counter potential 'free-rider' criticism and to increase the credibility of the alliance relationship. As the above discussion shows, Tokyo has acknowledged this role conflict and policy dilemma. The inconsistent response seems to be an attempt to remain faithful – as far as possible – to the different norms and values in Japan's role set.

Given Tokyo's de facto breach of the ban on collective self-defence, one may wonder if Japan's role conception of 'non-militarist country' is losing importance. There is no clear-cut answer to this question. While there is obvious discontent among political leaders about the strict limitations on military contributions, it seems erroneous to say that Japan, due to the weakening anti-militarism, is 'drift[ing] from its old moorings' and entering 'a new era', as Kenneth Pyle argues (2007a: 299 and 374). Rather, officials have adhered to a limited conception of Japan's international military role, despite the momentous changes in the international environment since the end of the Cold War and overwhelming US pressure for Tokyo to abandon its pacifist values. If the role conception of 'non-militarist country' no longer appealed to the Japanese, Tokyo would have more seriously considered joining boost phase missile defence research in the face of the North Korean threat. Moreover, officials' prudently seeking to evade a de jure exercise of the right of collective self-defence suggests a gradual change in Japan's *interpretation* of its self-conception as a 'non-militarist country', while the *relevance* of this role seems to be unaffected or declining only slightly. Missile defence has clearly exposed Japan's role conflict, thus serving as a driving force in its debate on the role conception of 'non-militarist country'. However, the case study findings do not suggest that Japan will abolish its pacifist-minded norms completely.

Conclusion

The explanatory power of role conceptions

The preceding analysis demonstrates the explanatory power of role conceptions, illuminating Germany's and Japan's policies on missile defence for territorial security, for the defence of soldiers deployed abroad and for assisting allies and partners. Conflicting ideational concepts account for apparent *inconsistencies between two policy fields* of the *same country*. For instance, German decision-makers assessed the utility of MD systems for territorial defence and for the protection of its soldiers very differently. Considering territorial MD as an inappropriate policy option, they sought security through cooperative multilateral efforts, thereby adhering to entrenched normative beliefs. However, political leaders were willing to develop MD for soldiers abroad, as they regarded such technology as a contribution to the transatlantic relationship and multilateral bodies like the UN.

Role conceptions also explain why *two countries* may choose *different approaches* in their foreign policies. Germany in its MEADS policy and Japan in its territorial defence posture chose to cooperate with other countries in developing complex technologies. However, in Germany's case, ideational factors worked in favour of a multilateral approach with emphasis on the NATO context, while in Japan's case, normative aspects negated a multilateral solution, with Tokyo preferring a bilateral setup with the US. Tokyo has in fact rejected cooperation with other countries such as South Korea due to constitutional stipulations (Takesada 2008).

Likewise, role conceptions help to explain why *two countries* under certain circumstances may choose *similar approaches* in their policy. Due to analogous configurations in role conceptions, both Germany and Japan acted as 'selective' exporters of security when faced with the question of helping allies and partners with MD-related capabilities. The two countries' policies were the outcomes of comparable, though not identical, role conflicts related to the conceptions of 'non-militarist country', 'exporter of security' and 'reliable partner'.

Finally, role conceptions help to account for *apparently irrational behaviour* by states. Japan insists that it will not intercept a missile as long as it is unclear whether it is targeted at its territory. As seen above, such a policy is risky, given the fact that North Korean missiles can reach Japan within a short span of time. The role conception of 'anti-militarist country' with its emphasis on an exclusively defence-oriented policy offers a convincing explanation for this policy choice.

While the analysis illustrates that both Germany's and Japan's approaches to MD are fundamentally driven by broadly shared norms and values, other factors also influence policy outcomes. Perceptions of threat, cost-effectiveness and technological feasibility are weighty aspects in a country's MD policy. However, it must be noted that these aspects are not assessed independently of a country's role conceptions, but rather *in view* of them. Additionally, in both countries economic interests motivated the participation in MD. Such economic considerations were evident in Germany's involvement in MEADS and Japan's decisions to build a territorial MD shield. Finally, domestic political settings had a decisive influence on policy outcomes. For example, considerations about the distribution of power in coalition governments caused the smaller party – the Green Party in Germany's case and the Komei Party in Japan's – to drop initial objections against policy plans of the dominant party. The Green Party thus went along with the SPD by voting for the MEADS procurement in April 2005, while the Komei Party refrained from blocking Koizumi's December 2002 Aegis decision. The domestic political atmosphere – characterized by frenzy vis-à-vis North Korea about the 'kidnapping issue'– also had a substantial effect on Japan's December 2003 decision to deploy a territorial MD shield.

Role conflicts and role tension

The analysed policy cases offer insights into how countries deal with role conflict or role tension. Germany and Japan displayed three interrelated methods of handling situations of conflicting behavioural expectations. A first set of techniques comprises the utilization of *semantic techniques* such as *conceptual ambiguity, emphasis and de-emphasis, as well as the broadening of interpretations* to lessen the strain from diverging behavioural expectations. For example, when explaining the conditions of SDF dispatches, Japanese policy-makers were vague in their definition of a 'non-combat' area. By leaving some ambiguity in the term, they alleviated Japan's role conflict between the conception of 'non-militarist country' and the ones of 'exporter of security' and 'reliable partner'. Japanese lawmakers furthermore used the technique of broadening conceptual interpretations when discussing whether Tokyo would be permitted to intercept missiles targeting the US mainland. By stretching the interpretive limits of what it means to be a 'non-militarist country', politicians sought to lessen the strain resulting from the need be a 'reliable partner' to the US.

The related technique of stressing only certain aspects was adopted both in Germany's MEADS policy and in Japan's territorial MD policy. In the 1990s, German MEADS supporters consciously de-emphasized the fact that they sought to expand the international role of the *Bundeswehr*, aware of the tensions with the role conception of 'non-militarist country'. In a similar vein, Japanese policy-makers stressed their territorial MD shield would be operated independently and at Tokyo's own discretion, even though this pledge may be difficult to uphold in practice. In doing so, they attempted to alleviate public concern about a possible breach of the ban on collective self-defence, encapsulated in the role conception of 'non-militarist country'.

A second method of handling role conflict was to *proactively seek to change the circumstances and conditions that gave rise to the conflict*. Germany attempted to break out of such a dilemma in the run-up to the Iraq war in 2003. While Berlin was opposed to a possible US-led pre-emptive strike on Iraq in line with the conception of 'non-militarist country', it did not want to block NATO preparations for an attack completely due to the role conceptions of 'reliable partner' and 'contributor to regional cooperation'. To get out of this dilemma, Germany chose to veto the proposed NATO war preparations, but signalled at the same time a willingness to provide defensive support to Turkey. Berlin successfully freed itself from the 'all or nothing' policy choice by convincing other countries to narrow the scope of the NATO decision to Turkey's support. This was an acceptable solution for Germany, because it would not have to act in contradiction of its role conceptions – at least not in an overt fashion.

A third method of dealing with role conflict was to *violate partially or fully one role conception's prescriptions in order to fulfil those of another*. For example, in defiance of the role conception of 'reliable partner' and 'contributor to regional cooperation', German policy-makers sided with Russia in their criticism of territorial missile defence, failing to consult first with other countries. While acting in line with perceived responsibilities as an 'anti-militarist country' and a 'regional stabilizer', this stance undermined chances of finding a consensus within NATO. The third method of handling role conflict was even more evident in Germany's and Japan's policies regarding the provision of missile defence-related equipment to partners before the 2003 Iraq war. In line with their conceptions of being 'non-militarist countries', they distanced themselves from US war preparations. However, faced with the need to act as 'reliable partners', both countries decided in the end to provide limited support – which they publicly claimed was not related to the Iraq war. Germany thus aided Turkey and Israel, while Japan sent an Aegis ship to the Indian Ocean. By providing indirect help in the Iraq war, both Berlin and Tokyo arguably violated their conception of being 'non-militarist countries'.

This analysis does not provide sufficient grounds for determining the circumstances under which a country may favour a particular method or technique of dealing with role conflict or role tension. However, it shows that countries often use several methods simultaneously and that other factors – such as the domestic atmosphere or economic interests – may lead them to favour one method over another. How long and to what extent a country can rely on the third method of violating one role conception in favour of another cannot be answered conclusively by this analysis either. Coping with role conflict in such a way may indicate a cognitive dissonance, in which a country holds incongruous beliefs and attitudes within its role set. If a country relies on this third method for an extended period of time, the role conception being violated will likely undergo gradual adjustment to fit new societal beliefs and values.

4 Policies on textbook talks

Comparing German–Polish and Japanese–South Korean dialogue

Introduction

Former adversaries of war often clash over diverging interpretations of the past and especially history textbook depictions. Since historical narratives are intimately linked to the construction, consolidation and reproduction of national identity, a country's approach to dealing with history textbook disputes is an intriguing area for role theoretical research. This chapter examines German and Japanese policies regarding such disputes and bilateral textbook talks with former opponents Poland and South Korea, respectively.

From a historical perspective, German–Polish and Japanese–South Korean relations exhibit many parallels. Strong cultural bonds have existed for centuries between the respective peoples. In both relations, one party brutally oppressed its immediate neighbour in the early 20th century. After 1945, the former oppressors, Germany and Japan, successfully rehabilitated from their defeat in the Second World War to become self-confident democratic and economic superpowers, while their neighbours Poland and South Korea faced economic hardship and authoritarian rule. History textbooks in all four countries were afflicted with misconceptions and antagonisms after 1945. While Polish and South Korean textbooks emphasized the belligerent and untrustworthy nature of their former oppressors, German and Japanese textbooks gave only scarce consideration to their neighbours, reflecting contempt for their former adversaries. Finally, both Poland and South Korea became full-fledged democracies after the Cold War, spurring new examinations of the past.

The chapter is divided into four main parts. The first section discusses the importance of textbook consultations, evaluating the role of governmental and civil society actors. The second and third sections explore the postures of the German and Japanese political leadership regarding bilateral textbook talks with Poland and South Korea, respectively. The last section compares the two cases, assessing the explanatory power of role conceptions. Overall, significant differences in the behaviours and attitudes exhibited by German and Japanese decision-makers regarding textbook talks are observed. Compared to their German counterparts, Japanese leaders reflect a lack of political will to engage in dialogue with Seoul about improving mutual depictions in textbooks. These different approaches pose a puzzle to rationalist explanations of international relations, which expect memory politics to be driven by strategic concerns. From this perspective, Seoul and Tokyo should have overcome their disputed history swiftly in the face of the communist threat. In contrast, strategic interests in German–Polish relations did not clearly point towards reconciliation, given the ideological confrontation during the Cold War. Role conceptions do help to explain the two countries' policies, but other factors also need to be taken into account.

This case study traces and analyses German and Japanese policies since 1945, thereby going beyond this book's general focus on the post-Cold War era. Such coverage is necessary because current progress can only be evaluated when considering prior developments. Moreover, as will be seen, strong continuity exists between pre- and post-Cold War attitudes and behaviour. Although more research is needed on this point, this finding suggests that the motivational factors in German and Japanese policies have not changed fundamentally since the end of the Cold War.

Textbook talks: goals and actors

History education is considered an essential vehicle for the cultivation of future generations' historical consciousness and the transmission of political and social norms (Chon 2007: 261). Textbooks are attributed international significance, because they are a tangible manifestation of how a society treats its past. Especially after traumatic experiences of war, textbooks tend to contain narrow-minded and one-sided nationalist narratives that become the basis for new mutual misperceptions and frictions. Thus, as Laura Hein and Mark Selden observe, 'people fight over textbook content because education is so obviously about the future, reaches so deeply into society, and is directed by the state' (2000: 3).

While first international attempts to combat nationalistic school education in the late 1920s and early 1930s largely failed, the task was taken up with renewed urgency after the Second World War by the United Nations Educational, Scientific and Cultural Organization (UNESCO). In 1974, the UNESCO's General Conference described the goal of textbook revision as ensuring that education materials are 'accurate, balanced, up-to-date and unprejudiced and will enhance mutual knowledge and understanding between different peoples' (Pingel 1999: 16). Textbook talks ultimately seek to promote a transnational reconstruction of the past that nurtures tolerance and inclusiveness as a basis for peaceful coexistence between former opponents. Historical writing must thus be 'objective' in the sense that it is 'acceptable to all parties concerned' (Lübbe 1977: 318).

The approach to international textbook talks has gradually changed, reflecting the evolution of the historical discipline. Textbook studies throughout most of the Cold War period relied primarily on the 'consensus model', in which the involved parties stress points of agreement rather than differences in their perspective (Pingel 1999: 13). More recent textbook talks have relied increasingly on the 'multiperspectivity model', in which participants seek to expose points of agreement, while recognizing that history can be reconstructed from a variety of perspectives. The aim is to make textbooks more pluralist and inclusive, teaching students to think critically and understand the complexity of historical situations (Stradling 2003).

Joint textbook studies can be conducted either as projects with official governmental backing or as purely civil society endeavours under the leadership of non-governmental organizations (NGOs). Despite the important role of non-state actors in supporting textbook talks however, this chapter maintains that political leadership is essential.[1] Doubtless, projects without government involvement have certain advantages, including the unofficial setting that allows for freedom, creativity and risk taking (Horvat 2007). Such projects also tend to progress more smoothly, since NGOs will assemble like-minded researchers sympathetic to the cause of reconciliation. However, as Falk Pingel contends, the implementation of joint study results 'often turns out to be the Achilles heel of projects conducted by NGOs. Ministries are not obliged to follow their advice and can ban their materials from schools' (Pingel 2008: 191). Moreover, civil society initiatives are often viewed as biased.[2]

Joint talks endorsed by the respective governments have important advantages over purely private ones. Government officials – in their role as representatives of their state – can lend legitimacy and credibility to joint history projects and thus help overcome domestic opposition. Furthermore, political leaders are crucial actors in the implementation of textbook changes, as they exert direct influence over teaching guidelines, curricular directives and textbook authorization criteria. On the downside, government-backed projects may take considerable time, and participants may have more difficulty in tackling contentious bilateral issues (Pingel 2008: 184, 191). Given the pivotal role of the state in the context of school education, the examination of German and Japanese policies in this chapter sheds new light on the ways in which decision-makers can influence the process of reconciliation.[3]

German politics on history textbook talks with Poland

After the Second World War, German and Polish history textbooks were beset by historical grievances as well as Cold War ideological antagonisms. Teaching materials in the Federal Republic moreover reflected strong resentment against Polish authorities for expelling approximately eight million Germans from their homelands in the aftermath of the war (Kamusella 2004: 29). The German government's evolving stance regarding textbook talks with Poland can be divided into three main phases. The first phase covers the post-war period until around 1970, when Bonn rejected joint work with Poland, while demonstrating a willingness to engage in such talks with countries from the capitalist bloc. During the second phase, lasting until the end of the Cold War, the German government began its active support for textbook improvements with Poland. Finally, in the period since 1990, political leaders in Berlin have continued to back textbook consultations, although bilateral frictions about historical remembrance have re-emerged at the same time.

1945–1970: Poland as an ideological enemy

Following the Second World War, initiatives for the improvement of textbooks between Germany and Poland seemed out of the question, given the deepening ideological division in Europe. As Gotthold Rhode, a historian who took part in the bilateral commission in the 1970s, observed:

> Whoever would have predicted in 1945 that Polish and German historians and geographers belonging to the war generation would meet in Warsaw to negotiate toughly, but cordially and collegially in German on the possibility of devising more objective school textbooks and teaching-methods would have been declared mad (*geistesgestört*).
>
> (Riemenschneider 1998: 75)

At the same time, the Federal Republic was willing to engage in textbook talks with countries of the 'Western' bloc. Most prominently, Germany and France agreed to establish a bilateral commission of historians under the umbrella of UNESCO, publishing a first set of recommendations as early as 1951. The bilateral work was critically supported by Georg Eckert, a professor who was an outspoken proponent of textbook talks and who set up the 'International Institute for the Improvement of School Books' in Brunswick (Braunschweig) in 1951. Policy-makers' espousal of such textbook work was motivated both by strategic concerns amid the Soviet threat and by the belief that rampant nationalism had led to the devastating Second World War (Kansteiner 2006: 109; Schneider 2004: 70).

With regard to Poland, German textbooks increasingly focused on the bitter memory of expulsion after the war. In 1956, the Standing Conference of the Ministers of Education and Cultural Affairs of the states (*Länder*) in Germany (*Kultusministerkonferenz*) adopted a decree called 'Recommendations on the Study of the East' (Empfehlungen zur Ostkunde, also called Ostkunde-Erlass). The directive required teachers to increase their coverage on the 'Eastern territories' in class, fostering in students a 'profound connection' with these areas (Gauger and Buchstab 2004: 92). To many Polish observers, Germany's apparent territorial claims demonstrated a lack of self-critical reflection about wartime crimes (Goehrke *et al.* 1977: 67).

From around the late 1950s and early 1960s, new discussions emerged in Germany about the need to come to terms with the past. The public was alerted to the importance of remembrance by a series of incidents, including a wave of anti-Semitic graffiti in 1958–9 as well as the trials of Adolf Eichmann and other Nazi leaders in the early 1960s (Kansteiner 2006: 112; Hirsch 2003). Impetus for a critical examination of the past also emanated from the East German leadership, which accused the Federal Republic of being unable to confront history squarely (Frei 2004: 43). In this context, civil society actors began to criticize mutual textbook depictions of Germany and Poland. In 1955, a small private conference was held between German and Polish historians at Georg Eckert's institute. The joint research was suspended after the Hungarian Uprising of 1956, but German history teacher Enno Meyer published a set of 47 propositions on textbook depictions, based on conference discussions (Ruchniewicz 2005: 237ff.). Another initiative was launched by Pastor Günter Berndt of the Protestant Academy of West Berlin, who organized a series of private conferences in 1969–70. In his 1971 book, Berndt strongly criticized the portrayals of Poland in German textbooks (Strobel 2008a). Lacking governmental backing, Berndt's publication – like Meyer's – had little impact on teaching practices in German schools, however.

1970–1990: détente and the first textbook project with Poland

It was not until the early 1970s that Chancellor Willy Brandt's *Ostpolitik* and the atmosphere of global détente permitted first steps towards reconciliation with Communist Poland. In an attempt to lessen regional tensions and ameliorate Germany's front-line status, Chancellor Willy Brandt sought to expand the Federal Republic's social, economic and political ties with countries of the Eastern bloc. The normalization of relations with Poland in the 1970 Treaty of Warsaw as well as Brandt's gesture of contrition in his famous 'Warsaw Genuflection' served as foundations for the subsequent establishment of a joint textbook commission.

Key political elites in the Federal Republic gradually began promoting the idea of textbook talks and setting up financial and institutional support. When the President of the German UNESCO commission Georg Eckert and his Polish counterpart called for schoolbook talks at the General Assembly in Paris in November 1970, German decision-makers reacted with cautious encouragement (Wernstedt 2000: 125). Eckert evidently considered political support vital and thus approached key decision-makers to convince them of his idea (Girgensohn 1981: 4). Policy-makers, including Chancellor Willy Brandt, began to embrace the idea of joint talks and to negotiate the establishment of a textbook commission. The Foreign Ministry demonstrated its espousal of Eckert's activities by beginning to provide regular budgetary support to his 'International Institute for the Improvement of School Books' in Brunswick in 1971 (Strobel 2005: 258). In the same year, German politicians agreed on holding joint talks under the auspices of the UNESCO. This institutional choice was influenced by Cold War conditions, with the UNESCO representing an ideal channel for contact with Communist Poland, because it was less official in character compared to direct talks. However, policy-makers in the Federal Republic were aware that the UNESCO – as an intergovernmental institution – also underlined the state's backing and gave legitimacy to the endeavour.

The first meeting of the commission took place in Poland in late February 1972, at a time when the Treaty of Warsaw had not yet been ratified in either country. Judging a favourable political environment critical for their work, participants of the talks were elated when the Treaty was ratified in May 1972. Retrospectively pondering on the decisive role of political support for textbook talks at the beginning of 1972, Wlodzimierz Borodziej, secretary of the Polish commission from 1979 to 1981, asserted 'the political establishment ... without doubt acted as a midwife for the commission' (Borodziej 2000: 157).

The first conference phase of the talks lasted until 1976, resulting in a set of 26 recommendations. During this time, German political leaders played a decisive, though not overly conspicuous, role in encouraging the successful conclusion of talks. Decision-makers sought to foster a beneficial atmosphere by backing the project, while also providing enough room for historians to deliberate without political interference and nationalistic pressure. The analysis reveals four strategies employed towards this end.

First, as mentioned above, political leaders relied on the UNESCO as the framework for bilateral talks. This approach allowed politicians to support the talks, while utilizing the authority and reputation of this esteemed organization as a shield against criticism (Borodziej 2003: 36). In other words, the UNESCO framework served the double function of demonstrating political endorsement while also protecting commission members against nationalistic pressures.

Secondly, political leaders used their position as governmental representatives to raise public awareness about the commission's activities and to demonstrate sincerity about the project to the Polish side. In response to a request by Eckert, the Minister of Education of the state of Northrhine-Westphalia Jürgen Girgensohn, for example, published the first interim results of the joint commission in 1972 in the state's gazette (*Amtsblatt*). As Girgensohn recollects, 'He [Eckert] needed this signal of governmental recognition of his work vis-à-vis his Polish partners. Doubts had emerged [among Polish representatives], whether the German delegation had sufficient official backing' (Girgensohn 1981: 3). By October 1972, seven other German states had followed Northrhine-Westphalia's lead, declaring solidarity with the project and publishing interim results of the talks (Strobel 2005: 254). Another symbolic gesture in support of the ongoing bilateral textbook talks with Poland was the awarding in 1972 of the Federal Cross of Merit to Georg Eckert at the request of the Foreign Ministry (Harstick 2000: 108). Coinciding with the first round of German–Polish textbook talks, the award was a powerful signal of political endorsement regarding Eckert's efforts.

Thirdly, political representatives took a deliberately low profile when it came to the actual work of the textbook commission and proactively sought to limit political pressure. SPD member and Federal President Gustav Heinemann for example declined an invitation to provide a greeting to the bilateral commission in 1972, explaining the government wanted to make clear it exerted no influence on the 'objective work' of the scholars (Strobel 2005: 263). Furthermore, the selection of commission members was fully entrusted to Georg Eckert in order to prevent biases due to political considerations. Cooperating with his close colleagues, Eckert ensured that the participants were reputable historians with in-depth knowledge, representing both the political left and right (Maier 2008; Strobel 2008a). German politicians who supported the joint talks also sought to ease some of the domestic pressure on historians regarding the contentious issue of expulsion. While the above-mentioned 1956 'Decree on the Study of the East' (*Ostkunde-Erlass*) was not completely revoked, the German states agreed in June 1973 on a new statement that declared the previous recommendations no longer fully adequate. History classes would no longer be required to cover the culture and history of the Eastern territories (Gauger and Buchstab 2004: 93). This new educational agreement helped to expand the leeway for historians in treating the delicate issue of expulsion.

Finally, German political leaders generously supported the legal institutionalization and the financing of Eckert's 'International School Textbook Institute'. The institute played a key role in the realization of bilateral textbook conferences with France from 1951 and with Poland from 1972. When Eckert died in January 1974, policy-makers were concerned that the institute might not be able to continue its work due to financial and organizational difficulties. Under the leadership of both Social Democratic Party (SPD) and Christian Democratic Union (CDU) politicians, the institute was given legal status as an independent institution and named the 'Georg-Eckert-Institute' (GEI) in 1974. In fact, the law on the establishment of the institute in Brunswick received support from all parliamentarians in Lower Saxony, including those from the ruling SPD and the opposition's CDU and FDP, making it the only law passed unanimously in the state during the legislative period between 1974 and 1976 (Oschatz 2000: 13). Decision-makers also ensured that the GEI received adequate funding, with seven German states pledging their support (Gabriel 2000: 11). Although the GEI is to a significant degree financed through governmental sources, it remains autonomous in its research activities – and thus is neither an official government organization nor a purely private institution. Rather, it may be described as a 'parapublic' institution, as it 'escape[s] the common binary distinctions of state-society or public-private' (Krotz 2007: 1). The reliance on a parapublic institution served policy-makers' dual goal of demonstrating their support for textbook talks, while maintaining distance from the actual work of the institute.

In 1976, the joint commission concluded its work with 26 concise suggestions on how German–Polish history should be dealt with in textbooks. The recommendations caused considerable controversy in Germany, with two issues dominating the public debate. First, a number of critics pointed out that the recommendations failed to mention important bilateral matters like the secret supplementary protocol to the Hitler–Stalin–Pact of 23 August 1939, which led to the division of Poland. In consideration of Poland's relationship with the Soviet Union, the commission had deliberately left this issue out from discussions (Borodziej 2001: 12). Secondly, the recommendations were widely criticized for downplaying the expulsion issue. Opponents asserted that describing Polish policies with the term 'transfer' was inadequate.[4] Reactions to the recommendations among the political leadership were mixed. Conservative politicians of the CDU-CSU tended to be more cautious and doubtful than representatives of the SPD.[5] However, the CDU-CSU did not consist of a monolithic block, with key politicians such as Richard von Weizsäcker, Rita Süssmuth, Ernst Albrecht or Bernhard Vogel, backing the bilateral commission's work (Maier 2008). While many conservative politicians were critical of the recommendations themselves, they agreed in principle on the necessity for joint textbook improvements. In their view, bilateral talks were futile with a Communist-ruled Poland in which historians could not speak freely.

Since the commission's recommendations were not binding and each German state was responsible for issuing its own teaching guidelines and approving textbooks, the effect on actual teaching practices was far from guaranteed. The difficulty of modifying textbook content was exacerbated by the sheer variety of teaching materials available in the Federal Republic. There were almost one hundred different history textbooks, issued by more than a dozen different publishers (Jacobmeyer 1979: 199). German politicians in favour of the recommendations adopted two related strategies to encourage consideration of the commission's work at schools.

First, top-level leaders including the Chancellor and the Foreign Minister took the lead in expressing their full support for the commission, appealing to individual state leaders in Germany to consider changes in history teaching. Even before the commission published its final and most controversial recommendations on the modern era in bilateral relations, Foreign Minister Dietrich Genscher on a visit to Warsaw in November 1975 advocated putting 'the recommendations into practice as soon as possible' (Jacobmeyer 1979: 199). Furthermore, Chancellor Helmut Schmidt worked behind the scenes to convince state leaders of the importance of the commission's work. In June 1977, he explained before the German–Polish Forum: '[Regarding the consideration of the recommendations in education,] I am often holding talks and exchanging letters with the prime ministers of the states, which have the highest executive authority in educational policies.' Schmidt asserted that 'persistent efforts and goodwill' would lead to success (Schmidt 1977: 618).

Secondly, German politicians in favour of the bilateral textbook talks ensured that the recommendations would be widely read. More than 300,000 copies of the document were printed in Germany, guaranteeing a broad distribution among the public and especially among teachers, textbook authors and publishers. Several state governments sent copies of the recommendations to schools, accompanied by a letter from the prime minister or the minister of education explaining the significance of the German–Polish work (Jacobmeyer 1979: 317). Northrhine-Westphalia took the lead among all German states in adopting a decree on the 'Education for International Understanding' (Erziehung zur Völkerverständigung) on 15 November 1977, thereby abrogating the 1956 directive 'Recommendations on the Study of the East' (Girgensohn 1981: 8). Following in-depth deliberations, a majority of German states announced their intention to consider the recommendations in their history textbooks and teaching, although they would not do so uncritically, they maintained. Bavaria, where former expellees represent an important voter constituency, was one of the states rejecting the recommendations. The CSU-led government explained it valued the goal of international understanding, but maintained this objective 'can be realized only on the basis of equality, mutual respect and the factual-objective depiction of historical-political circumstances' (Jacobmeyer 1979: 135).

The efforts by supporters of the recommendations bore fruit and led to improvements in textbook depictions. A 1978 survey among history teachers in the area of Oberhausen and Duisburg found that the purpose and content of the

German–Polish recommendations were generally well-known. It also revealed that many publishers had already begun to make changes in textbook content (Jacobmeyer 1979: 388). In comparison, a 1982 study on Polish textbooks revealed mixed results, with only some volumes taking the recommendations into account (Meyer 1982: 274).

The bilateral textbook commission continued its work after the 1976 publication, although it lost some of its importance in the 1980s. Amid political upheaval, many Polish historians were caught up with domestic issues and thus unable to participate consistently in the bilateral deliberations (Borodziej 2000). In Germany, the inauguration of the conservative federal government under Chancellor Helmut Kohl in 1982 had potential implications on bilateral textbook work. In his first policy declaration on 13 October 1982, Kohl criticized his predecessors' memory politics harshly. He stated Germany was facing a 'spiritual-moral crisis' (*geistig-moralische Krise*), which was 'the result of a decade-long questioning (*Verunsicherung*) in relationship to our history ... and ... questioning of our national self-image' (Limbach 2008). In Kohl's view, a new national historical identity – based on a factually accurate yet positive version of the past – would enhance political stability and render Germany more predictable in international politics (Kansteiner 2006: 126).[6] Nevertheless, there was little change in Germany's policies on joint textbook work with Poland. Kohl briefly considered suspending the bilateral work or making personnel changes (Kondo 2001: 21; Strobel 2005: 264). However, after deliberations involving historian Gotthold Rhode, the Chancellor decided to maintain governmental support for the existing commission. Kohl in fact issued a statement in April 1985, publicly expressing his support for the project (Kondo 1998: 127).

At the same time, Kohl provided more systematic assistance to the activities of former expellees by increasing the government's financial support for their foundations (Bergsdorf 2004: 64). He revived a tradition of post-war chancellors attending the annual meetings of expellees, a practice that had been abandoned under Brandt. While Kohl did not endorse the demands of the expellees politically, he defended their symbolic status as victims. Daniel Levy and Julian Dierkes observe: 'The memory of ethnic Germans' fate played a central role in Kohl's attempt to revive and rehabilitate old notions such as the "Vaterland" (fatherland) and the "Volk" (people). He sought to dissociate the ethno-cultural idiom from its Nazi connotation' (Levy and Dierkes 2002: 258). The expulsion issue also served as a symbolic counterweight to the focus on the victims of German aggression.

1990–2011: new textbook projects amid history-related frictions

After the fall of communism, relations between Poland and reunited Germany quickly improved, especially after the signing of the bilateral border treaty of 14 November 1990, fixing the Oder-Neisse Line as their common border under international law. The fundamental political changes appeared to offer a good opportunity to discuss both countries' history education and triggered debates on the need to revise the textbook recommendations of 1976. Emerging as a democracy in the early 1990s, Warsaw adopted a system of competing and pluralistic textbooks. The bilateral textbook commission thus suggested a new series of meetings, a proposal that was received positively by the Kohl government, with the Foreign Ministry agreeing to provide generous financial support (Maier 2008; Kondo 1993: 315).

Following extensive deliberations, the textbook commission agreed in 1997 to develop a book to be called *Germany and Poland in the 20th Century: Suggestions on History Teaching*, featuring didactic advice and primary source material for teachers. The book title deliberately omitted the term 'recommendations', as historians did not want to give the impression they were replacing and distancing themselves from the 1976 joint publications (Maier 2008). The 2001 publication of the teachers' handbook was hailed by Wlodzimierz Borodziej, a former secretary of the bilateral commission, observing the new, more than 400 page-long manual was 'twenty times as voluminous as the 1976 Recommendations, detailed and nuanced' (Borodziej 2003: 38). To increase awareness about the handbook, the Georg-Eckert-Institute issued press releases and publicized it at teachers' conferences. Policy-makers supported these efforts, for example by arranging a high-profile presentation in the parliament of Lower Saxony and by advertising the book on the website of the Federal Center for Political Education (Bundeszentrale für politische Bildung) (Maier 2008). The Foreign Ministers of Germany and Poland furthermore acknowledged the important contributions of the German–Polish textbook commission in 2002 by presenting it with the 'Award for Special Service in the Development of German–Polish Relations'. The book was a considerable success, with more than 26,000 copies of the German edition sold (Maier 2008).

Nevertheless, bilateral disputes in the post-Cold War era about the remembrance of the expulsion issue have confirmed a persistent need for history dialogue and joint research. Public interest in the issue of expulsion grew for at least three reasons. First, Kohl's decision to recognize the Oder-Neisse line as the common border with Poland was a bitter awakening for many former expellees and their descendants, stimulating debates (Hirsch 2004). Secondly, the Kohl government – aware the border recognition had been an unpopular move – increased financial support for expellee associations (Koschyk 2004: 140). This enabled expellees to raise public awareness through events and conferences. Thirdly, the policies of ethnic cleansing and persecution in the former Yugoslavia and in the Kosovo conflict led to a re-evaluation of the German experience. Many left-wing opinion leaders, including Günter Grass, admitted to having long 'overlooked' the suffering of millions of German expellees (Jach 2000; Frevert 2003).

The most controversial issue was the plan by the German Association of Expellees (Bund der Vertriebenen, BdV) to establish an exhibition centre, the 'Center against Expulsion', to depict the plight of Germans forced to leave their homeland at the end of the war. In Poland, politicians as well as the public expressed concern about the project, especially as BdV president Erika Steinbach was well-known for her controversial and hostile statements about Poland. They feared the centre would resort to a revisionist interpretation of history, in which the expulsion was not properly contextualized and perpetrators were portrayed as victims. Polish observers warned the centre might become a major setback for the bilateral textbook commission, which had worked hard to balance historical interpretations. Polish media went as far as to dub the planned exhibition a 'Centre against Reconciliation' (Lutomski 2004: 449).

The dispute over the planned 'Centre against Expulsion' was indirectly related to the textbook work between Germany and Poland in at least three ways. First, Warsaw's resentment against Erika Steinbach revealed the widespread concern about German revisionism in Poland, despite decades of success in improving depictions and narratives through textbook talks. Secondly, a growing number of German decision-makers, including Angela Merkel, have argued in favour of making the expulsion issue a mandatory subject in school curricula (Merkel 2005). At least four German states, Baden-Württemberg, Bavaria, Lower Saxony, and Northrhine-Westphalia, have added the issue as a compulsory topic in history classes (Strobel and Maier 2008: 7; Niedersächsisches Ministerium für Inneres Sport und Integration 2008). As coverage of the expulsion issue increases in history education, the continuation of joint research with Poland is indispensable to avert further frictions. Thirdly, the deterioration in German–Polish relations over the exhibition centre and other issues triggered two new initiatives in bilateral textbook work. Under the leadership of the state of Saxony, a small, regional project was started in 2005, followed by a more extensive project backed by the federal government in 2008.

Amid frictions in the German–Polish relationship, the state of Saxony sought to provide positive impetus in 2005 by supporting a bilateral group of historians in creating a joint supplementary textbook. A small project team was established under Kinga Hartmann of the Educational Agency of Saxony (Hartmann 2008). It was agreed that the book would serve as a complementary textbook and focus on the history of the German–Polish border region of Saxony and Lower Silesia (Niederschlesien). Saxony's Minister of Culture and Education Steffen Flath explained that his state hoped to 'arouse understanding and empathy among the students of the neighbouring regions ... for the experiences of the respective other side' (Schmidt and Flath 2008). The political leadership furthermore agreed to finance 25 per cent of the project costs, while the other 75 per cent would be covered by a special EU project fund (Hartmann 2008; Schmidt and Flath 2008). After two years of intensive work, the joint textbook called *Understanding History – Shaping the Future: German–Polish Relations in the Years 1933–1949* was thus published in 2007 in both languages (Hartmann 2008).

While Saxony's project was under way, German Foreign Minister Frank-Walter Steinmeier floated the idea for a similar initiative on the federal level in a speech in October 2006, pointing out that Germany and France had already succeeded in writing a joint textbook. He went on, 'Perhaps it is not impossible to also compile in the medium term a joint German–Polish history book that will help us understand each other better' (Steinmeier 2006). The project got under way with the inauguration of Prime Minister Donald Tusk in Poland and was officially kicked off in May 2008 with a project team supported by the

Georg-Eckert-Institute (Jasper 2008). The two countries agreed to finance the project on equal terms (Strobel 2008b: 27). According to Steinmeier, the goal is to create a textbook for high school students 'in which German guilt and German crimes are neither concealed nor relativized. But in which the suffering of the Germans who were displaced is also described' (Steinmeier 2008).

In December 2010, the project group presented politicians from Germany and Poland with a 140-page document providing recommendations and conceptual ideas on the development of the joint book (Steuerungsrat und Expertenrat des Projektes Deutsch-Polnisches Geschichtsbuch 2010). Subsequently, it issued a call for proposals by publishers interested in developing the joint textbook. Despite two bidding rounds in 2011, no publishing house could be found due to concerns about the financial risks involved. While the academic coordinator of the textbook team Krzysztof Ruchniewicz warned the project was in danger, director of the Georg-Eckert-Institute Simone Lässig was more optimistic, arguing that various publishers had shown interest (Deutschland Radio 2011; Götzke 2011). Lässig furthermore emphasized, 'we have the political support we need' (Götzke 2011).

Japanese politics on history textbook talks with South Korea

After the Second World War, history textbooks in Japan and South Korea reflected deep-seated mutual resentments. In Japan, textbooks revealed contempt and a lack of interest in Korean history (Chon 2007: 253). The Japanese government's stance regarding bilateral history textbook improvements with South Korea can be divided into four phases. During the first phase, covering the time period from after the Second World War until 1982, textbook depictions were discussed primarily in the domestic context. During the second phase, from 1982 to 1990, criticism about Japanese textbook narratives began to emerge from South Korea and China. While the Japanese government declared its intention to take into account regional views when authorizing textbooks, it did not consider the establishment of a bilateral history commission. The third phase, from 1990–2001 was marked by a growing willingness by Japanese politicians to confront the country's wartime responsibility squarely. However, initiatives to promote research on Japan's historical role in Asia were met by a backlash from conservative opinion leaders. During the fourth phase, since 2001, the Japanese government officially shifted towards a supportive stance on history textbooks with Korea. However, the joint historical research has been significantly hampered by controversial policies and statements by nationalist leaders in Japan.

1945–1982: domestic controversy and polarization of memory politics

During the first two decades after the Second World War, a polarization developed in Japan between views from the political left and right regarding the content of history textbooks, with decisive consequences for today's situation. While US occupation authorities at first emphasized reforming the educational system and increasing critical coverage of Japan's recent history of aggression, the Korean War of 1950–3 led to a 'reverse course' in policies. Consequently, the Japanese left wing was purged rather than the pre-war nationalists. After Japan regained sovereignty in 1952, conservative leaders used their political clout to ensure textbook screenings by the Ministry of Education (MoE) toned down accounts of wartime belligerence (Lee 2002). This policy reflected the growing political clout of conservative leaders, some of whom had served in government positions prior to 1945. Textbook authors, many belonging to the political left wing, protested the MoE's screenings (Kondo 2004). In particular, historian Ienaga Saburo filed a lawsuit in 1965, arguing that the government's authorization system violated the Constitution with its right for the freedom of expression.

Following the normalization of diplomatic relations between Japan and South Korea in the same year, the UNESCO headquarters in Paris proposed history textbook talks between the two countries as a means to complement the political process of reconciliation. Although Tokyo at first responded positively, talks were soon postponed with the Japanese side citing difficulties in choosing participants for textbook talks amid domestic controversy about the Ienaga lawsuit (Chung 2006: 23; Sakai 2002: 5). Many Japanese historians from the political left, agreeing with Ienaga about the unconstitutional nature of the MoE's textbook authorization, were suspicious of government involvement in the proposed project. For Japan's conservative-nationalist opinion leaders, the Ienaga lawsuit provided a welcome pretext for abandoning the bilateral project with South Korea.

Ienaga's lawsuit turned into a protracted legal battle, continuing until 1997.[7] Victories for Ienaga in lower courts in the 1970s and a consequent relaxation of MoE screening procedures triggered a backlash among right-wing conservative political leaders in the LDP, who maintained that Japanese textbooks lacked patriotism (Ide *et al.* 2010: 181; Nagahara 1983: 74). At the same time, the idea of holding bilateral textbook talks was not taken up by either Seoul or Tokyo. While South Korean leaders were focused on securing economic assistance, many decision-makers in Japan opposed textbook talks with other countries. As the newspaper *Asahi Shinbun* observed, there was a widespread belief among LDP politicians that 'the content of textbooks should be decided independently by each country' (*Asahi Shinbun* 1987).

Tokyo's leadership did not shy away from demanding changes in foreign textbooks, however. In 1958, the Ministry of Foreign Affairs established a non-profit organization, called International Society for Educational Information (ISEI; Kokusai Kyōiku Jōhō Sentā), to which it provided annual budgetary support. ISEI's primary aim was to 'rectify incorrect accounts by pointing out mistaken descriptions with regard to Japan and providing related documents and pictures' (Gaimusho 2000: 357). The organization initially focused on one-sided depictions about Japan as a country of 'Samurai' and 'Geisha'. Reportedly, ISEI later also submitted requests targeting 'anti-Japanese' descriptions in foreign history textbooks (*Chosun Ilbo* 2001; Kondo 2008a).[8]

1982–1990: international friction over textbooks

The first major international dispute about the content of Japanese history textbooks emerged in 1982 following an announcement of that year's textbook screening results (Satoh 1987: 247ff.). Media reports revealing the MoE had demanded authors erase or moderate descriptions of Japanese wartime atrocities triggered a storm of protests and outrage among South Korean and Chinese leaders. Tokyo was divided on how to respond. While the Foreign Ministry was willing to make concessions to avoid further friction, others, including many bureaucrats in the MoE, viewed international protests as interference in domestic affairs (Seddon 1987: 216). According to Satoh Komei, in charge of textbook authorization at the time, MoE officials furthermore believed that protests would eventually subside and therefore 'did not behave proactively' (*sekkyokuteki ni ugokou to wa shinakatta to iu*) on the issue (Satoh 1987: 275).

In autumn 1982, the MoE finally announced the so-called 'Neighbourhood Clause' (Kinrin shokoku jōkō) as a new criterion in its screening process, according to which Japan would exercise 'necessary care, in the interest of international friendship and cooperation' in the treatment of recent history (Satoh 1987: 281–2). The Japanese government never specified how it would judge whether textbook content was appropriate, however. The option of holding government-backed consultations with neighbours on this question was not discussed in Tokyo. Nevertheless, textbook descriptions of Japanese wartime belligerence and militarism generally increased after 1982. The introduction of the 'Neighbourhood Clause' thus did have an impact on textbooks, despite reluctance within the MoE to enforce the new authorization policy (Nozaki 2002: 608; Kondo 2004, 2001: 51; Chon 2007: 253). Among conservative-nationalist opinion leaders and politicians, the new policy caused indignation, however (Togo 2008c). Many, including Satoh Komei, contended that the entire dispute was based on a 'case of mistaken reporting' (*gohō jiken*) (Satoh 1987: 283).[9]

Frustrated about Japan's official policy, a major right-wing organization, the Citizen's Conference to Protect Japan (Nihon o mamoru Kokumin Kaigi), announced in autumn 1982 a plan to develop its own history textbook for high schools. In 1986, the MoE authorized the organization's textbook *Shinpen Nihonshi* (New Edition Japanese History) for use in schools. The approval met with protests from South Korea and China, where the book was seen as biased and whitewashing Japan's past. Within Japan, the book was also controversial (*Japan Economic Newswire* 1986). Seeking to prevent another major textbook dispute, the Japanese government quietly decided to request further changes in *Shinpen Nihonshi* after its official approval (Nozaki 2002: 610). This measure, combined with the low adoption rate of the book in schools, eased Korean and Chinese concerns.

1990–2001: contrition and conservative countermoves

In both Japan and South Korea, the end of the Cold War as well as the death of Showa Emperor Hirohito in January 1989 elicited new debates about historical memory and war responsibility. Tokyo's stance in the 1990s was characterized by a growing willingness to confront wartime responsibility. Especially after the monopoly of the LDP on government control was broken in 1993, political leaders offered various apologies to neighbouring countries. Prime Minister Hosokawa Morihito stated in August 1993 that Japan's military actions in the 1930s and 1940s amounted to 'an aggressive war and a wrong war' (Buruma 1994: 297). His successor, Prime Minister Murayama Tomiichi, also expressed remorse over Japan's imperial past on the fiftieth anniversary of the war's end (Wittig 2002: 42).

The willingness to deal with Japan's past was also reflected in Tokyo's textbook policies. References to the so-called 'comfort women' – women assembled against their will and forced into prostitution – were included in all high school books approved in 1994, and in all middle school books approved in 1997 (Richter 2003: 1–2). Textbook passages describing other wartime atrocities also increased (Togo 2008c). Moreover, Tokyo helped to launch two important initiatives promoting research on Japan's past role in Asia. One project involved the establishment of a historical document centre, the other focused on the promotion of academic exchanges between Japanese and South Korean historians. Neither initiative was directly concerned with the contents of history textbooks, but both constituted important elements in Japan's policy of remembrance.

The first project, the establishment of a document centre, was based on an idea by Murayama Tomiichi, Japan's first socialist prime minister. As part of his August 1994 Peace, Friendship and Exchange Initiative, Murayama proposed an Asian Historical Document Centre (Ajia Rekishi Shiryō Sentā) to support 'historical research, including the collection and cataloging of historical documents' (Murayama 1994). A government-appointed committee of experts enthusiastically endorsed the proposal in June 1995, recommending the inclusion of records that had thus far not been accessible to the public in government libraries and reference centres (Mizuno 2005: 119). However, as not everyone in Tokyo supported the proposal, foot-dragging among bureaucrats and politicians continued to delay the project (Fujisawa 2003: 43). Finally, the centre was established as part of the National Archives of Japan in 2001, following a Cabinet decision two years earlier. Contrary to the 1995 recommendation of the expert committee, the government did not approve the publication of documents that had been publicly unavailable, however (Mizuno 2005: 119). Some observers criticized this publication policy as overly reticent (ibid.). On the other hand, the Asian Historical Document Centre – with its 28 million historical records – now doubtless facilitates research about Japan's role in the region (Ajia Rekishi Shiryō Sentā 2001).

The second project, promoting cultural and intellectual exchanges with South Korea, was also triggered by Murayama's Peace, Friendship and Exchange Initiative. Following Murayama's proposal, the Japanese Ministry of Foreign Affairs helped to set up the Japan–Korea Joint Research Forum (Nikkan kyōdō kenkyū fōramu) in April 1995. The Forum was established as part of the Japan–Korea Foundation for Cultural Exchange (Nikkan bunka kōryū kikin), an independent, government-backed organization set up by Tokyo and Seoul in 1983 with the aim of increasing mutual understanding and trust. The joint research, which took place between 1996 and 2004, generated a total of 21 books, published in the Japan–Korea Joint Research Series (Nikkan kyōdō kenkyū sōsho). While the most controversial points in Japan–South Korea relations were not covered in the research, the publications include notable contributions on bilateral history (Okonogi 2008). However, public awareness of the research is low in Japan, both because the book series clearly targets an academic audience and because the government has not promoted it (Okonogi 2008).

While these two projects were under way, Murayama's efforts to demonstrate Japanese contrition caused indignation among right-leaning politicians. Controversial remarks by nationalist decision-makers on historical issues plagued relations with Asian countries. For example, in August 1995, Education Minister Shimamura Yoshinobu maintained that 'it is a matter of perspective whether or not' Japan had waged a war of invasion (Arai and Iga Toshiya 2001: 194; Tanaka 2007: 173). Three months later, Eto Takami, director general of the Management and Coordination Agency, commented that 'Japan also did some good' (*yoi koto mo shita*) during its 1910–45 occupation of Korea, including the construction of schools, railroads and ports (Chung 2006: 40; Kawano and Matsuo 2002: 216).

In response to the series of controversial remarks and verbal missteps, South Korean Foreign Minister Gong Ro-Myeong in November 1995 voiced the idea of Tokyo and Seoul supporting joint research between both countries' historians in order to narrow the gaps in historical understanding. While Gong refrained from touching upon the issue of textbooks directly, he insisted, 'It is desirable for the results [of this research] to be reflected in government [policy]' (Chung 2006: 40). Although Japan initially signalled consent, the creation of a joint research panel was delayed due to diverging opinions of Tokyo and Seoul about the content of research (*Yomiuri Shinbun* 1997). While Seoul clarified that it sought a semi-official commission with the potential to produce binding recommendations for the two governments and their textbooks, officials in Tokyo insisted that the panel be purely private (*Korea Times* 2000). According to media reports, the Japanese government feared 'frictions [would] arise about both governments' official stance regarding past treaties' if the talks were government-backed (Chung 2006: 44).

After prolonged debates between Japan and Korea, the panel was inaugurated in July 1997 as a private body and called the Japan–Korea Joint Committee for the Promotion of Historical Research (Nikkan rekishi kenkyū sokushin ni kan suru kyōdō iinkai). At Tokyo's insistence, the two governments agreed that the commission would 'neither conduct joint research on history nor strive towards a common historical perception of the two countries' (Chung 2006: 45). Rather, the purpose was to examine possibilities for joint history research and make recommendations to the two governments accordingly. Many observers accused Tokyo of 'buying time' with this arrangement, as the government continued to skirt controversial discussions on historical perceptions with South Korea (Kondo 2001: 50). The committee's final report, published in May 2000, urged the two governments to begin joint research and cooperation on the development of history teaching materials (Okonogi 2008).

However, filled with optimism about improved relations under the leadership of Korean President Kim Dae-Jung, Japanese political elites failed to translate the panel's proposal into action. The 1998 joint declaration stating both countries' intention to 'overcome their unfortunate history and to build a future-oriented relationship' was erroneously interpreted in Tokyo as a Korean pledge not to dwell on history issues anymore (Togo 2005: 460; 2008c).

In 1997, Japan had already refused another offer by South Korea for government-led textbook talks. In turning down the proposal by the Korean UNESCO commission, ministry officials in charge of textbook authorization explained that studies of this kind 'should be conducted by non-governmental researchers' and do 'not suit government involvement' (*Mainichi Shinbun* 1997). Officials also contended they could not enforce recommendations emerging from such talks, because the Japanese textbook screening system only permitted factual corrections (Kondo 2001: 50).

Right-wing opinion leaders in Tokyo nevertheless voiced frustration about official apologies and apparent 'concessions' to neighbouring countries. They were particularly dismayed about the increasing references to 'military comfort women' in textbooks in the mid-1990s. An influential right-wing group, the Japanese Society for History Textbook Reform (Atarashii rekishi kyōkasho o tsukurukai; abbreviated Tsukurukai) was established in December 1996, with the objective of working towards a more positive view of Japanese history in textbooks. Conservative politicians also voiced disapproval regarding the government's education policy. For example, in June 1998 Minister of Education Machimura Nobutaka described before the Diet his impression that 'many history textbooks ... write too much about the negative aspects' of the country's past (*Kokuritsu Kokkai Toshokan,* 8 June 1998). Furthermore, a group of over 100 LDP lawmakers lent behind-the-scenes support and financial backing to the Japanese Society for History Textbook Reform (McNeill 2005).

Efforts by conservative politicians to establish a more 'positive' view on Japanese modern history in textbooks made some headway when the MoE approached publishers with an unofficial appeal in January 1999, asking them to 'take more balance' in middle school textbooks (Arai and Iga Toshiya 2001: 184; Nozaki 2002: 616). Reportedly, the Prime Minister's Cabinet Secretariat further increased pressure by placing phone calls to all publishers and asking for restraint in descriptions of 'comfort women' (Chung 2006: 77). The apparent consequence was that middle school textbooks passing the 2001 screening process markedly reduced passages treating Japanese war atrocities, including the comfort women issue. While all seven middle school textbooks authorized in 1997 had made references to forced wartime prostitution, three of the seven editions in 2001 had removed all such references (Nozaki 2002: 616; Chon 2007: 253).

2001–2011: talks on history and textbooks amid growing tensions

Tokyo's stance regarding government-backed talks shifted amid a fierce dispute about Japanese history textbooks following the announcement of the MoE's screening results in April 2001. The authorized middle school books included one issued by the controversial Society for History Textbook Reform. The Korean government reacted with outrage, arguing the book embellished Japan's past and asking Tokyo to revise 35 items in textbook descriptions (Lee 2002: 15). However, officials in Tokyo rejected Seoul's demands, explaining there were 'no factual mistakes' in the narratives on modern history and that the MoE had screened all approved textbooks with full consideration of the Neighbourhood Clause (Arai and Iga Toshiya 2001: 187; Machimura 2001). Citing the constitutional right to the freedom of expression, they declared that the government would not interfere in the textbook authorization process for diplomatic reasons. As Foreign Minister Machimura Nobutaka explained, 'the judgment whether a historical perception of an author is right or wrong would violate the Constitution's provision protecting the freedom of thought and conscience', and therefore Japan does not conduct its textbook authorization 'from the standpoint of deciding on a particular historical perception' (Machimura 2001). This line of reasoning was, however, inconsistent with the pledge to consider the Neighbourhood Clause in textbook screenings – a commitment concerned not only with factual errors, but also with the contextualization and interpretation of the past. Since Tokyo had evidently failed to meet the expectations of regional countries in 2001, Kondo Takahiro went so far as to declare the Neighbourhood Clause 'de facto meaningless' (Kondo 2004).

After the Japanese government rejected demands for textbook revisions, Koreans shifted their attention to the adoption rate of the controversial textbook in schools. The Society for History Textbook Reform had set a target adoption rate of 10 per cent. However, in the summer of 2001, it became clear that only about 0.04 per cent of junior high schools had opted for the textbook, causing the issue to lose some of its significance in bilateral relations (Fuhrt 2005: 53).[10]

In October 2001, Tokyo's attitude towards government-backed talks on controversial historical issues changed unexpectedly. On 15 October, Prime Minister Koizumi paid a visit to Seoul – his first since coming to office in April – in an attempt to heal the rift in relations caused by the dispute about the Tsukurukai textbook and his visits to the controversial Yasukuni Shrine, where a number of convicted Japanese war criminals are commemorated. In his meeting with Korean President Kim Dae-Jung, Koizumi proposed founding a joint research committee on bilateral history (Chung 2001: 115). Although Koizumi did not mention talks on textbooks specifically, the initiative was clearly linked, given the recent disputes about historical perceptions. The sudden reversal of Tokyo's policy of rejecting government-backed talks seems to have been driven by at least three factors. First, due to Washington's focus on the Middle East after the 11 September 2001 terrorist attacks on the US, Tokyo and Seoul felt the need for better mutual cooperation amid ongoing tensions with North Korea. Secondly, leaders in both countries knew that improved relations were necessary for a successful joint hosting of the Soccer World Cup in 2002. Thirdly, the Japanese government apparently recognized the dispute over historical perceptions had grown more serious than ever with the authorization of the Tsukurukai book and that a diplomatic response was required (Kondo 2008b).

The jointly established committee, called the Japan–Korea Committee for Joint History Research (Nikkan Rekishi Kyōdō Kenkyū Iinkai), met between 2002 and 2005. The committee was set up in the Japan–Korea Cultural Foundation (Nikkan bunka kōryū kikin), an autonomous institution focused on the promotion of cultural and academic exchanges between the two countries. As both Tokyo and Seoul supply funds, the institution may be classified as a parapublic institution, as defined above. The selection of Japanese committee members was led by Tokyo University Professors Mitani Taichiro and Kitaoka Shinichi and Keio University Professor Okonogi Masao, in cooperation with the Ministry of Foreign Affairs (Okonogi 2008). Mitani, who became the Japanese side's chair of the joint committee, emphasized the need to establish a scholarly arena not directly influenced by the government and sought to include experts from across the political spectrum (Okonogi 2008).

From the start of the joint project, Tokyo and Seoul disagreed about whether the expected research results would have an impact on the content of textbooks. Korean Foreign Minister Han Seung-Su maintained 'the research results should be reflected in textbook narratives' (*Chosun Ilbo* 2002). The Japanese side rejected such demands, but promised to 'take measures to make widely known (*shūchi tettei*) those research results that can be used in the compilation of textbooks' (Chung and Kimura 2008b: 126). Prime Minister Koizumi even went as far as to state that Japan would 'use or mention' (*katsuyō, heiki*) the results in textbooks (Kim 2002). As before, Tokyo explained its restrained stance by the need to protect the freedom of expression. Due to bilateral disagreements, the joint research committee thus met with the goal of identifying and discussing divergences in historical perceptions rather than developing recommendations for teaching materials.

The research committee's joint work was complicated by political and public pressure, however. One participant explained he and his colleagues felt compelled to act as 'national representatives' (*kuni no daihyōsha*), charged with defending the national interest (Member of the Japan–Korea Joint Research Commission on History 2007). Another Japanese researcher similarly described his impression of the committee: 'The atmosphere was very formal and ceremonious, because both sides were carrying the weight of their governments on their shoulders' (*Asahi Shinbun* 2007). At least three factors contributed to such perceptions about a lack of academic freedom.

First, frequent controversial remarks by Japanese cabinet members and high-level politicians cast doubts about the leadership's support for the project, sparking discontent and mutual mistrust among participants. For example, in November 2004, then Education Minister Nakayama Nariaki stated that he thought it was 'good that such terms as sex slaves of the Japanese Imperial Army and forced Asian labor [are] less frequently mentioned in [recently authorized] school history books' (*Asahi Shinbun* 2005a). Complaints about budget shortages on the Japanese side of the project reinforced suspicions among Korean participants about a lack of political backing (Kuroda 2006: 99).

Secondly, the choice of participants in the talks has been problematic. Each side criticized the other for not drawing a clear line between academics and politics, as some of the appointed researchers had strong ties to the political establishment. Korean participants speculated that former government advisers like Kitaoka Shinichi and Okonogi Masao might be susceptible to political pressure, calling into question their academic objectivity. On the Korean side, Yi Mun-Yol and Kang Chang-Il embarked on political careers, the latter resigning his post in the committee mid-way through the talks (Chung 2006: 129). In Japan and Korea, researchers' involvement in government activities was criticized as causing 'ambiguity' and jeopardizing the neutrality of the joint committee (Chung 2006: 52; Kuroda 2006: 99).

Thirdly, among the Japanese public there is considerable opposition to joint history talks with Korea. Kimura Kan, a first- and second-round participant, observed that approximately 85 per cent of emails he received from Japanese citizens expressed disapproval of his work, making it difficult for him and his colleagues to sustain motivation (Kimura 2007). This strong opposition is at least partially rooted in common misunderstandings about the goals of such research projects, reflected in Japanese media reports. The respected journal *Nihon no Ronten,* for example, published an article in 2006 arguing that joint talks could never result in a shared historical interpretation. The article describes the German–Polish recommendations as little more than a 'data-book of historical facts' – an assessment which demonstrates the author's lack of knowledge about the joint endeavour (Matsumoto 2006: 257). Even Kitaoka Shinichi, participant in the joint research project with South Korea, seems to harbour similar doubts. In his 2007 book, he insisted that a common textbook could not be created with other countries and that it was only possible to 'confirm the facts' (Kitaoka 2007: 224).

In June 2005, the Japan–Korea Committee for Joint History Research published its final report comprising more than 1,000 pages, covering bilateral history from ancient times to the modern era. Rather than furnishing a common interpretation of the past, the report presents each side's viewpoints on particular historical events (Nikkan Rekishi Kyōdō Kenkyu Iinkai 2005). In Japan, opinions were divided on whether the report was a success or failure. While critics argued that the committee had achieved little more than making explicit the differences in historical perceptions, others maintained the project's goal had been precisely to determine where divergences existed (Kang 2006: 254; Okonogi 2008). The report's effect on the broader public seems to have been minimal, however. Having received only limited publicity, it is not well known in Japan. Although it is accessible on the internet, the report is not available for purchase in bookstores, which means anyone interested has to print the lengthy document (Chung 2008). Furthermore, average citizens and even history teachers will find it difficult to read the report, given its size and technical content (Kondo 2008b).

Just as the joint committee published its final report in June 2005, criticism regarding Japanese textbooks and historical consciousness resurfaced in Korea. The April 2005 authorization of the second edition of the controversial, nationalistic history book by the Society for History Textbook Reform infuriated the Korean public (Richter 2005: 97). Again, the Japanese government refused to make revisions to the book, emphasizing the need to protect freedom of expression (Chiba 2005). Tensions in bilateral relations concurrently rose over an unresolved territorial dispute concerning the South Korean-controlled island of Takeshima.

In an attempt to mend relations, the Japanese and Korean heads of state agreed in June 2005 to establish a second panel of researchers. This time, Koizumi agreed to a subcommittee covering the issue of history textbooks (Chon 2007: 260). It was the first time that Japan showed itself willing to establish a government-backed joint committee to deal with textbooks. However, Japanese policy-makers disagreed whether joint research results should be considered in textbook screenings in the future. While some politicians supported such a step, other officials, especially from the MoE, argued this was not possible given the need to respect freedom of thought (*Mainichi Shinbun* 2005; *Kyodo News* 2007).

After a delay the second research committee was finally launched in June 2007, following extensive debates about the selection of Japanese participants. Given the plan to treat textbook issues, many first-round participants feared that this project would be even more politicized than the previous attempt and thus refused to take part. Prime Minister Abe Shinzo and Foreign Minister Aso Taro, both well known for their right-wing positions, indeed sought to exercise influence by insisting on the inclusion of certain historians, resulting in a commission with markedly more nationalistic viewpoints (Member of the Japan–Korea Joint Research Commission on History 2007). One participant argued that the Abe administration was mainly interested in 'assertive diplomacy' (*shuchō gaikō*), rather than in a true exchange of opinions to reach mutual understanding (Okonogi 2008).

While the second round of talks was in progress, four issues triggered new debates about the Japanese government's historical consciousness and educational policies. First, in 2006 Tokyo passed a revised version of the country's Basic Law on Education (Kyōiku kihonhō), containing a controversial passage requiring schools to instil national pride in students (Sakata 2007: 93). The revision heightened concern domestically and internationally that textbooks might increasingly play down Japanese atrocities in their pursuit of patriotism. Second, doubts about the government's policies intensified when it was revealed that the MoE had ordered publishers in 2007 to tone down descriptions on the military's involvement in mass suicides by Okinawans during the Battle of Okinawa in 1945 (*Japan Times* 2007).[11] Third, the authorization by the MoE of the new textbook edition by the Japanese Society for History Textbook Reform in April 2009 met with protest from Seoul (*Sankei Shinbun* 2009).[12] Finally, Koreans were also infuriated by the March 2010 revelation that all five social studies textbooks for elementary schools to be used from 2011 clearly identified the Seoul-controlled islet of Takeshima as Japanese territory (Brown 2010). Reportedly, the MoE had demanded that publishers draw a national border line between South Korea and the islets (Kang and Lee 2010: 113).[13]

The second-round Japan–Korea Committee for Joint History Research released its report on 23 March 2010, after nearly three years of discussion. Like the first report, the new publication (more than 2,000 pages long) covered bilateral history from ancient to modern times, with each side presenting its viewpoints in separate chapters (Nikkan Rekishi Kyōdō Kenkyu Iinkai 2010). Of particular interest was the school textbooks subgroup, charged with examining the two countries' history textbooks. The subgroup's report comprises almost 500 pages and deals with issues such as the evolution of the bilateral textbook dispute, the textbook authorization systems and the depiction of Japan's colonization of Korea in textbooks of both countries (Nikkan Rekishi Kyōdō Kenkyu Iinkai 2010). Participants were clearly able to further deepen their understanding of each other's viewpoints, highlighting many points of contention. However, they failed to provide any joint guidance to Japanese and Korean textbook publishers and authors on how to depict bilateral history. Perhaps due to this lack of suggestions, Japanese politicians did not publicly address the implications for textbook contents. *Asahi Shinbun* concluded that the report 'once again illustrated the difficulty of understanding each other's historical consciousness' (2010). *Tokyo Shinbun* similarly observed there were many gaps in how the countries viewed their history, although it 'evaluate[d] highly that differences in opinion are not concealed in the report' (2010).

The DPJ-led government under Hatoyama generated some optimism with a proposal from Foreign Minister Okada Katsuya on 7 October 2009. Speaking at the Foreign Correspondents' Club of Japan, Okada said it would be 'ideal' if South Korea, China and Japan published a common history textbook to clear up controversies over the interpretation of historical events, although he warned that such a project would take considerable time (Yoo 2009). It was the first time a Japanese government representative had officially raised the possibility of a shared textbook with Korea and China. Following the publication of the second report by the Japan–Korea Committee for Joint History Research, Okada reiterated his hopes for a common textbook with Korea, stating in July 2010, 'Although this is a thing of the future, it would be ideal (*risōteki*) for Korea and Japan to jointly compile a history textbook' (*JoongAng Ilbo* 2010).

Nevertheless, it remains an open question whether Japan and Korea can successfully establish a government-backed commission to compile a common textbook. Participants of the two rounds of government-backed talks so far are sceptical, with a Japanese participant maintaining 'we've reached the limit of joint research' (Brown 2010). Another participant similarly cautioned: 'the attitudes [among Japanese and Koreans] towards history research are too different' (*Tokyo Shinbun* 2010). Many Koreans were furthermore infuriated by the April 2011 revelation that all seven Japanese civics textbooks authorized for use in middle schools from 2012 describe the disputed islets of Takeshima as Japanese territory. Three of the texts maintained that the islets were 'unlawfully occupied' by South Korea (Hanano 2011). The Korean newspaper *Hankyoreh* also noted that some of the screened history textbooks still claim that Japan ruled southern Korea from the fourth to sixth centuries, a theory revealed to be false by the second-round Japan–Korea Committee for Joint History Research (Choi 2011).

Explaining German and Japanese policies

Characteristics and analysis

The case study reveals significant differences in German and Japanese behaviour regarding textbook disputes with Poland and South Korea, respectively. While Berlin's policy-makers generally played an active support role in textbook talks, Tokyo's lawmakers have been markedly more hesitant or even opposed to such an undertaking. To characterize and compare each country's approach in detail, it is useful to consider *four stages* in textbook talks: the initiation, conference, implementation and follow-up phases.[14] In the *initiation stage*, the period leading up to the start of talks, German policy-makers played a key role in launching the bilateral textbook commission with Poland. They overcame domestic resistance by publicly endorsing the talks and thereby giving legitimacy to the project. Japanese policy-makers, on the other hand, repeatedly rejected offers to begin government-backed joint work on schoolbooks with South Korea.

In the *conference phase*, the period during which government-backed bilateral textbook talks are held, German and Japanese behaviour also differed considerably. Relying on a number of tactics, German politicians were able to establish a beneficial balance between providing political backing while simultaneously shielding the joint commission from overwhelming nationalistic pressure, especially during the initial set of conferences in the 1970s. In contrast, researchers in the Japanese–Korean talks since 2002 have complained about overt interference by government leaders, for example in the choice of commission participants.

The institutional choices made by German political elites contributed to a more favourable balance between political support and non-interference. The UNESCO framework was one means by which German and Polish politicians were able to support the commission's work, but Japanese decision-makers have explicitly rejected the UNESCO model. Furthermore, while both Germany and Japan relied on parapublic institutions to provide institutional support for the joint talks, the nature of the two institutions is somewhat different. The Georg-Eckert-Institute (GEI) is charged specifically with the task of holding international textbook talks and making recommendations to enhance objectivity in German education and textbooks. The Japan–Korea Cultural Foundation, on the other hand, focuses on the promotion of cultural and academic exchanges between Japan and Korea, and thus – as an institution – does not hold a mandate to make recommendations for textbook improvements. Furthermore, with its focus on cultural exchange, the Foundation seems unlikely to develop the extensive expertise, experience and reputation in textbook talks of the GEI.

The *implementation phase* covers the period in which politicians undertake efforts to reform history education and modify textbooks based on the results from bilateral talks. Many high-level German politicians encouraged consideration of the commission's work in history teaching, for example by appealing to individual state leaders and by distributing copies of the recommendations to schools. Japanese policy-makers, on the other hand, have shown more reluctance in initiating changes. Although the first- and second-round joint research reports are available for download on the internet, there have been no initiatives by Tokyo to raise public awareness and inform history teachers. Moreover, Japanese officials seem disinclined to promote changes in textbooks. Many argue the MoE cannot make corrections to the historical perceptions and interpretations expressed in textbooks. However, this stance is contradictory to Japan's pledge since 1982 to take into account the feelings of its neighbours in the authorization process of textbooks, which suggests that historical perceptions are considered. This policy ambiguity casts doubt on the Japanese willingness to make changes in textbooks or to compile a joint textbook, as suggested by Foreign Minister Okada.

The final stage in textbook talks, the *follow-up phase,* involves new joint projects in the context of history education, after major changes in textbooks have already been implemented. Only German–Polish talks have reached this stage. Berlin's policy-makers have continued to back cooperation with Poland actively since 1990, helping to launch one regional and two federal initiatives in the area of textbooks. Progress on joint teaching materials during the follow-up phase was overshadowed, however, by renewed tensions over the commemoration of the expulsion issue.

Overall, the analysis reveals radically different attitudes towards textbook talks in Germany and Japan. According to Kondo Takahiro, Japan has taken a 'posture diametrically opposed' (*seihantai no shisei*) to that of Germany when it comes to dealing with history disputes (Kondo 1993: 3). While politicians in Berlin consistently and actively encourage and support textbook talks, their counterparts in Tokyo seem to lack the political will to hold such talks. Moreover, bilateral reconciliation initiatives with Korea have been spoiled and disrupted by nationalist backlashes in Japan. Lawmakers from Germany and Japan furthermore differ in their expectations for joint textbook commissions. Political elites in the Federal Republic consistently saw bilateral talks as a means to overcome nationalism. In Japan by contrast, many decision-makers are sceptical about the fundamental goal of a transnational reconstruction of the past. Instead, they believe history disputes can only be 'managed' by letting both sides vent their anger and 'agreeing to disagree'.

The picture is more complex than that of 'a good Germany and a bad Japan', however. In the Federal Republic's case, the question of how to commemorate the plight of German expellees from Eastern territories has led to growing frictions with Poland since the end of the Cold War. On the other hand, there has been some progress in Japan's case, with textbooks nowadays depicting Japanese wartime atrocities in greater detail than those of the late 1970s. As Kathleen Woods Masalski observes, Japan's books offer 'a far more self-critical narrative' now, including issues like the Nanjing massacre and Korean anti-Japanese resistance (Masalski 2000: 284). In addition, only very few Japanese schools have chosen to use the controversial textbook by the Society for History Textbook Reform.

A striking characteristic in Japan's policy is that reconciliation efforts have been offset in part by domestic backlashes, eliciting suspicions among neighbouring countries. Park Soon-Won for example maintained Japan has played a 'double game' regarding textbook talks with South Korea. He observed that, while Tokyo had agreed to set up a bilateral commission, it still authorized right-wing textbooks (Park 2008). In Germany, reforms in textbooks also elicited countermoves by conservative opinion leaders, as seen during the historians' dispute of the 1980s. However, these conservatives never received a critical level of backing and did not have a detectable effect on education policies. On the whole, German conservative backlashes were more confined in scope and often had the effect of strengthening the Federal Republic's culture of contrition.

The explanatory power of role conceptions

Germany's supportive stance on textbook talks can be explained by examining the country's role conceptions. Politicians in the Federal Republic are 'determined *never again* to allow militarism and nationalism to threaten European stability' and peace (Maull 2004: 89; emphasis added). The associated role conception 'contributor to regional cooperation' helps to account for German acceptance of foreign participation in crafting a new narrative of the country's past. After 1945, policy-makers in the Federal Republic embraced a new vision of an integrated region comprising equal and tamed states. Their fundamental objective was to overcome narrow-minded nationalist thinking, which had given rise to disastrous wars in the past. Decision-makers were thus prepared to promote an international narrative of the past in textbooks with various viewpoints rather than presenting a linear national perspective. The Federal Republic's faith in international organizations, reflected in its role set, also explains Bonn's decision to conduct joint textbook talks under the auspices of the UNESCO.

Secondly, the general receptiveness to the idea of holding bilateral talks with Poland can be understood in light of the role conception 'regional stabilizer'. Policy-makers display enthusiasm for advancing multilateral consultations, bargaining and compromise, seeking to ensure compatibility between national interests and viewpoints among neighbours. This role conception gained particular relevance in the 1970s, as the government under Chancellor Brandt's leadership stepped up efforts to establish cooperative relations with communist countries. Textbook talks with Poland were seen as a means to reduce tensions and encourage bilateral exchange. It should be kept in mind, however, that Brandt's policies towards Eastern Europe met with considerable scepticism among conservatives in the initial years. Thus, the Chancellor's visionary and determined leadership was a key factor in establishing reconciliation as a 'high profile component of [Germany's] relations with [central-east Europe]' (Phillips 1998: 65).

Erika Steinbach's possible role in the planned establishment of the 'Centre against Expulsion' caused considerable irritation in Poland. In view of the above-mentioned role conceptions, it seems puzzling that German politicians did not act more decisively by quickly rejecting Steinbach's nomination to the project's council. The analysis suggests two reasons, which are not directly linked to Germany's role set. First and most importantly, expellees and their organizations enjoy strong and well-established ties especially to the CSU, sister party of the CDU (of which Steinbach is a member), providing them with considerable political clout (Phillips 1998: 78). Secondly, a growing number of politicians and opinion leaders sympathize with the expellees' demands for remembering their fate, after debates on this issue were often suppressed during the Cold War.

Explaining Japan's behaviour regarding history textbook disputes with South Korea is more complex. The general reluctance and rightist-nationalists' outright opposition to textbook projects are at odds with the role conceptions of 'contributor to regional cooperation' and 'reliable partner'. According to the former role conception, Japan seeks to play a constructive and supportive role in bi- and multilateral cooperation, although not with the same focus on overcoming nationalism as Germany. The role conception would thus suggest that Japan would make a more determined effort to resolve history-related disagreements – for example by holding textbook talks – in order to ensure other regional projects are not negatively affected.

Similarly, the role conception 'reliable partner' would suggest a more cooperative and forthcoming attitude in solving history-related quarrels with South Korea. According to this conception, Japanese policy-makers seek to support the US in providing military deterrence in the region. Cooperation between Japan and Korea can significantly bolster the credibility of US deterrence, because the bilateral relation comprises the 'third leg' of the US alliance system in Northeast Asia (Cha 1999). The role conception of 'reliable partner' would thus imply active steps by Japan to resolve history-related disputes in order to guarantee a functioning alliance system. A closer examination reveals this role conception indeed has some impact on Tokyo's behaviour. Particularly at times when the security situation in East Asia was tense – for example, when North Korea made a show of force by launching missiles – Japanese policy-makers exhibited a more forthcoming stance in dealing with history-related issues. Thereby, they responded to alter-part expectations by the US to strengthen ties with Seoul. However, the prevalent reluctance to hold history textbook talks demonstrates that alter-part expectations have not been internalized by Tokyo's lawmakers. Rather, such expectations have been taken into account only through temporary adjustments.

Why has Japan's policy not been in line with the two role conceptions of 'contributor to regional cooperation' and 'reliable partner'? Japanese lawmakers have repeatedly rejected government-backed textbook talks by referring to their country's role as 'promoter of universal values', defending democracy and human rights. They argue Japan must protect freedom of speech by refraining from imposing particular interpretations of the past. However, Japan's stance is unconvincing and seems cynical. Since Tokyo has influenced historical interpretations and depictions in textbooks through its screening process in numerous cases, the focus on freedom of speech seems to be no more than an excuse to avoid textbook talks.

A more convincing explanation for Japan's stance is the nationalistic tendency among the political elite. As seen in the analysis, many decision-makers resent foreign criticism of Tokyo's treatment of its past – an aspect observed in the role conception 'respected and trusted country'. Politicians seek to move beyond the humiliating memory of war and set Japan on equal footing with other countries. Frustration about persistent foreign criticism of Japanese textbooks has resulted in a tendency towards self-assertion and defiance. Textbook talks are seen as counterproductive to the goal of establishing Japan as a 'respected and trusted country', as they call new attention to past mistakes and aggressive policies.

A *distinction* must be made between far-right nationalist politicians and more moderate leaders, however. A *minority of vocal far-right* opinion leaders seem to hold a role conception based on narrow-minded historical revisionism emphasizing Japan's superiority and uniqueness. They deny mistakes in Japan's wartime foreign policy conduct, focusing rather on the alleged positive impact of Japanese rule in Asia. Right-wing nationalists furthermore reject the condemnation of Japan's past as 'victor's justice'. The *majority of more moderate decision-makers*, however, do not deny Japanese atrocities and war crimes (Togo 2008a, 2008b). Why have these politicians not provided stronger backing for textbook talks?

The analysis suggests a number of reasons. First, supporters of reconciliation with Korea are aware that initiatives like textbook talks tend to trigger backlashes among nationalists, due to the sharp division in opinion about war responsibility among Japan's political elite. Thus, they have rather focused on the promotion of academic and cultural exchanges – activities that are relatively uncontroversial in Japan. To avoid prompting a backlash, they moreover avoid explicitly declaring that research activities have the goal of 'reconciliation' (*wakai*), preferring instead a 'gentle' (*yurui*) approach (Okonogi 2008). In other words, lawmakers realize that policies of atonement may be diplomatically counterproductive if they prove to be domestically polarizing (Lind 2008).

In this context, it is furthermore important to recognize that the struggle between the rightist-nationalist and moderate forces in Japan extends beyond the mere issue of history education. The battle is closely connected to debates about Japanese national identity and the founding principles of post-1945 Japan, embodied for instance in the Peace Constitution. The evaluation of Japan's past raises questions about what should be learned from historical experiences and what kind of country Japan should strive to be. Many rightist-nationalists seek to free Japan from the constraints of its past, which in their eyes causes Tokyo to act with undue subservience and submissiveness vis-à-vis regional neighbours and the US. By presenting the country's history in a more 'positive' light, they hope to raise national self-esteem and encourage Japan to exercise full self-determination in its policies without constantly paying heed to other countries' viewpoints. The battle over history education and textbooks is thus tied to far-reaching questions about Japan's future foreign policy course, explaining why it is fought with such immense passion and vigour.

Secondly, moderate politicians are concerned about the potential personal consequences if they enthusiastically endorse textbook talks. Especially those lawmakers in the 'catch-all' party LDP fear damage to their career. Broad support from different LDP factions is crucial for being chosen as a party leader and to be made prime minister. By standing up for textbook talks, a politician is likely to stir opposition among rightist-nationalist party members and thereby lower his own chances of advancing within the party hierarchy. Furthermore, politicians also fear 'losing the most passionately nationalist segments of their constituency' by staking out critical positions on Japan's wartime role and calling for textbook talks (Hein and Selden 2000: 25).

Thirdly, as discussed above, many decision-makers doubt whether textbook talks can accomplish more than an 'agreement to disagree'. There are at least two reasons for this sceptical attitude. Japanese domestic polarization is seen as an obstacle to talks, complicating both the selection of participants for a joint project and the process of reaching agreements even among the Japanese researchers themselves. Furthermore, many Japanese worry that the history issue may be used for political purposes, especially by China. Such fears are not completely unfounded: when Prime Minister Murayama offered a series of apologies and proposed various reconciliation initiatives in 1995, for example, Beijing reacted with a major exhibition at Chinese middle schools on Japanese war atrocities in Nanjing. This raised doubts among Japanese politicians on whether China is really interested in a joint reflection on the past (Togo 2008c).

Overall, role conceptions offer important insights into Germany's supportive and Japan's more ambiguous stance on textbook talks. In Japan's case, the analysis finds a role conflict between the conceptions of 'contributor to regional cooperation' and 'reliable ally' on the one hand, and the nationalist tendencies reflected in the role of 'respected and trusted country'. As seen above, additional factors should be considered to understand why moderate politicians do not challenge rightist-nationalist tendencies more vigorously. The next section will examine other factors that influence Germany's and Japan's policies.

Consideration of other factors

As seen in the discussion above, views about remembrance and reconciliation are polarized in Japan. Thomas Berger accurately observes that, as a result, the 'consensus on what are the boundaries of permissible rhetoric about the past is far weaker in Japan than it is in the Federal Republic' (2009: 13). The lack of a firm Japanese consensus on contrition and self-critical reflection on the past has at least four sources.

First, while the atrocities committed by both countries were horrendous, public memory has been influenced by the particular historical circumstances and experiences. Unparalleled in history, the systematic, state-organized killing of millions of Jews in the Holocaust contributed to a strong sense of shame among Germans in the post-war era. In Japan, on the other hand, the terrifying use of the two atomic bombs on Hiroshima and Nagasaki has shaped a feeling of victimhood, despite Japan's colonial and wartime policies of aggression in Asia.

Secondly, occupation policies in the post-war era differed in Germany and Japan, with the US keeping Japan more insulated from Asia and from its war responsibility, for example by shielding Emperor Hirohito from war crime charges (Shin 2010; Selden 2008). Moreover, the US focused its purges on the armed forces, while seeking to administer Japan through existing domestic bureaucracies, a decision that permitted significant continuity in government entities from the pre-1945 era. In Germany, on the other hand, purges and war crime trials targeted former political leaders associated with the Nazi regime (Berger 2009: 24).

Thirdly, geopolitical circumstances, including Japan's status as an island nation facing economically weak countries in Asia contributed to a lack of impetus towards atonement in Tokyo's post-war policy vis-à-vis its neighbours. By contrast, Germany – divided into different occupation zones and surrounded by advanced, industrialized countries – had to overcome the mistrust of its neighbours in order to achieve political and economic rehabilitation. After 1945, policy-makers in the Federal Republic thus embraced the integration of Europe and rejected narrow-minded nationalist thinking.

Fourthly, in domestic politics, Japan's ruling by the conservative Liberal Democratic Party (LDP) for practically the entire Cold War era also had an undeniable effect on the country's dealing with its past. In the German case, the inauguration of the left-leaning SPD government under Chancellor Brandt in 1969 provided new momentum to confront Germany's past squarely and to begin textbook talks with Poland. Some of the most unsettling historical issues like the Holocaust, which had been avoided in public debates previously, were finally addressed during this period (Kansteiner 2006: 117). Japan's Socialist Democratic Party similarly sought a more critical examination of wartime responsibility but was unable to influence memory politics directly without government control during the Cold War. When Japan's first socialist prime minister took office in 1994–5, he initiated efforts related to history issues including the Asian Historical Document Centre. However, compared to its German counterpart, the Japanese left came into office significantly later, for a shorter time period and its power was more constrained due to the coalition with the LDP. Its impact on Japanese perceptions of the past was therefore more limited.

Furthermore, there are important differences between the two countries' education systems, facilitating a critical treatment of recent history in Germany more than in Japan. The Federal Republic's system emphasizes the role of history education in nurturing students' political perspectives and critical thinking (Miyakawa 2001). As teaching and exam questions are geared towards discussion and interpretation, it is thus relatively easy to incorporate multiple perspectives into textbook narratives. The Japanese system, on the other hand, is dominated by the need to prepare students to pass high school and university entrance exams (Nicholls 2006: 51). Most of these exams contain multiple choice questions emphasizing right or wrong answers. Schools tend to choose those textbooks deemed best for students' exam preparation, and these are often books presenting a single linear account of history rather than discussing multiple perspectives. A further difference in education systems is that German schools teach history as a single subject – comprising both national and world history – whereas Japanese schools offer these two components separately (Mitani 2007: 243). The split between national and world history in Japan makes it more difficult to compare different viewpoints and discuss the effects of Japanese foreign policy on other countries (Chon 2007: 253).

In conclusion, German and Japanese role conceptions provide important insights into each country's policy on history textbook disputes, although other factors throw further light on the different approaches. Challenges in textbook narratives remain in both cases. While German and Japanese students continue to learn relatively little about the history of their neighbours, Polish and Korean students cover Germany and Japan in detail (Chon 2007: 253). Although Germany and Poland have made significant progress in developing a transnational narrative on their bilateral history, a number of obstacles remain. Warsaw's post-Cold War integration into the EU strengthened political ties with Berlin, but it also revived some old prejudices. While Germans have been anxious about an influx of cheap labour from their Eastern neighbours, the Polish public has harboured suspicions about Berlin's dominance in the EU. Textbook talks will need to address such concerns to prevent new bilateral friction. Moreover, as seen in the dispute about the 'Centre against Expulsion' in Berlin, Germany and Poland will need to cooperate in finding an acceptable narrative on the expulsion of ethnic Germans.

5 Conclusion

Through the content analysis of foreign policy speeches and the two case studies, this book systematically demonstrates how cognitive and ideational variables affect foreign policy-making in Germany and Japan. The analysis reveals that decision-makers hold distinct ideas and beliefs about the roles their respective countries should play in regional security affairs. The comparative method, developed to help identify role conceptions in major foreign policy speeches, is based on inductive categorization techniques. National objectives are thus explored through the eyes of German and Japanese politicians. The case studies in this book illustrate how cognitive and social factors motivate and legitimate particular decisions and actions in the investigated policy fields. Distinct *attitudes* and persistent patterns of *reasoning* and *behaviour* are identified in Germany's and Japan's policies on missile defence and history textbook disputes. As seen, role conceptions exert a powerful influence on how issues are framed and on the range of options perceived by policy-makers in formulating their response.

Despite broad similarities in their aims, the qualitative analysis reveals marked differences in policy preferences and strategies between the two countries. While the German role set is characterized by a *transformationalist* mindset about international relations, the Japanese one comprises *transformationalist* as well as *traditionalist* elements (see also Chapter 2). In other words, German policy-makers are confident they can overcome the security dilemma in international relations by nurturing mutual interdependence, advancing multilateral cooperation and mediation, and fostering supranationalism. Japanese policy-makers, on the other hand, pay more attention to the balance of power and regard the US–Japan alliance as a deterrent and thus anchor of stability in East Asia. The deeply ingrained norm of prioritizing the bilateral alliance permeates Tokyo's overall approach to regional security. Multilateral cooperation is thus considered a supplement rather than an alternative to ensure stability. Nevertheless, some aspects in Japan's normative framework suggest policy-makers do not have an exclusively 'realist' outlook on international relations. Like their German counterparts, Japanese policy-makers prefer economic over military forms of power, exhibit an aversion to exercising unilateralism and dominance over other countries, and reflect a strong attachment to universal values such as democracy and human rights.

The case study on territorial missile defence was particularly useful for exposing these different attitudes of German and Japanese decision-makers. Political elites in Berlin are reluctant to consider the strategic need for a territorial defence system, while being remarkably receptive to Russian criticism about US plans. They emphasize that adequate security can only be achieved diplomatically through consultation and compromise with Russia as well as Iran. Focused on promoting multilateral mediation, policy-makers neglect MD as an option for dealing with urgent security risks. Based on their *transformationalist* outlook, they seek to escape the security dilemma through multilateralism and negotiation.

In Japan, politicians tend to evaluate a territorial missile defence system positively, arguing that it is conducive to regional stability under current circumstances. Through participation in the US project, Japan confirms loyalty to its alliance partner, thus cementing the bilateral relationship with its deterrence function. Furthermore, developing the MD potential ensures that Japan 'does not itself become a power vacuum that would be a destabilizing factor in [the] regional environment', especially in view of North Korea's and China's growing missile capabilities (Ministry of Defence Japan 2007). This reasoning indicates the *traditionalist* mindset of Japanese politicians, who aspire to a regional balance of power. Japanese policy-makers equally stress that MD as a non-offensive system corresponds to Japan's defensive, non-militarist strategy. The latter argument reflects the *transformationalist* element in Japanese thinking, focused on overcoming the security dilemma through self-restraint. Many contemporary observers and commentators overlook this line of reasoning, as they pay exclusive attention to the 'realist' aspects of Japanese MD policy.

Overall, role theory proves to be a useful tool for explaining policy choices identified in the case studies, although additional factors often help to further illuminate why decision-making elites favour particular approaches. The analysis confirms that a 'purely structural understanding of international politics is impoverished', because power structures and foreign policy choices are meaningless in the absence of a set of shared normative convictions and ideas (Malici 2006: 58). Power and material interests matter, but they are perceived and evaluated through a cognitive lens comprising the norms and values embodied in the role set. Thus, an explanation of Germany's and Japan's post-Cold War regional security policies must pay attention to the normative standards of behaviour guiding the decisions and approaches of government representatives.

The remainder of this concluding chapter will address five central issues pertaining to this study. First, it will return to the key questions underlying this study. Are Germany's and Japan's post-Cold War policies characterized by change or continuity? Drawing on a classification scheme adopted from Charles Hermann, this section seeks to evaluate the type and extent of change in the two countries (Hermann 1990). It finds that incremental adaptations in foreign policy preferences can be identified in both Germany and Japan. However, recent depictions of a drastic change in Tokyo's foreign policy course are misguided and exaggerated. This section also discusses the nationalistic sentiments reflected in Japan's recent foreign policy thinking. The subsequent section succinctly evaluates major strengths and weaknesses of role theory. It readdresses the issue of role conflict, applying the empirical findings of this book. Although this study sheds light on the question of how nations cope with role conflict, the difficulty of predicting behaviour remains a weak point in the role theoretical approach and needs to be investigated further. The conclusion then takes a broader perspective by asking whether role conceptions will continue to guide foreign policies in Germany and Japan for the foreseeable future. Although recent trends in both countries may indicate a diminishing influence, the section concludes that it is too early for a definitive answer. Finally, potential areas of further study are discussed.

Change and continuity in German and Japanese foreign policies

Based on role theoretical analysis, this book seeks to re-evaluate the question of continuity and change in German and Japanese regional security policies. Has Japan – in comparison to Germany – indeed been undergoing sweeping changes in its foreign policy orientation, as numerous scholars claim? Neither the qualitative analysis of foreign policy speeches nor the case studies corroborate such a judgement. Rather, a remarkable degree of continuity is found in *both* German and Japanese *speeches* and *patterns of foreign policy behaviour*. The study demonstrates a persistence of role conceptions and foreign policy behaviour across different government coalitions in both countries. Neither the long-awaited change in government from LDP- to DPJ-leadership in Japan in 2009 nor the more frequent post-Cold War government changes in Germany led to a comprehensive rethinking in foreign policy.

The question of change and continuity nevertheless warrants further attention, because of its academic relevance. A major problem in recent foreign policy studies is that the term 'change' is generally 'under-theorized' and lacks conceptual clarity (Hagström and Williamsson 2009: 243). Most scholars seek to *explain* foreign policy change rather than *define* and *assess* it. In order to evaluate with more precision the extent and type of change in German and Japanese foreign policies, Charles Hermann's classification model proves useful (Hermann 1990). Hermann identifies four graduated levels of foreign policy change, adapted here to fit the role theoretical approach (see Figure 5.1). Before classifying the changes identified in German and Japanese foreign policy, the four levels are described below:

1   *Change in the scope or salience of a national role conception (NRC)*: The first and most limited type of change involves a modification in the scope of activity covered by an NRC. A country may alter the *level of effort* or the *range of recipients or target countries* of its policies. At the same time, 'What is done, how it is done, and the purpose for which it is done remain unchanged' (Hermann 1990: 5). This type of change most likely results from a re-evaluation of the salience of an NRC within a role set after an experience of perceived policy success or failure.

2   *Partial NRC change regarding preferred means:* The second type of change refers to an adjustment in collectively shared understandings about

CLASSIFICATION OF ROLE CHANGE

	Description		Hermann's corresponding category
	Change regards:	Continuity regards:	
① Change in scope/ salience of NRC	• Change in NRC regarding either: – Level of effort oriented towards goal or – Range of activity (e.g. scope of recipients/ targets of policy)	• Role conceptions not altered in main content (aims, instruments)	• 'Adjustment change'
② Partial NRC change regarding preferred means	• Change in views of appropriate instruments/ means	• Purpose and aim of policy remain fixed	• 'Program change'
③ Complete change of one NRC	• Emergence of new NRC with distinct set of aims, purposes, instruments	• Other NRCs in role set remain in place	• 'Problem/ goal change'
④ Change of role set (multiple NRCs affected)	• Emergence of multiple new NRCs • Rejection of prior ideas and foreign policy approaches	• Little / no continuity in role set	• 'International orientation change'

Figure 5.1. Categorization of Change

Adapted from Charles Hermann's classification scheme (Hermann 1990)

the appropriate instruments or means associated with a particular role conception. However, continuity persists in the fundamental aims and purposes underlying the NRC. Change thus pertains to the *means* of foreign policy, while the general *goals* of an actor remain stable. This kind of change most likely occurs when previous policy instruments prove ineffective or inefficient under new circumstances.

3 *Complete change of one NRC:* The third type of change implies more fundamental change with regard to one of the NRCs in the role set. A new role conception comprising a distinct set of purposes and instruments emerges, either replacing a previously held NRC or complementing the existing role set. The change does not concern more than one NRC in the role set, however. This kind of change may arise for example when new policy challenges necessitate the definition of additional goals and roles or when external developments recurrently challenge a shared understanding or idea.

4 *Change of role set:* The fourth and most extensive type of change involves the simultaneous emergence of multiple new NRCs in the role set, replacing former shared understandings. As policy-makers reject prior ideas, the role set changes significantly. This type of change is most likely to occur when a country is at a turning point in the face of a major foreign policy event, shaping new considerations about the state's objectives in international affairs.[1]

From a role theoretical perspective, which of these types of change can be considered 'drastic'? Without doubt, the fourth type has far-reaching consequences on foreign policy orientation and behaviour, based on a profound redefinition of the normative guidelines in foreign policy. The third type, the complete change of one NRC, implies more circumscribed but nevertheless substantial change in foreign policy goals and behaviour, as new, shared normative understandings emerge. In contrast, the aims and objectives in foreign policy-making remain unaffected in the first and second types of change. Here, the structure of normative beliefs is amended rather than fundamentally altered. These two types of change lead to a modification of behaviour, but – from a role theoretical perspective – they do not entail complete redefinitions of guiding principles. In other words, these two types of change do not imply *new* foreign policy strategies as a result of rejecting earlier ones. Rather, the existing framework of orientation is *refurbished and adjusted.*[2]

The adapted categorization scheme could be further refined, for example by adding grading levels or categories to classify alterations like the one in Germany's role conception of 'contributor to regional cooperation', which does not fit clearly into the above scheme. Although the content of this role conception did not change significantly, the underlying rationale for pursuing it seemed to shift over the time period investigated. Whereas policy-makers in the early 1990s frequently raised emotional, history-focused arguments to justify their commitment for European multilateralism, a decade later debates were dominated by practical reasoning (e.g. economic advantages), although historical motives did not disappear completely. Germany's policy was portrayed more as a deliberate choice rather than an inevitable destiny. The shift had no obvious effect on Germany's role conception in terms of behavioural prescriptions (what and how something should be done). The NRC was apparently 'updated' for a new post-war generation of politicians and voters by introducing a new rationale, while shared ideas about appropriate policy conduct and instruments remained unaffected.

Aside from this particular case of change, the four categorization levels adapted from Hermann's research seem sufficiently detailed to assess the other changes observed in German and Japanese regional security policies. The qualitative content analysis does not reveal *type (3) or (4) changes* in either Germany or Japan, as no new role conceptions are identified throughout the time period investigated. Some *type (1) change* is found in both Germany's and Japan's role conception of 'exporter of security'. Speeches in both countries clearly reflect the intention to play a more extensive role in ensuring global security and to exert a greater effort towards it. However, the most important change in both German and Japanese policies is a *type (2) change*: a re-evaluation of the utility and legitimacy of military force in connection with the role conceptions of 'exporter of security' and 'non-militarist country'. Seeking to ensure global security and stability, both countries' policy-makers were increasingly willing to dispatch military forces to multilateral missions. As a result, the number of *Bundeswehr* and Self-Defence Force personnel engaged in missions abroad grew throughout the post-Cold War era. As seen in Chapter 2, Japan's adjustment with regard to the use of military force has involved a greater conceptual step than in Germany's. The qualitative analysis shows that in the early 1990s, Japan held a more restrictive notion of being a non-militarist country, accepting the use of military means only for national self-defence. Germany, on the other hand, did not principally reject collective self-defence and exhibited a willingness to send troops to multilateral missions to assist other NATO members. The dispatch of troops to global missions in conflict areas thus corresponded more closely to Germany's previous foreign policy concept.[3]

However, in both countries incremental changes regarding international dispatches were anchored firmly within the established normative guidelines. This highlights the limited nature of the type (2) changes and the overall continuity in the role sets. First, policy-makers in both countries exhibited – and still do – a deep scepticism about using military measures, instead favouring diplomatic means of conflict resolution. Tokyo and Berlin rely on narrowly defined rules of engagement for their troops, focusing on reconstruction efforts rather than offensive combat missions. Secondly, the increased global engagements in security affairs were predicated on traditional foreign policy parameters: While Germany concentrated on the institutionalized and multilateral contexts of the UN, NATO and the EU in guiding its policies, Japan's international contributions rested primarily on the allegiance to the US, although Tokyo sought to reinforce UN-led activities as well. In gradually reconstructing their role in international security, both countries thus relied on familiar frameworks as normative reference points.

Two concurrent processes drove the expansion of Germany's and Japan's military roles.[4] First, *alter-part expectations* were crucial in initiating extensive debates and internal reassessments about military contributions for international security. As they sought to uphold their reputations as 'reliable partners', Berlin and Tokyo were particularly inclined to accommodate the demands to assume more responsibility in security affairs after the Cold War. The influence of alter-part expectations was reflected in such terms as 'responsibility', 'duty', 'burden-sharing' and 'solidarity' in German as well as in Japanese debates. Secondly, the realization that global dispatches of military troops may be necessary to secure peace in conflict areas triggered a *learning process* in both countries' foreign policy outlook.[5] Berlin grew markedly more willing to send troops abroad as policy-makers recognized the potentially disastrous humanitarian consequences in case of diplomatic failure, as during the Bosnian and Kosovo conflicts. Similarly, Japanese politicians gave up some of their reservations against military missions and sent troops to such unstable areas as Zaire and Kenya in order to alleviate the tragic plight of refugees. At the same time, Tokyo eased the stringent restrictions and conditions imposed upon its UN contributions, for policy-makers acknowledged them to be unrealistic and irresponsible.

As depicted above, the role theoretical analysis permits a reassessment of recent academic evaluations of Japan's foreign policy course. Scholars have clearly overstated and misconstrued the changes under way by asserting that Japan is undergoing a fundamental 'transformation' (Samuels 2007b: 64) and that it stands on the 'threshold of a new era' (Pyle 2007a: 374) in its international orientation. First, many observers have exaggerated the *extent of change* in Tokyo's foreign policy. Like their German counterparts, Japanese decision-makers have not fundamentally challenged the normative framework guiding their country's foreign policy behaviour. New foreign policy strategies are discernible in neither Berlin nor Tokyo, as deeply ingrained role conceptions continue to shape preferences and decisions. As seen above in the application of Hermann's classification, change in both countries was essentially limited to the preferred instruments of foreign policy and the level of effort exerted towards particular policy goals. Although these changes are doubtlessly important, they do not reflect a fundamental reorientation.

Second, many scholars have misinterpreted the *purpose and motivation* driving the changes in Japan. Accusations that Tokyo was developing military ambitions linked to national interests and discarding its post-war ideals are mistaken. Like in Germany, the primary motivation for Japan to expand its international security role has been the desire to take on a greater share of the burden of maintaining regional and international stability, thereby demonstrating solidarity with key partners, especially the US.[6] For both Germany and Japan, role conflicts between the conception of 'anti-militarist country' on the one hand and those of 'reliable partner' and 'exporter of security' on the other hand gave rise to discussions about necessary adjustments. Changes in both countries resulted from the interrelated processes of transnational socialization and learning and were accompanied by intense debates and domestic soul-searching. Scholarly accounts of Japan's 'militarization' tend to overlook the enormous US normative pressure on Tokyo to extend its international contributions. Japan has not renounced its anti-militarist values, but sought to redefine its shared understandings in order to fulfil perceived duties in the bilateral alliance with the US and in multilateral security missions. Thus, Japanese anti-militarism has *evolved*, rather than *weakened*.

On the whole, both Germany's and Japan's regional security policies are characterized by a 'modified continuity' (Harnisch 2001: 48). Despite some gradual adjustments, overall continuity has prevailed in both countries' role sets. This finding raises a further question: why have scholars *perceived* more change in Japan's foreign policy than in Germany's? Part of the answer may be that most of the academic work is not comparative, as pointed out in the Introduction. However, this answer is not fully satisfying. The book's analysis suggests three reasons for the different academic perceptions of the two countries.

First, compared to Germany, change has been more patent in Japan. During the Cold War, Tokyo was generally seen as a passive and reactive actor in security affairs and international issues, whose foreign policy was linked to the pursuit of economic interests. In contrast, Germany became actively involved in regional political and security issues through the development of multilateral European institutions from the early stages of the Cold War. Bonn evolved into a key actor promoting regional cooperation and integration and proposing new initiatives and projects. Furthermore, Germany developed its own distinctive foreign policy ideas, especially with its *Ostpolitik* of the 1970s. Thus, as the expansion of Germany's international security role corresponds to the tradition of earlier foreign policy activism, it appears less striking. On the other hand, Japanese changes in its restrictive notion of being a non-militarist country are easily traceable. During the Cold War, Tokyo's normative framework was enshrined in an array of laws and non-binding Diet resolutions, such as the peaceful use of space resolution or the three non-nuclear principles. Changes in these regulations are conspicuous.

Second, the realist elements in Japan's role set may cause analysts to overestimate current changes in foreign policy. As seen in the content analysis, Tokyo's attention to power constellations reflects a partially realist outlook on international relations. Politicians' statements and decisions thus often lend credence to the predictions and interpretations of realist IR theory. When applied to Japan, realism is inclined to perceive major change in Japan's policy, as the country departs from its 'abnormal' state of affairs and embarks on policies of power maximization. Explicitly or implicitly, realist theory has informed many of the recent accounts of Japan's foreign policy, leading to erroneous descriptions of the country's course.

Third, the expansion of Japan's international security role has been accompanied by nationalist rhetoric, fuelling perceptions of a fundamental change. Far-right groups, such as the Association for Textbook Reform (Tsukurukai) spawn an image of a Japan abandoning the lessons of history and reverting to pre-war militarism. As a result, the Japanese domestic movement to amend the Constitution has frequently been misinterpreted. Many observers fear that changing the current ban on using military force in international conflicts would amount to a renunciation of Japan's post-war ideals (Watanabe 2005). However, as seen in the qualitative content analysis, this interpretation does not correspond to mainstream views in Japan. The majority of politicians do not aspire to a muscular Japan with genuine independence from the US.

Japan's nationalist tendencies: the importance of trust and respect

Japan's nationalist tendencies should not be ignored, however. The case studies, particularly the one on history textbook disputes, reveal a growing trend towards self-assertion and defiance in the country's foreign policy in recent years, due to a rise in nationalist sentiments. At the core of the issue is Japan's role conception of being a 'trusted and respected country'. Rather than resolving the unsettled history issue through unequivocal apologies and compensation, a domestic cycle of negative emotions and frustration has pulled Japan in a different direction: Tokyo increasingly takes an uncompromising, nationalistic stance on many foreign policy issues. Self-assertion and defiance are fuelled by an *unfulfilled desire* to become a trusted and respected country – a country neither constantly admonished for its past wrongs nor relegated to a subservient follower role in its alliance relationship with the US.

After the Second World War, both German and Japanese policy-makers sought their country's international rehabilitation in order to gain leeway in regional and global affairs and to establish the basis for a positive and confident national spirit. However, while Tokyo's elites display a sense of failure in their endeavour,

Berlin's leaders generally seem content with the level of respect and trust Germany receives. The analysis in this book exposes multiple reasons for these differing outlooks. Berlin's decision-makers gradually achieved equality with key partner countries through the mutual relinquishment of sovereignty to the European supranational level. Furthermore, they gained room to manoeuvre by establishing their country as a privileged link between France and the US. They demonstrated persistent support for European integration and provided bold and unambiguous apologies for past misdeeds, and thus were able to build up trust reserves as a key asset for exercising international influence. The peaceful reunification of Germany after the Cold War enhanced the sense of achievement and confirmation about the adopted strategy among political elites. In contrast, Japanese decision-makers were unable to boost their country's international influence by cultivating equality vis-à-vis the US alliance partner. They failed to build up trust among regional neighbours due to a cautious and reluctant stance in dealing with Japan's record of aggression. The economic recession has furthermore damaged Japanese self-confidence and cast doubts on Tokyo's ability to earn international respect.

The tendency towards a more defiant and self-assertive posture does not indicate that Japanese politicians are abandoning the basic parameters guiding their foreign policy, however. Lawmakers are likely to challenge Washington occasionally, while being careful not to jeopardize the alliance relationship itself, which remains the centrepiece of Japan's regional and global security strategy. Furthermore, lawmakers may refuse to automatically give in to Korean or Chinese demands on history issues, but they will simultaneously support multilateral regional cooperation and assure neighbours of Tokyo's peaceful intentions. Based on Japan's current role set, Tokyo's foreign policy will most likely be characterized by somewhat paradoxical and contradictory behaviour for the foreseeable future.

Advantages and disadvantages of role theory

Among role theory's many strengths, two stand out. First, as a constructivist approach, role theory pays attention to individual state characteristics rather than presuming homogeneous actor preferences based on universal assumptions about foreign policy conduct, as other mainstream theories do. Thus, it is suitable to explain variations in policy approaches and preferences across different countries, such as the ones found between German and Japanese regional security policies. As Ted Hopf accurately observes, 'the promise of constructivism is to restore a kind of partial order and predictability to world politics that derives not from imposed homogeneity, but from an appreciation of difference' (1998: 200). It should be noted, however, that focusing on individual state characteristics has ramifications for research projects. The identification of national role conceptions requires extensive efforts in data collection and analysis. In order to heighten sensitivity to particular connotations or meanings, chosen materials should preferably be analysed in the original language. Moreover, since NRCs may be modified or altered, role theoretical analyses for different countries will need to be updated from time to time. Nevertheless, as shown, such analyses offer insights into distinct foreign policy styles that may be inexplicable through structural accounts.

Secondly, role theory stands out among constructivist approaches in providing concrete research tools. Through the analysis of key foreign policy speeches or other government documents, it enables the systematic examination of how cognitive and ideational factors are translated into policy preferences. Many of the existing constructivist works have been criticized for their conceptually, empirically and methodologically loose application of the term 'identity' (Ashizawa 2008: 573). In contrast to other constructivist approaches, role theory keeps a clearly defined analytical focus on national role conceptions and offers tools for empirical investigation and comparison of normative-ideational factors. It furthermore recognizes and captures the effects of different levels of analysis to the extent that such aspects are reflected and absorbed in the collectively held conceptions. Role theory can thus reveal how material factors are interpreted, given meaning and related to behavioural guidelines by policy-makers.

As an interpretive-explanatory approach, role theory has an important shortcoming: it has difficulty in predicting state behaviour. NRCs motivate rather than cause state behaviour and often contain ambiguity and room for interpretation. Behavioural inferences are particularly challenging in cases of role conflict, because of the variety of coping strategies countries can resort to. The number of such cases evaluated in this book is too limited to draw definite conclusions about preferred coping strategies. It seems, however, that politicians generally refrain from negotiating completely new role conceptions, unless they are under severe domestic and international pressure. As was seen, both Germany and Japan changed their shared understandings only partially with respect to preferred policy instruments, after re-evaluating the utility and legitimacy of military force. The analysis suggests that decision-makers tend to utilize semantic techniques in case of role conflict, drawing on conceptual ambiguities in their conceptions. Thereby, politicians avoid obvious NRC violations and redefinitions of shared conceptions. This finding confirms that role conceptions are generally 'sticky' and cannot be changed easily or quickly.

Role conceptions and their impact on policy-making

Role theory proved to be a useful tool in explaining the observed patterns of behaviour in German and Japanese foreign policy. But will shared role conceptions continue to guide politicians' decisions in the future? In fact, several recent developments indicate that role conceptions may lose some of their impact on foreign policy-making in the two countries. Although these trends should not be overestimated at this point, they merit further attention. First of all, the financial crisis and growing national debts have led to shrinking resources in foreign policy in both countries. Fiscal constraints may severely complicate Germany's and Japan's abilities to live up to their international commitments. In particular, experts in both countries have complained about lacking resources for the military, prohibiting them from investing in new equipment and technology for troop deployments in crisis areas. As a result, there is a growing gap between the declared goal of playing a more active role in international security and the material capacity to meet the resulting commitments (Wagner 2005). In a June 2010 interview, SPD parliamentarian Hans-Peter Bartels reflected on the potential negative consequences of Germany's cost-cutting programme, as the country seeks to comply with a legal ruling whereby it is bound by the 'Schuldenbremse' (debt-brake). Referring to a potential German withdrawal from the MEADS project, Bartels cautioned that the Federal Republic runs the risk of relying on the 'debt-brake as a strategy substitute' (*Schuldenbremse als Strategieersatz*) in foreign policy (Bartels 2010).

In the future, the intensifying resource crunch may have effects on other important areas of foreign policy as well. Berlin may react to demands for financial transfers to poorer EU member states with increasing reluctance and objections. Furthermore, Germany's willingness to promote regional cooperation may weaken as the country is no longer able to 'contain the negative side-effects of further integration through side payments in the domestic realm' (Harnisch 2001: 46). Lobbyists may put pressure on decision-makers to pay closer attention to national rather than regional interests. In Japan, political leaders are also forced to deal with numerous urgent domestic policy issues such as growing income disparity, pension payments, healthcare costs, as well as the reconstruction requirements following the destructive 2011 Tohoku earthquake. As they seek to allocate resources to these policy areas, Japan's massive financial support for US troops stationed in the country (the so-called 'sympathy budget') may cause public controversy, with major ramifications for the alliance relationship.

Secondly, a number of scholars have called attention to the process of 'domestication' in Germany's foreign policy, a development that could undermine the influence of role conceptions on decision-making in certain policy areas.[7] The term 'domestication' refers to an increasing number of domestic political actors who seek to shape foreign policy. Because of the strong tradition of federalism in Germany, the *Länder* have played a particularly important role in this process. Over recent years, EU competencies have increasingly intruded upon policy areas, which traditionally had been the sole preserve of the German *Länder*. In response, individual states have sought to exercise more influence within intergovernmental negotiations, through the Committee of the Regions for example, providing them with a direct voice within the EU's institutional framework. Therefore, the *Länder* are practising an auxiliary foreign policy (*Nebenaußenpolitik*), based on their particular interests (Knodt 2001: 173). Nevertheless, *Länder* influence should not be overestimated. The German states do not have consistent interests that would allow them to operate as an autonomous player through coordinated efforts.

Thirdly, in Japan, recent reforms and changes in the political system have opened up the process of policy-making to societal pressures. This increases the risk of politicians engaging in short-sighted populist behaviour and thereby deviating from established role conceptions. The 1993–4 electoral reform and subsequent administrative restructuring significantly strengthened the prime ministerial position, while weakening the power of the bureaucracy in decision-making. With the introduction of a mixed-member election system in the Upper House that combines proportional and majoritarian voting systems, individual party leaders gained more influence. Prime ministers and other top-level politicians have thus relied more and more on popularity, skillfully using the media to buttress their domestic standing. Former Prime Minister Abe Shinzo for example owed his prominence to his tough stance on North Korea in the emotional 'kidnapping issue'.

Research perspectives

This study's findings suggest three promising issue areas for further research. First, the inductive method for qualitative content analysis, specially devised to conduct the study at hand, could be applied to other countries in order to investigate and compare their role sets. The approach helped to determine similarities and differences between Germany and Japan, thereby enabling a deeper understanding of the distinct foreign policy strategies. It thus seems sensible to examine whether this method can yield good results in other cases as well. Quite likely, the inductive approach will prove most useful for comparing countries with broad similarities, since the coding process involves the identification of corresponding themes to group specific foreign policy ideas.

Secondly, the issue of role conflict and coping strategies should be examined in more detail in future studies. In the limited number of observed incidents, this book was able to expose the way Germany and Japan dealt with such conflicts, drawing some preliminary conclusions about preferred strategies. However, further research will be indispensable to substantiate these results, to develop a clearer understanding of the conditions under which particular strategies may be favoured, and to compare the coping behaviour of different countries.

A third area for further investigation concerns such concepts as reputation, respect, dignity, esteem and trust in international relations. These concepts apparently played an important role in both the German and the Japanese foreign policy perspectives (especially reflected in Tokyo's NRC 'trusted and respected country'). Reputation and the above-mentioned terms mirror a country's 'soft power' resources.[8] Such resources are particularly valuable for nations lacking substantial military capabilities. Further constructivist research on these concepts may shed light on how different countries conceive of their international reputation and how much it means to them. Furthermore, such research may reveal whether a perceived lack of respect from important partner countries generally prompts nationalist tendencies, as in the Japanese case.

Notes

Introduction

1 See e.g. Kinkel 1993d for Germany and Kaifu 1990a for Japan.

2 To name a few: Maull 1990/1991; Waltz 1993; Garten 1989/1990, 1992; Buruma 1994; Grieco 1996; Mearsheimer 1990a; Berger 1996; Becker and Rüland 1997; Katzenstein and Shiraishi 1997.

3 Of course, differences between Germany and Japan should not be overlooked. While Germany is geographically located in the middle of Europe and shares borders with a number of countries, Japan is an island nation isolated in geographic terms from the rest of East Asia. Moreover, Peter Katzenstein points out that economic disparities between Japan and other Asian countries are much greater than those between Germany and some of its key regional partner countries, such as France and Great Britain (Katzenstein 2005: 220.)

4 A notable exception is Katzenstein's valuable comparative work (2005) on Germany and Japan, discussed in further detail below.

5 Aside from the ones mentioned below, studies that emphasize overwhelming continuity in German foreign policy include (among others): Risse 2001, 2004; Schneider *et al.* 2002; Meiers 2002; Malici 2006; Speck 2007; Bierling 2006; Duffield 1999; Boekle *et al.* 2001. Only few studies have raised doubts about the continuity thesis, see: Schöllgen 2003; Hellmann 2004; Baumann 2006; Fröhlich 2008. These studies focus particularly on changes during the government of Chancellor Gerhard Schröder.

6 Schröder, born in 1944, has no personal recollection of World War II. Hence he has been counted as part of the post-war generation of leaders.

7 See e.g. Algieri 2011; Frankenberger and Maull 2011; Overhaus 2004: 552; Harnisch and Schieder 2006; Maull 2006a.

8 Although Samuels does not stress the end of the Cold War as a sharp discontinuity (as Pyle does), he still sees it as a key factor. Samuels argues 'there was no single "big bang" forcing the transformation, though the end of the cold war comes close' (2007b: 86).

9 Mike Mochizuki agrees that Japan is undergoing important adjustments, but not a transformation (2007, 2006). Christopher Hughes sees fundamental changes, with Japan increasingly 'becoming a more assertive or "normal" military power,' but he points out that these changes have taken place within the traditional framework in Japan's security policy: the US-Japan alliance (2004a: 18; 2007).

10 Samuel's book is vague on this point. On the one hand, he gives the impression that the expansion of Japan's military role has been primarily driven by revisionists who have a nationalist agenda and who – picking up on a shift in popular sentiment after the Gulf War – 'began to paint Article 9 as an obstacle to "international cooperation"' (Samuels 2007b: 1). This would suggest that revisionists with a narrow-minded nationalist

policy agenda might have significant sway over the future use of military force. On the other hand, Samuels maintains that revisionists will not be able to push through all their objectives, since other ideological groups will also seek to influence policies.

11 In total, the analysis covers 129 German and 130 Japanese documents. In addition to speeches, a small number of major interviews and newspaper articles by policy-makers are used.

12 The case studies consider policy developments until Dec. 2011.

13 Older works include an essential role theoretical comparison between Germany, Japan and the US. See Frenkler *et al.* 1997.

1 Theoretical and methodological frameworks

1 See among others Risse 1999, 2003; Duffield 1999; Checkel 2001.

2 Role theory shares many of the assumptions of 'identity' literature. However, a key difference lies in the fact that a nation's identity is deemed to develop and consolidate during a process of distinguishing between the 'self' and the 'other' – an assumption not made by role theory. As Kai Schulze observes, 'To construct one's own identity, an entity defines what is perceived as unique to it*self* and therefore different to the *other*. In this sense the *other* could also serve as a negative description of the *self*' (2010: 3). As will be seen in detail below, another difference is that role conceptions consist of an ego- and an alter-part. According to role theory, other countries' behavioural expectations thus can influence the foreign policy behaviour of a nation. In contrast, identity theory generally does not presuppose or examine such a connection.

3 In addition to foreign policy speeches, a small number of major interviews and newspaper articles by policy-makers are used.

4 The standard method for ensuring reproducability is to use several coders. This study could not rely on such an approach, as it is based on a doctoral dissertation, in which collaborative work is not allowed. To ensure transparency, the book provides a systematic explanation of the coding process.

2 Role conceptions in German and Japanese speeches

1 Some policy-makers are more hesitant, however. Prime Minister Koizumi Junichiro noted that Japan should respect East Asia's diversity and 'not foist our values on our neighbours' (*kachikan o oshitsukenai*) (Koizumi 2002f).

2 The term is adopted and slightly modified from a paper by Christopher Hughes and Akiko Fukushima, which uses the term 'bilateralism-plus' (Hughes and Fukushima 2004: 56). Here, the prefix 'US' is added to emphasize that, of all its bilateral relationships, Japan attaches by far the greatest importance to the one with Washington.

3 German and Japanese missile defence policies

1 Foreign Ministry official Jürgen Schnappertz points out that MEADS could help ward off a missile attack from the sea, e.g. the North Sea (Schnappertz 2010, interview with A. Sakaki)

2 Karsten Voigt maintains that most of the security experts of the SPD disagreed with the view of an imminent arms race with Russia. These experts, he notes, were aware of the growing danger from Iranian WMD programmes (Voigt 2010, interview with A. Sakaki). Hans-Ulrich Klose contends that such expert voices were largely sidelined in the debate by those following Russian arguments (Klose 2010, interview with A. Sakaki). SPD members were in clear agreement, however, about the need for cooperation with Russia.

3 Compared to 2000–1, members from the CDU-CSU were more openly sceptical about Russian arguments. This had at least four reasons: (1) party members in 2007 were concerned about the increasingly authoritarian tendencies in Russia (Staff member of the CDU/CSU parliamentary grouping 2010, interview with A. Sakaki), (2) the CDU-CSU was in the governing coalition in 2007, and thus felt a stronger need to react and consider German security interests (Keller 2010, interview with A. Sakaki; Sinjen 2010, interview with A. Sakaki), (3) MD was an even more unpopular topic around 2001, as the US was moving towards withdrawal from the ABM Treaty, and (4) knowledge about MD among policy-makers was even more shallow in the earlier phase, as the topic had not been debated intensely (Sinjen 2010, interview with A. Sakaki).

4 Mützenich warned, however, that other countries may perceive MD as part of an offensive strategy in order to reduce an enemy's second strike capability. Thus, countries such as Russia or Iran may feel compelled to build up their offensive capabilities if the US and its allies pursue MD (Mützenich 2010, interview with A. Sakaki).

5 This was confirmed in a number of interviews with A. Sakaki: Voigt 2010; Bartels 2010; Katsioulis 2010; Schnappertz 2010.

6 These three areas are related, of course. The existence of particular role conceptions may influence policy-makers' perceptions of threats, technological feasibility and cost aspects. Nevertheless, separate consideration of each of these aspects helps clarify the reasons for the identified policy characteristics.

7 In an interview, the chair of the rapporteurs group, Hans-Peter Bartels (SPD) explained that the parliamentarians had charged the members from the Defence Ministry to take minutes on the results from their meetings, which later served as a first draft for the report. He insists that the structure and content of both documents were determined by the parliamentarians (Bartels 2010, interview with A. Sakaki).

8 Rolf Mützenich notes that many fellow politicians were not fully aware of the actual risks faced by soldiers abroad at this time. The security situation for NATO troops in Afghanistan was only beginning to deteriorate, and thus many politicians had not given in-depth consideration to the needs of soldiers. With the worsening security situation in Afghanistan in the following years, the general awareness grew, however (Mützenich 2010, interview with A. Sakaki)

9 Scholars and experts actively participated in the debate. Papers critical of MEADS include Landmann 2005; Lange 2005. Papers in support of the project include Krause 2005; Grams 2005; Bauer and Agüera 2005.

10 According to insiders, the decision to develop IRIS-T was based less on strategic rationale than on political considerations. Since defence industry giant EADS had received the contract for the MEADS project, the other major company involved in missile technology, Diehl, was given the contract for IRIS-T.

11 The financial terms of the deal were not disclosed (*New York Times* 2003).

12 According to an official from the National Institute for Defence Studies (2008, interview with A. Sakaki), the reaction of the Japanese government concerning the missile shot was limited, because party politics were in disarray at the time.

13 See e.g. the arguments by Tsukihara Shigeaki on 24 April 1998 in the Diet or the Upper House Diet session on 2 Oct. 1997 (*Kokuritsu Kokkai Toshokan*).

14 See e.g. the Upper House Diet sessions on 5 Nov. 1997 and on 2 Nov. 1994 (*Kokuritsu Kokkai Toshokan*).

15 See e.g. the Diet session on 24 April 1998 (*Kokuritsu Kokkai Toshokan*).

16 See e.g. the 18 Nov. 1999 Diet session (*Kokuritsu Kokkai Toshokan*).

17 The exact costs of the research efforts were not disclosed, but officials did not contradict reports that put the figure at between US$400 and 524 million, which were to be split equally between the two countries (Sims 1999).

18 Japan later increased the planned number of MD systems to 16 PAC-3 fire units and four Aegis ships equipped with SM-3 interceptors (Toki 2008).

19 After the Defence Agency was elevated in status to Defence Ministry in Jan. 2007, the Defence Minister had the same power.

20 See the 9 May 2008 Diet debate (*Kokuritsu Kokkai Toshokan*).

21 See *Asahi Shinbun* 2005b: 261.

22 Or US$1.2 billion. See *Asahi Shinbun* 2006. Currency conversion at www.oanda.com; the given number is only a rough estimate, since currency fluctuations may change costs considerably.

23 Or €1.6 billion. See CNN 2005.

24 The Japanese government has not disclosed specific figures for the operation costs.

25 See e.g. the 9 Nov. 2001 debate in the Diet (*Kokuritsu Kokkai Toshokan*).

26 The Komei Party, in the coalition government with the LDP, opposed the dispatch, but asserted in early Dec. that it would not risk breaking up the coalition over the issue (Berkofsky 2002a).

27 See the 13 Nov. 2002 debate in the Diet (*Kokuritsu Kokkai Toshokan*).

4 Policies on textbook talks

1 The role of civil society actors is discussed in Lilly Gardner-Feldman (Feldman 2008, 2007).

2 A recent trilateral civil society project between Japanese, Korean and Chinese scholars demonstrates these obstacles. Sales figures of the jointly published history book indicate that most buyers are individuals, rather than teachers or schools with bulk orders. Furthermore, among the Japanese public, the project was criticized for being biased and representing the political left (Wang 2009: 117–18).

3 Textbook talks are obviously not a magical remedy to overcome historical resentments. They need to be accompanied by other gestures of atonement and reconciliation. On the range of policy fields, see Torpey 2003: 6.

4 The term was in fact borrowed from the Potsdam Agreement of 1945. For a comprehensive overview of the controversy, see Jacobmeyer 1979.

5 The CSU in particular was opposed to the recommendations. With the support of the CSU and the Association of Expellees (*Bund der Vertriebenen*), three German historians published the so-called 'Alternative Recommendations on the Treatment of German–Polish History in Schoolbooks' in 1978. These recommendations, however, were not written in cooperation with Polish historians.

6 For more detailed accounts of Kohl's stance, see e.g. Fischer and Lorenz 2007; Levy and Dierkes 2002.

7 For a detailed overview of the Ienaga lawsuit see Petersen 2001 or Ide *et al.* 2010: 179.

8 Not much is known publicly about ISEI's requests and activities. According to the *Asahi Shinbun*, one controversial demand in the early 1980s was for Moscow to change Soviet textbooks describing the four disputed islands of the 'Northern Territories' as Soviet territory. ISEI insisted that the four islands were Japanese territory (*Asahi Shinbun* 1984). According to Kondo Takahiro, ISEI's demands for textbook revisions have been 'counterproductive' (Kondo 2008a). ISEI went bankrupt in Nov. 2004, following years of financial mismanagement (Japanese Diet 2005).

9 This portrayal had a lasting effect, as there is a widespread misconception among Japanese even today that the 1982 dispute was sparked by entirely incorrect reporting. The government's press secretary reflected this view in 2005, stating the textbook controversy 'was based on a false report' (Chiba 2005).

10 The market share of 0.04% corresponds to about 520–70 copies sold to schools (Nozaki 2002: 619).

11 Following public demonstrations in Okinawa in Sept. 2007, the MoE announced a compromise solution by which textbook publishers were allowed to apply for

modifications to their texts. For more information on the Okinawa controversy, see also *Japan Focus* 2008; Ito 2009; *Okinawa Times* 2008.

12 Seoul's reaction was more restrained compared to 2001 and 2005, however, especially due to security concerns about North Korea following the regime's test-firing of a long-range missile.

13 This development was preceded by a controversy over the inclusion of a reference to Japan's Takeshima claim in the Teaching Guidelines (*Gakushū shidō yōryō*) for social studies in middle schools. See e.g. *Yomiuri Shinbun* 2008; *Japan Times* 2008b; *Mainichi Shinbun* 2008)

14 The division into phases is adopted from Pingel 2007b. Falk Pingel suggests three main phases corresponding to the first three stages in this chapter. Here, a fourth phase is added to delineate the new developments in German–Polish talks since the end of the Cold War.

5   Conclusion

1 A major foreign policy event for both Germany and Japan was clearly the two countries' defeat in the Second World War. Both countries significantly altered their foreign policy outlook after 1945. See e.g. Berger 1998.

2 Interestingly, Charles Hermann defines the last three forms of change (termed programme change, problem/goal change, international orientation change) as 'major foreign policy redirections'. He does not explain this categorization, but his perception may be related to the fact that his analysis is focused on the *visibility* of change, which is significantly lower in the first type.

3 It must be stressed that to this day, German global military contributions are more extensive in both size (i.e. number of troops deployed) and type of mission (e.g. involvement in combat) than Japanese ones. Thus, it would be mistaken to conclude that Japan's role set has necessarily undergone greater change than Germany's.

4 These processes are also discussed in Harnisch 2001; Maull 2006b, 1999; Webber 2001.

5 For a detailed examination of foreign policy learning, see Levy 1994.

6 In academic debates, the process of Japan's foreign policy learning is frequently underestimated or overlooked. Richard Samuels appears to discount foreign policy learning as a cause for change, as he stresses that Japan's 'revisionists began to paint Article 9 as an obstacle to "international cooperation"', 'opportunistically slic[ing] away at antimilitarist restrictions' and 'secur[ing] several major legislative victories in the 1990s' (Samuels 2007b: 81 and 91).

7 See e.g. Maull 2006a; Harnisch 2009; Overhaus 2004.

8 On the notion of soft power, see Nye 2004.

References

References used in content analysis

German documents

Fischer, Joschka (1998) Interview des Bundesministers des Auswärtigen, Joschka Fischer, zur Außenpolitik der neuen Bundesregierung mit der Zeitung 'Der Tagesspiegel' vom 5. November 1998 (Interview with Foreign Minister Joschka Fischer on the foreign policy of the new Federal Government with *Der Tagesspiegel* on 5 November 1998), *Internationale Politik*, 12/1998.

—— (1999a) Rede des Bundesministers des Auswärtigen und EU-Ratsvorsitzenden Joschka Fischer vor dem Europäischen Parlament in Straßburg (Speech by Foreign Minister and EU-Council Chairman Joschka Fischer before the European Parliament in Strasbourg), 21 July, *Internationale Politik*, 11/1999.

—— (1999b) Rede des deutschen Außenministers, Joschka Fischer, am 6. Februar 1999 auf der Konferenz für Sicherheitspolitik in München (Speech by German Foreign Minister Joschka Fischer on 6 February 1999 at the Conference for Security Policy in Munich), *Internationale Politik*, 2/1999.

—— (1999c) Rede des deutschen Außenministers, Joschka Fischer, vor der 54. Generalversammlung der Vereinten Nationen am 22. September 1999 in New York (Speech by German Foreign Minister Joschka Fischer before the 54th General Assembly of the United Nations on 22 September 1999 in New York), *Internationale Politik*, 12/1999.

—— (1999d) Rede vor der französischen Nationalversammlung: Zukunftsfähigkeit und Legitimität der Europäischen Union (Speech before the French National Assembly: sustainability and legitimacy of the European Union), 20 Jan., Berlin: Auswärtiges Amt, www.france-allemagne.fr/Rede-von-Aussenminister-Fischer-in,361. html (accessed May 2008).

—— (2000a) Multilateralismus als Aufgabe deutscher Außenpolitik: Rede des Bundesministers des Auswärtigen, Joschka Fischer (Multilateralism as a task of German foreign policy: speech by Foreign Minister Joschka Fischer), 4 Sept., *Bulletin*, 53(4)/2000.

—— (2000b) Rede des Bundesministers des Auswärtigen Joschka Fischer am 12. Mai 2000 in der Humboldt Universität in Berlin (Speech by Foreign Minister Joschka Fischer on 12 May 2000 at Humboldt University in Berlin), *Bulletin*, 29/2000.

—— (2001) Rede des Bundesministers des Auswärtigen, Joschka Fischer, zum eingebrachten Entwurf eines Gesetzes zum Vertrag von Nizza vor dem Deutschen Bundestag in Berlin (Speech by Foreign Minister Joschka Fischer on the proposal for

154   *References*

a law on the agreement of Nizza before the German Parliament in Berlin), 18 Oct., *Bulletin*, 73(2)/2001.

—— (2002) Rede von Bundesaußenminister Joschka Fischer im Rahmen der Debatte über die transatlantischen Beziehungen vor dem Deutschen Bundestag am 27. Juni 2002 in Berlin (Speech by Foreign Minister Joschka Fischer on the debate about the transatlantic relationship before the German Parliament on 27 June 2002 in Berlin), *Internationale Politik*, 9/2002.

—— (2003a) Rede des Bundesministers des Auswärtigen, Joschka Fischer, vor dem Deutschen Bundestag in Berlin (Speech by Foreign Minister Joschka Fischer before the German Parliament in Berlin), 16 Jan., *Bulletin*, 4(1)/2003.

—— (2003b) Rede des deutschen Außenministers, Joschka Fischer, zur Erweiterung der Europäischen Union vor dem Deutschen Bundestag am 3. Juli 2003 in Berlin (Speech by German Foreign Minister Joschka Fischer on the enlargement of the European Union before the German Parliament on 3 July 2003 in Berlin), *Internationale Politik*, 9/2003.

—— (2003c) Regierungserklärung des Bundesministers des Auswärtigen, Joschka Fischer, zum Europäischen Rat in Brüssel vor dem Deutschen Bundestag (Government policy statement by Foreign Minister Joschka Fischer regarding the European Council in Brussels before the German Parliament), 11 Dec., *Bulletin*, 112(1)/2003.

—— (2004a) Europa auf der Suche nach politischer Ordnung: Rede zur Eröffnung des Internationalen Bertelsmann Forums in Berlin (Europe in search of a political order – speech at the opening of the International Bertelsmann Forum in Berlin), 9 Jan, *Bulletin*, 3(1)/2004.

—— (2004b) Rede des Bundesministers des Auswärtigen, Joschka Fischer, zur aktuellen Europapolitik vor dem Deutschen Bundestag (Speech by Foreign Minister Joschka Fischer on current European Politics before the German Parliament), 13 Feb., *Bulletin*, 14(1)/2004.

—— (2005a) Rede des Bundesministers des Auswärtigen, Joschka Fischer, zum Gesetzesentwurf zu dem Vertrag vom 29. Oktober 2004 über eine Verfassung für Europa vor dem Deutschen Bundestag in Berlin (Speech by Foreign Minister Joschka Fischer on the draft legislation for the agreement of 29 October 2004 on the Constitution for Europe before the German Parliament in Berlin), 24 Feb., *Bulletin*, 14(1)/2005.

—— (2005b) Rede des Bundesministers des Auswärtigen, Joschka Fischer, zur Ratifizierung der europäischen Verfassung vor dem Deutschen Bundestag am 12. Mai 2004 in Berlin (Speech by Foreign Minister Joschka Fischer regarding the ratification of the European Constitution before the German Parliament on 12 May 2004 in Berlin), 12 May, *Bulletin*, 41(2)/2005.

Genscher, Hans-Dietrich (1990a) Rede bei der 45. Generalversammlung der Vereinten Nationen (Speech at the 45th General Assembly of the United Nations), 26 Sept., in Auswärtiges Amt (ed.), *Außenpolitik der Bundesrepublik Deutschland: Dokumente von 1949 bis 1994* (Foreign Policy of the Federal Republic of Germany: Documents from 1949 to 1994) pp. 708–714, Cologne: Verlag Wissenschaft und Politik, 1995.

—— (1990b) Verpflichtende Erklärung zur deutschen Truppenreduzierung (Binding Declaration on the German Reduction of Troops), 30 Aug., in Auswärtiges Amt (ed.), *Außenpolitik der Bundesrepublik Deutschland: Dokumente von 1949 bis 1994* (Foreign Policy of the Federal Republic of Germany: Documents from 1949 to 1994) pp. 685–688, Cologne: Verlag Wissenschaft und Politik, 1995.

—— (1991) Rede des Bundesministers des Auswärtigen, Genscher, am 25. September 1991 vor der 46. Generalversammlung der Vereinten Nationen in New York (Speech by

Foreign Minister Genscher on 25 September 1991 before the 46th General Assembly of the United Nations in New York), 25 Sept., in Auswärtiges Amt (ed.), *Außenpolitik der Bundesrepublik Deutschland: Dokumente von 1949 bis 1994* (Foreign Policy of the Federal Republic of Germany: Documents from 1949 to 1994) pp. 821–826, Cologne: Verlag Wissenschaft und Politik, 1995.

—— (1992) Abschiedsrede des Bundesministers des Auswärtigen, Genscher, vor dem Diplomatischen Korps am 15. Mai 1992 auf dem Petersberg in Königswinter (Farewell speech by Foreign Minister Genscher before the Diplomatic Corps on 15 May 1992 on the Petersberg in Königswinter), in Auswärtiges Amt (ed.), *Außenpolitik der Bundesrepublik Deutschland: Dokumente von 1949 bis 1994* (Foreign Policy of the Federal Republic of Germany: Documents from 1949 to 1994) pp. 857–860, Cologne: Verlag Wissenschaft und Politik, 1995.

—— (1997) Rede von Bundesminister a.D. Hans-Dietrich Genscher auf einer Konferenz über Zusammenarbeit in Europa am 5. September 1997 in Wien (Speech by former Minister Hans-Dietrich Genscher at a conference on cooperation in Europe on 5 September 1997 in Vienna), *Internationale Politik*, 10/1997.

Herzog, Roman (1995) Die Grundkoordinaten deutscher Außenpolitik (The basic principles of German foreign policy), *Internationale Politik* (April).

—— (1998) Partnerschaft für das 21. Jahrhundert: Die neue Qualität im euro-atlantischen Dialog (Partnership for the 21st century: the new quality in Euro-Atlantic dialogue), 1 Feb., *Internationale Politik*, 2/1998.

Jung, Franz J. (2006) Verteidigung neu definieren: Interview mit der *Frankfurter Allgemeinen Zeitung* (Redefining defence: interview with *Frankfurter Allgemeinen Zeitung*), 2 May, *Bundesregierung Online*, http://archiv.bundesregierung.de/Content/DE/Archiv16/Interview/2006/05/2006-05-02-verteidigung-neu-definieren.html (accessed March 2012).

—— (2007) Rede des deutschen Verteidigungsministers Josef Jung zu aktuellen Herausforderungen der europäischen Sicherheits- und Verteidigungspolitik (Speech by German Defence Minister Franz Josef Jung on the current challenges in European security and defence policy), 10 April, *Internationale Politik*, 5/2007.

—— (2008) Die Welt in Unordnung: Veränderte Machtverhältnisse, fehlende Strategien. Rede bei der Münchner Sicherheitskonferenz (The world in disarray: changing relations of power, lack of strategies. Speech at the Munich Security Policy Conference), 8 Feb., *Internationale Politik*, 3/2008.

Kinkel, Klaus (1992a) NATO's enduring role in European security, *NATO Review*, 40 (Oct.).

—— (1992b) Rede des Bundesministers des Auswärtigen, Dr. Kinkel am 23. September 1992 bei der 47. Generalversammlung der Vereinten Nationen in New York (Speech by Foreign Minister Dr Kinkel on 23 September 1992 at the 47th General Assembly of the United Nations in New York), in Auswärtiges Amt (ed.), *Außenpolitik der Bundesrepublik Deutschland: Dokumente von 1949 bis 1994* (Foreign Policy of the Federal Republic of Germany: Documents from 1949 to 1994) pp. 875–879., Cologne: Verlag Wissenschaft und Politik, 1995.

—— (1993a) Das Konzept der 'Erweiterten Sicherheit': Baustein einer Europäischen Sicherheitsarchitektur, Beitrag in der Frankfurter Rundschau vom 16. Dezember 1993 (The Concept of 'Extended Security': Building Block of a European Security Architecture, Contribution in the Frankfurter Rundschau on 16 December 1993), in Auswärtiges Amt (ed.), *Außenpolitik der Bundesrepublik Deutschland: Dokumente von 1949 bis 1994* (Foreign Policy of the Federal Republic of Germany: Documents from 1949 to 1994) pp. 1007–1012, Cologne: Verlag Wissenschaft und Politik, 1995.

156   *References*

—— (1993b) Deutsche Sicherheitspolitik in den 90er Jahren: Rede des Bundesministers des Auswärtigen, Dr. Kinkel, vor der Führungsakademie der Bundeswehr am 9. November 1993 in Hamburg (German foreign policy in the 1990s: speech by Foreign Minister Dr Kinkel before the Leader's Academy of the Bundeswehr on 9 November 1993 in Hamburg), in Auswärtiges Amt (ed.), *Außenpolitik der Bundesrepublik Deutschland: Dokumente von 1949 bis 1994* (Foreign Policy of the Federal Republic of Germany: Documents from 1949 to 1994) pp. 975–978, Cologne: Verlag Wissenschaft und Politik, 1995.

—— (1993c) Deutschland und Großbritannien: Partner in Europa, Beitrag in der Tageszeitung *Die Welt* vom 25. November 1993 (Germany and Great Britain: partner in Europe, contribution in *Die Welt* on 25 November 1993), in Auswärtiges Amt (ed.), *Außenpolitik der Bundesrepublik Deutschland: Dokumente von 1949 bis 1994* (Foreign Policy of the Federal Republic of Germany: Documents from 1949 to 1994) pp. 985–986, Cologne: Verlag Wissenschaft und Politik, 1995.

—— (1993d) Verantwortung, Realismus, Zukunftssicherung: Deutsche Außenpolitik in einer sich neu ordnenden Welt, Beitrag in der *Frankfurter Allgemeinen Zeitung* vom 19. März 1993 (Responsibility, realism, securing the future: German foreign policy in a reorganized world, contribution in *Frankfurter Allgemeine Zeitung* of 19 March 1993), in Auswärtiges Amt (ed.), *Außenpolitik der Bundesrepublik Deutschland: Dokumente von 1949 bis 1994* (Foreign Policy of the Federal Republic of Germany: Documents from 1949 to 1994) pp. 904–910, Cologne: Verlag Wissenschaft und Politik, 1995.

—— (1994a) Deutsche Außen- und Sicherheitspolitik: Rede von Bundesminister Dr. Kinkel in der Graf-Stauffenberg-Kaserne in Sigmaringen am 29. April 1994 (German foreign and security policy: speech by Foreign Minister Dr Kinkel in the Graf-Stauffenberg-Caserne in Sigmaringen on 29 April 1994), in Auswärtiges Amt (ed.), *Außenpolitik der Bundesrepublik Deutschland: Dokumente von 1949 bis 1994* (Foreign Policy of the Federal Republic of Germany: Documents from 1949 to 1994) pp. 1054–1057, Cologne: Verlag Wissenschaft und Politik, 1995.

—— (1994b) Deutsche Außenpolitik in einer neuen Weltlage: Rede vom Bundesminister des Auswärtigen, Kinkel, vor der Deutschen Gesellschaft für Auswärtige Politik am 24. August 1994 in Bonn (German foreign policy in the new international situation: speech by Foreign Minister Kinkel before the German Association for Foreign Policy on 24 August 1994 in Bonn), in Auswärtiges Amt (ed.), *Außenpolitik der Bundesrepublik Deutschland: Dokumente von 1949 bis 1994* (Foreign Policy of the Federal Republic of Germany: Documents from 1949 to 1994) pp. 1081–1085, Cologne: Verlag Wissenschaft und Politik, 1995.

—— (1994c) Deutsche Präsidentschaft im Rat der Europäischen Union: Erklärung der Bundesregierung, abgegeben vom Bundesminister des Auswärtigen, Kinkel, vor dem Deutschen Bundestag (German presidency in the European Union Council: Statement of the German Government, delivered by Foreign Minister Kinkel before the German Parliament), 29 June, in Auswärtiges Amt (ed.), *Außenpolitik der Bundesrepublik Deutschland: Dokumente von 1949 bis 1994* (Foreign Policy of the Federal Republic of Germany: Documents from 1949 to 1994) pp. 1067–1070, Cologne: Verlag Wissenschaft und Politik, 1995.

—— (1994d) Erklärung des deutschen Außenministers Klaus Kinkel vor dem Nordatlantischen Kooperationsrat am 2. Dezember 1994 in Brüssel (Statement by German Foreign Minister Klaus Kinkel before the Northatlantic Cooperation Council on 2 December 1994 in Brussels), *Internationale Politik,* 2/1995.

—— (1994e) Eröffnungsstatement des Bundesministers des Auswärtigen Kinkel vor dem Bundesverfassungsgericht zum Auslandseinsatz der Bundeswehr am 19. April

1994 in Karlsruhe (Opening statement of Foreign Minister Kinkel before the Federal Court on the deployment abroad of the Bundeswehr on 19 April 1994 in Karlsruhe), in Auswärtiges Amt (ed.), *Außenpolitik der Bundesrepublik Deutschland: Dokumente von 1949 bis 1994* (Foreign Policy of the Federal Republic of Germany: Documents from 1949 to 1994) p. 1050, Cologne: Verlag Wissenschaft und Politik, 1995.

—— (1994f) Rede vor der 49. Generalversammlung der Vereinten Nationen am 27. September 1994 in New York (Speech before the 49th General Assembly of the United Nations on 27 September 1994 in New York), in Auswärtiges Amt (ed.), *Außenpolitik der Bundesrepublik Deutschland: Dokumente von 1949 bis 1994* (Foreign Policy of the Federal Republic of Germany: Documents from 1949 to 1994) pp. 1111–1118, Cologne: Verlag Wissenschaft und Politik, 1995.

—— (1995a) Ansprache von Bundesaußenminister Klaus Kinkel anläßlich der Feier des 125jährigen Jubiläums des Auswärtigen Amtes am 16. Januar 1995 in Bonn (Speech by Foreign Minister Klaus Kinkel on the 125th anniversary of the Foreign Ministry on 16 January 1995 in Bonn), *Internationale Politik,* 4/1995.

—— (1995b) Rede des deutschen Außenministers, Klaus Kinkel, am 19. Juni 1995 in Paris vor der Parlamentarischen Versammlung der Westeuropäischen Union über das Konzept einer kooperativen Sicherheitsstruktur für ganz Europa (Speech by Foreign Minister Klaus Kinkel on 19 June 1995 in Paris before the Parliamentary Assembly of the Western European Union on the concept of a cooperative security structure for the whole of Europe), *Internationale Politik,* 8/1995.

—— (1995c) Rede von Bundesaußenminister Klaus Kinkel auf der Münchner Konferenz für Sicherheitspolitik (Speech by Foreign Minister Klaus Kinkel at the Munich Conference for Security Policy), 5 Feb., *Internationale Politik,* 4/1995.

—— (1996) Rede von Bundesaußenminister Klaus Kinkel vor der 51. Generalversammlung der Vereinten Nationen in New York (Speech by Foreign Minister Klaus Kinkel before the 51st General Assembly of the United Nations in New York), 25 Sept., *Internationale Politik,* 2/1997.

—— (1997a) Interview des Bundesministers des Auswärtigen, Klaus Kinkel, mit der Kölnischen/Bonner Rundschau vom 18. Juli 1997 (Interview with Foreign Minister Klaus Kinkel with the Kölnischen/Bonner Rundschau of 18 July 1997), *Internationale Politik,* 10/1997.

—— (1997b) Interview des deutschen Außenministers Klaus Kinkel mit dem Deutschlandfunk anläßlich der Unterzeichnung des Vertrags von Amsterdam (Interview with German Foreign Minister Klaus Kinkel by Deutschlandfunk on the signing of the Treaty of Amsterdam), 2 Oct., *Internationale Politik,* 11/1997.

—— (1998) Rede von Bundesaußenminister Klaus Kinkel beim Neujahrsempfang der Amerikanischen Handelskammer in Deutschland am 22. Januar 1998 in Stuttgart (Speech by Foreign Minister Klaus Kinkel at the New Year Reception of the US Chamber of Commerce in Germany on 22 January 1998 in Stuttgart), *Internationale Politik,* 2/1998.

—— and Hervé de Charette (1996) Gemeinsamer Beitrag des deutschen und des französischen Außenministers für die Tageszeitung *Le Figaro, Financial Times* und die *Frankfurter Allgemeine Zeitung,* veröffentlicht am 29. März 1996 (Joint contribution by the German and French Foreign Ministers to *Le Figaro, Financial Times* and *Frankfurter Allgemeine Zeitung,* published on 29 March 1996), *Internationale Politik,* 8/1996.

—— and Douglas Hurd (1994) Eine strategische Vision für Europa: Beitrag in der *Süddeutschen Zeitung* und der *Times* (A strategic vision for Europe: Contribution in the *Süddeutsche Zeitung* and the *Times*), 26 April, in Auswärtiges Amt (ed.), *Außenpolitik der Bundesrepublik Deutschland: Dokumente von 1949 bis 1994* (Foreign Policy of the Federal Republic of Germany: Documents from 1949 to 1994) pp. 1051–1053, Cologne: Verlag Wissenschaft und Politik, 1995.

Kohl, Helmut (1990a) Ansprache von Bundeskanzler Dr. Kohl zur Eröffnung der Konferenz für Wirtschaftliche Zusammenarbeit in Europa (KWZE) in Bonn am 19. März 1990 (Opening speech by Chancellor Dr Kohl at the Conference for Economic Cooperation in Europe in Bonn on 19 March 1990), in Auswärtiges Amt (ed.), *Außenpolitik der Bundesrepublik Deutschland: Dokumente von 1949 bis 1994* (Foreign Policy of the Federal Republic of Germany: Documents from 1949 to 1994) pp. 661–666, Cologne: Verlag Wissenschaft und Politik, 1995.

—— (1990b) Ansprache zur Eröffnung der Konferenz für Wirtschaftliche Zusammenarbeit in Europa (Speech on the opening of the Conference for Economic Cooperation in Europe), 19 March, in Auswärtiges Amt (ed.), *Außenpolitik der Bundesrepublik Deutschland: Dokumente von 1949 bis 1994* (Foreign Policy of the Federal Republic of Germany: Documents from 1949 to 1994) p. 661, Cologne: Verlag Wissenschaft und Politik, 1995.

—— (1990c) Botschaft von Bundeskanzler Dr. Kohl zum Tag der Deutschen Einheit an alle Regierungen der Welt, mit denen das vereinte Deutschland diplomatische Beziehungen unterhält (Message by Chancellor Dr Kohl on the day of the German unification to all governments in the world, with which the unified Germany has diplomatic relations), 3 Oct., in Auswärtiges Amt (ed.), *Außenpolitik der Bundesrepublik Deutschland: Dokumente von 1949 bis 1994* (Foreign Policy of the Federal Republic of Germany: Documents from 1949 to 1994) pp. 718–720, Cologne: Verlag Wissenschaft und Politik, 1995.

—— (1990d) Regierungserklärung von Bundeskanzler Dr. Kohl vom 3. Oktober 1990 (Government policy statement by Chancellor Dr Kohl on 3 October 1990), in Auswärtiges Amt (ed.), *Außenpolitik der Bundesrepublik Deutschland: Dokumente von 1949 bis 1994* (Foreign Policy of the Federal Republic of Germany: Documents from 1949 to 1994) pp. 727–732, Cologne: Verlag Wissenschaft und Politik, 1995.

—— (1991a) Regierungserklärung von Bundeskanzler Dr. Kohl vor dem Deutschen Bundestag vom 30. Januar 1991 (Government policy statement by Chancellor Dr Kohl on 30 January 1991 before the German Parliament), in Auswärtiges Amt (ed.), *Außenpolitik der Bundesrepublik Deutschland: Dokumente von 1949 bis 1994* (Foreign Policy of the Federal Republic of Germany: Documents from 1949 to 1994) pp. 784–787, Cologne: Verlag Wissenschaft und Politik, 1995.

—— (1991b) Regierungserklärung zu den Ergebnissen des Europäischen Rates in Maastricht von Bundeskanzler Dr. Kohl am 13. Dezember 1991 vor dem Deutschen Bundestag (Government policy statement on the results of the European Council in Maastricht by Chancellor Dr Kohl on 13 December 1991), in Auswärtiges Amt (ed.), *Außenpolitik der Bundesrepublik Deutschland: Dokumente von 1949 bis 1994* (Foreign Policy of the Federal Republic of Germany: Documents from 1949 to 1994) pp. 846–850, Cologne: Verlag Wissenschaft und Politik, 1995.

—— (1993a) Ansprache des Bundeskanzlers Dr. Kohl anläßlich des Festaktes in der Kunst- und Ausstellungshalle der Bundesrepublik Deutschland am 21. Januar 1993 in Bonn: Dreißigjähriges Bestehen des Elysée-Vertrages (Speech by Chancellor Dr Kohl at the Ceremony at the Art and Exhibition Hall of Federal Germany on 21 January 1993 in Bonn: 30th anniversary of the Elysée Agreement), in Auswärtiges Amt (ed.), *Außenpolitik der Bundesrepublik Deutschland: Dokumente von 1949 bis 1994* (Foreign Policy of the Federal Republic of Germany: Documents from 1949 to 1994) pp. 899–901, Cologne: Verlag Wissenschaft und Politik, 1995.

—— (1993b) Erklärung der Bundesregierung zur Sondertagung des Europäischen Rates in Brüssel, abgegeben von Bundeskanzler Helmut Kohl vor dem Deutschen Bundestag (Statement by the government on the Special Conference of the European Council in Brussels, delivered by Chancellor Helmut Kohl before the German Parliament), 11 Nov., *Bulletin,* 99/1993.

—— (1996a) Beitrag von Bundeskanzler Helmut Kohl für die französische Wochenzeitung 'Le Nouvel Observateur', veröffentlicht am 28. November 1996 (Contribution by Chancellor Helmut Kohl for the French weekly *Le Nouvel Observateur,* on 28 November 1996), *Internationale Politik,* 2/1997.

—— (1996b) Rede des deutschen Bundeskanzlers, Helmut Kohl, vor dem Nordatlantischen Kooperationsrat am 4. Juni 1996 in Berlin (Speech by German Chancellor Helmut Kohl before the Northatlantic Cooperation Council on 4 June 1996 in Berlin), *Internationale Politik,* 10/1996.

—— (1996c) Rede von Bundeskanzler Helmut Kohl anläßlich der Verleihung der Ehrendoktorwürde durch die Katholische Universität am 2. Februar 1996 in Löwen, Belgien (Speech by Chancellor Helmut Kohl on the awarding of an honorary doctorate by the Catholic University on 2 February 1996 in Leuven, Belgium), *Internationale Politik,* 8/1996.

—— (1996d) Rede von Bundeskanzler Helmut Kohl anläßlich der Verleihung des Eric-M.-Warburg-Preises der Atlantik Brücke am 18. Juni 1996 in Berlin (Speech by Chancellor Helmut Kohl on the awarding of the Eric-M.-Warburg Prize of the Atlantic Bridge on 18 June 1996 in Berlin), *Internationale Politik,* 2/1997.

—— (1997a) Erklärung des deutschen Bundeskanzlers, Helmut Kohl, zum Abschluß der NATO-Gipfelkonferenz am 9. Juli 1997 in Madrid (Statement by German Chancellor Helmut Kohl at the closing of the NATO Summit on 9 July 1997 in Madrid), *Internationale Politik,* 9/1997.

—— (1997b) Rede von Bundeskanzler Helmut Kohl über Europa und Amerika als Partner in einer sich wandelnden Welt vor dem Chicago Council on Foreign Relations am 19. Juni 1997 in Chicago (Speech by Chancellor Helmut Kohl on Europe and America as partners in a changing world, before the Chicago Council on Foreign Relations on 19 June 1997 in Chicago), *Internationale Politik,* 2/1998.

Köhler, Horst (2005a) Rede von Bundespräsident Horst Köhler beim Abendessen zum Auftakt der 41. Münchner Sicherheitskonferenz (Speech by President Horst Köhler at the opening dinner for the 41st Munich Security Conference), 11 Feb., *Bulletin,* 13(1)/2005.

—— (2005b) Rede von Bundespräsident Horst Köhler zum 50. Jahrestag der Gründung der Deutschen Gesellschaft für Auswärtige Politik am 3. Juni 2005 in Berlin (Speech by President Horst Köhler on the 50th anniversary of the establishment of the German Association for Foreign Policy on 3 June 2005 in Berlin), *Bulletin,* 52(1)/2005.

Maizière, Thomas de (2006) Rede des Chefs des Bundeskanzleramts Thomas de Maizière bei der Bundesakademie für Sicherheitspolitik am 26. Januar 2006 (Speech by the Chief of the Chancellery Thomas de Maizière at the Federal Academy for Security Policy on 26 January 2006), *Bundesregierung Online,* http://archiv.bundesregierung.de/Content/DE/Archiv16/Rede/2006/01/2006-01-26-rede-chef-des-bundeskanzleramts-thomas-de-maizi%C3%A8re-bei-der-bundesakademie-fuer-sicherheitspoli.html (accessed March 2012).

Merkel, Angela (2005) Nie wieder Politik zu Lasten unserer Nachbarn: Interview mit polnischer Zeitschrift 'Fakt' (Never again policy at the expense of our neighbours: interview with the Polish journal *Fakt*), 2 Dec., *Bundesregierung Online,* http://archiv.bundesregierung.de/Content/DE/Archiv16/Interview/2005/12/2005-12-02-nie-wieder-politik-zu-lasten-unserer-nachbarn.html (accessed March 2012).

—— (2006a) Handlungsfähigkeit der NATO stärken: Rede bei der Deutsch-Atlantischen Gesellschaft in Berlin (Strengthening NATO's capacity to act: speech at the German-Atlantic Association in Berlin), 25 Oct., *Bundesregierung Online*, http://archiv. bundesregierung.de/Content/DE/Archiv16/Rede/2006/10/2006-10-24-rede-bkin-dt-atlantische-gesellschaft.html (accessed March 2012).

—— (2006b) Rede von Bundeskanzlerin Angela Merkel anlässlich der Tagung 'Impulse 21: Berliner Forum Sicherheitspolitik' (Speech by Chancellor Angela Merkel at the conference 'Impulse 21: Berlin Forum for Security Policy'), 10 Nov., *Bundesregierung Online*, http://archiv.bundesregierung.de/Content/DE/Archiv16/Rede/2006/11/2006-11-10-rede-bkin-impulse21.html (accessed March 2012).

—— (2006c) Rede von Bundeskanzlerin Angela Merkel bei der Deutschen Gesellschaft für Auswärtige Politik (Speech by Chancellor Angela Merkel at the German Association for Foreign Policy), 8 Nov., *Bundesregierung Online*, http://archiv.bundesregierung. de/Content/DE/Archiv16/Rede/2006/11/2006-11-08-rede-bkin-deutsche-gesellschaft-fuer-auswaertige-politik.html (accessed March 2012).

—— (2006d) Rede von Bundeskanzlerin Angela Merkel anlässlich der Eröffnung des Internationalen Bertelsmann Forums: Die Zukunft der Europäischen Union (Speech by Chancellor Angela Merkel at the opening of the International Bertelsmann Forum: The Future of the European Union), 22 Sept., *Bundesregierung Online*, http://archiv. bundesregierung.de/Content/DE/Archiv16/Rede/2006/09/2006-09-23-bertelsmann.html (accessed March 2012).

—— (2006e) Wertegebundene Europapolitik (Value-bound European policy), 1 Nov., *KAS-Portal*, 444/2006.

—— (2007a) Leidenschaft für Europa: Interview mit der 'Irish Times' (Passion for Europe: interview with the *Irish Times*), 13 Jan., *Bundesregierung Online*, http://archiv. bundesregierung.de/Content/DE/Archiv16/Interview/2007/01/2007-01-13-merkel-irish-times.html?nn=273424 (accessed March 2012).

—— (2007b) Rede anlässlich des Festaktes zur Euro-Einführung in Slowenien (Speech at the ceremony for the introduction of the euro in Slovenia), 15 Jan., *Bundesregierung Online*, http://archiv.bundesregierung.de/Content/DE/Archiv16/Rede/2007/01/2007-01-15-rede-bkin-euroeinfuehrung-slowenien.html (accessed March 2012).

—— (2007c) Rede von Bundeskanzlerin Angela Merkel im Europäischen Parlament (Speech by Chancellor Angela Merkel in the European Parliament), 17 Jan., *Bundesregierung Online*, http://archiv.bundesregierung.de/Content/DE/Archiv16/Rede/2007/01/2007-01-17-bkin-rede-ep.html (accessed March 2012).

—— (2008a) Rede von Bundeskanzlerin Angela Merkel anlässlich der Frühjahrstagung der Parlamentarischen Versammlung der NATO (Speech by Chancellor Angela Merkel at the spring conference of the Parliamentarian Assembly of NATO), 26 May, *Internationale Politik*, 7(8)/2008.

—— (2008b) Rede von Bundeskanzlerin Angela Merkel beim 'National Forum on Europe' in Dublin (Speech by Chancellor Angela Merkel at the 'National Forum on Europe' in Dublin), 14 April, *Internationale Politik*, 5/2008.

—— (2008c) Rede von Bundeskanzlerin Angela Merkel vor der Parlamentarischen Versammlung des Europarats am 15. April 2008 in Straßburg (Speech by Chancellor Angela Merkel before the Parliamentarian Assembly of the European Council on 15 April 2008, in Strasbourg), *Internationale Politik*, 5/2008.

—— (2010a) Rede von Bundeskanzlerin Dr. Angela Merkel beim Neujahrsempfang für das Diplomatische Corps am 25. Januar 2010 in Berlin (Speech by Chancellor Dr Angela Merkel at the New Year reception of the Diplomatic Corps on 25 January

2010 in Berlin), *Bundesregierung Online*, www.bundesregierung.de/Content/DE/ Bulletin/2010/01/09-3-bk-neujahrsempfang.html (accessed March 2012).

—— (2010b) Rede von Bundeskanzlerin Dr. Angela Merkel auf der Veranstaltung 'Die Europa-Rede' am 9. November 2010 in Berlin (Speech by Chancellor Dr Angela Merkel at the 'Europe Speech' event on 9 November 2010 in Berlin), *Bundesregierung Online*, www.bundesregierung.de/Content/DE/Rede/2010/11/2010-11-09-merkel-europarede. html (accessed March 2012).

—— (2011a) Rede von Bundeskanzlerin Angela Merkel anlässlich des Neujahrsempfangs für das Diplomatische Corps (Speech by Chancellor Angela Merkel at the New Year reception of the Diplomatic Corps), 24 Jan. 2011, *Bundesregierung Online*, www. bundesregierung.de/Content/DE/Rede/2011/01/2011-01-24-merkel-diplomatische-corps.html (accessed March 2012).

—— (2011b) Rede von Bundeskanzlerin Dr. Angela Merkel auf der 47. Münchner Sicherheitskonferenz am 5. Februar 2011 in München (Speech by Chancellor Dr Angela Merkel at the 47th Munich Security Conference on 5 February 2011), *Bundesregierung Online*, www.bundesregierung.de/Content/DE/Bulletin/2011/02/15-2-bk-sicherheitskonferenz.html (accessed March 2012).

Pflüger, Friedbert (1999) Europa muss Weltmacht werden: Weichenstellungen der deutschen Ratspräsidentschaft: Beitrag des außenpolitischen Sprechers der CDU/CSU Bundestagsfraktion (Europe must become a global power: far-reaching consequences of the German Council Presidency), 1 Jan., *Internationale Politik*, 1/1999.

Rau, Johannes (2002a) Das 21. Jahrhundert durch globale und regionale Zusammenarbeit gestalten: Neujahrsansprache (Shaping the 21st century through global and regional cooperation), 11 Jan., *Bulletin*, 2(2)/2002.

—— (2002b) Rede von Bundespräsident Johannes Rau über die Zukunft Europas anlässlich seines Staatsbesuchs in Italien am 16. April 2002 in Rom (Speech by President Johannes Rau on the future of Europe on his state visit to Italy), 16 April, *Internationale Politik*, 9/2002.

Rühe, Volker (1995a) Rede des deutschen Verteidigungsministers, Volker Rühe, am 11. Mai 1995 in Bonn über die Nordatlantische Allianz als Fundament einer neuen Friedensordnung in Europa (Speech by German Defence Minister Volker Rühe on 11 May 1995 in Bonn on the North Atlantic Alliance as a basis for a new peace order in Europe), *Internationale Politik*, 8/1995.

—— (1995b) Rede von Bundesverteidigungsminister Volker Rühe über Europa und Amerika, gehalten auf der Münchner Konferenz für Sicherheitspolitik (Speech by Defence Minister Volker Rühe about Europe and America, delivered at the Munich Conference for Security Policy), 4 Feb., *Internationale Politik*, 4/1995.

—— (1996) Vortrag von Verteidigungsminister Volker Rühe vor dem Royal Institute of International Affairs und der Konrad Adenauer Stiftung in London (Address by Defence Minister Volker Rühe before the Royal Institute of International Affairs and the Konrad Adenauer Foundation in London), 19 Nov., *Internationale Politik*, 2/1997.

Scharping, Rudolf (1995a) Deutsche Außenpolitik muss berechenbar sein (German foreign policy must be predictable), 1 Aug., *Internationale Politik*, 8/1995.

—— (1995b) Rede des Vorsitzenden der SPD, Rudolf Scharping, über die gemeinsame transatlantische Sicherheit auf der Münchner Konferenz für Sicherheitspolitik (Speech by the chairman of the SPD, Rudolf Scharping, regarding common transatlantic security at the Munich Conference for Security Policy), 5 Feb., *Internationale Politik*, 4/1995.

—— (1999a) Rede des deutschen Verteidigungsministers, Rudolf Scharping, am 6. Februar 1999 auf der Konferenz für Sicherheitspolitik in München (Speech by German Defence

Minister Rudolf Scharping on 6 February 1999, at the Conference for Security Policy in Munich), *Internationale Politik,* 2/1999.

—— (1999b) Rede des deutschen Verteidigungsministers, Rudolf Scharping, zu 'Grundlinien deutscher Sicherheitspolitik' am 8. September 1999 an der Führungsakademie der Bundeswehr in Hamburg (Speech by German Defence Minister Rudolf Scharping on 'Basics in German Security Policy' on 8 September 1999 at the Leader's Academy of the Bundeswehr in Hamburg), *Internationale Politik,* 10/1999.

Schröder, Gerhard (1998a) Ansprache von Bundeskanzler Gerhard Schröder beim Jahresempfang für das Diplomatische Corps am 23. November 1998 (Speech by Chancellor Gehard Schröder at the annual reception for the Diplomatic Corps on 23 November 1998), *Internationale Politik,* 12/1998.

—— (1998b) Regierungserklärung von Bundeskanzler Gerhard Schröder, abgegeben am 10. November 1998 vor dem Deutschen Bundestag in Bonn (Government statement by Chancellor Gerhard Schröder, delivered on 10 November, 1998 before the German Parliament in Bonn), *Internationale Politik,* 12/1998.

—— (1999) Rede von Bundeskanzler Gerhard Schröder zum Thema 'Deutsche Sicherheitspolitik an der Schwelle des 21. Jahrhunderts' auf der Konferenz für Sicherheitspolitik in München (Speech by Chancellor Gerhard Schröder on 'German security policy on the edge of the 21st century' at the Conference for Security Policy in Munich), 6 Feb., *Internationale Politik,* 4/1999.

—— (2000a) Deutsche Politik zu Beginn des neuen Jahrhunderts: Rede von Bundeskanzler Gerhard Schröder (German policy at the beginning of the new century: speech by Chancellor Gerhard Schröder), 4 Sept., *Bulletin,* 53(2)/2000.

—— (2000b) Rede von Bundeskanzler Gerhard Schröder bei der Entgegennahme des World Statesmen Award der 'Appeal of Conscience Foundation' am 7. September 2000 in New York (Speech by Chancellor Gerhard Schröder on accepting the World Statesmen Award of the 'Appeal of Conscience Foundation' on 7 September 2000 in New York), *Bulletin,* 55(2)/2000.

—— (2001a) Nach der Reform: Zukunftsstrategien für Gesamteuropa: Rede von Bundeskanzler Gerhard Schröder auf dem Internationalen Bertelsmann Forum (After the reform: future strategies for the whole of Europe. Speech by Chancellor Gerhard Schröder at the International Bertelsmann Forum), 19 Jan., *Bulletin,* 10(2)/2001.

—— (2001b) Rede von Bundeskanzler Gerhard Schröder auf der 37. Münchner Konferenz für Sicherheitspolitik (Speech by Chancellor Gerhard Schröder at the 37th Munich Conference for Security Policy), 3 Feb., *Bulletin,* 11(2)/2001.

—— (2001c) Regierungserklärung von Bundeskanzler Gerhard Schröder zur Tagung des Europäischen Rates vor dem Deutschen Bundestag in Berlin (Government policy statement by Chancellor Gerhard Schröder on the Convention of the European Council before the German Parliament in Berlin), 12 Dec., *Bulletin,* 89(1)/2001.

—— (2001d) Regierungserklärung von Bundeskanzler Gerhard Schröder zu den Ergebnissen des Europäischen Rates in Nizza vor dem Bundestag in Berlin (Government policy statement by Chancellor Gerhard Schröder on the results of the European Council Meeting in Nizza before the German Parliament in Berlin), 19 Jan., *Bulletin,* 6(2)/2001.

—— (2002a) Interview mit Bundeskanzler Gerhard Schröder mit der Wochenzeitung 'Die Zeit' vom 15. August 2002 (Interview with Chancellor Gerhard Schröder with *Die Zeit* on 15 August 2002), *Internationale Politik,* 9/2002.

—— (2002b) Rede von Bundeskanzler Gerhard Schröder vor dem Frankreich-Zentrum der Albert-Ludwigs-Universität Freiburg (Speech by Chancellor Gerhard Schröder before the France-Centre of the Albert-Ludwigs-University Freiburg), 12 April, *Bulletin,* 27(2)/2002.

—— (2003a) Rede von Bundeskanzler Gerhard Schröder beim Festakt zum Tag der Deutschen Einheit am 3. Oktober 2003 in Magdeburg (Speech by Chancellor Gerhard Schröder at the ceremony for the anniversary of German Unification on 3 October 2003 in Magdeburg), *Bulletin,* 81(2)/2003.

—— (2003b) Regierungserklärung des deutschen Bundeskanzlers, Gerhard Schröder, zu den Ergebnissen des Europäischen Rates in Brüssel vor dem Deutschen Bundestag am 3. April 2003 in Berlin (Government policy statement of the German Chancellor on the result of the European Council in Brussels before the German Parliament on 3 April 2003 in Berlin), *Internationale Politik,* 9/2003.

—— (2004a) Rede von Bundeskanzler Gerhard Schröder an der Erasmus-Universität 'World Leader Cycle' in Rotterdam (Speech by Chancellor Gerhard Schröder at the Erasmus University 'World Leader Cycle' in Rotterdam), 15 April, *Bulletin,* 34(1)/2004.

—— (2004b) Rede von Bundeskanzler Gerhard Schröder auf der Konferenz für Europäische Kulturpolitik in Berlin (Speech by Chancellor Gerhard Schröder at the Conference for European Culture Policy in Berlin), 26 Nov., *Bulletin,* 108(1)/2004.

—— (2004c) Rede von Bundeskanzler Gerhard Schröder zur Eröffnung der Bundesakademie für Sicherheitspolitik in Berlin (Speech by Chancellor Gerhard Schröder on the opening of the Federal Academy for Security Policy in Berlin), 19 March, *Bulletin,* 25(3)/2004.

—— (2005a) Rede von Bundeskanzler Gerhard Schröder auf dem III. Europaratsgipfel am 17. Mai 2005 in Warschau (Speech by Chancellor Gerhard Schröder at the III. European Council Summit on 17 May 2005 in Warsaw), *Bulletin,* 44(2)/2005.

—— (2005b) Regierungserklärung von Bundeskanzler Gerhard Schröder zur Ratifizierung der europäischen Verfassung vor dem Deutschen Bundestag (Government policy statement by Chancellor Gerhard Schröder regarding the ratification of the European Constitution before the German Parliament), *Bulletin,* 41(1)/2005, www. bundesregierung.de/nn_774/Content/DE/Bulletin/2001__2005/2005/05/2005-05-12-regierungserklaerung-von-bundeskanzler-gerhard-schroeder-zur-ratifizierung-der-europaeischen-v.html (accessed May 2007).

Steinmeier, Frank-Walter (2005) Deutsche Außenpolitik im Zeichen der Kontinuität: Interview mit der 'Bild am Sonntag' (German foreign policy on the track of continuity: interview with *Bild am Sonntag*), 28 Nov., *Bundesregierung Online,* http://archiv. bundesregierung.de/Content/DE/Archiv16/Interview/2005/11/2005-11-28-deutsche-aussenpolitik-im-zeichen-der-kontinuitaet.html (accessed March 2012).

—— (2006) Wunder können wir nicht vollbringen: Interview mit der *Süddeutschen Zeitung* (We cannot work wonders: interview with *Süddeutsche Zeitung*), 21 Dec., *Bundesregierung Online,* http://archiv.bundesregierung.de/Content/DE/Archiv16/Interview/2006/12/2006-12-22-interview-steinmeier.html?nn=273424 (accessed March 2012).

—— (2007a) Diese Ratspräsidentschaft bedeutet eine große zusätzliche Verantwortung: Interview mit der *Bild am Sonntag* (This Council Presidency means big additional responsibility: interview with *Bild am Sonntag*), 7 Jan., *Bundesregierung Online,* http://archiv.bundesregierung.de/Content/DE/Archiv16/Interview/2007/01/2007-01-07-steinmeier-bams.html (accessed March 2012).

—— (2007b) Rede auf der 43. Münchner Konferenz für Sicherheitspolitik (Speech at the 43rd Munich Conference for Security Policy), 11 Feb., *Internationale Politik,* 3/2007.

—— (2007c) Rede des Bundesministers des Auswärtigen Dr. Frank-Walter Steinmeier zum Thema 'Aktuelle Fragen der deutschen Außenpolitik' (Speech by Foreign Minister Dr Frank-Walter Steinmeier on 'current issues in German foreign policy'), 11 Sept., *Internationale Politik,* 10/2007.

—— (2007d) Rede von Bundesaußenminister Frank-Walter Steinmeier anlässlich des 10. WDR-Europa Forums in Berlin (Speech by Foreign Minister Frank-Walter Steinmeier on the 10th WDR-Europe Forum in Berlin), 9 May, *Internationale Politik*, 6/2007.

—— (2008a) A new transatlantic agenda in a changing world: speech by Foreign Minister Frank-Walter Steinmeier at the 'Conference on Germany in the Modern World' at Harvard University 12 April 2008, *Internationale Politik*, 5/2008.

—— (2008b) Auf dem Weg zu einer europäischen Ostpolitik: Die Beziehungen Deutschlands und der EU zu Russland und den östlichen Nachbarn: Rede bei der Willy-Brandt-Stiftung (On the road to a European 'Ostpolitik': the relations of Germany and the EU to Russia and the Eastern neighbours. Speech at the Willy-Brandt-Stiftung), 4 March, *Internationale Politik*, 4/2008.

—— (2008c) Außenminister Frank-Walter Steinmeier vor der Schwarzkopf-Stiftung – 'Historische Reden an Europa' – am 10. Dezember 2008 in Berlin (Foreign Minister Frank-Walter Steinmeier before the Schwarzkopf-Foundation: 'Historical Speeches to Europe' on 10 December 2008 in Berlin), *Internationale Politik*, 1/2009.

—— (2008d) Die Welt in Unordnung – veränderte Machtverhältnisse, fehlende Strategien: Rede bei der Münchner Konferenz für Sicherheitspolitik (The world in disarray – changing relations of power, lack of strategies: speech at the Munich Conference for Security Policy), 9 Feb., *Internationale Politik*, 3/2008.

—— (2009a) Die Welt im Umbruch – wo steht Europa: Rede von Außenminister Steinmeier (The world in upheaval: how Europe is positioned. Speech by Foreign Minister Frank-Walter Steinmeier), 25 Jan., *Auswärtiges Amt Online*, www.auswaertiges-amt.de/DE/ Infoservice/Presse/Reden/2009/090125-BM.html (accessed March 2012).

—— (2009b) Rede von Außenminister Frank-Walter Steinmeier bei der 45. Münchner Sicherheitskonferenz (Speech by Foreign Minister Frank-Walter Steinmeier at the 45th Munich Security Conference), 6 Feb., *Auswärtiges Amt Online*, www.auswaertiges-amt.de/DE/Infoservice/Presse/Reden/2009/090206-BM-Sicherheitskonferenz.html (accessed March 2012).

Süssmuth, Rita (1990) Die Zukunft der Deutschen in Europa: Statement der Präsidentin des Deutschen Bundestages, Prof. Dr. Rita Süssmuth (The future of the Germans in Europe: statement of the President of the German Parliament, Prof. Dr Rita Süssmuth), 26 June, in Auswärtiges Amt (ed.), *Außenpolitik der Bundesrepublik Deutschland: Dokumente von 1949 bis 1994* (Foreign Policy of the Federal Republic of Germany: Documents from 1949 to 1994) pp. 677–678, Cologne: Verlag Wissenschaft und Politik, 1995.

Thierse, Wolfgang (2005) Rede des Präsidenten des Deutschen Bundestages, Wolfgang Thierse, beim Festakt zum 15. Jahrestag der Deutschen Einheit am 3. Oktober 2005 in Potsdam (Speech by the President of the German Parliament, Wolfgang Thierse, at the ceremony on the 15th anniversary of German Unification on 3 October 2005, in Potsdam), *Bulletin*, 77(1)/2005.

Weizsäcker, Richard von (1990) Ansprache von Bundespräsident Dr. von Weizsäcker in der Philharmonie in Berlin am 3. Oktober 1990 (Speech by President Dr von Weizsäcker in the Philharmonic in Berlin on 3 October 1990), in Auswärtiges Amt (ed.), *Außenpolitik der Bundesrepublik Deutschland: Dokumente von 1949 bis 1994* (Foreign Policy of the Federal Republic of Germany: Documents from 1949 to 1994) pp. 721–726, Cologne: Verlag Wissenschaft und Politik, 1995.

—— (1993) Zur deutschen Außenpolitik: Ansprache des Bundespräsidenten beim Symposium des Instituts für Friedensforschung und Sicherheitspolitik im Rathaus Hamburg am 2. Dezember 1993 (Regarding German foreign policy: speech by the President at the Symposium of the Institute for Peace Research and Peace Policy at the

City Hall in Hamburg on 2 December 1993), in Auswärtiges Amt (ed.), *Außenpolitik der Bundesrepublik Deutschland: Dokumente von 1949 bis 1994* (Foreign Policy of the Federal Republic of Germany: Documents from 1949 to 1994) pp. 989–997, Cologne: Verlag Wissenschaft und Politik, 1995.

Westerwelle, Guido (2009) Rede des Bundesministers des Auswärtigen, Dr. Guido Westerwelle, im Rahmen der Aussprache zur Regierungserklärung der Bundeskanzlerin vor dem Deutschen Bundestag am 10. November 2009 in Berlin (Speech by Foreign Minister Dr Guido Westerwelle in the context of the debate on the government declaration before the German Parliament on 10 November 2009 in Berlin), *Bundesregierung Online*, www.bundesregierung.de/Content/DE/Bulletin/2009/11/112-2-bmaa-bt.html (accessed March 2012).

—— (2010a) Rede des Bundesministers des Auswärtigen, Dr. Guido Westerwelle, auf der 46. Münchner Sicherheitskonferenz am 6. Februar 2010 in München (Speech by Foreign Minister Guido Westerwelle at the 46th Munich Security Conference on 6 February 2010 in Munich), *Bundesregierung Online*, www.bundesregierung.de/nn_774/Content/DE/Bulletin/2010/02/13-2-bmaa-sicherheitskonferenz.html (accessed March 2012).

—— (2010b) Rede von Bundesaußenminister Guido Westerwelle vor der 65. Generalversammlung der Vereinten Nationen am 25. September 2010 in New York (Speech by Foreign Minister Guido Westerwelle before the 65th UN General Assembly on 25 September 2010 in New York), *Auswärtiges Amt Online*, www.bundesregierung.de/nn_1272/Content/DE/Pressemitteilungen/AA/2010/09/2010-09-25-rede-von-bundesauenminister-guido-westerwelle-vor-der-65-generalversammlung-der-vere.html (accessed March 2012).

—— (2010c) Rede von Bundesminister Westerwelle beim Forum des Goethe-Instituts zum Thema 'Illusion der Nähe? Ausblicke auf die europäische Nachbarschaft von morgen' (Speech by Minister Westerwelle at the Goethe-Institute Forum 'Illusion of closeness? Outlook on tomorrow's European neighbourhood'), 29 Oct., *Auswärtiges Amt Online*, www.auswaertiges-amt.de/DE/Infoservice/Presse/Reden/2010/101029-BM-Europ-Nachbarschaft.html (accessed March 2012).

—— (2011) 'Europäische Stabilitätsunion: globale Gestaltungsmacht': Rede von Bundesaußenminister Guido Westerwelle vor Studierenden der Universität Leiden in Den Haag ('European stability union: global power that shapes', speech by Foreign Minister Guido Westerwelle, The Hague), 4 Oct., *Auswärtiges Amt Online*, www.auswaertiges-amt.de/nn_582138/sid_B77EDBCAB29EFAAEBCBAC7EA43C5AFA7/DE/Infoservice/Presse/Reden/2011/111004_BM_NL.html?nnm=582150 (accessed March 2012).

Japanese Documents

Abe, Masatoshi (2004) Dai 2 kai Nichi-OSCE kyōsai kaigi 'Aratana anzen hosho kankyō ni okeru kōkatekina funsō yobō no mosaku' Abe gaimu fuku daijin kichō kōen (Keynote speech by Vice Foreign Minister Abe Masatoshi at the second Japan–OSCE conference 'Search for effective conflict prevention under new security circumstances'), 15 March, Tokyo: Gaimushō, www.mofa.go.jp/mofaj/press/enzetsu/16/ef_0315.html (accessed March 2007).

Abe, Shinzo (2006a) APEC shunō kaigi shuseki – Betonamu kōshiki hōmon ni okeru naigai kisha kaiken (Press conference by Prime Minister Abe Shinzo during his official visit to Vietnam – attending the APEC Leader's Meeting), 20 Nov., Tokyo: Kantei, www.kantei.go.jp/jp/abespeech/2006/11/20vietnampress.html (accessed March 2007).

—— (2006b) Dai 165 kai kokkai ni okeru Abe naikaku sōri daijin shoshin hyōmei enzetsu (Policy speech by Prime Minister Abe Shinzo to the 165th session of the Diet), 29 Sept., Tokyo: Kantei, www.kantei.go.jp/jp/abespeech/2006/09/29syosin.html (accessed Feb. 2007).

—— (2007a) Dai 166 kai kokkai ni okeru Abe naikaku sōri daijin shisei hōshin enzetsu (Policy Speech by Prime Minister Abe Shinzo at the 166th Session of the Diet), 26 Jan., Tokyo: Kantei, www.kantei.go.jp/jp/abespeech/2007/01/26sisei.html (accessed April 2007).

—— (2007b) Dai 168 kai kokkai ni okeru Abe naikaku sōri daijin shoshin hyōmei enzetsu (Policy speech by Prime Minister Abe Shinzo at the 168th Session of the Diet), 10 Sept., Tokyo: Kantei, www.kantei.go.jp/jp/abespeech/2007/09/10syosin.html (accessed Nov. 2007).

—— (2007c) Dai 168 kai kokkai ni okeru Abe naikaku sōri daijin (Policy speech by Prime Minister Abe Shinzo at the 168th Session of the Diet), 10 Sept. 2007, Tokyo: Kantei. www.kantei.go.jp/jp/abespeech/2007/09/10syosin.html (accessed Oct. 2009).

Aso, Taro (2005) Watakushi no ajia senryaku: Nihon ha ajia no jissenteki senkusha, Thought Leader tarubeshi (My Asian strategy: Japan as the practical pioneer or thought leader), 7 Dec., Tokyo: Gaimushō, www.mofa.go.jp/mofaj/press/enzetsu/17/easo_1207.html (accessed Oct. 2007).

—— (2006a) Ajian Woru Sutorito Janaru shi he no Aso daijin kikō 'nihon wa chugoku no minshutekina shōrai o kangei suru' (Contribution by Foreign Minister Aso Taro to the *Asian Wall Street Journal* 'Japan welcomes China's democratic future'), 13 March, Tokyo: Gaimushō, www.mofa.go.jp/mofaj/press/enzetsu/18/easo_0313.html (accessed Feb. 2007).

—— (2006b) Dai 164 kai kokkai ni okeru Aso gaimu daijin no gaikō enzetsu (Foreign policy speech by Foreign Minister Aso Taro at the 164th session of the Diet), 20 Jan., Tokyo: Gaimushō, www.mofa.go.jp/mofaj/press/enzetsu/18/easo_0120.html.

—— (2006c) 'Jiyu to hanei no yumi' o tsukuru: hirogaru nihon gaikō no chihei (Making an 'arc of freedom and prosperity': Japan's expanding diplomatic horizons), 30 Nov., Tokyo: Kantei, www.mofa.go.jp/mofaj/press/enzetsu/18/easo_1130.html (accessed March 2007).

—— (2006d) Kokusai kōryu kaigi 'Ajia no mirai' 2006 'Ajia kyōdōtai' he no michi – kōsō to tenbō ni okeru Aso Taro gaisho supichi 'Nettowaku gata Ajia' no mirai o kōsō suru (International Exchange Conference 'The Future of Asia' 2006, Foreign Minister Aso Taro's speech 'A networked Asia' on the topic of 'the road to an Asian community: conception and outlook'), 26 May, Tokyo: Gaimushō, www.mofa.go.jp/mofaj/press/enzetsu/18/easo_0526.html (accessed March 2007).

—— (2006e) Working together for a stable and prosperous East Asia: lessons of the past, a vision for the freedom to dream – address by Foreign Minister Taro Aso at the Center for Strategic and International Studies, Washington, DC, May 3, 2006, Tokyo: Gaimushō, www.mofa.go.jp/announce/fm/aso/address0605.html (accessed Jan. 2007).

—— (2007) Dai 166 kai kokkai ni okeru Aso gaimu daijin no gaikō enzetsu (Policy speech by Foreign Minister Aso Taro at the 166th session of the Diet), 24 May, Tokyo: Gaimushō, www.mofa.go.jp/mofaj/press/enzetsu/19/easo_0126.html (accessed May 2007).

—— (2008) Dai 170 kai kokkai ni okeru Aso sōri daijin shoshin hyōmei enzetsu (Policy speech by Prime Minister Aso Taro at the 170th Session of the Diet), 29 Sept., Tokyo: Kantei, www.kantei.go.jp/jp/asospeech/2008/09/29housin.html (accessed Oct. 2008).

Fukuda, Yasuo (2007) Dai 168 kai kokkai ni okeru Fukuda sōri daijin shoshin hyōmei enzetsu (Policy speech by Prime Minister Fukuda Yasuo at the 168th session of the Diet), 1 Oct., Tokyo: Kantei, www.kantei.go.jp/jp/hukudaspeech/2007/10/01syosin. html (accessed 20 October, 2007).

—— (2008) Fukuda Yasuo nihonkoku naikaku sōri daijin supichi o kokusai kōryū 'Ajia no mirai' 2008 taiheiyō ga 'naigai' to naru hi he 'tomo ni ayumu' mirai no ajia ni 5tsu no yakusoku (Speech by Japanese Prime Minister Fukuda Yasuo at the 2008 International Conference on the 'Future of Asia': towards the Pacific Ocean becoming an 'inland sea': five pledges to a future Asia that 'walks together'), 22 May, Tokyo: Gaimushō, www.mofa.go.jp/mofaj/press/enzetsu/20/efuk_0522.html (accessed Oct. 2008).

Hashimoto, Ryutaro (1996a) Dai 126 kai kokkai ni okeru Hashimoto naikaku sōri daijin shisei hōshin enzetsu (Policy speech by Prime Minister Hashimoto Ryutaro at the 136th session of the Diet), 22 Jan., Tokyo: Gaimushō, www.mofa.go.jp/mofaj/press/ enzetsu/08/eha_0122.html (accessed Jan. 2007).

—— (1996b) Dai 139 kai rinji kokkai Hashimoto sōri shoshin hyōmei enzetsu (Policy speech by Prime Minister Hashimoto Ryutaro at the special meeting of the 139th session of the Diet), 29 Nov., Tokyo: Gaimushō, www.mofa.go.jp/mofaj/press/enzetsu/08/ eha_1129.html (accessed Feb. 2007).

—— (1997a) Dai 140 kai kokkai ni okeru Hashimoto naikaku sōri daijin shisei hōshin enzetsu (Policy speech by Prime Minister Hashimoto Ryutaro at the 140th session of the Diet), 20 Jan., Tokyo: Gaimushō, www.mofa.go.jp/mofaj/gaiko/bluebook/97/1st/194-203. html (accessed March 2007).

—— (1997b) Press conference by Prime Minister Hashimoto Ryutaro at the Japan-ASEAN Summit Meeting in Malaysia: December 16, 1997, Tokyo: Gaimushō, www.mofa.go.jp/region/asia-paci/asean/pmv9712/conference_RH.html (accessed Jan. 2007).

Hata, Tsutomu (1994a) Dai 129 kai kokkai ni okeru Hata fuku sōri ken gaimu daijin no gaikō enzetsu (Foreign policy speech of Vice Prime Minister and Foreign Minister Hata Tsutomu at the 129th session of the Diet), 4 March, Tokyo: Gaimushō, www.mofa. go.jp/mofaj/gaiko/bluebook/1995_1/h07-shiryou-1-1.htm#a2 (accessed Jan. 2007).

—— (1994b) Dai 129 kai kokkai ni okeru Hata naikaku sōri daijin shoshin hyōmei enzetsu (Policy speech by Prime Minister Hata at the 129th session of the Diet), 10 May, Tokyo: Gaimushō, www.mofa.go.jp/mofaj/gaiko/bluebook/1995_1/h07-shiryou-1-1.htm#a3 (accessed Jan. 2007).

Hatoyama, Yukio (2009a) Address by H.E. Dr. Yukio Hatoyama Prime Minister of Japan: Japan's new commitment to Asia – toward the realization of an East Asian community, 15 Nov., Tokyo: Kantei, www.kantei.go.jp/foreign/hatoyama/ statement/200911/15singapore_e.html (accessed Nov. 2010).

—— (2009b) Dai 173kai kokkai ni okeru Hatoyama naikaku sōri daijin shoshin hyōmei enzetsu (Policy speech by Prime Minister Hatoyama Yukio at the 173rd session of the Diet), 26 Oct., Tokyo: Kantei, www.kantei.go.jp/jp/hatoyama/ statement/200910/26syosin.html (accessed Nov. 2010).

Hosokawa, Morihiro (1993a) Dai 127 kai kokkai ni okeru Hosokawa naikaku sōri daijin shoshin hyōmei enzetsu (Policy speech by Prime Minister Hosokawa Morihiro at the 127th session of the Diet), 23 Aug., Tokyo: Gaimushō, www.mofa.go.jp/mofaj/gaiko/ bluebook/1993_1/h05-1-shiryou-1.htm#a3 (accessed Jan. 2007).

—— (1993b) Dai 128 kai kokkai ni okeru Hosokawa naikaku sōri daijin shoshin hyōmei enzetsu (Policy speech by Prime Minister Hosokawa Morihiro), 21 Sept., Tokyo:

Gaimushō,   www.mofa.go.jp/mofaj/gaiko/bluebook/1993_1/h05-1-shiryou-1.htm#a4 (accessed Jan. 2007).

—— (1994a) Beikoku Jōjitaun Daigaku ni okeru Hosokawa sōri daijin enzetsu (Speech by Prime Minister Hosokawa Morihiro at Georgetown University in the US), 2 Nov., Tokyo: Gaimushō, www.mofa.go.jp/mofaj/gaiko/bluebook/1995_1/h07-shiryou-1-2. htm#a1 (accessed Jan. 2007).

—— (1994b) Dai 129 kai kokkai ni okeru Hosokawa naikaku sōri daijin shisei hōshin enzetsu (Policy speech by Prime Minister Hosokawa Morihiro at the 129th session of the Diet), 4 March, Tokyo: Gaimushō, www.mofa.go.jp/mofaj/gaiko/bluebook/1995_1/ h07-shiryou-1-1.htm#a1 (accessed Jan. 2007).

Ikeda, Yukihiko (1996a) ASEAN kakudai gaishō kaigi kobetsu kaigō ('7+1' kaigō) ni okeru Ikeda gaimu daijin sutetomento (Statement by Foreign Minister Ikeda Yukihiko at the post-ministerial conference (7+1 session)), 24 July, Tokyo: Gaimushō, www.mofa.go.jp/mofaj/gaiko/bluebook/97/1st/211-213.html.

—— (1996b) Dai 136 kai kokkai ni okeru Ikeda zengaimudaijin no gaikō enzetsu (Foreign policy speech by Foreign Minister Yukihiko Ikeda to the 136th session of the Diet), 22 Jan., Tokyo: Gaimushō, www.mofa.go.jp/mofaj/press/enzetsu/08/ei_0122.html (accessed March 2007).

—— (1997) Dai 140kai kokkai ni okeru Ikeda gaimu daijin no gaikō enzetsu (Foreign policy speech by Foreign Minister Ikeda Yukihiko at the 140th session of the Diet), 20 Jan., Tokyo, www.mofa.go.jp/mofaj/press/enzetsu/09/ei_0120.html (accessed Jan. 2007).

Kaifu, Toshiki (1990a) Dai 119kai kokkai ni okeru Kaifu naikaku sōri daijin shoshin hyōmei enzetsu (Policy speech by Prime Minister Kaifu in the 119th Diet session), 12 Oct., Tokyo: Gaimushō, www.mofa.go.jp/mofaj/gaiko/bluebook/1991/h03-shiryou-1. htm#a1 (accessed Jan. 2007).

—— (1990b) Georgia Nichibei kyōkai shusai bansan ni okeru Kaifu naikaku sōri daijin enzetsu (Speech by Prime Minister Kaifu at the US–Japan Association in Georgia), 12 July, Tokyo: Gaimushō, www.mofa.go.jp/mofaj/gaiko/bluebook/1990/h02-shiryou-2. htm#a5 (accessed Feb. 2007).

—— (1990c) Japan's vision, *Foreign Policy*, 80: 28–39.

—— (1991a) Dai 120kai kokkai ni okeru Kaifu naikaku daijin shisei hōshin enzetsu (Policy speech by Prime Minister Kaifu in the 120th session of the Diet), 25 Jan., Tokyo: Gaimushō,   www.mofa.go.jp/mofaj/gaiko/bluebook/1991/h03-shiryou-1. htm#a2 (accessed March 2007).

—— (1991b) Dai 121kai kokkai ni okeru Kaifu naikaku sōri daijin shoshin hyōmei enzetsu (Policy speech by Prime Minister Kaifu in the 121th session of the Diet), 5 Aug., Tokyo: Gaimushō, www.mofa.go.jp/mofaj/gaiko/bluebook/1991/h03-shiryou-1. htm#a4 (accessed Jan. 2007).

Kakizawa, Koji (1992) ASEAN kakudai gaishō kaigi zentaikaigi (6+7) ni okeru Kakizawa gaimu seimujikan stetomento (Statement by Parliamentary Vice Minister for Foreign Affairs Kakizawa Koji to the General Session of the ASEAN Post-Ministerial Conference), 24 July, Tokyo: Gaimushō, www.mofa.go.jp/mofaj/gaiko/bluebook/1992/ h04-shiryou-2.htm#b6 (accessed Jan. 2007).

Kan, Naoto (2010a) Dai 174 kai kokkai ni okeru Kan naikaku sōri daijin shoshin hyōmei enzetsu (Policy speech by Prime Minister Kan Naoto at the 174th session of the Diet), 11 June, Tokyo: Kantei, www.kantei.go.jp/jp/kan/statement/201006/11syosin.html (accessed March 2011).

—— (2010b) Dai 176 kai kokkai ni okeru Kan naikaku sōri daijin shoshin hyōmei enzetsu (Policy speech by Prime Minister Kan Naoto at the 176th session of the Diet), 1 Oct.,

Tokyo: Kantei, www.kantei.go.jp/jp/kan/statement/201010/01syosin.html (accessed Nov. 2010).

—— (2011) Kan sōri daijin gaikō ni kan suru enzetsu 'Rekishi no bunsuirei ni tatsu nihon gaikō' (Speech on foreign policy by Prime Minister Kan 'Japanese diplomacy at a historic watershed'), 20 Jan., Tokyo: Kantei, www.kantei.go.jp/jp/kan/statement/201101/20speech.html (accessed July 2011).

Kawaguchi, Yoriko (2002a) Dai 154 kai kokkai ni okeru Kawaguchi gaimu daijin no gaikō enzetsu (Policy speech by Foreign Minister Kawaguchi Yoriko at the 154th session of the Diet), 4 Feb., Tokyo: Gaimushō, www.mofa.go.jp/mofaj/press/enzetsu/14/ekw_0204.html (accessed April 2007).

—— (2002b) Kyōtsu no chōsen: Beikoku to Nihon, genzai no nihon no mikata (Common challenges: US and Japan: current Japanese view), 16 Sept., Tokyo: Gaimushō, www.mofa.go.jp/mofaj/press/enzetsu/14/ekw_0916.html (accessed April 2007).

—— (2002c) Nihon kisha kurabu ni okeru Kawaguchi gaimu daijin seisaku enzetsu (Policy speech by foreign Minister Kawaguchi Yoriko at the Japanese Press Club), 18 March, Tokyo: Gaimushō, www.mofa.go.jp/mofaj/press/enzetsu/14/ekw_0318.html (accessed April 2007).

—— (2003) Dai 156 kai kokkai ni okeru Kawaguchi gaimu daijin no gaikō enzetsu (Foreign policy speech by Foreign Minister Kawaguchi Yoriko at the 156th session of the Diet), 31 Jan., Tokyo: Gaimushō, www.mofa.go.jp/mofaj/press/enzetsu/15/ekw_0131.html (accessed Jan. 2007).

—— (2004) Foreign Correspondents Club Japan Press Conference: September 16, 2004, Tokyo: Gaimushō, www.mofa.go.jp/announce/fm/kawaguchi/press040916.html (accessed April 2007).

Koizumi, Junichiro (2001a) Dai 151kai kokkai ni okeru Koizumi naikaku sōri daijin shoshin hyōmei enzetsu (Policy speech by Prime Minister Koizumi Junichiro at the 151st session of the Diet), 7 May, Tokyo: Gaimushō, www.kantei.go.jp/jp/koizumispeech/2001/0507syosin.html (accessed Jan. 2007).

—— (2001b) Dai 153kai kokkai ni okeru Koizumi naikaku sōri daijin shoshin hyōmei enzetsu (Policy speech by Prime Minister Koizumi Junichiro at the 153rd session of the Diet), 27 Sept., Tokyo: Gaimushō, www.kantei.go.jp/jp/koizumispeech/2001/0927syosin.html (accessed Oct. 2007).

—— (2001c) Nikkei Shinbun shusai 'Ajia no mirai' bansankai Koizumi sōri enzetsu (Speech by Prime Minister Koizumi Junichiro at the 'Future of Asia' Conference Dinner hosted by *Nikkei Shinbun*), 7 June, Tokyo: Gaimushō, www.mofa.go.jp/mofaj/press/enzetsu/13/ekoi_0607.html (accessed Jan. 2007).

—— (2002a) 21 seiki no nichibei dōmei: mitsu no chōsen (The Japan–US Alliance in the 21st century: three challenges), 10 Sept., Tokyo: Gaimushō, www.mofa.go.jp/mofaj/press/enzetsu/14/ekoi_0910.html (accessed April 2007).

—— (2002b) Boao Ajia Foramu ni okeru supichi 'Ajia no shin seiki chōsen to kikai' (Speech by Prime Minister Koizumi Junichiro at the Boao Forum for Asia 'Asia's new century: challenge and opportunity'), 12 April, Tokyo: Gaimushō, www.mofa.go.jp/mofaj/press/enzetsu/14/ekoi_0412.html (accessed April 2007).

—— (2002c) Dai 154kai kokkai ni okeru Koizumi naikaku sōri daijin shisei hōshin enzetsu (Policy speech by Prime Minister Koizumi Junichiro at the 154th session of the Diet), 4 Feb., Tokyo: Kantei, www.kantei.go.jp/jp/koizumispeech/2002/02/04sisei.html (accessed April 2007).

—— (2002d) Dai 155 kai kokkai ni okeru Kozumi naikaku sōri daijin shoshin hyōmei enzetsu (General policy speech by Prime Minister Koizumi Junichiro at the 155th session of the

Diet), 18 Oct., Tokyo: Kantei, www.kantei.go.jp/jp/koizumispeech/2002/10/18syosin.html (accessed April 2007).

—— (2002e) Koizumi sōri daijin no ASEAN shokoku hōmon ni okeru seisaku enzetsu 'Higashi Ajia no naka no nihon to ASEAN – Socchokuna patonashippu o motomete' (Speech by Prime Minister Koizumi Junichiro on his visit to ASEAN countries 'Japan and ASEAN in East Asia – calling for a sincere partnership'), Tokyo: Gaimushō, www. mofa.go.jp/mofaj/press/enzetsu/14/ekoi_0114.html (accessed March 2007).

—— (2002f) Sōzōteki patonashippu ni mukete: Ajia kikai shusai kōenkai (Speech by Prime Minister Koizumi Junichiro hosted by the Asia Society 'Towards a creative partnership'), Tokyo: Gaimushō, www.mofa.go.jp/mofaj/press/enzetsu/14/ekoi_0501. html (accessed April 2007).

—— (2003a) ASEAN Bijinesu tōshi samitto sōri supichi (Speech by Prime Minister Koizumi Junichiro at the ASEAN Business and Investment Summit), Tokyo: Gaimushō, www.mofa.go.jp/mofaj/press/enzetsu/15/ekoi_1007.html (accessed April 2007).

—— (2003b) Dai 156 kai kokkai ni okeru Koizumi naikaku sōri daijin shisei hōshin enzetsu (General policy speech by Prime Minister Koizumi Junichiro at the 156th session of the Diet), 31 Jan., Tokyo: Kantei, www.kantei.go.jp/jp/koizumispeech/2003/01/31sisei. html (accessed Jan. 2007).

—— (2003c) Dai 156 kai tsūjō kokkai shūryōji ni okeru Koizumi naikaku sōri daijin kisha kaiken (Press conference by Prime Minister Koizumi Junichiro on the closing of the 156th regular Diet session), 29 July, Tokyo: Kantei, www.kantei.go.jp/jp/ koizumispeech/2003/07/29press.html (accessed April 2007).

—— (2003d) Dai 157kai kokkai ni okeru Koizumi naikaku sōri daijin shoshin hyōmei enzetsu (Policy speech by Prime Minister Koizumi Junichiro at the 157th session of the Diet), 26 Sept., Tokyo: Kantei, www.kantei.go.jp/jp/koizumispeech/2003/09/26syosin. html.

—— (2003e) Koizumi naikaku sōri daijin kisha kaiken (Press conference by Prime Minister Koizumi Junichiro), 9 Dec., Tokyo: Kantei, www.kantei.go.jp/jp/ koizumispeech/2003/12/09press.html (accessed March 2007).

—— (2004a) Dai 159 kai kokkai ni okeru Koizumi naikaku sōri daijin shisei hōshin enzetsu (General policy speech by Prime Minister Koizumi Junichiro at the 159th session of the Diet), 19 Jan., Tokyo: Kantei, www.kantei.go.jp/jp/koizumispeech/2004/01/19sisei. html (accessed April 2007).

—— (2004b) Dai 161 kai kokkai ni okeru Koizumi naikaku sōri daijin shoshin hyōmei enzetsu (General policy speech by Prime Minister Koizumi Junichiro at the 161st session of the Diet), 12 Oct., Tokyo: Kantei, www.kantei.go.jp/jp/koizumispeech/2004/10/12syosin. html (accessed April 2007).

—— (2004c) Nikkei Shinbun shusai 'Ajia no mirai' bansankai Koizumi sōri daijin aisatsu (Greeting by Prime Minister Koizumi Junichiro at the conference banquet 'The Future of Asia' hosted by *Nikkei Shinbun*), 3 June, Tokyo: Gaimushō, www.mofa.go.jp/mofaj/ press/enzetsu/16/ekoi_0603.html (accessed April 2007).

—— (2005a) APEC shunō kaigigo no naigai kisha kaiken (Press conference by Prime Minister Koizumi Junichiro following the APEC leader's meeting), 19 Nov., Tokyo: Gaimushō, www.kantei.go.jp/jp/koizumispeech/2005/11/19press.html (accessed April 2007).

—— (2005b) Dai 162kai kokkai ni okeru Koizumi naikaku sōri daijin shisei hōshin enzetsu (Policy speech by Prime Minister Koizumi Junichiro at the 162nd session of the Diet), 21 Jan., Tokyo: Kantei, www.kantei.go.jp/jp/koizumispeech/2005/01/21sisei. html (accessed March 2007).

—— (2005c) Dai 163 kai kokkai ni okeru Koizumi naikaku sōri daijin shoshin hyōmei enzetsu (Policy speech by Prime Minister Koizumi Junichiro at the 163rd session of the Diet), 26 Sept., Tokyo: Gaimushō, www.kantei.go.jp/jp/koizumispeech/2005/09/26syosin. html (accessed April 2007).

—— (2005d) US President and Prime Minister of Japan discuss strong relationship: press conference: November 16, 2005, Washington, DC, White House, www.whitehouse. gov/news/releases/2005/11/print/20051116-5.html (accessed Aug. 2008).

—— (2006a) Dai 164 kai kokkai ni okeru Koizumi naikaku sōri daijin shisei hōshin enzetsu (General policy speech by Prime Minister Koizumi Junichiro at the 164th session of the Diet), 20 Jan., Tokyo: Kantei, www.kantei.go.jp/jp/koizumispeech/2006/01/20sisei. html (accessed March 2007).

—— (2006b) Koizumi sōri daijin nentō kisha kaiken (New Year's press conference by Prime Minister Koizumi Junichiro), 4 Jan., Tokyo: Kantei, www.kantei.go.jp/jp/ koizumispeech/2006/01/04press.html (accessed May 2007).

Komura, Masahiko (1999a) Ajia no mirai ni mukete nihon no Ridashippu (Japan's leadership for the future of Asia), 3 June, Tokyo: Gaimushō, www.mofa.go.jp/mofaj/ press/enzetsu/11/eko_0603.html (accessed Feb. 2007).

—— (1999b) ASEAN kakudai gaishō kaigi zentai kaigō de no Komura gaimu daijin enzetsu (Speech by Foreign Minister Komura Masahiko at the ASEAN PMC meeting), 27 July, Tokyo: Gaimushō, www.mofa.go.jp/mofaj/press/enzetsu/11/eko_727a.html (accessed Feb. 2007).

—— (1999c) Dai 145 kai kokkai ni okeru gaimu dajin no gaikō enzetsu (Foreign policy speech by Foreign Minister Komura Masahiko at the 145th session of the Diet), 19 Jan., Tokyo: Gaimushō, www.mofa.go.jp/mofaj/press/enzetsu/11/eko_0119.html (accessed Feb. 2007).

—— (1999d) Nichi-ASEAN gaishō kaigi de no Komura gaimu daijin enzetsu (Speech by Foreign Minister Komura Masahiko at the Japan-ASEAN Foreign Ministers' meeting), 27 July, Tokyo: Gaimushō, www.mofa.go.jp/mofaj/press/enzetsu/11/eko_727b.html (accessed Feb. 2007).

—— (2008a) 'Ajia no seiki' no jitsugen ni mukete (Towards the realization of an 'Asian century'), 2 June, Tokyo: Gaimushō, www.mofa.go.jp/mofaj/press/enzetsu/20/ ekmr_0602.html (accessed Oct. 2008).

—— (2008b) Ajia: Kokusaiteki antei no kōchiku (Asia: building the international stability (speech at the 44th Munich Conference on Security Policy)), 10 Feb., Tokyo: Gaimushō, www.mofa.go.jp/mofaj/press/enzetsu/20/ekmr_0210.html (accessed Nov. 2008).

—— (2008c) Dai 169 kai kokkai ni okeru Komura gaimu daijin no gaikō enzetsu (Policy speech by Foreign Minister Komura Masahiko at the 169th session of the Diet), 18 Jan., Tokyo: Gaimushō, www.mofa.go.jp/mofaj/press/enzetsu/20/ekmr_0118.html (accessed Dec. 2008).

Kono, Yohei (1994a) ASEAN kakudai gaishōkaigi zenkaigi (6+7) ni okeru Kono fuku sōri ken gaimu daijin sutetomento (Statement by Vice Prime Minister and Foreign Minister Kono Yohei at the ASEAN post-ministerial conference (6+7)), 26 July, Tokyo: Gaimushō, www.mofa.go.jp/mofaj/gaiko/bluebook/1995_1/h07-shiryou-1-2.htm# a4 (accessed Jan. 2007).

—— (1994b) ASEAN Chiiki Fōramu (ARF) ni okeru Kono Fukusōri ken gaimu daijin hatsugen (Statement by Vice Prime Minister and Foreign Minister Kono Yohei at the ASEAN Regional Forum), 25 July, Tokyo: Gaimushō, www.mofa.go.jp/mofaj/gaiko/ bluebook/1995_1/h07-shiryou-1-2.htm#a3 (accessed Jan. 2007).

—— (1994c) Dai 49kai kokuren sōkai ni okeru Kono fuku sōri ken gaimu daijin ippan tōron enzetsu (Regular debate speech by Vice Prime Minister and Foreign Minister Kono Yohei at the 49th UN General Assembly), 27 Sept., Tokyo: Gaimushō, www.mofa.go.jp/mofaj/gaiko/bluebook/1995_1/h07-shiryou-1-2.htm#a6 (accessed Jan. 2007).

—— (1995a) A path for the future of Japan's foreign policy, 5 Jan., Tokyo: Gaimushō, www.mofa.go.jp/announce/announce/archive_3/path.html (accessed March 2007).

—— (1995b) Foreign Minister's major speeches and articles: foreign policy speech to the 132th session of the Diet, 20 Jan., Tokyo: Gaimushō, www.mofa.go.jp/announce/announce/archive_3/speech.html (accessed Feb. 2007).

—— (1995c) Japan's role in Asia-Pacific regional cooperation, 28 July, Tokyo: Gaimushō, www.mofa.go.jp/announce/announce/archive_3/asia.html (accessed Feb. 2007).

—— (2000) Dai 147kai kokkai ni okeru Kono Yohei gaimu daijin no gaikō enzetsu (Policy speech by Foreign Minister Kono Yoei at the 147th session of the Diet), 28 Jan., Tokyo: Gaimushō, www.mofa.go.jp/mofaj/press/enzetsu/12/ekn_0128.html (accessed March 2007).

—— (2001a) 21 seiki higashi ajia gaikō no kōsō (The conception for diplomacy in East Asia in the 21st century), 23 Jan., Tokyo: Gaimushō, www.mofa.go.jp/mofaj/press/enzetsu/13/ekn_0123.html (accessed Oct. 2008).

—— (2001b) Dai 151 kai kokkai ni okeru Kono gaimu daijin no gaikō enzetsu (Policy speech by Foreign Minister Kono Yohei at the 151st session of the Diet), 31 Jan., Tokyo: Gaimushō, www.mofa.go.jp/mofaj/press/enzetsu/13/ekn_0131.html (accessed Nov. 2008).

Machimura, Nobutaka (2005a) Dai 162kai kokkai ni okeru Machimura gaimu daijin no gaikō enzetsu (Foreign policy speech by Foreign Minister Machimura Nobutaka at the 162nd session of the Diet), 21 Jan., Tokyo: Gaimushō, www.mofa.go.jp/mofaj/press/enzetsu/17/emc_0121.html (accessed April 2007).

—— (2005b) Machimura gaimu daijin no nyu yoku ni okeru seisaku supichi 'sengo 60 nen o mukaeta nihon no sekai senryaku to nichibei kankei' (Policy speech by Foreign Minister Machimura Nobutaka in New York 'Japan's global strategy and the Japan–US relationship on the 60th Anniversary of the end of World War II'), 29 April, Tokyo: Gaimushō, www.mofa.go.jp/mofaj/press/enzetsu/17/emc_0429.html (accessed March 2007).

Maehara, Seiji (2011) Dai 177 kai kokkai ni okeru Maehara gaimu daijin no gaikō enzetsu (Foreign policy speech by Foreign Minister Maehara Seiji at the 177th session of the Diet), 24 Jan., Tokyo: Gaimushō, www.mofa.go.jp/mofaj/press/enzetsu/23/emhr_0124.html (accessed June 2011).

Matsumoto, Takeaki (2011) Dai 17 kai kokusai kōryū kaigi 'Ajia no Mirai' ni okeru Matsumoto gaimu daijin enzetsu (Speech by Foreign Minister Matsumoto Takeaki at the 17th International Exchange Conference 'Future of Asia'), 26 May, Tokyo: Gaimushō, www.mofa.go.jp/mofaj/press/enzetsu/23/emtm_0526.html (accessed Sept. 2011).

Miyazawa, Kiichi (1991) Dai 122 kai lokkai ni okeru Miyazawa naikaku sōri daijin shoshin hyōmei enzetsu (Policy speech by Prime Minister Miyazawa Kiichi at the 122nd session of the Diet), 8 Nov., Tokyo: Gaimushō, www.mofa.go.jp/mofaj/gaiko/bluebook/1992/h04-shiryou-1.htm#a1 (accessed Jan. 2007).

—— (1992a) Dai 123 kai kokkai ni okeru Miyazawa naikaku sōri daijin shisei hōshin enzetsu (Policy speech by Prime Minister Kiichi Miyazawa to the 123rd session of the Diet), 24 Jan., Tokyo: Gaimushō, www.mofa.go.jp/mofaj/gaiko/bluebook/1992/h04-shiryou-1.htm#a2 (accessed Jan. 2007).

—— (1992b) Dai 125 kai kokkai ni okeru Miyazawa maikaku Sōri daijin shoshin hyōmei enzetsu (Policy speech by Prime Minister Kiichi Miyazawa to the 125th session of the National Diet), 30 Oct., Tokyo: Gaimushō, www.mofa.go.jp/mofaj/gaiko/ bluebook/1992/h04-shiryou-1.htm#a4 (accessed Jan. 2007).

—— (1992c) Miyazawa naikaku sōri daijin no Daikanminkoku hōmon ni okeru seisaku enzetsu (Policy speech by Prime Minister Miyazawa Kiichi during his visit to the Republic of Korea), 17 Jan., Tokyo: Gaimushō, www.mofa.go.jp/mofaj/gaiko/ bluebook/1992/h04-shiryou-2.htm#b2 (accessed Jan. 2007).

—— (1992d) Nashonaru puresu kurabu ni okeru Miyazawa maikaku sōri daijin supichi (Speech by Prime Minister Miyazawa Kiichi at the National Press Club), 2 July, Tokyo: Gaimushō, www.mofa.go.jp/mofaj/gaiko/bluebook/1992/h04-shiryou-2.htm#b8 (accessed Jan. 2007).

—— (1993a) ASEAN hōmon ni okeru Miyazawa naikaku sōri daijin seisaku enzetsu (Policy speech by Prime Minister Miyazawa Kiichi during his ASEAN visit [to Indonesia]), 16 Jan., Tokyo: Gaimushō, www.mofa.go.jp/mofaj/gaiko/bluebook/1993_1/h05-1-shiryou-2. htm#a2 (accessed Jan. 2007).

—— (1993b) Dai 126 kai kokkai ni okeru Miyazawa naikaku sōri daijin shisei hōsei enzetsu (Policy speech by Prime Minister Miyazawa Kiichi at the 126th session of the Diet), 22 Jan., Tokyo: Gaimushō, www.mofa.go.jp/mofaj/gaiko/bluebook/1993_1/h05- 1-shiryou-1.htm#a1 (accessed Jan. 2007).

Mori, Yoshiro (2000a) 'Ajia no Mirai' bansankai ni okeru Mori sōri aisatsu (Remarks by Prime Minister Mori Yoshiro at 'The Future of Asia' dinner conference), 8 June, Tokyo: Gaimushō, www.mofa.go.jp/mofaj/press/enzetsu/12/ems_0608.html (accessed March 2007).

—— (2000b) Dai 147 kai kokkai ni okeru Mori naikaku sōri daijin shoshin hyōmei enzetsu (Policy speech by Prime Minister Mori Yoshiro at the 147th session of the Diet), 7 April, Toyko: Gaimushō, www.kantei.go.jp/jp/morisouri/mori_speech/2000/0407syosin.html (accessed Feb. 2007).

—— (2000c) Dai 149 kai kokkai ni okeru Mori naikaku sōri daijin shoshin hyōmei enzetsu (Policy speech by Prime Minister Yoshiro Mori at the 149th session of the Diet), 28 July, Tokyo: Gaimushō, www.kantei.go.jp/jp/morisouri/mori_speech/2000/0728syosin.html (accessed March 2007).

—— (2001) Dai 151kai kokkai ni okeru Mori naikaku sōri daijin no shisei hōshin enzetsu (Policy speech by Prime Minister Mori Yoshiro at the 151st session of the Diet), 31 Jan., Tokyo: Gaimushō, www.kantei.go.jp/jp/morisouri/mori_speech/2001/0131syosin.html (accessed Jan. 2007).

Murayama, Tomiichi (1994a) Dai 130 kai kokkai ni okeru Murayama naikaku sōri daijn shoshin hyōmei enzetsu (Policy speech by Prime Minister Murayama Tomiichi at the 130th session of the Diet), 18 July, Tokyo: Gaimushō, www.mofa.go.jp/mofaj/gaiko/ bluebook/1995_1/h07-shiryou-1-1.htm#a4 (accessed Jan. 2007).

—— (1994b) Dai 131 kai kokkai ni okeru Murayama sōri daijin shoshin hyōmei enzetsu (Policy speech by Prime Minister Murayama Tomiichi at the 131st session of the Diet), 30 Sept., Tokyo: Gaimushō, www.mofa.go.jp/mofaj/gaiko/bluebook/1995_1/h07- shiryou-1-1.htm#a5 (accessed Jan. 2007).

—— (1995a) Dai 134 kai kokkai ni okeru Murayama sōri daijin shoshin hyōmei enzetsu (Policy speech by Prime Minister Murayama Tomiichi at the 134th session of the Diet), 29 Sept., Tokyo: Kantei, www.kantei.go.jp/jp/murayamasouri/speech/kokkai-134.html (accessed Jan. 2007).

—— (1995b) Sengo 50 shūnen no shūsenkinenbi ni attate (On the 50th anniversary of the end of the war), 15 Aug., Tokyo: Gaimushō, www.mofa.go.jp/mofaj/press/danwa/07/dmu_0815.html (accessed Jan. 2007).

Nakasone, Hirofumi (2009) Dai 171 kai kokkai ni okeru Nakasone gaimu daijin no gaikō enzetsu (Policy speech by Foreign Minister Nakasone Hirofumi at the 171st session of the Diet), 28 Jan., Tokyo: Gaimushō, www.mofa.go.jp/mofaj/press/enzetsu/21/enks_0128.html (accessed Nov. 2010).

Nakayama, Taro (1991a) ASEAN kakudai gaishō kaigi – zentai kaigi ni okeru Nakayama gaimu daijin sutetomento (ASEAN Post-Ministerial Conference: Speech by Foreign Minister Nakayama at the Plenary Meeting), 22 July, Tokyo: Gaimushō, www.mofa.go.jp/mofaj/gaiko/bluebook/1991/h03-shiryou-2.htm#a5 (accessed May 2007).

—— (1991b) Dai 120 kai kokkai ni okeru Nakayama gaimu daijin no gaikō enzetsu (Foreign policy speech by Foreign Minister Nakayama at the 120th session of the Diet), 25 Jan., Tokyo: Gaimushō, www.mofa.go.jp/mofaj/gaiko/bluebook/1991/h03-shiryou-1.htm#a3 (accessed Jan. 2007).

—— (1991c) Dai 46 kai kokuren sōkai Nakayama gaimu daijin ippan enzetsu (Statement by Foreign Minister Nakayama Taro at the 46th session of the General Assembly of the United Nations), 24 Sept., Tokyo: Gaimushō, www.mofa.go.jp/mofaj/gaiko/bluebook/1992/h04-shiryou-2.htm#b1 (accessed Jan. 2007).

Noda, Yoshihiko (2011) Dai 178 kai kokkai ni okeru Noda naikaku sōri daijin shoshin hyōmei enzetsu (Policy speech by Prime Minister Noda Yoshihiko at the 178th session of the Diet), 13 Sept., Tokyo: Kantei, www.kantei.go.jp/jp/noda/statement/201109/13syosin.html (accessed Sept. 2011).

Obuchi, Keizo (1998a) 142 kai kokkai ni okeru Obuchi gaimudaijin no gaikō enzetsu (Foreign policy speech by Foreign Minister Obuchi Keizo at the 142nd session of the Diet), 16 Feb., Tokyo: Gaimushō, www.mofa.go.jp/mofaj/press/enzetsu/10/eo_0216.html (accessed March 2007).

—— (1998b) 21 seiki he no tenbō: Nihon to Higashi Ajia (Outlook into the 21st century: Japan and East Asia), 4 May, Tokyo: Gaimushō, www.mofa.go.jp/mofaj/press/enzetsu/10/eo_0504.html (accessed Feb. 2007).

—— (1998c) Ajia no akarui mirai no sōzō ni mukete (Towards the creation of a bright future for Asia), 16 Dec., Tokyo: Gaimushō, www.mofa.go.jp/mofaj/press/enzetsu/10/eos_1216.html (accessed March 2007).

—— (1998d) Ajia no asu no tsukuru chiteki taiwa (Intellectual dialogue on creating tomorrow's Asia), 2 Dec., Tokyo: Gaimushō, www.mofa.go.jp/mofaj/press/enzetsu/10/eos_1202.html (accessed Feb. 2007).

—— (1998e) Ajia no mirai to Nihon no yakuwari (Asia's future and Japan's role), 4 June, Tokyo: Gaimushō, www.mofa.go.jp/mofaj/press/enzetsu/10/eo_0604.html (accessed Feb. 2007).

—— (1998f) Dai 143 kai kokkai ni okeru Obuchi naikaku sōri daijin shoshin hyōmei enzetsu (Policy speech by Prime Minister Keizo Obuchi at the 143rd session of the Diet), 7 Aug., Tokyo: Gaimushō, www.kantei.go.jp/jp/obutisouri/speech/1998/0807syosin.html (accessed Feb. 2007).

—— (1998g) Dai 144 kai kokkai ni okeru Obuchi sōri dajin shoshin hyōmei enzetsu (Policy speech by Prime Minister Obuchi Keizo at the 144th session of the Diet), 27 Nov., Tokyo: Gaimushō, www.kantei.go.jp/jp/obutisouri/speech/1998/1127syoshinhyoumei.html (accessed Feb. 2007).

—— (1999a) Chikago Nichibei Kyōkai Rengō 20 shunen kinen yushoku kai ni okeru Obuchi sōri daijin supichi (Dinner speech by Prime Minister Obuchi Keizo at the 20th anniversary of the US–Japan Society), 30 April, Tokyo: Gaimushō, www.mofa.go.jp/mofaj/press/enzetsu/11/eos_0430.html (accessed March 2007).

——(1999b) Dai 145 kai kokkai ni okeru Obuchi naikaku sōri daijin shisei hōshin enzetsu (Policy speech by Prime Minister Obuchi Keizo at the 145th session of the Diet), 19 Jan., Tokyo: Gaimushō, www.kantei.go.jp/jp/obutisouri/speech/1999/0119sisei.html (accessed Jan. 2007).

—— (1999c) Dai 146 kai kokkai ni okeru Obuchi naikaku sōri daijin shoshin hyōmei enzetsu (Policy speech by Prime Minister Obuchi Keizo to the 146th session of the Diet), 29 Oct., Tokyo: Gaimushō, www.kantei.go.jp/jp/obutisouri/speech/1999/1029syosin.html (accessed Feb. 2007).

—— (1999d) Nikkei Shinbun shusai dai 5 kai kokusai kōryū kaigi 'Ajia no mirai' bansankai ni okeru Obuchi sōri aisatsu (International conference on 'The Future of Asia' hosted by *Nihon Keizai Shinbun*: welcome speech by Prime Minister Obuchi Keizo at the banquet), 3 June, Tokyo: Gaimushō, www.mofa.go.jp/mofaj/press/enzetsu/11/eos_0603.html (accessed March 2007).

—— (2000) Dai 147 kai kokkai ni okeru Obuchi naikaku sōri daijin shisei hōshin enzetsu (Policy speech by Prime Minister Obuchi Keizo at the 147th session of the Diet), 28 Jan., Tokyo: Gaimushō, www.kantei.go.jp/jp/obutisouri/speech/2000/0128sisei.html (accessed Feb. 2007).

Okada, Katsuya (2010) Dai 174 kai kokkai ni okeru Okada gaimu daijin no gaikō enzetsu (Foreign policy speech by Foreign Minister Okada Katsuya at the 174th session of the Diet), 29 Jan., Tokyo: Gaimushō, www.mofa.go.jp/mofaj/press/enzetsu/22/eokd_0129.html (accessed Nov. 2010).

Shiozaki, Yasuhisa (2006) Speech by Mr. Yasuhisa Shiozaki Senior Vice-Minister for Foreign Affairs of Japan at the 42nd Munich Conference on Security Policy, 5 Feb., Tokyo: Gaimushō, www.mofa.go.jp/policy/security/speech0602.html (accessed Jan. 2007).

Sugiura, Seiken (2001) Nikkei Shinbun shusai 'Ajia no mirai' Sugiura fuku daijin enzetsu (Speech by Vice Foreign Minister Sugiura Seiken at the 'Future of Asia' conference hosted by *Nikkei Shinbun*), 7 June, Tokyo: Gaimushō, www.mofa.go.jp/mofaj/press/enzetsu/13/ear_0607.html (accessed March 2007).

Tanaka, Makiko (2001a) ASEAN+3 (Ni-chū-kan) gaishō kaigi de no Tanaka daijin sutetomento (Statement by Foreign Minister Tanaka Makiko on the occasion of the ASEAN + 3 (Japan, China, Korea) meeting), 25 July, Tokyo: Gaimushō, www.mofa.go.jp/mofaj/press/enzetsu/13/etn_0724.html (accessed Jan. 2007).

—— (2001b) Dai 151 kai kokkai sangiin gaikō bōei iinkai ni okeru Tanaka gaimudaijin shoshin (Policy speech by Foreign Minister Tanaka Makiko to the committee on Foreign Affairs and Defence of the House of Councillors at the 151st session of the Diet), 17 May, Tokyo: Gaimushō, www.mofa.go.jp/mofaj/press/enzetsu/13/etn_0517.html (accessed March 2007).

—— (2001c) San Furanshisuko heiwa jōyaku shomei 50 shūnen kinenshikiten ni okeru Tanaka gaimu daijin enzetsu (Speech by Foreign Minister Tanaka Makiko at the ceremony to commemorate the 50th anniversary of the signing of the Japan–US Security Treaty), 8 Sept., Tokyo: Gaimushō, www.mofa.go.jp/mofaj/press/enzetsu/13/etn_0908.html (accessed Jan. 2007).

Watanabe, Michio (1992a) Dai 123 kai kokkai ni okeru Watanabe gaimu daijin no gaikō enzetsu (Foreign policy speech by Foreign Minister Watanabe Michio to the 123rd session of the Diet), 24 Jan., Tokyo: Gaimushō, www.mofa.go.jp/mofaj/gaiko/bluebook/1992/h04-shiryou-1.htm#a3 (accessed Jan. 2007).

—— (1992b) Dai 47 kai kokuren sōkai ni okeru Watanabe gaimu daijin ippan enzetsu (Speech by Foreign Minister Watanabe Michio at the 47th Session of the General Assembly of the United Nations), 22 Sept., Tokyo: Gaimushō, www.mofa.go.jp/mofaj/gaiko/bluebook/1992/h04-shiryou-2.htm#b9 (accessed Jan. 2007).

—— (1993) Dai 126 kai kokkai ni okeru Watanabe gaimu daijin no gaikō enzetsu (Foreign policy speech by Foreign Minister Watanabe Michio at the 126th session of the Diet), 22 Jan., Tokyo: Gaimushō, www.mofa.go.jp/mofaj/gaiko/bluebook/1993_1/h05-1-shiryou-1.htm#a2 (accessed Jan. 2007).

Other References

Abe, Shinzo (2006) *Utsukushi kuni he* (Towards a Beautiful Country), Tokyo: Bunshun Shinsho.

Adomeit, Hannes (2001) *Putin und die Raketenabwehr: Moskaus Haltung zu NMD im Kontext der russisch-amerikanischen Beziehungen* (Putin and Missile Defence: Moscow's Stance on NMD in the Context of Russian–American Relations), SWP-Studie, 29 Sept, Berlin: Dt. Inst. für Internat. Politik und Sicherheit.

Aerospace Daily (1992) Threat from North Korea, China spurs JDA bid for missile defense, LexisNexis, 16 March.

—— (1993) Japan's Prime Minister urges debate over TMD proposal, LexisNexis, 6 Oct.

Aggestam, Lisbeth (2000) A common foreign and security policy: role conceptions and the politics of identity in the EU, in Lisbeth Aggestam and Adrian Hyde-Price (eds), *Security and Identity in Europe: Exploring the New Agenda* (pp. 86–115), Basingstoke: Macmillan Press.

—— (2004) *A European Foreign Policy? Role Conceptions and the Politics of Identity in Britain, France and Germany,* Stockholm: Stockholm University.

Agüera, Martin (2003) Germans doubt U.S. plan to merge MEADS, Patriot, *Defense News,* LexisNexis, 21 July.

—— (2005) MEADS debate looms in Berlin, *Defense News,* LexisNexis, 7 March.

—— (2007) *Worum streiten sie eigentlich? Deutschlands Rüstungspolitik während der rot-grünen Regierungskoalition 1998–2005 an den Beispielen MEADS und A400M* (What are they Fighting about? Germany's Armament Policy during the Red-Green Coalition Government 1998–2005: The Examples of MEADS and A400M), Kieler Schriften zur politischen Wissenschaft, 18, Frankfurt am Main: Peter Lang Verlag.

Ajia Rekishi Shiryō Sentā (2001) *Sentā no shōkai* (Introduction of the Center), www.jacar.go.jp/center/center.html (accessed June 2009).

Akita, Hiroyuki, Akio Takahara, Masayuki Tadokoro, and Takeo Mori (2009) Nihon gaikō no aidentiti to wa nani ka (What is the identity of Japanese foreign diplomacy?), *Gaikō Fōramu,* 247(2): 44–53.

Algieri, Franco (2011) Deutsche Außen- und Sicherheitspolitik im europäischen Kontext: Das abnehmende Strahlen der Integrationsleuchttürme (German foreign and security politics in a European context: the diminishing shining of the integration lighthouses), in Thomas Jäger, Alexander Hoese and Kai Oppermann (eds), *Deutsche Außenpolitik: Sicherheit, Wohlfahrt, Institutionen und Normen* (German Foreign Policy: Security, Welfare, Institutions and Norms), 2nd edn (pp. 126–47), Wiesbaden: VS Verlag für Sozialwissenschaften/Springer Fachmedien Wiesbaden.

Arai, Shinichi, and Iga Toshiya (2001) Rekishi Mondai Kanren Nenpyō, Shiryō (Time line and records regarding history problem), *Sekai,* 696 (Dec.): 178–96.

Arbeitsgruppe Friedensforschung an der Universität Kassel (2005) *'Abwehrwaffen' als Teil einer offensiven Strategie?* ('Defense Weapons' as a Part of an Offensive Strategy?), www.uni-kassel.de/fb5/frieden/themen/ABM-Vertrag/meads3.html.

Armed Forces Newswire Service (1998) Germany: MEADS key test case for int'l cooperation, LexisNexis, 27 April.

Arnhold, Klaus (2001) *Russlands Vorschlag zur nicht-strategischen Raketenabwehr für Europa* (Russia's Proposal for Non-Strategic Missile Defence for Europe), SWP-Studie, Berlin: SWP.

Asahi Shinbun (1984) 'Nihon, ima mo rōdō 10 jikan': gaikokukyōkasho, nishiki ni izen zure ('(In) Japan, the working time (is) still 10 hours': in textbooks of foreign countries, still a gap in perception), 15 Aug.

—— (1987) Gaimusho, nikkan kyōkasho kyōgi o kentō – Kenjinkaigi ni bunkakai (Foreign Ministry examining Japan–Korea textbook consultation: subcommittee in the advisory council), 3 Jan.

—— (2001) Nakatani bōei chōkan: misairu bōei de dokuji no jōhō shūshū o mezasu (Defense Agency Chief Nakatani: seeking independent information gathering (capabilities)), 29 June.

—— (2005a) 'Asian neighbors' clause, 10 March, www.asahi.com/english/opinion/ TKY200503100126.html (accessed Oct. 2007).

—— ed. (2005b) *Jieitai: shirarezaru henyō* (The Self Defense Forces: The Unknown Transformation), Tokyo: Asahi Shinbun Sha.

—— (2006) Abe shushō 'kenkyū' hatsugen, hamon seifu kenkai, fumikosu amerika-muke? Misairu geigeki (Prime Minister Abe's 'research' utterance – stepping over the government's interpretation – and its repercussion: leaning towards the US? Intercepting missiles), 17 Nov.

—— (2007) Changing history education, 28 June, www.asahi.com/english/Herald-asahi/ TKY200706150138.html (accessed July 2008).

—— (2010) Kyōkasho meguri, sōgo ni hihan nikkan kyōdō kenkyū dai ni ki hōkokusho (Mutual criticism on textbooks: the second report by the Japan–Korea committee for joint history research), 23 March, www.asahi.com/international/update/0323/ TKY201003230343.html (accessed July 2010).

Ashizawa, Kuniko P. (2008) When identity matters: state identity, regional institution-building, and Japanese foreign policy, *International Studies Review*, 10: 571–98.

Aßmann, Lars (2007) *Theater Missile Defense (TMD) in East Asia: Implications for Beijing and Tokyo*, Zugl. Bochum, Univ., Diss., 2005; Berlin: LIT Verlag.

Aviation Week and Space Technology (1995) MEADS moves ahead, but funding shaky, LexisNexis, 30 Oct.

Backman, Carl W. (1970) Role theory and international relations: a commentary and extension, *International Studies Quarterly*, 14(3): 310–19.

Barnett, Michael (1993) Institutions, roles and disorder: the case of the Arab states system, *International Studies Quarterly*, 37(3): 271–96.

Bartels, Hans-Peter (2010) Interview with A. Sakaki, 22 June, Berlin.

Bauer, Thomas (2007) *Missile Defence: The Debate in Germany,* Fondation pour la Recherche Stratégique, www.frstrategie.org/barreFRS/publications/pv/ defenseAntimissile/pv_20070625_eng.pdf.

—— and Martin Agüera (2005) *MEADS ist unverzichtbar: Kritische Auseinandersetzung mit der Debatte um das Luftabwehrraketensystem* (MEADS is Indispensable: Critical Examination of the Debate about the Aerial Missile Defense System), CAP Working Paper, Munich: Universität München.

Baumann, Rainer (2006) *Der Wandel des Deutschen Multilateralismus: Eine diskursanalytische Untersuchung deutscher Außenpolitik* (The Change in German Multilateralism: A Discourse Analytical Examination of German Foreign Policy), Baden-Baden: Nomos Verlagsgesellschaft.

BBC (2000) Putin warns against enlarging Nato, 15 June, http://news.bbc.co.uk/1/hi/world/europe/792492.stm (accessed July 2008).

—— (2002) Germany to supply missiles to Israel, 27 Nov., http://news.bbc.co.uk/2/hi/middle_east/2517431.stm (accessed Oct. 2008).

—— (2005) Growing opposition to air defence project in German ruling parties, *BBC Monitoring,* LexisNexis, 24 Jan.

—— (2007) Japan tests anti-missile system, *BBC News*, 18 Dec., http://news.bbc.co.uk/1/hi/world/asia-pacific/7149197.stm (accessed July 2010).

—— (2009) Iran tests longest range missiles, *BBC Online*, 28 Sept., http://news.bbc.co.uk/2/hi/middle_east/8278026.stm (accessed March 2010).

Becher, U. A. J., W. Borodziej, and R. Maier, eds (2001) *Deutschland und Polen im 20. Jahrhundert: Analysen – Quellen – didaktische Hinweise* (Germany and Poland in the 20th Century: Analyses, Sources, Didactic Suggestions), Hanover: Verlag Hahnsche Buchhandlung.

Becker, B., and J. Rüland, eds (1997) *Japan und Deutschland in der internationalen Politik: Neue Herausforderungen nach dem Ende des Kalten Krieges* (Japan and Germany in International Politics: New Challenges after the End of the Cold War), Mitteilungen des Instituts für Asienkunde, 283, Hamburg: Institut für Asienkunde.

Bender, Bryan (2003) NATO impasse seen slowing a US attack from Turkey, *Global Security*, 13 Feb., www.globalsecurity.org/org/news/2003/030213-turkey01.htm (accessed Oct. 2008).

Berg, Bruce L. (2004) *Qualitative Research Methods for the Social Sciences,* 5th edn, Boston, MA: Pearson Education.

Berger, Thomas U. (1996) Norms, identity, and national security in Germany and Japan, in Peter J. Katzenstein (ed.), *The Culture of National Security: Norms and Identity in World Politics* (pp. 317–56), New York: Columbia University Press.

—— (1998) *Cultures of Antimilitarism: National Security in Germany and Japan,* Baltimore, MD: Johns Hopkins University Press.

—— (2003) Power and purpose in Pacific East Asia: a constructivist interpretation, in G. J. Ikenberry and Michael Mastanduno (eds), *International Relations Theory and the Asia-Pacific* (pp. 387–419), New York: Columbia University Press.

—— (2009) *Different Beds, Same Nightmare: The Politics of History in Germany and Japan: AICGS Policy Report,* Washington, DC: American Institute for Contemporary German Studies.

Bergsdorf, Wolfgang (2004) Der Stellenwert ostdeutscher Kulturpflege in der Ära Kohl (The significance of East German cultural support in the Kohl era), in Jörg-Dieter Gauger and Manfred Kittel (eds), *Die Vertreibung der Deutschen aus dem Osten in der Erinnerungskultur* (The Expulsion of Germans from the East in the Culture of Memory), (pp. 53–67), Sankt Augustin: Konrad-Adenauer-Stiftung e.V.

Berichterstattergruppe Bodengebundene Luftverteidigung (2004) *Abschlussbericht* (Final Report), www.geopowers.com/Machte/Deutschland/Rustung/Rustung_2004/MEADS_VertA.pdf (accessed Sept. 2008).

Berkofsky, Axel (2002a) Aid and comfort: Japan's Aegis sets sail, *Asia Times Online*, 19 Dec., www.atimes.com/atimes/Japan/DL19Dh01.html (accessed May 2008).

—— (2002b) Japan navy's salvo catches politicians off guard, *Asia Times Online*, 16 May, www.atimes.com/japan-econ/DE16Dh01.html (accessed Sept. 2008).

Bernstein, Richard (2003) Germany says NATO rift over Turkey is near an end, *New York Times Online*, 14 Feb., http://query.nytimes.com/gst/fullpage.html?res=9E01E1DB153 AF937A25751C0A9659C8B63 (accessed Oct. 2008).

Biddle, Bruce J. (1986) Recent development in role theory, *Annual Review of Sociology*, 12: 67–92.

Bierling, Stephan (2006) *No More 'Sonderweg': German Foreign Policy under Chancellor Angela Merkel*, www.kas.de/wf/doc/kas_9114-544-1-30.pdf (accessed March 2009).

Bittner, Jochen (2008) Schlappe für Bush? Von wegen (Setback for Bush? Not at all), *Die Zeit Online*, 3 April, http://blog.zeit.de/bittner-blog/2008/04/03/deutschlands-nato-schlappe_50 (accessed July 2008).

Boehmer, George (1995) U.S. signs statement of intent with Germany, *Associated Press Worldstream*, LexisNexis, 20 Feb.

Boekle, Henning, Jörg Nadoll, and Bernhard Stahl (2000) Identität, Diskurs und vergleichende Analyse europäischer Außenpolitiken: Theoretische Grundlegung und methodische Vorgehensweise (Identity, discourse, and comparative analysis of European foreign policies: theoretical basics and methodological approach), *PAFE-Arbeitspapiere*, 1 (Dec.): 1–41.

—— Volker Rittberger, and Wolfgang Wagner (2001) Constructivist foreign policy theory, in Volker Rittberger (ed.), *German Foreign Policy since Unification: Theories and Case Studies* (pp. 105–37), Manchester: Manchester University Press.

Borodziej, Wlodzimierz (2000) Die Deutsch-Polnische Schulbuchkommission 1972–1999 (The German–Polish Textbook Commission 1972–1999), in Ursula A. J. Becher and Rainer Riemenschneider (eds), *Internationale Verständigung: 25 Jahre Georg-Eckert-Institut für internationale Schulbuchforschung in Braunschweig* (International Understanding: 25 Years Georg-Eckert Institute for International Textbook Research in Brunswick) (pp. 157–65), Hanover: Verlag Hahnsche Buchhandlung.

—— (2001) Vorwort (Preface), in Ursula A. J. Becher, Wlodzimierz Borodziej and Robert Maier (eds), *Deutschland und Polen im 20. Jahrhundert: Analysen – Quellen – didaktische Hinweise* (Germany and Poland in the 20th Century: Analyses, Sources, Didactic Suggestions) (pp. 11–15), Hanover: Verlag Hahnsche Buchhandlung.

—— (2003) The German–Polish textbook dialogue, in Andrew Horvat and Gebhard Hielscher (eds), *Sharing the Burden of the Past: Legacies of War in Europe, America, and Asia* (pp. 35–8), Tokyo: Asia Foundation and Friedrich-Ebert Stiftung.

Brinkley, Joel (1991a) Seven Iraqi missiles are fired at cities in Israel and two at Saudi Arabia's capital; Patriots stop Scuds but Israeli man is killed by debris, *New York Times Online*, 26 Jan., http://query.nytimes.com/gst/fullpage.html?res=9D0CE5D7113DF935 A15752C0A967958260&sec=&spon=&pagewanted=print (accessed July 2008).

—— (1991b) War in the Gulf: Israel gets $670 million in German aid, *New York Times Online*, 1 Feb., http://query.nytimes.com/gst/fullpage.html?res=9D0CE5DF123EF932 A35751C0A967958260&sec=&spon=&pagewanted=print (accessed Oct. 2007).

Brown, Peter J. (2010) Japan and Korea thumb a poisoned ledger, *Asia Times Online*, 9 April, www.atimes.com/atimes/Japan/LD09Dh01.html (accessed July 2010).

Bundesministerium für Verteidigung (2006) *Weißbuch 2006 zur Sicherheit Deutschlands und zur Zukunft der Bundeswehr: Online Ausgabe* (White Book 2006 on German Security and the Future of the Armed Forces), Berlin: Bundesministerium für Verteidigung, www.bmvg.de/portal/PA_1_0_12D/PortalFiles/C1256EF40036B05B/

W26UYEPT431INFODE/WB_2006_dt_mB.pdf?yw_repository=youatweb (accessed July 2008).

Burkeman, Oliver, and Michael Howard (2003) Turkish troops enter northern Iraq: Ankara ignores US warning of secondary battle front, *Guardian*, 22 March, www.guardian. co.uk/world/2003/mar/22/turkey.iraq (accessed Oct. 2008).

Buruma, Ian (1994) *The Wages of Guilt: Memories of War in Germany and Japan,* 1st edn, New York: Farrar Straus Giroux.

Busse, Nikolas (2007) Thema verfehlt (Missing the Point), *Frankfurter Allgemeine Zeitung*, 10 April.

Cambone, Stephen, Ivo Daalder, Stephen J. Hadley, and Christopher J. Makins (2000) *European Views of National Missile Defense,* Washington, DC: Atlantic Council of the United States.

Castle, Stephen (2003) Turkey plan to enter north puts Nato deal at risk, *Independent*, 25 March, www.independent.co.uk/news/world/politics/turkey-plan-to-enter-north-puts-nato-deal-at-risk-592314.html (accessed Oct. 2008).

Cha, Victor D. (1999) *Alignment despite Antagonism: The United States–Korea–Japan Security Triangle,* Studies of the East Asian Institute, Columbia University, Stanford, CA: Stanford University Press.

Chafetz, Glenn, Hillel Abramson, and Suzette Grillot (1996) Role theory and foreign policy: Belarusian and Ukrainian compliance with the nuclear nonproliferation regime, *Political Psychology,* 17(4): 727–57.

Checkel, Jeffrey T. (2001) The Europeanization of citizenship? in Maria G. Cowles, James A. Caporaso, and Thomas Risse (eds), *Transforming Europe: Europeanization and Domestic Change* (pp. 180–97), Ithaca, NY: Cornell University Press.

Chiba, Akira (2005) Press conference on April 5th, 2005: Assistant Press Secretary Akira Chiba, Toyko, www.mofa.go.jp/announce/press/2005/4/7 (accessed Sept. 2007).

Choi, Won-Hyung (2011) Japanese textbooks escalate country's claims on Dokdo, *Hankyoreh*, 31 March, http://english.hani.co.kr/arti/english_edition/e_national/470809. html (accessed Dec. 2011).

Chon, Jo-Chon (2007) Kan-nichi ni tsukimatou rekishi no kage to sono kokufuku no tame no kokoromi (The historical shadow that haunts Korea–Japan relations and the attempt to overcome it), in Hiroshi Mitani (ed.), *Rekishi kyokasho mondai* (The History Textbook Problem) (pp. 248–69), Tokyo: Nihontosho.

Chosun Ilbo (2001) Nihon, kinrinkoku ni kyōkasho shūsei o shitsuyō yōkyū (Japan stubbornly demands revisions in neighboring countries' textbooks), 20 April, www. chosunonline.com/article/20010420000015 (accessed Oct. 2007).

—— (2002) Nihon 'rekishi kyōdō kenkyū no seika, kyōkasho ni hanei shinai' (Japan: 'no reflection of the joint history research results in textbooks'), 4 Jan., www.chosunonline. com/news/20020104000012 (accessed May 2007).

Chung, Jae-Jeong (2001) *South Korea–Japan History Reconciliation: A Progress Report,* www.tafjapan.org/forums/pdf/20011113pdf/83-119-e.pdf (accessed July 2009).

—— (2008) Experience of the joint compilation of a history textbook for Korean and Japanese students aimed at historical reconciliation, paper at conference, History Education and Reconciliation: Comparative Perspectives on East Asia, Brunswick, 15 Oct.

Chung, Nami (2006) *Shūshi ronbun: Naze 'nikkan rekishi kyōdō kenkyū' nanoka* (Why a 'joint Japan–Korea history research'?), masters thesis at the Graduate School of International Cooperation Studies, Kobe University.

—— and Kan Kimura (2008a) 'Rekishi ninshiki' mondai to dai-ichiji nikkan rekishi kyōdō kenkyū o meguru ichikōsatsu (1) (Consideration about the 'historical perception' problem and the first Japan–Korea joint history research, part 1), *Kokusai Kyōryoku Ronshū*, 16(1): 155–84, www.research.kobe-u.ac.jp/gsics-publication/jics/chung&kimura_16-1.pdf (accessed Aug. 2009).

—— (2008b) 'Rekishi ninshiki' mondai to dai-ichiji nikkan rekishi kyōdō kenkyū o meguru ichikōsatsu (2) (Consideration about the 'historical perception' problem and the first Japan-Korea joint history research, part 2), *Kokusai Kyōryoku Ronshū*, 16(2): 121–45, www.research.kobe-u.ac.jp/gsics-publication/jics/chung&kimura_16-2.pdf (accessed Aug. 2009).

CNN (2005) Japan rocket lifts with satellite, 24 Jan., http://edition.cnn.com/2006/WORLD/asiapcf/01/23/japan.rocket.launch.ap/index.html (accessed Jan. 2005).

Collina, Tom Z. (2010) U.S. taps Romania for missile defense, *Arms Control Today*, 40 (March), www.armscontrol.org/act/2010_03/MissileDefense (accessed May 2010).

Cooney, Kevin J. (2007) *Japan's Foreign Policy since 1945*, Armonk, NY: Sharpe.

Covault, Craig, and John D. Morocco (1994) U.S., Europe advance missile defense options, *Aviation Week and Space Technology*, LexisNexis, 5 Sept.

Defense News (2011) Japan launches spy satellite, 12 Dec., www.defensenews.com/story.php?i=8541177&c=ASI&s=TOP (accessed Dec. 2011).

Dehéz, Dustin (2005) *Umfassender Schutz für Truppe und Heimat? Das Flugabwehrsystem MEADS in der Kritik: Kommentar* (Comprehensive Protection for Troops and for the Homeland? Criticism of the Missile Defence System MEADS: A Commentary), http://dias-online.org/fileadmin/templates/downloads/050301_27.pdf (accessed July 2009).

Dempsey, Judy (2011) Russia seeks pledge from NATO on missile defense, *New York Times Online*, 21 May, www.nytimes.com/2011/05/22/world/europe/22nato.html (accessed Dec. 2011).

Deutsche Welle Online (2007) Raketenabwehr: NATO einig, Russland dagegen (Missile defense: NATO in agreement, Russia opposed), www.dw-world.de/dw/article/0,2144,2448704,00.html (accessed Oct. 2007).

Deutschland Radio (2011) Deutsch-Polnisches Geschichtsbuch findet keinen Verlag (German–Polish history book not finding publisher), 27 July, http://wissen.dradio.de/nachrichten.59.de.html?drn:news_id=47266&drn:date=1311760800 (accessed Dec. 2011).

Donahue, Patrick (2011) German government under pressure to scrap Meads missile project, *Bloomberg*, 15 Feb., www.bloomberg.com/news/2011-02-15/german-government-under-pressure-to-scrap-meads-missile-project.html (accessed Dec. 2011).

Ducke, Isa (2002) *Status Power: Japanese Foreign Policy-Making toward Korea*, New York: Routledge.

Duffield, John S. (1999) Political culture and state behavior: why Germany confounds neorealism, *International Organization*, 53(4): 765–803.

—— (2003) Asia-Pacific security institutions in comparative perspective, in G. J. Ikenberry and Michael Mastanduno (eds), *International Relations Theory and the Asia-Pacific* (pp. 243–70), New York: Columbia University Press.

Edström, Bert (1988) *Japan's Quest for a Role in the World: Roles Ascribed to Japan Nationally and Internationally 1969–1982*, Stockholm: University of Stockholm.

—— (2004) The Yoshida doctrine and the unipolar world, *Japan Forum*, 16(1): 63–84.

European Commission (2006) *Eurobarometer 65: Die Öffentliche Meinung in der Europäischen Union: Nationaler Bericht Deutschland* (Eurobarometer 65: Public Opinion in the European Union. National Report on Germany), http://ec.europa.eu/public_opinion/archives/eb/eb65/eb65_de_nat.pdf (accessed July 2008).

Feldman, Lily G. (2007) The role of non-state actors in Germany's foreign policy of reconciliation: catalysts, complements, conduits, or competitors? in Anne-Marie Le Gloannec (ed.), *Non-State Actors in International Relations: The Case of Germany* (pp. 15–45), Manchester: Manchester University Press.

—— (2008) *German–Polish Reconciliation: How Similar, How Different? Lecture given at the German Historical Institute in Warsaw, Poland,* Warsaw: Center for International Relations, www.csm.org.pl/images/rte/File/Aktualnosci/LGFeldman_WarsawEssay308.pdf (accessed Aug. 2008).

Filipiak, Rainer (2006) *Europäische Sicherheitspolitik und amerikanische Verteidigungskonzeptionen* (European Security Policy and American Defense Conceptions), Duisburg-Essen: Dissertation im Fachbereich Gesellschaftswissenschaften.

Fischer, Torben, and Matthias N. Lorenz (2007) *Lexikon der 'Vergangenheitsbewältigung' in Deutschland: Debatten und Diskursgeschichte des Nationalsozialismus nach 1945* [Encyclopedia of 'Coming to Terms with the Past' in Germany: Debates and Discourse History of National Socialism after 1945], Bielefeld: Transcript-Verlag.

Focus (2006) Iran: BM-25-Raketen können Europa erreichen. Iran-Krise (Iran: BM-25-missiles can reach Europe. Iran crisis), 27 April, www.focus.de/politik/ausland/iran/iran_aid_108191.html (accessed July 2008).

Foreign Press Center Japan (2002) Seifu, AEGIS kan o Indoyō ni hakken (Government sending Aegis ship to Indian Ocean], Tokyo, http://fpcj.jp/old/j/mres/japanbrief/jb_197.html (accessed Sept. 2008).

Forsberg, Tuomas (2005) German foreign policy and the war on Iraq: anti-Americanism, pacifism or emancipation? *Security Dialogue,* 36(2): 213–31.

Fouse, David (2003) Japan gets serious about missile defense, *Asia-Pacific Center for Security Studies,* 2(4) (June): 1–4.

Frankenberger, Klaus-Dieter, and Hanns W. Maull (2011) 'Gimme a break': in foreign policy, Germany takes time out from a complex world, *Foreign Policy in Focus,* 494, www.deutsche-aussenpolitik.de/index.php?/digest/zeige_oped.php?was=59 (accessed March 2011).

Frankfurter Allgemeine Zeitung (2003a) Auch Deutschland widerspricht Nato-Planung für Türkei (Germany also contradicts NATO-planning for Turkey), 10 Feb., www.faz.net/s/RubA24ECD630CAE40E483841DB7D16F4211/Doc~E0E16C9A8699048EEAFE2F2B13CAD6439~ATpl~Ecommon~Scontent.html (accessed Oct. 2008).

—— (2003b) Schröder schließt Ja zur Kriegsresolution aus (Schröder rules out yes on war resolution), 22 Jan., www.faz.net/s/RubA24ECD630CAE40E483841DB7D16F4211/Doc~E32C8579B82894ED09988DF916C3B8365~ATpl~Ecommon~Scontent.html (accessed Oct. 2008).

—— (2011) Meads: FDP und Grüne fordern Ausstieg aus Raketenabwehrsystem (Meads: FDP and Greens demand exit from missile defense system), 15 Feb., http://m.faz.net/aktuell/politik/ausland/meads-fdp-und-gruene-fordern-ausstieg-aus-raketenabwehrsystem-1593870.html (accessed Dec. 2011).

Freedman, Lawrence, and Efraim Karsh (1993) *The Gulf Conflict, 1990–1991: Diplomacy and War in the New World Order,* Princeton, NJ: Princeton University Press.

Frei, Norbert (2004) Deutsche Lernprozesse: NS-Vergangenheit und Generationenfolge seit 1945 (German processes of learning: NS-past and generational succession since 1945), in Wolfgang Meseth, Matthias Proske, and Frank-Olaf Radtke (eds), *Schule und Nationalsozialismus: Anspruch und Grenzen des Geschichtsunterrichts* (School and National Socialism: Requirements and Constraints on History Education) (pp. 33–48), Frankfurt: Campus.

Frenkler, Ulf, Sebastian Harnisch, Knut Kirste, Hanns W. Maull, and Wolfram Wallraf (1997) *DFG-Projekt 'Zivilmächte': Schlussbericht und Ergebnisse. Deutsche, amerikanische und japanische Außenpolitikstrategien 1985–1995: Eine vergleichende Untersuchung zu Zivilisierungsprozessen in der Triade* (DFG-Project 'Civilian Powers': Final Report and Results. German, American and Japanese Foreign Policy Strategies 1985–1995: A Comparative Examination of Civilizing Processes in the Triad), Trier: Universität Trier.

Frevert, Ute (2003) Der jüngste Erinnerungsboom in der Kritik (Criticism of the most recent memory boom) *Aus Politik und Zeitgeschichte*, B: 40–1, www.bpb.de/Publikationen/ ZX3176,0,Der_j%FCngste_Erinnerungsboom_in_der_Kritik.html (accessed Aug. 2009).

Fröhlich, Stefan (2008) Deutsche Außen- und Sicherheitspolitik im Rahmen der EU (German Foreign and Security Policy in the Context of the EU), *Aus Politik und Zeitgeschichte*, 43: 15–21.

Frühling, Stephan, and Svenja Sinjen (2007) Raketenabwehr, NATO und die Verteidigung Europas (Missile Defense, NATO and the Protection of Europe). Analysen & Argumente, Konrad-Adenauer-Stiftung, no. 40 (March) www.kas.de/wf/doc/kas_10599-544-1-30. pdf?070807144036 (accessed March 2012).

Fuhrt, Volker (2005) Der Schulbuchdialog zwischen Japan und Südkorea: Entstehung, Zwischenergebnisse und Perspektiven (The textbook dialogue between Japan and South Korea: origins, intermediate results, perspectives), *Internationale Schulbuchforschung,* 27(1): 45–57.

Fujisawa, Hoei (2003) Commentary, on Andrew Horvat and Gebhard Hielscher (eds), *Sharing the Burden of the Past: Legacies of War in Europe, America, and Asia* (pp. 43–4), Tokyo: Asia Foundation and Friedrich-Ebert Stiftung.

Fukuda, Yasuo (2003) Naikaku kanbōchōkan danwa (Statement by Chief Cabinet Secretary Fukuda Yasuo (19 Dec.), www.kantei.go.jp/jp/tyokan/koizumi/2003/1219danwa.html (accessed Nov. 2008).

Gabriel, Sigmar (2000) Grußwort (Niedersächsischer Ministerpräsident) (Greeting (Minister-President of Lower Saxony)), in Ursula A. J. Becher and Rainer Riemenschneider (eds), *Internationale Verständigung: 25 Jahre Georg-Eckert-Institut für internationale Schulbuchforschung in Braunschweig* (International Understanding: 25 Years Georg-Eckert Institute for International Textbook Research in Brunswick) (pp. 11–12), Hanover: Verlag Hahnsche Buchhandlung.

Gaimusho (2000) *Wa ga gaikō no kinkyō* (Current situation of Japan's foreign policy), Tokyo: Gaimusho.

Garten, Jeffrey E. (1989/1990), Japan and Germany: American concerns, *Foreign Affairs,* 68(5): 84–101.

—— (1992) *A Cold Peace: America, Japan, Germany, and the Struggle for Supremacy,* New York: Times Books.

Gauger, Jörg-Dieter, and Günter Buchstab (2004) Schule als gesellschaftlicher und politischer Seismograph: Der historische deutsche Osten im Unterricht (School as a seismograph of society and politics: the historical German East in class), in Jörg-Dieter Gauger and Manfred Kittel (eds), *Die Vertreibung der Deutschen aus dem Osten in der Erinnerungskultur* (The Expulsion of Germans from the East in the Culture of Memory) (pp. 85–109), Sankt Augustin: Konrad-Adenauer-Stiftung e.V.

Girgensohn, Jürgen (1981) Nordrhein-Westfalen und die Umsetzung der Deutsch-Polnischen Schulbuchempfehlungen, Rede des Kultusministers von NRW: Tagung zum Thema Die deutsch-polnischen Beziehungen am Beispiel der Umsetzung der Schulbuchempfehlungen im Lande Nordrhein-Westfalen (Northrhine-Westphalia and the implementation of the

German–Polish textbook recommendations, speech of the Minister of Education of NRW at the conference on German–Polish Relations in Light of the Implementation of the Textbook Recommendations in the State of Northrhine-Westphalia), Friedrich-Ebert Stiftung in Zusammenarbeit mit dem Kultusministerium NRW, Bergneustadt.

Goehrke, Carsten, Manfred Hellmann, Erwin Oberländer, and Dieter Wojtecki (1977) *Östliches Europa: Spiegel der Geschichte* (Eastern Europe: Mirror of History), Quellen und Studien zur Geschichte des östlichen Europa, 9, Wiesbaden: Steiner.

Goozner, Merrill (1994) Japan balks at buying into Mini-SDI system, *Chicago Tribune,* LexisNexis, 3 Nov.

Götzke, Manfred (2011) Deutsch-polnisches Schulgeschichtsbuch ohne Verlag (German–Polish school history book without publisher), *Deutschlandfunk,* 3 Aug., www.dradio. de/dlf/sendungen/campus/1520331/ (accessed Dec. 2011).

Grams, Christoph (2003) *Das mittlere erweiterte Luftverteidigungssystem MEADS: Geschichte, Idee, Realisierung* (The Medium Extended Air Defense System MEADS: History, Idea, Realization), Schriftenreihe 'strategische Analysen' des Instituts für Strategische Analysen e.V. (ISA), Frankfurt am Main and Bonn: Report-Verlag.

—— (2005) *Das Medium Extended Air Defense System (MEADS): Ein Prüfstein für Deutschlands Streitkräftetransformation?* (The Medium Extended Air Defense System (MEADS): A Touchstone for Germany's Transformation of Armed Forces), DGAP Analyse 2.

Grieco, Joseph M. (1996) *Realism and Regionalism: American Power and German and Japanese Institutional Strategies During and After the Cold War*, Working Paper, Berkeley, CA: Center for German and European Studies, University of California at Berkeley.

Hacke, Christian (2008) Germany's foreign policy under Angela Merkel, *AICGS Advisor* (8 Aug.): 1–3, www.aicgs.org/documents/advisor/hacke.vuln0808.pdf (accessed February 2009).

Haftendorn, Helga (2001) *Deutsche Außenpolitik zwischen Selbstbeschränkung und Selbstbehauptung, 1945–2000* (German Foreign Policy between Self-Restraint and Self-Assertion, 1945–2000), Stuttgart and Munich: Deutsche Verlags-Anstalt.

Hagen, Regina, and Jürgen Scheffran (2001) Zwischen Raketenabwehr und Weltraumrüstung: Was macht Europa? (Between missile defence and armament and space: what is Europe doing?), *Wissenschaft und Frieden*, 2, www.wissenschaft-und-frieden.de/seite.php?artikelID=0105 (accessed July 2009).

Hagström, Linus, and Jon Williamsson (2009) 'Remilitarization' really? Assessing change in Japanese foreign security policy, *Asian Security,* 5(3): 242–72.

Hanano, Yuta (2011) More junior high textbooks mention Takeshima, Senkaku, *Asahi Shinbun*, 1 April, www.asahi.com/english/TKY201103310159.html (accessed Dec. 2011).

Harden, Blaine (2009) Japan prepares to shoot down North Korean missile in case of accident, *Washington Post*, 28 March, www.washingtonpost.com/wp-dyn/content/article/2009/03/27/AR2009032700501.html (accessed July 2010).

Harnisch, Sebastian (2001) Change and continuity in post-Unification German foreign policy, *German Politics,* 10(1): 35–60.

—— (2009) The politics of domestication, *German Politics,* 18(4): 455–68.

—— and Siegfried Schieder (2006) Germany's new European policy: weaker, leaner, meaner, in Hanns W. Maull (ed.), *Germany's Uncertain Power: Foreign Policy of the Berlin Republic* (pp. 95–108), Basingstoke: Palgrave Macmillan.

Harstick, Hans-Peter (2000) Georg Eckert (1912–1974), in Ursula A. J. Becher and Rainer Riemenschneider (eds), *Internationale Verständigung: 25 Jahre Georg-Eckert-Institut für internationale Schulbuchforschung in Braunschweig* (International Understanding: 25 Years Georg-Eckert Institute for International Textbook Research in Brunswick) (pp. 105–15), Hanover: Verlag Hahnsche Buchhandlung.

Hartmann, Kinga (2008) Personal correspondence, 10 Aug.

Harvey, Cole (2009) Obama shifts gears on missile defense, *Arms Control Today*, 39 (Oct.), www.armscontrol.org/act/2009_10/missiledefense (accessed May 2010).

He, Yinan (2009) *The Search for Reconciliation: Sino-Japanese and German–Polish Relations since World War II*, Cambridge: Cambridge University Press.

Hegmann, Gerhard, and Thomas Steinmann (2011) Lockheed Martin gibt Meads nicht auf (Lockheed Martin does not give up Meads), *Financial Times Deutschland*, 11 Sept, www.ftd.de/unternehmen/industrie/:raketenabwehrsysten-lockheed-martin-gibt-meads-nicht-auf/60102927.html (accessed Dec. 2011).

Hein, Laura, and Mark Selden (2000) The lessons of war, global power, and social change, in Laura Hein and Mark Selden (eds), *Censoring History: Citizenship and Memory in Japan, Germany, and the United States* (pp. 3–50), London and New York: M. E. Sharp.

Hellmann, Gunther (2004) Von Gipfelstürmern und Gratwanderern: 'Deutsche Wege' in der Außenpolitik (From summiteer to hiker on the ridge: 'German ways' in foreign policy), *Aus Politik und Zeitgeschichte*, B11 (8 March): 32–9.

Hermann, Charles F. (1990) Changing course: when governments choose to redirect foreign policy, *International Studies Quarterly*, 34(1) (March): 3–21.

Hirsch, Helga (2003) Kollektive Erinnerung im Wandel (Collective Memory in Flux), *Aus Politik und Zeitgeschichte*, B40–1, www.bpb.de/publikationen/7GE5AG,0,Kollektive_Erinnerung_im_Wandel.html (accessed Aug. 2009).

—— (2004) Flucht und Vertreibung – die Rückkehr eines Themas (Escape and expulsion: the return of a topic), in Jörg-Dieter Gauger and Manfred Kittel (eds), *Die Vertreibung der Deutschen aus dem Osten in der Erinnerungskultur* (The Expulsion of Germans from the East in the Culture of Memory) (pp. 113–22), Sankt Augustin: Konrad-Adenauer-Stiftung e.V.

Holsti, K. J. (1970) National role conceptions in the study of foreign policy, *International Studies Quarterly*, 14(3): 233–309.

Hopf, Ted (1998) The promise of constructivism in international relations theory, *International Security*, 23(1) (Summer): 171–200.

Horvat, Andrew (2007) Obstacles to European style historical reconciliation between Japan and South Korea: a practitioner's perspective, in David K. W. Hock (ed.), *Legacies of World War II in South and East Asia* (pp. 152–82), Singapore: Institute of Southeast Asian Studies.

Hosoda, Hiroyuki (2004) Naikaku kanbōchōkan danwa: Heisei 17 nendo ikō ni kakaru bōei keikaku no taikō ni tsuite (Statement by Chief Cabinet Secretary Hosoda Hiroyuki: regarding the defence guidelines for the time from 2005 onwards), www.kantei.go.jp/jp/tyokan/koizumi/2004/1210danwa.html (accessed Nov. 2008).

Howland, Jonathan, and Stoyan Stoyanov (2007) A German role in Europe-based missile defense: Dr. Peter Ramsauer, CSU Bundestag Leader addresses JINSA on September 4, 2007, Wasington DC: Jewish Institute for National Security Affairs, www.jinsa.org/articles/print.html/documentid/3910 (accessed May 2008).

Hughes, Christopher W. (2004a) *Japan's Reemergence as a 'Normal' Military Power*, Adelphi Paper, London: Routledge.

—— (2004b) *Japan's Security Agenda: Military, Economic, and Environmental Dimensions*, London: Lynne Rienner Publishers.

—— (2004c) Japan's security policy, the US–Japan alliance, and the 'War on Terror': incrementalism confirmed or radical leap? *Australian Journal of International Affairs,* 58(4) (Dec.): 427–45.

—— (2007) Japan's doctoring of the Yoshida doctrine, *Asia Policy,* 4: 199–204.

—— and Akiko Fukushima (2004) US–Japan security relations: toward bilateralism plus? in Ellis S. Krauss and T. J. Pempel (eds), *Beyond Bilateralism: U.S.–Japan Relations in the New Asia-Pacific* (pp. 55–86), Stanford, CA: Stanford University Press.

Hyde-Price, Adrian, and Lisbeth Aggestam (2000) Conclusion: exploring the new agenda, in Lisbeth Aggestam and Adrian Hyde-Price (eds), *Security and Identity in Europe: Exploring the New Agenda* (pp. 234–62), Basingstoke: Macmillan Press.

Ide, Hiroto, Hiroyuki Fukushima, and Masaharu Ishida (2010) Sengō no nikkan ni okeru kyōkasho mondai o meguru kyōiku seisaku, kyōikugaku no shosō (Education politics and phases of pedagogics in the post-war Japan–Korea textbook problem), in Nikkan Rekishi Kyōdō Kenkyu Iinkai (ed.), *Dai 2 ki nikkan rekishi kyōdō kenkyū hōkokusho* (Report of the Second Joint Japan–Korea Research Commission on History) (pp. 151–89), Tokyo: Nikkan Bunka Kōryū Kikin.

Independent (1998) Japan earmarks $3.5m for missile defence uplift, LexisNexis, 18 Aug.

Inoguchi, Takashi (2005) *Japanese Politics: An Introduction,* Melbourne: Trans Pacific Press.

Inside Missile Defense (2007) Germans ask Krieg not to make changes to MEADS program plan, LexisNexis, 28 Feb.

Iokibe, Makoto, ed. (2006) *Sengo nihon gaikōshi (Shinpan)* (The Diplomatic History of Postwar Japan), 2nd edn, Tokyo: Yūhikaku.

—— Katsuyuki Yakushiji, and Motoshige Itō (2006) *90 nendai no shōgen Miyazawa Kiichi: Hoshuhonryū no kiseki* (Testimony from the 1990s: Miyazawa Kiichi. The Locus of the Conservative Mainstream), Tokyo: Kyōdō Insatsu.

Ishiba, Shigeru (2005) Nihon no bōei seisaku no zenpantekina kadai (General issues in Japan's defence policy), *Kokusai Mondai,* 543: 2–20.

—— (2006) Dai-8kai nichibei anpo senryaku kaigi: Kichō kōen (8th Strategic Conference on the Japan–US Security Treaty: keynote address), www.ja-nsrg.or.jp/f2006-8.htm.

Ishizuka, Katsumi (2004) Japan and UN peace operations, *Japanese Journal of Political Science,* 5(1): 137–57.

Ito, Masami (2009) No Okinawa clause for textbooks, *Japan Times,* 4 Feb., http://search.japantimes.co.jp/cgi-bin/nn20090204a4.html (accessed Feb. 2009).

Jach, Michael (2000) Ende eines Feindbilds (The end of an enemy image), *Focus,* 35: 48, www.focus.de/politik/deutschland/geschichte-ende-eines-feindbilds_aid_186343.html (accessed July 2009).

Jacobmeyer, W., ed. (1979) *Die Deutsch-Polnischen Schulbuchempfehlungen in der öffentlichen Diskussion der Bundesrepublik Deutschland: Eine Dokumentation* (The German–Polish Textbook Recommendations in the Public Discussion in the Federal Republic of Germany: A Documentation), Brunswick: Georg-Eckert Institut für internationale Schulbuchforschung.

Japan Economic Newswire (1986) Textbook screening reflects government policy, report says, LexisNexis, 25 June.

—— (2003a) Intercepting missiles over Japan seen constitutional, LexisNexis, 22 June.

—— (2003b) Koizumi downplays concern missile defense will anger N. Korea, LexisNexis, 19 Dec.

Japan Focus (2008) Mass suicides in Okinawa, first published in *Asahi Shinbun,* 27 Dec., http://japanfocus.org/products/details/2629 (accessed Feb. 2008).

Japan Policy and Politics (2003a) Japan could share intelligence with U.S. in Iraq War: Ishiba, 10 Feb., http://findarticles.com/p/articles/mi_m0XPQ/is_2003_Feb_10/ai_97400070 (accessed May 2008).

—— (2003b) Japan security policy likely to stand at crossroads, LexisNexis, 6 Jan.

—— (2008) Japan officials stay calm over Aso's 'collective self defense' remark, 6 Oct., http://findarticles.com/p/articles/mi_m0XPQ/is_/ai_n30895973 (accessed Oct. 2008).

Japan Times (2002) AEGIS kan hakken mondai (The problem of AEGIS surveillance), 20 Dec., www.japantimes.co.jp/shukan-st/english_news/editorial/2002/ed20021220.htm (accessed Sept. 2008).

—— (2007) Military 'forced' Okinawa mass suicides: expert defies ministry to go public with criticism of textbook revisions, 28 Nov., http://search.japantimes.co.jp/cgi-bin/nn20071128a5.html (accessed Nov. 2007).

—— (2008a) 'Noncombat zone' not vague, Machimura says, 19 April, http://search.japantimes.co.jp/cgi-bin/nn20080419a3.html (accessed Nov. 2008).

—— (2008b) Takeshima Japanese, schools to be told, 20 May, http://search.japantimes.co.jp/cgi-bin/nn20080520a1.html (accessed May 2008).

—— (2009a) New spy satellite launched into orbit, 29 Nov., http://search.japantimes.co.jp/print/nn20091129a1.hml (accessed March 2010).

—— (2009b) North Korea fires rocket over Tohoku, 5 April, http://search.japantimes.co.jp/print/nn20090405x1.html (accessed April 2009).

Japanese Diet (2005) Dai 162 kai tsūjō kokkai – Kessan iinkai: Kokusai kyōiku jōhō senta no tōsan ni tsuite (162nd Diet Session – Budget Committee, About the bankruptcy of the International Society for Education Information) 16 May.

Japanese Government (2008) *Uchū kihon hō* (Basic Law on Outer Space), 20 May, http://law.e-gov.go.jp/announce/H20HO043.html (accessed Nov. 2008).

Jasper, Martin (2008) Lehrbuch gegen die Angst voreinander (Textbook against mutual fear), *Braunschweiger Zeitung*, 31 Jan., www.newsclick.de/index.jsp/menuid/2184/artid/7908824 (accessed July 2009).

Jimbo, Ken (2002) A Japanese perspective on missile defense and strategic coordination, *Nonproliferation Review* (Summer): 56–62.

JoongAng Ilbo (2010) Interview: Okada gaishō, 'kan-nichi, anpo, bōei bunya demo kyōryoku no dankai ga kita' (Interview: Foreign Minister Okada, 'The time has come for Japan–Korea cooperation on security and defence'), 14 July, http://japanese.joins.com/article/article.php?aid=131154&servcode=A00&sectcode=A10 (accessed July 2010).

Kahler, Tobias (2001) *Die verunsicherte Gemeinschaft: Probleme transatlantischer Rüstungskooperation am Beispiel des MEADS* (Unsettled Society: Problems in Transatlantic Armament Cooperation: The Example of MEADS), Berlin: Diplomarbeit im Fachbereich Politische Wissenschaft an der Freien Universität.

Kamusella, Tomasz (2004) The expulsion of the population categorized as 'Germans' from the post-1945 Poland, in Steffen Prauser and Arfon Rees (eds), *The Expulsion of the 'German' Communities from Eastern Europe at the End of the Second World War* (pp. 21–32), EUI Working Paper HEC, San Domenico: European University Institute.

Kaneda, Hideaki, Kazumasa Kobayashi, Hiroshi Tajima, and Hirofumi Tosaki (2006) *Nihon no misairu bōei: Henyō suru senryaku kankyō ka no gaikō, anzenhoshō sesaku* (Japan's Missile Defence: Foreign and Security Policy under a Changing Strategic Environment), Tokyo: Nihon Kokusai Mondai Kenkyūsho.

—— (2007) *Japan's Missile Defense: Diplomatic and Security Policies in a Changing Strategic Environment*, Tokyo: Japan Institute of International Affairs: Japan Institute of International Affairs.

Kang, David, and Ji-Young Lee (2010) Japan–Korea relations: same as it ever was, *Comparative Connections,* 12(1): 109–18.

Kang, Sang-Jung (2006) Ikkokushi kara tohoku ajia shi he, sorega rekishi ninshiki no soukoku ni shokou o motarasu (From one-country history to a northeast Asia history: that will be a breakthrough in the conflict of historical perception), *Nihon No Ronten,* 252–5.

Kansteiner, Wulf (2006) Losing the war, winning the memory battle: the legacy of Nazism, World War II, and the Holocaust in the Federal Republic of Germany, in Richard N. Lebow, Wulf Kansteiner, and Claudio Fogu (eds), *The Politics of Memory in Postwar Europe* (pp. 102–46), Durham, NC: Duke University Press.

Katayama, Yoshihiro (2008) Interview with A. Sakaki, 24 March, Tokyo.

Katsioulis, Christos (2010) Interview with A. Sakaki, 7 May, Berlin.

Katzenstein, Peter J. (1996) Introduction: alternative perspectives on national security, in Peter J. Katzenstein (ed.), *The Culture of National Security: Norms and Identity in World Politics* (pp. 1–32), New York: Columbia University Press.

—— (2005) *A World of Regions: Asia and Europe in the American Imperium,* London: Cornell University Press.

—— and Takashi Shiraishi (1997) Conclusion: regions in world politics – Japan and Asia – Germany in Europe, in Peter J. Katzenstein and Takashi Shiraishi (eds), *Network Power: Japan and Asia* (pp. 341–81), Ithaca, NY: Cornell University Press.

Kaufman, Stephen (2010) Romania agrees to host ballistic missile interceptor, America (US Department of State), 4 Feb., www.america.gov/st/eur-english/2010/February/201 00204155405esnamfuak0.8593866.html (accessed May 2010).

Kawakami, Takahashi, and Ken Jimbo (2002) Dandō misairu bōei to nichibei dōmei (Ballistic missile defence and the Japan–US alliance), in Satoshi Morimoto (ed.), *Misairu bōei – atarashii kokusai anzen hosho no kōzu* (Missile Defence: Outline of the New International Security Policy) (pp. 262–81), Tokyo: Nihon Kokusai Mondai Kenkyusho.

Kawano, Noriyuki, and Masatsugu Matsuo (2002) Political outcomes of the slips of the tongue of Japanese Ministers, *Hiroshima Peace Science,* 24: 197–221, http://home.hiroshima-u.ac.jp/heiwa/JNL/24/KawaMatsu.PDF (accessed August 2009).

Keller, Patrick (2010) Interview with A. Sakaki, 20 May, Berlin.

Kim, Gi-Chol (2002) Yureru 'kan-nichi rekishi kyōdō kenkyū iinkai' (The 'Korea–Japan Joint History Research Committee' shaking), *Chosun Ilbo,* 22 April, www.chosunonline.com/article/20020422000032 (accessed September 2008).

Kimura, Kan (2007) Roundtable discussion/commentary at conference, 19 Oct., Symposium des Goethe Instituts, de la Maison Franco-Japonaise und de L'Institut Franco-Japonais, Der Prozeß der deutsch-französischen Aussöhnung und das gemeinsame Schulbuchprojekt (The process of German–French reconciliation and the joint textbook project), Tokyo.

Kington, Tom, and Michael Hoffman (2011) Qatar discusses MEADS partnership with Germany, Italy, *Defense News,* LexisNexis, 17 Nov., www.defensenews.com/story.php?i=8291353 (accessed December 2011).

Kirste, Knut (1998) *Rollentheorie und Außenpolitikanalyse: Die USA und Deutschland als Zivilmächte* (Role theory and foreign policy analysis: the US and Germany as civilian powers), Europäische Hochschulschriften, 359, Frankfurt am Main: Peter Lang Verlag.

Kitaoka, Shinichi (2007) *Kokuren no seiji rikigaku: Nihon wa doko ni iru no ka* (The Political Dynamics of the United Nations: Where does Japan Stand?), Chūkō Shinsho, 1899, Tokyo: Chūōkōronsha.

Klaeden, Eckart von (2007) Europe needs a debate on missile defense, Atlantic Community, www.atlantic-community.org/index/articles/view/Europe_Needs_a_Debate_on_Missile_Defense (accessed May 2008).

Klien, Susanne (2002) *Rethinking Japan's Identity and International Role: An Intercultural Perspective,* London and New York: Routledge.

Klose, Hans-Ulrich (2010) Interview with A. Sakaki, 23 June, Berlin.

Knodt, Michèle (2001) External representation of German Länder interests, in Wolf-Dieter Eberwein and Karl Kaiser (eds), *Germany's New Foreign Policy: Decision-Making in an Interdependent World* (pp. 173–88), Basingstoke: Palgrave.

Koizumi, J., and Jijigahosha 'Cabi Netto' Henshubu, eds (2006) *Koizumi Junichiro desu* (I am Koizumi Junichiro), Tokyo: Jijigaho.

Kokuritsu Kokkai Toshokan (Various dates) *Kokkai kaigiroku kensaku shisutemu* (Search System for Meeting Transcripts of the National Diet), Tokyo: Diet Library Japan, http://kokkai.ndl.go.jp/cgi-bin/KENSAKU/swk_srch.cgi?SESSION=9028&MODE=2.

Kondo, Takahiro (1993) *Doitsu gendaishi o kokusai kyōkasho kaizen: Posuto kokumin kokka no rekishi ishiki* (International Textbook Improvement of Contemporary History of Germany: Post-National Historical Consciousness), Nagoya: Nagoya Daigaku Shuppankai.

—— (1998) *Kokusai rekishi kyōkasho taiwa: Yōroppa ni okeru 'kako' no saihen* (International History Textbook Dialogue: The Reconstitution of the 'Past' in Europe), Tokyo: Chūōkōronsha.

——(2001) *Rekishi kyōiku to kyōkasho: Doitsu, Osutoria, soshite Nihon* (History Education and Textbooks: Germany, Austria, and Japan), Iwanami Booklet, 545, Tokyo: Iwanami.

—— (2004) *Der japanisch-südkoreanische Schulbuchstreit: Probleme und aktuelle Entwicklungen* (The Japanese–South Korean Textbook Dispute: Problems and Current Developments), Vortrag an der Universität Siegen, www2.fb1.uni-siegen.de/history/dgng/dokumente/schulbuchstreit.pdf (accessed July 2008).

—— (2008a) Author's email correspondence with Kondo Takahiro.

—— (2008b) Progress in and future issues of the dialogue on history in East Asia, 15 Oct., History Education and Reconciliation: Comparative Perspectives on East Asia, Brunswick.

Korea Times (2000) Seoul, Tokyo have long way to go to reach shared view on Korea–Japan history, LexisNexis, 1 June.

Koschyk, Hartmut (2004) Der neue Stellenwert von Flucht und Vertreibung in der Erinnerungskultur (The new significance of escape and expulsion in the culture of remembrance), in Jörg-Dieter Gauger and Manfred Kittel (eds), *Die Vertreibung der Deutschen aus dem Osten in der Erinnerungskultur* (The Expulsion of Germans from the East in the Culture of Memory) (pp. 139–44), Sankt Augustin: Konrad-Adenauer-Stiftung e.V.

Krause, Joachim (2000) The new crisis over national missile defense, *Internationale Politik* (transatlantic edn), 1(2) (Summer): 35–9.

—— (2001) Raketenabwehr: Sprengstoff für die atlantische Allianz? (Missile defense: explosive for the Atlantic Alliance?), *Jahrbuch für internationale Sicherheitspolitik,* 465–95.

—— (2005) *MEADS in der Kritik: Braucht die Bundesrepublik Deutschland ein Bodengebundenes taktisches Luftverteidigungssystem?* (Criticism of MEADS: does the Federal Republic of Germany need a ground-based tactical air defense system?), *Kieler Analysen zur Sicherheitspolitik,* 13, www.ispk.org/fileadmin/user_upload/Kieler%20 Analysen%20zur%20Sicherheitspolitik/KAzS13.pdf (accessed March 2012).

Krotz, Ulrich (2002) *National Role Conceptions and Foreign Policies: France and Germany Compared,* Working Papers of the Program for the Study of Germany and Europe, 2/1, Cambridge, MA: Harvard University.

——— (2007) *Parapublic Underpinnings of International Relations: The Franco-German Construction of International Social Purpose*, Tokyo: Friedrich-Ebert Stiftung, www.festokyo.com/krotz_eg.pdf (accessed August 2008).

Kubbig, Bernd W. (2000) *Problematische Kooperation im Dreieck: Das trilaterale Raketenabwehrprojekt MEADS* [Problematic cooperation in the triangle: the trilateral Missile Defense Project MEADS]. Raketenabwehrforschung International, Bulletin 18 (Fall), www.hsfk.de/abm/bulletin/pdfs/kubbka.pdf (accessed March 2012).

——— (2005a) *Als Entscheidungsgrundlage für das Raketenabwehrprojekt MEADS ungeeignet: Eine Analyse der Dokumente von BMVg und Berichterstattergruppe* (Inadequate as a Basis for Decision-Making on the Missile Defense Project MEADS: An Analysis of Documents of the Defense Ministry and the Rapporteurs Group), HSFK-Report, Frankfurt am Main: Hessische Stiftung Friedens- und Konfliktforschung.

——— (2005b) America: escaping the legacy of the ABM treaty, *Contemporary Security Policy,* 26(3): 410–30.

——— (2005c) Introduction: the domestic politics of missile defense, *Contemporary Security Policy,* 26(3) (Dec.): 385–409.

——— (2005d) *Raketenabwehrsystem MEADS: Entscheidung getroffen, viele Fragen offen* (Missile Defense System MEADS: Decision Taken, Many Questions Open), HSFK-Report, 10, Frankfurt am Main: Hessische Stiftung Friedens- und Konfliktforschung.

——— and Axel Nitsche (2005) Germany: selective security provider in the Schröder/ Fischer era, *Contemporary Security Policy,* 26(3) (Dec.): 520–43.

Kuroda, Katsuhiro (2006) Dainiji nikkan rekishi kyōdō kenkyū de nihon o mochiukeru 'kyōkasho' 'Takeshima' 'Nihon-kai' 3 ten setto (The three issues awaiting Japan in the second round of Japan–Korea joint history research: 'textbooks', 'Takeshima', 'Sea of Japan'), *Sapio,* 18(22): 97–9.

Kyodo News (2007) Japan, S. Korea begin 2nd round of history talks focused on textbook, 23 June, http://asia.news.yahoo.com/070623/kyodo/d8pu7sjg0.html (accessed July 2008).

Landler, Mark (2002) 'Clear as glass' against war with Iraq, Germans still agree to aid U.S. and Israel, *New York Times Online*, 28 Nov., http://query.nytimes.com/gst/fullpage.ht ml?res=9804E3DB1538F93BA15752C1A9649C8B63&sec=&spon=&pagewanted=p rint (accessed Oct. 2008).

Landmann, Jan (2005) *Bedeutung von Bedrohungsperzeptionen in der außen- und sicherheitspolitischen Debatte am Beispiel der Diskussion über das bodengestützte Luftabwehrsystem MEADS* (The Importance of Threat Perceptions in the Foreign and Security Policy Debates: Taking the Example of Discussions on the Ground-Based Air Defense System MEADS), Raketenabwehrforschung International, Bulletin. www.hsfk.de/abm/uniforum/pdfs/landmann.pdf (accessed Sept. 2007).

Lange, Sascha (2005) *Teilfähigkeitsverlust durch MEADS: Entspricht das Abwehrsystem den Verteidigungspolitischen Richtlinien?* (Partial Loss of Capability through MEADS: Does the Defence System Meet Defence Policy Guidelines?), Berlin: SWP-Aktuell, www.swp-berlin.org/fileadmin/contents/products/aktuell/aktuell2005_04_lgs_ks.pdf (accessed March 2012).

——— (2010) Interview with A. Sakaki, 20 May, Berlin.

Layne, Christopher (1993) The unipolar illusion: why new great powers will rise, *International Security,* 17(4) (Spring): 5–51.

Le Gloannec, Anne-Marie (2004) The unilateralist temptation: Germany's foreign policy after the cold war, *Internationale Politik und Gesellschaft,* 1: 27–39.

Lee, Dong-Hoo (2002) Media discourses on the other: Japanese history textbook controversies in Korea, proceedings of the Media Ecology Association, 3rd Annual Convention, 21–23 June, Marymount Manhattan College, www.media-ecology.org/publications/MEA_proceedings/v3/Lee03.pdf (accessed July 2008).

Levy, Daniel, and Julian Dierkes (2002) Institutionalizing the past: shifting memories of nationhood in German education and immigration legislation, in Jan-Werner Müller (ed.), *Memory and Power in Post-War Europe: Studies in the Presence of the Past* (pp. 244–64), Cambridge: Cambridge University Press.

Levy, Jack S. (1994) Learning and foreign policy: sweeping a conceptual minefield, *International Organization*, 48(2) (Spring): 279–312.

Lim, Robyn (2004) Missile defense: Japan faces tough choices over U.S. alliance, *International Herald Tribune*, 11 Feb., www.iht.com/articles/2004/02/11/edlim_ed3_.php (accessed Oct. 2008).

Limbach, Manuel (2008) *Vergangenheitsbewältigung in der Ära Kohl: Der 'Historikerstreit'* (Coming to Terms with the Past in the Kohl Era: The 'Historians' Dispute'), Norderstedt: Grin Verlag.

Lind, Jennifer (2008) Memory, apology, and international reconciliation, *Japan Focus*, 47(7), www.japanfocus.org/-Jennifer-Lind/2957 (accessed September 9, 2009).

Lisagor, Megan (2000) How others view U.S. missile defense, *National Journal*, LexisNexis, 8 July.

Lohse, Eckart (2010) Iran: Was schützt uns vor den Raketen? (Iran: What Protects us from missiles?), *Frankfurter Allgemeine Zeitung*, 14 Feb., www.faz.net/s/Rub868F8FFABF0341D8AFA05047D112D93F/Doc~E0C64274D3B2B45358E04EA5E6B938B1B~ATpl~Ecommon~Scontent.html (accessed Feb. 2010).

Lübbe, Hermann (1977) Wer kann sich historische Aufklärung leisten? (Who can afford historical enlightenment?), in Willi Oelmüller (ed.), *Wozu noch Geschichte? Zur Funktion der Geschichte in den Wissenschaften* (History for What? On the Function of History in Scholarship) (pp. 310–28), Munich: Fink.

Luppes, Jeffrey (2005) Never again war, never again Auschwitz: the German Greens and military intervention in the 1990s, paper at The Ethical Dimension of European Foreign Policy conference, London: LSE/KCL.

Lutomski, Pavel (2004) The debate about a center against expulsions: an unexpected crisis in German–Polish relations? *German Studies Review*, 27(3): 449–68.

Machimura, Nobutaka (2001) *Daijin Danwa* (Commentary of the Minister), 3 April, www.mext.go.jp/b_menu/houdou/13/04/010402.htm (accessed Aug. 2008).

McNeill, David (2005) *History Redux: Japan's Textbook Battle Reignites*, Japan Policy Research Institute Working Paper, 107 (June), www.jpri.org/publications/workingpapers/wp107.html (accessed Aug. 2008).

Maehara, Seiji (2006) Nihon no misairu bōei o dō kangaeruka: Kakasenai senryakuteki torikumi (How to think about Japan's missile defense: the necessary strategic approach), *Kaikakusha*, 555 (Oct.): 30–3.

Maier, Robert (2008) Interview with A. Sakaki, 16 Oct., Brunswick.

Mainichi Shinbun (1997) Tokyo rejects Seoul's call for textbook review, LexisNexis, 23 July.

—— (2005) Japan to propose Tokyo, Seoul review history textbooks, LexisNexis, 8 June.

—— (2008) Takeshima no kyōkasho no kaisetsu ga, naze mondai nan desu ka (Why is there a problem with the description of Takeshima in textbooks?), 19 Oct., http://mainichi.jp/life/edu/guideline/news/20081019ddm013070048000c.html (accessed Oct. 2008).

—— (2011) Multilateral diplomacy indispensable to improve ties with China, 23 June, http://mdn.mainichi.jp/perspectives/editorial/archive/news/2011/06/20110623p2a00m 0na007000c.html (accessed Dec. 2011).

Malici, Akan (2006) Germans as Venutians: the culture of German foreign policy behavior, *Foreign Policy Analysis*, 2: 37–62.

Martin, David (1996) Towards an alliance framework for extended air defence/ theatre missile defence, *NATO Review*, 3 (May): 32–5, www.nato.int/docu/review/1996/9603-7. htm (accessed June 2008).

Masaki, Hisane (2007) Japan shields itself from attack, *Asia Times Online*, 23 March, www.atimes.com/atimes/Japan/IC23Dh03.html (accessed May 2007).

Masalski, Kathleen W. (2000) Teaching democracy, teaching war: American and Japanese educators teach the Pacific war, in Laura Hein and Mark Selden (eds), *Censoring History: Citizenship and Memory in Japan, Germany, and the United States* (pp. 258–87), London and New York: M. E. Sharpe.

Mataichi, Seiji (2002) *AEGIS kan no indo yō hakken ni hantai suru* (Opposing the dispatch of the Aegis ship to the Indian Ocean), www.s-mataichi.com/message/20021210.html (accessed Sept. 2008).

Matsui, Kazuhiko (2000) Beihondo misairu bōei to ajia taiheiyō no anzen hoshō (The national missile defense of the US and Asia-Pacific security), *Shin Bōei Ronshū*, 28(3) (Dec.): 47–61.

Matsumoto, Kenichi (2006) 'Ajia' no imi sae kuni doko ni chigau no ni rekishi ninshiki no kyōyu nado arienai (Even the understanding of 'Asia' is different – it is impossible to have a joint historical perception), *Nihon no Ronten*: 256–9.

Matthews, Eugene A. (2003) Japan's new nationalism, *Foreign Affairs*, 82(6): 74–90.

Maull, Hanns W. (1990/1991) Germany and Japan: the new civilian powers, *Foreign Affairs*, 69(5): 91–106.

—— ed. (1998) *Regionalismus in Asien-Pazifik* (Regionalism in Asia-Pacific), Arbeitspapiere zur Internationalen Politik, 98, Bonn: Europa Union Verlag.

—— (1999) Germany and the use of force: still a civilian power? *Trierer Arbeitspapiere zur Internationalen Politik*, 2, www.deutsche-aussenpolitik.de/resources/tazip/tazip2. pdf (accessed March 2012).

—— (2004) Germany and the use of force: still a civilian power? in Saori N. Katada, Hanns W. Maull, and Takashi Inoguchi (eds), *Global Governance: Germany and Japan in the International System* (pp. 89–110), Aldershot: Ashgate.

—— (2006a) Conclusion: uncertain power. German foreign policy into the twenty-first century, in Hanns W. Maull (ed.), *Germany's Uncertain Power: Foreign Policy of the Berlin Republic* (pp. 273–86), Basingstoke: Palgrave Macmillan.

—— (2006b) Introduction, in Hanns W. Maull (ed.), *Germany's Uncertain Power: Foreign Policy of the Berlin Republic* (pp. 1–14), Basingstoke: Palgrave Macmillan.

—— (2007) Deutschland als Zivilmacht (Germany as a civilian power), in Gunther Hellmann, Siegmar Schmidt, and Reinhard Wolf (eds), *Handbuch zur deutschen Außenpolitik* (Reference Book on German Foreign Policy) (pp. 73–84), Opladen: VS Verlag für Sozialwissenschaften.

Mayring, Philipp (1990) *Qualitative Inhaltsanalyse: Grundlagen und Techniken* (Qualitative Content Analysis: Basic Foundations and Techniques), Weinheim: Deutscher Studien Verlag.

—— (2005) Neuere Entwicklungen in der qualitativen Forschung und der qualitativen Inhaltsanalyse (New developments in qualitative research and qualitative content analysis), in Philipp Mayring and Michaela Gläser-Zikuda (eds), *Die Praxis der qualitativen Inhaltsanalyse* (The Practical Use of Qualitative Content Analysis) (pp. 7–19), Beltz Pädagogik, Weinheim: Beltz.

Mearsheimer, John J. (1990a) Back to the future: instability in Europe after the cold war', *International Security*, 15(1): 5–56.

—— (1990b) Why we will soon miss the cold war, *Atlantic Monthly*, 266(2): 35–50.

Meiers, Franz-Josef (2002) A change of course? German foreign and security policy after Unification, *German Politics*, 11(3): 195–216.

Member of the Japan–Korea Joint Research Commission on History (Nikkan Rekishi Kyōdō Kenkyu Iinkai) (2007) Interview with A. Sakaki, 30 Oct., Tokyo.

Merkel, Angela (2005) Rede der Vorsitzenden der CDU/CSU-Bundestagsfraktion und Vorsitzenden der CDU Deutschlands, Dr. Angela Merkel anlässlich des 'Tages der Heimat' am 6. August 2005 in Berlin (Speech by the Chairperson of the CDU/CSU Bundestag Fraction and Chairperson of the CDU Germany, Dr Angela Merkel, on 'Homeland Day' on 6 August 2005 in Berlin), www.bund-der-vertriebenen.de/files/redemerkel.pdf (accessed July 2009).

Mey, Holger H. (1995) German–American relations: the case for a preference, *Comparative Strategy*, 14(2): 205–9.

Meyer, Enno (1982) Deutschland, die Deutschen und die deutsch-polnischen Beziehungen in den polnischen Geschichtslehrbüchern seit 1972 (Germany, the Germans and German–Polish relations in Polish history textbooks since 1972), *Internationale Schulbuchforschung*, 4(4): 261–74.

Midford, Paul (2003) Japan's response to terror: dispatching the SDF to the Arabian Sea, *Asian Survey*, 43(2): 329–51.

Miller, Judith (1985) Western Europeans, some with doubts, support 'Star Wars', *New York Times*, LexisNexis, 30 Dec.

Ministry of Defence Japan (2007) *Bōei hakusho* (Defence White Paper), Tokyo, www.clearing.mod.go.jp/hakusho_data/2007/2007/html/j2213200.html (accessed Feb. 2009).

—— (2008) *Bōei hakusho* (Defence White Paper), Tokyo, www.clearing.mod.go.jp/hakusho_data/2008/2008/html/k2212200.html (accessed Nov. 2008).

Ministry of Foreign Affairs Japan (2002) Press conference with Press Secretary Hatsuhisa Takashima, 6 Dec., www.mofa.go.jp/announce/press/2002/12/1206.html#7 (accessed May 2008).

Mitani, Hiroshi (2007) Kinrinshokoku – rekishi kyōkasho to nashonarizumu – kaisetsu (Nearby countries – history textbooks and nationalism – comment), in Hiroshi Mitani (ed.), *Rekishi kyokasho mondai* (The History Textbook Problem) (pp. 243–47), Tokyo: Nihontosho.

Miyakawa, Mikiko (2001) Learning from German textbooks, *Daily Yomiuri*, LexisNexis, 1 May.

Mizuno, Naoki (2005) Nikkan rekishi shiryō no kyōyūka o (Towards the joint sharing by Japan and Korea of historical records), *Sekai*, 741 (July), 116–123.

Mochizuki, Mike M. (2006) Japan's changing international role, in Thomas U. Berger, Mike M. Mochizuki, and Jitsuo Tsuchiyama (eds), *Japan in International Politics: The Foreign Policy of an Adaptive State* (pp. 1–22), Boulder, CO: Lynne Rienner Publishers.

—— (2007) Change in Japan's grand strategy: why and how much? *Asia Policy*, 4: 191–6.

Morimoto, Satoshi (2002) Misairu bōei to anzen hoshō (Missile defence and security), in Satoshi Morimoto (ed.), *Misairu bōei: Atarashii kokusai anzen hosho no kōzu* (Missile Defence: Outline of the New International Security Policy) (pp. 1–26), Tokyo: Nihon Kokusai Mondai Kenkyusho.

—— and Sugio Takahashi (2002) BMD to nihon no bōei seisaku (BMD and Japan's defence policy), in Satoshi Morimoto (ed.), *Misairu bōei: Atarashii kokusai anzen hosho no kōzu* (Missile Defence: Outline of the New International Security Policy) (pp. 303–21), Tokyo: Nihon Kokusai Mondai Kenkyusho.

Morris-Suzuki, Tessa (2003) Hisuterii no sejigaku: America no iraku, nihon no kitachōsen (The politics of hysteria: America's Iraq, Japan's North Korea), *Sekai*, 710 (Feb.): 230–40.

Müller-Brandeck-Bocquet, Gisela (2010) Deutsche Europapolitik unter Angela Merkel: Enge Gestaltungsspielräume in Krisenzeiten (German European policy under Angela Merkel: little leeway in times of crisis), in Gisela Müller-Brandeck (ed.), *Deutsche Europapolitik: Von Adenauer bis Merkel* (German European policy: from Adenauer to Merkel) (pp. 255–349), 2nd edn, Wiesbaden: VS Verlag für Sozialwissenschaften.

Muradian, Vago (2000a) German reluctance to fund MEADS may force restructuring of program, *Defense Daily*, LexisNexis, 22 Sept.

—— (2000b) Germany reverses stance, to join U.S. and Italy on next MEADS phase, *Defense Daily*, LexisNexis, 8 Dec.

Murayama, Tomiichi (1994) 'Heiwa yūkō kōryū keikaku' ni kan suru Murayama naikaku sōri daijin no danwa (Statement by Prime Minister Murayama Tomiichi on the 'peace, friendship, and exchange initiative'), www.mofa.go.jp/%5Cmofaj/area/taisen/murayama.html (accessed Aug. 2009).

Murayama, Yūzō (2002) TMD to nichibei dōmei: gijutsu kyōryoku (TMD and the Japan–US alliance: technology cooperation), in Satoshi Morimoto (ed.), *Misairu bōei: Atarashii kokusai anzen hosho no kōzu* (Missile Defence: Outline of the New International Security Policy) (pp. 283–301), Tokyo: Nihon Kokusai Mondai Kenkyusho.

Mützenich, Rolf (2004) MEADS, das Rad soll neu erfunden werden! (MEADS: reinventing the wheel), www.gruene-linke.de/themen/meads/muetzenich_mdb-spd.pdf (accessed Sept. 2008).

—— (2010) Interview with A. Sakaki, 22 June, Berlin.

Nachtwei, Winfried (2005) Kontroverse um Raketenabwehrsystem MEADS (Controversy about missile defence system MEADS), www.nachtwei.de/downloads/position/MEADS_info_20050228.pdf (accessed March 2008).

Nagahara, Yoko (1983) Krieg und Frieden in japanischen Schulgeschichtsbüchern: Ein Bericht zur jüngsten Schulbuchdiskussion in Japan (War and peace in Japanese history textbooks: a report on the recent textbook discussion in Japan), *Internationale Schulbuchforschung*, 5: 71–5.

Nassauer, Otfried (2009) Aus alt mach neu: Die Raketenabwehrpläne der USA (Forging (something) new from (something) old: the missile defence plans of the US), www.uni-kassel.de/fb5/frieden/themen/Raketen/obama4.html (accessed March 2010).

Nasu, Hitoshi (2005) Article 9 of the Japanese Constitution: revisited in the light of international law, *Journal of Japanese Law*, 18: 50–66.

National Institute for Defense Studies (2007) *East Asian Strategic Review 2007*, Tokyo, www.nids.go.jp/english/dissemination/east-asian/e2007.html (accessed May 2008).

NATO (2003) Decision sheet of the Defence Planning Committee of the North Atlantic Treaty Organization: NATO support to Turkey within the framework of Article 4, NATO press release, 16 Feb., www.nato.int/docu/pr/2003/p030216e.htm (accessed Oct. 2008).

—— (2011) *Missile Defense Fact Sheet*, www.nato.int/nato_static/assets/pdf/pdf_2011_06/20110608_Factsheet-Missile_Defence.pdf (accessed Dec. 2011).

Neuneck, Götz (2001) The NMD debate: technology, threats and implications for international security, in Paolo Cotta-Ramusion and Maurizio Martellini (eds), *Missile*

Threats and Ballistic Missile Defense: Technology, Strategic Stability and Impact on Global Security (pp. 147–74), Rome: Landau Forum – Centro Volta.

New York Times (2003) Threats and responses: German missile lease to Israel, 17 Jan., http://query.nytimes.com/gst/fullpage.html?res=9407E7DF1630F934A25752C0A965 9C8B63&sec=&spon=&pagewanted=print (accessed Oct. 2008).

NGO Online (2006) Bundeswehr soll knapp 25 Milliarden Euro erhalten (Armed forces to receive just under 25 billion euro), 30 March, www.ngo-online.de/ganze_nachricht. php?Nr=13284 (accessed Sept. 2008).

Nicholls, Jason (2006) Are students expected to critically engage with textbook perspectives of the Second World War? A comparative and international study, *Research in Comparative and International Education*, 1(1): 40–55.

Niedersächsisches Ministerium für Inneres Sport und Integration (2008) *Flucht und Vertreibung verbindlich im Unterricht* (Escape and expulsion compulsory in class), www.mi.niedersachsen.de/master/C49057555_N13619_L20_D0_I522.html (accessed July 2009).

Nikkan Rekishi Kyōdō Kenkyu Iinkai, ed. (2005) *Hōkokusho* (Report of the Joint Japan–Korea Research Commission on History), Tokyo: Nikkan Bunka Kōryū Kikin.

—— ed. (2010) *Dai 2 ki nikkan rekishi kyōdō kenkyū hōkokusho* (Report of the Second Joint Japan–Korea Research Commission on History), Tokyo: Nikkan Bunka Kōryū Kikin.

Nōsei, Nobuyuki (2007) *Misairu bōei: Nihon wa kyōi ni dō tachimukau no ka (*Missile Defence: How does Japan Face Threats?), Tokyo: Shinchosha.

Nozaki, Yoshiko (2002) Japanese politics and the history textbook controversy, 1982–2001, *International Journal of Educational Research*, 37: 603–22.

Nye, Joseph S. (2004) *Soft Power: The Means to Success in World Politics*, New York: Public Affairs.

Oe, Hiroshi (2007) *Gaikō to kokueki: Hōkatsuteki anzen hoshō to ha nanika* (Diplomacy and the National Interest: What is a Comprehensive Security Policy?), Tokyo: NHK Books.

Ogawa, Shinichi (2002) Missile defense and deterrence, *NIDS Security Reports*, 3 (March): 24–55.

Okinawa Times (2008) A political decision that obscures historical reality: 'involvement' approved, 'coercion' (Kyousei) disapproved in Okinawa mass suicide textbook treatment, originally publ. 27 Dec. 2007, *Japan Focus*, http://japanfocus.org/products/details/2629 (accessed Aug. 2008).

Okonogi, Masao (2008) Interview with A. Sakaki, 27 March, Tokyo.

Oros, Andrew L. (2008) *Normalizing Japan: Politics, Identity, and the Evolution of Security Practice*, Stanford, CA: Stanford University Press.

Oschatz, Georg-Bernd (2000) Zu dieser Festschrift (About this commemorative publication), in Ursula A. J. Becher and Rainer Riemenschneider (eds), *Internationale Verständigung: 25 Jahre Georg-Eckert-Institut für internationale Schulbuchforschung in Braunschweig* (International Understanding: 25 Years Georg-Eckert Institute for International Textbook Research in Braunschweig) (pp. 13–14), Hanover: Verlag Hahnsche Buchhandlung.

Overhaus, Marco (2004) In search of a post-hegemonic order: Germany, NATO and the European Security and Defence Policy, *German Politics*, 13(4): 551–68.

—— (2005) German foreign policy and the shadow of the past, *SAIS Review*, 15(2) (Summer/Fall): 27–41.

Park, Soon-Won (2008) A history that opens to the future: the first common East Asian history guide, paper at conference (15 Oct.), History Education and Reconciliation: Comparative Perspectives on East Asia, Brunswick.

People's Daily (2008) Japanese PM rules out possibility of collective self-defense, 4 Nov., http://english.people.com.cn/90001/90777/90851/6527208.html (accessed Nov. 2008).

Petersen, Susanne (2001) Die Schulbuchprozesse: Geschichtspolitik in japanischen Schulbüchern (Textbook trials: politics of history in Japanese textbooks), in Dietmar Rothermund (ed.), *Periplus 2001: Jahrbuch für Außereuropäische Geschichte* (Periplus 2001: Yearbook for History beyond Europe) (pp. 59–82), Münster: LIT Verlag.

Phillips, Ann L. (1998) The politics of reconciliation: Germany in Central-East Europe, *German Politics,* 7(2): 64–85.

Pingel, Falk (1999) *UNESCO Guidebook on Textbook Research and Textbook Revision,* Studien zur Internationalen Schulbuchforschung, Hanover: Hahnsche Buchhandlung.

—— (2007a) Interview with Alexandra Sakaki, 1 Dec., Osaka.

—— (2007b) *Von bilateraler 'Schulbuchdiplomatie' zu multilateraler Schulbuchforschung* (From Bilateral 'Textbook Diplomacy' to Multilateral Textbook Research), Kansai University and Goethe Institute, Geschichtsbewusstsein und Geschichtserziehung, Kontroversen um Geschichtsbücher und das Beispiel der deutsch-polnischen Annäherung, Osaka: Kansai University.

—— (2008) Can truth be negotiated? History Textbook revision as a means to reconciliation, *Annals of the American Academy of Political and Social Science,* 617(1): 181–98.

Pond, Elizabeth (1992) Germany in the new Europe, *Foreign Affairs,* 71(2): 114–30.

Pradetto, August (2006) The polity of German foreign policy: changes since Unification, in Hanns W. Maull (ed.), *Germany's Uncertain Power: Foreign Policy of the Berlin Republic* (pp. 15–28), Basingstoke: Palgrave Macmillan.

Putin, Vladimir W. (2007) Speech at the 43rd Munich Conference on Security Policy, 2 Oct., www.securityconference.de/konferenzen/rede.php?sprache=en&id=179 (accessed July 2008).

Pyle, Kenneth B. (2006) Abe Shinzo and Japan's change of course, *NBR Analysis,* 17(4): 5–31.

—— (2007a) *Japan Rising: The Resurgence of Japanese Power and Purpose,* New York: Public Affairs.

—— (2007b) The primacy of foreign policy in modern Japan: author's response, *Asia Policy,* 4: 208–11.

Reagan, Ronald (1983) Reagan's 'Star Wars' speech, www.cnn.com/SPECIALS/cold.war/episodes/22/documents/starwars.speech (accessed June 2008).

Researcher at the National Institute for Defense Studies (2008a) Interview with A. Sakaki, 19 March, Tokyo.

—— (2008b) Interview with A. Sakaki, 19 March, Tokyo.

—— (2008c) Interview with A. Sakaki, 27 March, Tokyo.

Richter, Steffi (2003) Zurichtung von Vergangenheit als Schmerzlinderung der Gegenwart (Shaping history as pain relief in the present), in Steffi Richter and Wolfgang Höpken (eds), *Vergangenheit im Gesellschaftskonflikt: Ein Historikerstreit in Japan* (Societal Conflict on the Past: A Historians' Dispute in Japan) (pp. 1–26), Cologne: Böhlau Verlag.

—— (2005) Alle vier Jahre wieder und nichts Neues? Das umstrittene 'Neue Geschichtslehrbuch' für japanische Mittelschulen (Every four years and nothing new? The controversial 'new history textbook' for Japanese middle schools), *Internationale Schulbuchforschung,* 27(1): 91–8.

Riemenschneider, Rainer (1998) Transnationale Konfliktbearbeitung: Die deutsch-französischen und die deutsch-polnischen Schulbuchgespräche im Vergleich, 1935–1997 (Transnational conflict management: comparison of the German–French and German–Polish textbook talks, 1935–1997), *Internationale Schulbuchforschung,* 20: 71–9.

Risse, Thomas (1999) Identitäten und Kommunikationsprozesse in der internationalen Politik: Sozialkonstruktivistische Perspektiven zum Wandel in der Außenpolitik (Identity and communication processes in international politics: social-constructivist perspective on change in foreign policy), in Monika Medick-Krakau (ed.), *Außenpolitischer Wandel in theoretischer und vergleichender Perspektive: Die USA und die Bundesrepublik Deutschland* (Foreign Policy Change in Theoretical and Comparative Perspective: The USA and the Federal Republic of Germany) (pp. 33–57), Baden-Baden: Nomos Verlagsgesellschaft.

—— (2001) A European identity? Europeanization and the evolution of nation-state identities, in Maria G. Cowles, James A. Caporaso, and Thomas Risse (eds), *Transforming Europe: Europeanization and Domestic Change* (pp. 198–216), Ithaca, NY: Cornell University Press.

—— (2003) Deutsche Identität und Außenpolitik (German identity and foreign policy), http://se2.isn.ch/serviceengine/FileContent?serviceID=10&fileid=5CBDE882-E9BD-94A8-E524-9D2C70D13288&lng=de (accessed Sept. 2008).

—— (2004) Kontinuität durch Wandel: Eine 'neue' deutsche Außenpolitik? (Continuity through change: a 'new' German foreign policy?), *Aus Politik und Zeitgeschichte*, B11 (8 March): 24–31.

Rittberger, Volker (2001) Introduction, in Volker Rittberger (ed.), *German Foreign Policy since Unification: Theories and Case Studies* (pp. 1–10), Manchester: Manchester University Press.

Rozman, Gilbert (2002) Japan's quest for great power identity, *Orbis*, 46(1): 73–91.

—— (2004) *Northeast Asia's Stunted Regionalism: Bilateral Distrust in the Shadow of Globalization*, Cambridge: Cambridge University Press.

Ruchniewicz, Krzystof (2005) Der Entstehungsprozess der gemeinsamen deutsch-polnischen Schulbuchkommission 1937/38–1972 (The origins of the joint German-Polish textbook commission, 1937/38–1972), *Archiv für Sozialgeschichte*, 45: 237–52.

Rudolf, Peter (2005) The myth of the 'German way': German foreign policy and transatlantic relations, *Survival*, 47(1): 133–52.

Rundfunk Berlin-Brandenburg Online (2003) *Neue Raketen für die Bundeswehr: Wie Milliarden sinnlos verpulvert werden* (New Missiles for the Bundeswehr: How Billions are Wasted Pointlessly), www.rbb-online.de/_/kontraste/beitrag_jsp/key=rbb_beitrag_1173371.html (accessed Nov. 2008).

Sakai, Toshiki (2002) *Nihon ni okeru kokusai kyōkasho kōryū* (International Textbook Exchange in Japan), www.festokyo.com/text_sakai.doc (accessed July 2009).

Sakata, Takashi (2007) *Shin kyōiku kihonhō* (The New Basic Law on Education), Tokyo: Kyōiku kaihatsu kenkyūsho.

Samuels, Richard J. (2007a) How Japan balances strategy and constraint: author's response, *Asia Policy*, 4: 204–8.

—— (2007b) *Securing Japan: Tokyo's Grand Strategy and the Future of East Asia*, Cornell Studies in Security Affairs, Ithaca, NY: Cornell University Press.

Sanger, David E. (1993) New missile defense in Japan under discussion with U.S., *New York Times*, LexisNexis, 18 Sept.

Sankei Shinbun (2009) Kankoku 'kako o bika' Jiyūsha kyōkasho no kentei gōkaku ni (Korea 'embellishing the past': Jiyusha textbooks passes screening), 9 April, http://sankei.jp.msn.com/life/education/090409/edc0904091710002-n1.htm (accessed Aug. 2009).

Sato, Yoichiro (2003) Defense precedents: Japan breaks ground in naval cooperation, *International Herald Tribune*, 18 Feb., www.iht.com/articles/2003/02/18/_edsato.php (accessed May 2008).

Satoh, Komei (1987) *Kyōkasho kentei no genba kara* (From the Scenes of the Textbook Authorization), Tokyo: Waseda Shuppan.

Schäfer, Paul (1996) MEADS oder: Schutz für unsere Expeditions-Truppen (MEADS or: protection for our expedition-troops), *Wissenschaft und Frieden*, 14(2) (June), www.uni-muenster.de/PeaCon/wuf/wf-96/9620206m.htm (accessed June 2008).

Scheffran, Jürgen, and Regina Hagen (2001) Europa und die Raketenabwehr (Europe and missile defence), *Blätter für deutsche und internationale Politik*, 4: 436–46.

Schmidt, Helmut (1977) Ansprache des Bundeskanzlers vor dem Deutsch-Polnischen Forum am 15. Juni 1977 (Speech by the Federal Chancellor before the German–Polish Forum on 15 June 1977), *Bulletin*, 56 (23 June): 617–19.

Schmidt, Mirko, and Steffen Flath (2008) Kleine Anfrage vom 16. April 2008 im Sächsischen Landtag zum Thema Deutsch-Polnisches Schulbuchprojekt 'Geschichte Verstehen – Zukunft Gestalten': Drucksache 4/11949 (Short inquiry on 16 April 2008 in the Landtag of Saxony regarding the German–Polish textbook project 'Understanding History – Shaping the Future'), www.svp-sachsen.de/assets/applets/160408_Anfrage_Schulbuchprojekt.pdf (accessed July 2009).

Schnappertz, Jürgen (2010) Interview with A. Sakaki, 19 May, Berlin.

Schneider, Connie (2004) *Abschied von der Vergangenheit? Umgangsweisen mit der nationalsozialistischen Vergangenheit in der dritten Generation in Ost- und Westdeutschland* (Farewell from the Past? The Handling of the National Socialist Past in the Third Generation in East and West Germany), Munich: Martin Meidenbauer Verlag.

Schneider, H., M. Jopp, and U. Schmalz, eds (2002) *Eine neue deutsche Europapolitik? Rahmenbedingungen, Problemfelder, Optionen* (A New German European Policy? Basic Conditions, Problem Areas, Options), Europäische Schriften des Instituts für Europäische Politik, 77, Bonn: Europa-Union-Verlag.

Schöllgen, Gregor (2003) *Der Auftritt: Deutschlands Rückkehr auf die Weltbühne* (The Performance: Germany's Return to the World's Stage), Munich: Propyläen.

—— (2005) Deutsche Außenpolitik in der Ära Schröder (German foreign policy in the Schröder era), *Aus Politik und Zeitgeschichte*, 32–3 (8 Aug.): 3–8.

Schreer, Benjamin (2010) Interview with A. Sakaki, 6 May, Berlin.

Schulze, Kai (2010) The rise of China and changes in Japan's identity construction, paper presented at the annual meeting of the ISA Convention 2010: Theory vs. Policy? Connecting Scholars and Practitioners (17 Feb.), www.allacademic.com/meta/p416713_index.html (accessed July 2010).

Schwarz, Hans-Peter (1985) *Die gezähmten Deutschen: Von der Machtbesessenheit zur Machtvergessenheit* (The Tamed Germans: From [Self-Aggrandizement] to [Low Profile in International Diplomacy and Abstention from Traditional Power Politics]), Stuttgart: Dt. Verl.-Anst.

Seddon, Terri (1987) Politics and curriculum: a case study of the Japanese history textbook dispute, 1982, *British Journal of Sociology of Education*, 8(2): 213–26.

Selden, Mark (2008) Japanese and American war atrocities, historical memory and reconciliation: World War II to today. War crimes, atrocities and state terrorism, *Japan Focus*, http://japanfocus.org/products/details/2724 (accessed May 2008).

Shanker, Thom, and Nicholas Kulish (2008) US and Poland set missile deal, *New York Times Online*, 14 Aug., www.nytimes.com/2008/08/15/world/europe/15poland.html?_r=1 (accessed May 2010).

Sherman, Jason (2003) Japan eyes U.S. sea-based missile defense, *Defense News*, LexisNexis, 24 Feb.

Shibuya, Kaoru (1999) Jieitai kanbu ga buchimaketa – 'Kitachōsen tepodon, nichibei anpo, bōeichō oshoku . . . Ima koso kekki no toki da' (The leadership of the self-defense forces has revealed 'North Korea's Taepodong, the Japan-US Security Alliance, corruption in the defence agency... now is the time to act'), *Shūkan Gendai* (3 April): 192–6.

Shin, Gi-Wook (2010) Perspective: historical disputes and reconciliation in Northeast Asia: the US role, *Pacific Affairs,* 83(4): 663–73.

Sims, Calvin (1999) U.S. and Japan agree to joint research on missile defense, *New York Times,* LexisNexis, 17 Aug.

Sinjen, Svenja (2010) Interview with A. Sakaki, 22 June, Berlin.

Soeya, Yoshihide (2005) *Nihon no 'midoru pawa' gaikō: Sengo nihon no sentaku to kōsō* (Japan's 'Middle Power' Diplomacy: Japan's Postwar Choices and Framework), Tokyo: Chikuma.

Speck, Ulrich (2007) The Merkel government: Germany still in search of a foreign policy, *Fride Working Paper,* 32: 6–8, www.aicgs.org/documents/speck0207.pdf (accessed Nov. 2008).

Spiegel (2002a) Streit über Waffen: Schröder liefert Israel Patriot-Raketen (Arguments about weapons: Schröder supplies Israel with Patriot-Missiles), 26 Nov., www.spiegel. de/politik/deutschland/0,1518,224482,00.html (accessed Oct. 2008).

—— (2002b) USA bitten Deutschland für den Kriegsfall um Hilfe (US ask Germany for help in case of war), 21 Nov., www.spiegel.de/politik/ausland/0,1518,223795,00.html (accessed Oct. 2008).

—— (2003) Die Türkei bekommt, was sie braucht (Turkey gets what it needs), 12 Feb., www.spiegel.de/politik/ausland/0,1518,234844,00.html (accessed Oct. 2008).

—— (2005) Grünen-Fraktion will Meads zustimmen (Green-Fraction intends to approve Meads), 19 April, www.spiegel.de/politik/deutschland/0,1518,352284,00.html (accessed Nov. 2009).

—— (2007a) America's controversial missile shield, 26 March, www.spiegel.de/ international/world/0,1518,473952,00.html (accessed July 2007).

—— (2007b) Ex-Nato-General wirft deutschen Politikern Ahnungslosigkeit vor (Ex-Nato-general accuses German politicians of being clueless), www.spiegel.de/politik/ ausland/0,1518,472722,00.html.

—— (2007c) Irans Atompläne: Jung befürwortet US-Raketenabwehr für Europa (Iran's nuclear plans: Jung supports US missile defence for Europe), 12 April, www.spiegel. de/politik/deutschland/0,1518,476780,00.html (accessed April 2007).

—— (2007d) Merkel mahnt Europa zur Einigkeit gegenüber US-Plänen (Merkel urges Europe to find consensus on US-plans), 21 March, www.spiegel.de/politik/ deutschland/0,1518,472871,00.html (accessed July 2008).

—— (2007f) Steinmeier warnt USA vor neuem Wettrüsten (Steinmeier warns US of new arms race), 17 March, www.spiegel.de/politik/deutschland/0,1518,472289,00.html (accessed Nov. 2007).

Staff member of the CDU/CSU parliamentary grouping (2010) Interview with A. Sakaki, 7 May, Berlin.

Steinmeier, Frank-Walter (2006) Polen und Deutschland – Gemeinsam Europas Zukunft gestalten: Rede von Bundesaußenminister Steinmeier zur Eröffnung des Akademischen Jahres an der Viadrina-Universität in Frankfurt (Oder) am 26.10.2006 (Poland and Germany – shaping a common Europe's future, speech by Foreign Minister Steinmeier at the beginning of the academic year at the Viadrina University in Frankfurt (Oder) on 26 October 2006), www.auswaertiges-amt.de/diplo/de/Infoservice/Presse/Reden/ 2006/061026-Viadrina.html (accessed Aug. 2008).

Steinmeier, Frank-Walter (2008) Warsaw and Berlin can change Europe: Federal Foreign Minister Steinmeier in the Polish newspaper *Dziennik* on 5 April 2008, http://www.

auswaertiges-amt.de/diplo/en/Infoservice/Presse/Interview/2008/080405-BM-Dziennik.
html (accessed Aug. 2008).
Stern (2003) Türkei bekommt nun doch deutsche 'Patriot'-Raketen (Turkey now to receive
German 'Patriot' missiles), 9 Feb., www.stern.de/politik/ausland/:Raketenlieferung-
T%FCrkei/503682.html (accessed Oct. 2007).
—— (2007) Raketenabwehr in Deutschland? (Missile defence in Germany?), 10 April,
www.stern.de/politik/deutschland/586602.html?nv=ct_mt (accessed April 2007).
Steuerungsrat und Expertenrat des Projektes Deutsch-Polnisches Geschichtsbuch (2010)
Schulbuch Geschichte: Ein deutsch-polnisches Projekt – Empfehlungen (Textbook
History: A German–Polish Project – Recommendations), www.gei.de/fileadmin/bilder/
pdf/Projekte/Schulbuch%20Geschichte.%20Ein%20deutsch-polnisches%20Projekt-
Empfehlungen.pdf (accessed Dec. 2011).
Stradling, Robert (2003) *Multiperspectivity in History Teaching: A Guide for Teachers,*
Strasbourg: Council of Europe Publishing, www.coe.int/t/e/cultural_co-operation/education/
history_teaching/european_dimension/Multiperspectivity-E.pdf (accessed April 2008).
Strobel, Thomas (2005) Die Gemeinsame deutsch-polnische Schulbuchkommission: Ein
spezifischer Beitrag zur Ost-West-Verständigung 1972–1989 (The Joint German–Polish
Textbook Commission: a specific contribution to the understanding between East and
West 1972–1989), *Archiv für Sozialgeschichte*, 45: 253–68.
—— (2008a) Interview with A. Sakaki, 16 Oct., Brunswick.
—— (2008b) Startschuss für ein gemeinsames deutsch-polnisches Geschichtsbuch
(Starting signal for a joint German-Polish history book), *Eckert: Das Bulletin*, 3: 26–8.
—— and Robert Maier (2008) Einführung (Introduction), in Thomas Strobel and Robert
Maier (eds), *Das Thema Vertreibung und die deutsch-polnischen Beziehungen
in Forschung, Unterricht und Politik* (The Expulsion Topic and German–Polish
Relations in Research, Teaching, and Politics) (p. 7), Studien zur Internationalen
Schulbuchforschung, Hanover: Hahnsche Buchhandlung.
Struck, Doug (2001) Japan divided on U.S. call for missile defense: constitutional bar
creates anxiety, *Washington Post*, LexisNexis, 8 Feb.
Süddeutsche Zeitung (2007) Koalition streitet über US-Pläne: Neues Konfliktfeld
Raketenabwehr (Coalition argues about US plans: missile defense new area of conflict), 19
March, www.sueddeutsche.de/deutschland/artikel/410/106304/ (accessed March 2007).
Swaine, Michael D., Rachael M. Swanger, and Takashi Kawakami (2001) *Japan and
Ballistic Missile Defense,* RAND Monograph Report, 1374, Santa Monica, CA: Rand.
Szechenyi, Nicholas (2006) A turning point for Japan's self-defense forces, *Washington
Quarterly*, 29(4): 139–50.
Tagesschau (2011) Rüstungsprojekt Meads wird begraben (Armament project Meads
buried), 16 Feb., www.tagesschau.de/inland/meads106.html (accessed Dec. 2011).
Takesada, Hideshi (2008) *Hideshi Takesada on the New South Korean Administration:
February 29, 2008,* Korea–Japan Group, Tokyo: Temple University.
Tanaka, Akihiko (2000) Sengo nihon gaikō ni okeru ajia: Sōri enzetsu no bunseki o tooshite
(Asia in Japan's postwar foreign diplomacy: through the analysis of prime minister
speeches), *Shakai Kagaku Kenkyu,* 5–6(51): 33–41.
—— (2007) *Ajia no naka no Nihon* (Japan in Asia), Tokyo: NTT Shuppan.
Tanaka, Hitoshi (2008a) Defining normalcy: the future course of Japan's foreign policy,
East Asia Insights, 3(1): 1–4.
—— (2008b) Interview with A. Sakaki, 18 March, Tokyo.
—— and Soichiro Tahara (2005) *Kokka to Gaikō* (The Nation and Diplomacy), Tokyo:
Kodansha Japan.

Tanida, Kuniichi (2011) Japan–U.S. missile project canceled, *Asahi Shinbun*, 3 Jan., www.asahi.com/english/TKY201101020016.html (accessed Dec. 2011).

Tanter, Richard (2006) Japan's Indian Ocean naval deployment: blue water militarization in a 'normal country', *Japan Focus*, http://japanfocus.org/products/details/1700 (accessed May 2008).

—— and Masaru Honda (2006) *Does Japan have a National Strategy?* www.zmag.org/content/print_article.cfm?itemID=10347&selectionID=1 (accessed May 2007).

Togo, Kazuhiko (2005) *Japan's Foreign Policy 1945–2003: The Quest for a Proactive Policy*, 2nd edn, Leiden: Brill Academic Publishers.

—— (2008a) Japan's historical memory: reconciliation with Asia, *Japan Focus*, 52(4), www.japanfocus.org/-Kazuhiko-TOGO/2997 (accessed Sept. 2009).

—— (2008b) *Rekishi to gaikō: Yasukuni – ajia – tōkyō saiban* (History and Foreign Policy: Yasukuni – Asia – Tokyo Tribunal), Tokyo: Kodansha Japan.

—— (2008c) Interview with A. Sakaki, 21 March, Tokyo.

Toki, Masako (2008) Under Fukuda, Japan accelerates ballistic missile defense cooperation with the United States, *WMD Insights*, 22, www.wmdinsights.com/I22/I22_EA5_JapanAcceleratesBMD.htm (accessed July 2009).

—— and Sarah Diehl (2007) Japan takes steps to integrate with US ballistic missile defense, *WMD Insights*, 17 (July/Aug.), http://wmdinsights.com/I17/I17_EA3_JapanTakesSteps.htm (accessed Feb. 2009).

Tokyo Shinbun (2009) Nichibei kankei, minshuseiken nara Ozawashi 'taitō' o kyōchō (In case of Democratic Party Government: regarding Japan–US relations Ozawa emphasizes 'equality'), 26 Feb., www.tokyo-np.co.jp/article/politics/scope/CK2009022602000109.html (accessed March 2009).

—— (2010) Nikkan rekishi kenkyū: Koto naru shikan mitome susumou (Japan–Korea history research: let's continue accepting different historical perceptions), 26 March, www.tokyo-np.co.jp/article/column/editorial/CK2010032602000076.html (accessed July 2010).

Torpey, John C. (2003) Introduction: politics and the past, in John C. Torpey (ed.), *Politics and the Past: On Repairing Historical Injustices* (pp. 1–36), Lanham, MD: Rowman & Littlefield.

Toyoshita, Narahiko (2005) Misairu bōei ni honrō sareru nihon gaikō (Japanese foreign policy being controlled by missile defense), *Sekai*, 737 (March): 36–43.

Ueki, Chikako Kawakatsu (2008) Interview with A. Sakaki, 18 March, Tokyo.

Voigt, Karsten (2010) Interview with A. Sakaki, 6 May, Berlin.

Wagner, Wolfgang (2005) From vanguard to laggard: Germany in European security and defense policy, *German Politics*, 14(4): 455–69.

Walker, Stephen G., and Sheldon W. Simon (1987) Role sets and foreign policy analysis in Southeast Asia, in Stephen G. Walker (ed.), *Role Theory and Foreign Policy Analysis* (pp. 141–59), Durham, NC: Duke University Press.

Waltz, Kenneth N. (1993) The emerging structure of international politics, *International Security*, 18(2): 44–79.

Wang, Zheng (2009) Old wounds, new narratives: joint history textbook writing and peacebuilding in East Asia, *History and Memory*, 21(1): 101–26.

Watanabe, Akio (2005) Revising the constitution and reforming the UN: Japan's parallel agenda, *Japan Echo*, 32(special issue), www.japanecho.co.jp/sum/2005/32sp08.html (accessed Nov. 2009).

Watanabe, Hirotaka (2004) Helping out in Iraq, *Japan Echo* 31(2) (April), www.japanecho.co.jp/sum/2004/310205.html (accessed Nov. 2008).

Webber, Douglas (2001) German European and foreign policy before and after Unification, *German Politics*, 10(1): 1–18.

Welt (2005) SPD und Grüne streiten um teure Luftabwehr: Milliardenprojekt auf der Kippe (SPD and Greens argue about expensive air defense: billion euro project on a knife edge), *Welt am Sonntag*, 23 Jan.

Wernstedt, Rolf (2000) Die Gründung des Georg-Eckert-Instituts für internationale Schulbuchforschung aus politischer und parlamentarischer Sicht (The establishment of the Georg-Eckert-Institute for International Textbook Research from the political and parlamentary perspective), in Ursula A. J. Becher and Rainer Riemenschneider (eds), *Internationale Verständigung: 25 Jahre Georg-Eckert-Institut für internationale Schulbuchforschung in Braunschweig* (International Understanding – 25 Years of Georg-Eckert Institute for International Textbook Research in Brunswick) (pp. 124–8), Hanover: Verlag Hahnsche Buchhandlung.

Weske, Simone (2006) *Deutschland und Frankreich: Motor einer Europäischen Sicherheits- und Verteidigungspolitik?* (Germany and France: Motor of European Security and Defense Policy?), Baden-Baden: Nomos Verlagsgesellschaft.

Whitlock, Craig (2010) Pentagon resists army's desire to stop development of MEADS missile system, *Washington Post*, 9 March, www.washingtonpost.com/wp-dyn/content/article/2010/03/08/AR2010030804865.html (accessed July 2010).

Wish, Naomi B. (1980) Foreign policy makers and their national role conceptions, *International Studies Quarterly*, 24(4): 532–54.

Wittig, Alexandra (2002) Japan's emerging role on the Korean Peninsula: the dynamics of Japan–South Korea relations in the post-cold war era, BA thesis, Princeton University.

Wuebbels, Mark (2004) Japan revises the three arms export principles, *Asian Export Control Observer*, 11(5): 10–12.

Xinhua News Agency (1985) Federal Germany not to take independent action on outer-space missile defense, *Xinhua General Overseas News Service*, LexisNexis, 7 Oct.

Yamaguchi, Mari (2008) Japan Parliament OKs bill allowing space programs for national security, *Daily Yomiuri*, LexisNexis, 21 May.

Yamaoka, Kunihiko, and Yasuhisa Shiozaki (2000) Gaikō wa naisei de aru: Shinryaku naki nihon no meiun (Foreign policy is a domestic affair: the fate of Japan without a strategy), *Kōken*, 38(11): 24–33.

Yomiuri Shinbun (1997) Japan, South Korea discuss 'shared history', LexisNexis, 18 Sept.

—— (2008) Nikkan shunō ga 15 funkan 'tachibanashi', Takeshima mondai mo wadai ni (Japanese, Korean heads of state 'chat' for 15 minutes, also talking about Takeshima problem), 9 July, www.yomiuri.co.jp/feature/20080625-3057808/news/20080709-OYT1T00429.htm (accessed Aug. 2008).

—— (2011) Noda to brief Obama on arms exports: relaxing ban to enable joint development, 15 Oct., www.yomiuri.co.jp/dy/national/T111014004781.htm (accessed Dec. 2011).

Yoo, Jee-Ho (2009) Japanese Foreign Minister suggests joint history text, *JoongAng Ilbo*, 9 Oct., http://joongangdaily.joins.com/article/print.asp (accessed July 2010).

Yoshizaki, Tomonori (2008) Interview with A. Sakaki, 19 March, Tokyo.

Yuzawa, Takeshi (2008) Interview with A. Sakaki, 19 March, Tokyo.

Zettel, Philipp (2003) *Patriot-Abwehrraketen und AWACS-Aufklärungsflugzeuge für Israel sowie die Türkei: Die deutsche Diskussion im Kontext des Irakkrieges* (Patriot Interception Missiles and AWACS-Reconnaissance Planes for Israel and Turkey: The German Discussion in the Context of the Iraq War), www.hsfk.de/abm/print/bulletin/zettel1.html (accessed March 2009).

Index

For Product Safety Concerns and Information please contact our EU
representative GPSR@taylorandfrancis.com
Taylor & Francis Verlag GmbH, Kaufingerstraße 24, 80331 München, Germany

www.ingramcontent.com/pod-product-compliance
Lightning Source LLC
Chambersburg PA
CBHW050706280326
41926CB00088B/2805